March of Dimes Birth Defects Foundation
Birth Defects: Original Article Series,
Volume 20, Number 5, 1984

Social Support and Families of Vulnerable Infants

Conference Coordinators—Consulting Editors
Kathryn E. Barnard, R.N., Ph.D., FAAN
Professor
Parent Child Nursing
University of Washington, Seattle

Patricia A. Brandt, R.N., Ph.D.
Assistant Professor
Parent Child Nursing
University of Washington, Seattle

Editor
Beverly S. Raff, R.N., Ph.D.
Vice President for Professional Education
March of Dimes Birth Defects Foundation

Associate Editor
Patricia Carroll, M.S.
Assistant Director
Nursing and Allied Health Education
March of Dimes Birth Defects Foundation

Library of Congress Cataloging in Publication Data

Main entry under title:
Social support and families of vulnerable infants.
    (Birth defects : original article series ; v. 20, no. 5, 1983)
    Includes index.
    1. Family social work—Addresses, essays, lectures. 2. Medical social work—Addresses, essays, lectures. 3. Developmentally disabled children—Family relationships—Addresses, essays, lectures. I. Barnard, Kathryn E. II. Brandt, Patricia A. III. Raff, Beverly S. IV. Carroll, Patricia. V. Series : Birth defects original article series ; v. 20, no. 5. [DNLM: 1. Family—congresses. 2. Social Environment—congresses. 3. Child Welfare— congresses. WI BI966 v.20 no.5 / WA 320 S6775 1982] RG626.B63 vol. 20, no. 5 616'.043 s [362.8'2]
84-7838
[HV697]
ISBN 0-86525-030-8

Printed in U.S.A.

Contents

Contributors and Participants 5

Preface

   Beverly S. Raff 7

Introduction

   Kathryn E. Barnard and Patricia A. Brandt 9

Social Support and Vulnerability: State of the Art in Relation to Families and Children

   Patricia MacElveen-Hoehn and Sandra J. Eyres 11

   Critique by Toni C. Antonucci 29

   Discussion 34

The Norbeck Social Support Questionnaire

   Jane S. Norbeck 45

Evaluation of the Personal Resource Questionnaire: A Social Support Measure

   Clarann Weinert 59

   Critique by Nancy Ewald Jackson 78

   Discussion 88

Social Support as a Factor in the Development of Parents' Attachment to Their Unborn

   Mecca S. Cranley 99

   Critique by Mary Ann Curry 109

   Discussion 115

Information Needs and Problem Solving Behavior of Parents of Infants

   Karen F. Pridham 125

   Critique by Lorraine O. Walker 150

   Discussion 156

Social Networks and Social Support of Primigravida Mothers and Fathers

   Linda R. Cronenwett 167

   Critique by Jacqueline Fawcett 186

   Discussion 192

Social Support and Negative Life Events of Mothers with Developmentally Delayed Children

Patricia A. Brandt 206

Critique by Suzanne L. Feetham 223

Discussion 232

Social Support of Teenage Mothers

Ramona T. Mercer, Kathryn C. Hackley, and Alan Bostrom 245

Critique by Gretchen Crawford 272

Discussion . . . . : . . . . : 280

Supportive Measures for High-Risk Infants and Families

Kathryn E. Barnard, Charlene Snyder, and Anita Spietz 291

Critique by Sharron S. Humenick 315

Discussion 320

Summary

Sandra J. Eyres 330

Index 335

Contributors and Participants

Gene Cranston Anderson, R.N., Ph.D., FAAN, Professor and Research Coordinator, College of Nursing, Box J197, J. Hillis Miller Health Center, University of Florida at Gainesville, Gainesville, FL 32610

Toni C. Antonucci, Ph.D., Associate Research Scientist, Institute for Social Research, Assistant Professor, Department of Family Practice, University of Michigan, P.O. Box 1248, Ann Arbor, MI 48106

Kathryn E. Barnard, R.N., Ph.D., FAAN, Professor, Parent Child Nursing (WJ-10), University of Washington, Seattle, WA 98195

Barbara E. Bishop, R.N., M.N., FAAN, Editor, MCN, The American Journal of Maternal/Child Nursing, 555 West 57th Street, New York, NY 10019

Alan Bostrom, Ph.D., Principal Statistician, University of California, San Francisco, Computer Center, U-76, San Francisco, CA 94143

Patricia A. Brandt, R.N., Ph.D., Assistant Professor, Parent Child Nursing (WJ-10), University of Washington, Seattle, WA 98195

Judith A. Bumbalo, R.N., M.S., formerly Lecturer, Parent Child Nursing (WJ-10), University of Washington, Seattle, WA 98195; currently a doctoral student, College of Nursing, Wayne State University, Detroit, MI

Mecca S. Cranley, R.N., Ph.D., Associate Professor, School of Nursing, University of Wisconsin-Madison, 600 Highland Avenue, Madison, WI 53792

Gretchen Crawford, R.N., Ph.D., Lecturer, The Ohio State University, College of Nursing, Columbus, OH

Linda R. Cronenwett, R.N., Ph.D., Assistant Research Scientist, Center for Nursing Research, School of Nursing, and Clinical Nurse Specialist and Lecturer, Department of Family Practice, School of Medicine, The University of Michigan, 400 N. Ingalls, Box 050, Ann Arbor, MI 48109

Nia Johnson-Crowley, R.N., M.S.N., Research Instructor, Parent Child Nursing (WJ-I0), University of Washington, Seattle, WA 98195

Mary Ann Curry, R.N., D.N.Sc., FAAN, Associate Professor, Department of Family Nursing, School of Nursing, The Oregon Health Sciences University, 3181 S.W. Sam Jackson Park Road, Portland, OR 97201

Gunnel Elander, Doctoral Student, Konualivagen 14, 24021 Loddekopinge, Sweden

Sandra J. Eyres, R.N., Ph.D., Associate Dean, Graduate Programs, University of Washington, School of Nursing, Seattle, WA 98195

Jacqueline Fawcett, Ph.D., FAAN, Associate Professor, Chairperson, Science Role Development, University of Pennsylvania, School of Nursing, Philadelphia, PA 19104

Suzanne L. Feetham, Ph.D., FAAN, Associate Director of Nursing for Education and Research, Children's Hospital National Medical Center, 111 Michigan Avenue, N.W., Washington, DC 20010

Kathryn C. Hackley, M.S.N., Staff Nurse, Alternative Birth Center, Mount Zion Hospital, San Francisco, CA 94115

Sharron S. Humenick, R.N., Ph.D., Associate Professor, College of Health Sciences, School of Nursing, University of Wyoming, Box 3065, University Station, Laramie, WY 82071

Nancy Ewald Jackson, Ph.D., Research Associate Professor, Parent and Child Nursing, Nursing Research Office SM-27, University of Washington, Seattle, WA 98195

Regina Lederman, Ph.D., Professor & Project Director, Center for Health Sciences, School of Nursing, University of Wisconsin-Madison, 600 Highland Avenue, Madison, WI 53792

Patricia MacElveen-Hoehn, R.N., Ph.D., Research Associate, Parent Child Nursing (WJ-10), University of Washington, Seattle, WA 98195

Diane Magyary, R.N., Ph.D., Research Associate, Parent Child Nursing (WJ-10), University of Washington, Seattle, WA 98195

Ramona T. Mercer, R.N., Ph.D., FAAN, Professor, Department of Family Health Care Nursing, School of Nursing, University of California, San Francisco, San Francisco, CA 94143

Jane S. Norbeck, R.N., D.N.Sc., Assistant Professor, Department of Mental Health and Community Nursing, Room N505-Y, School of Nursing, University of California, San Francisco, San Francisco, CA 94143

Karen F. Pridham, R.N., Ph.D., FAAN, Professor, School of Nursing and Department of Family Medicine & Practice, Center for Health Sciences, University of Wisconsin-Madison, 600 Highland Avenue, Madison, WI 53792

Marion Rose, R.N., Ph.D., Associate Professor, Parent Child Nursing, University of Washington, Seattle, WA 98195

Charlene Snyder, R.N., M.S.N., Research Assistant Professor, Parent Child Nursing (WJ-10), University of Washington, Seattle, WA 98195

Anita Spietz, R.N., M.S.N., Research Assistant Professor, Parent Child Nursing, University of Washington, Seattle, WA 98195

Georgina Sumner, R.N., M.S.N., Project Director, Nursing Child Assessment Satellite Training, University of Washington, WJ-10, Seattle, WA 98195

Lorraine O. Walker, R.N., Ed.D., FAAN, Professor, School of Nursing, University of Texas at Austin, 1700 Red River Street, Austin, Texas 78701

Clarann Weinert, R.N., S.C., Ph.D., Education Director/Assistant Professor, College of Nursing, Montana State University, Bozeman, MT 59717

Preface

Beverly S. Raff, R.N., Ph.D.

The goal of this research roundtable is to examine social support in relation to families of vulnerable infants in order to determine client needs and examine clinical interventions to meet these needs. These presentations, critiques, and discussions are valuable sources of information to researchers concerned with social support and professionals working with vulnerable infants and their families.

The research presented concerns social support in relation to infant vulnerability, attachment, primigravida parents, developmentally delayed children, teenage mothers, high-risk infants, and the development of questionnaires. In addition to the research, multiple definitions of social support are examined, as are related concepts of coping behavior and adaptation; patients' needs, attitudes, and preferred sources of social support; and intervention programs that have been successful. Evaluations of research designs, the need for more precisely defined terminology, data on the strengths and weaknesses of questionnaires, and inventories currently used to evaluate social support are extremely important aspects of this volume. Questions are raised and recommendations are made that require careful consideration in future research. This publication will be particularly useful to clinical practitioners since it examines social support in relation to patient needs and perceptions, and it presents and evaluates a variety of methods in which support can be provided.

The March of Dimes is very grateful to Drs. Kathryn Barnard and Patricia Brandt for coordinating this conference and enlisting the participation of the presenters, critiquers, and discussants for this research roundtable. Their efforts have provided a forum for exchange which may lead to new creative efforts and has raised additional questions, and it will provide a valuable foundation for future research. The ultimate goal is to help patients to learn how to cope and to know how to obtain additional support when necessary in order to achieve an optimal outcome for both infant and family.

Introduction

Kathryn E. Barnard, R.N., Ph.D., FAAN, and **Patricia A. Brandt,** R.N., Ph.D.

This nursing research roundtable was the third in the series that have been sponsored by the March of Dimes Birth Defects Foundation. These small conferences, designed to promote significant exchanges among nurse investigators and their colleagues from other topic related disciplines, are important stimuli for the developing science of nursing. It is fortunate that the conference proceedings can also be shared through publication with the larger community of scholars and practitioners.

The topic of the conference, "Social Support and Families of Vulnerable Infants," fits in with the rapidly developing scientific interest in the relationship between social support and health status. In regard to child and parenting health outcomes, the positive benefits of support from family, friends, and community appear to be more evident in stressful family situations.

A major issue discussed during the conference was how to define and measure social support. Several investigators presented their methodological work through which tools have evolved to measure support. Clearly this work represents beginning advances toward describing complex phenomena in the social environment that promote coping and mastery. Although the individual's perception of support appears to have potential as a health predictor, it became evident during the conference that perceived support is best studied in the context of other coping strategies and parental competencies. Furthermore, actions may not be perceived as "support" because the person needing help is uncomfortable with the self-reliance promoted by the helper. Over-dependence on others for support may actually erode one's coping behavior by decreasing control and problem solving. Therefore, supportive strategies that enhance outcomes of personal or family development which may involve some discomfort need to be studied rather than only those strategies which encourage perceived support or acceptance.

Another feature of support addressed was the importance the individual has in initiating and maintaining a supportive network, his or her social competence. Professionals may provide opportunities for clients to obtain support from others, but the responsibility resides with clients to mobilize and develop their own social network. When assisting individuals or families who are socially isolated, it is doubtful that "giving them support" as the only helping strategy will remove the risk accompanying the lack of support. Clients without support systems are difficult to help. However, these very families with high-risk infants are especially vulnerable for maladaptive parenting and child outcomes. We need to know much more about the relationship between helping, social competence, and social networks. The vulnerability of the high-risk infant and family makes it probable that they would benefit from a support system.

This nursing research roundtable provided a forum for presenting conceptual and empirical knowledge about social support and vulnerable individuals and for reaching a consensus about future research directions. We now need to move ahead with the knowledge we shared and discover what features of the social environment promote positive health behaviors for the child and family. In addition, we need to explore what type of supportive strategies best match the client's needs and situation. What is the most efficient, economical, and desirable supportive strategy to encourage growth or diminish stress? For example, would help from one's personal network produce different outcomes than help from a parent support group or volunteer linking network? How can mutually beneficial connections between professional and lay support systems be developed? Scientific investigations which focus on these research questions will further our understanding of the links which connect the individual, the environment, and health outcomes.

Social Support and Vulnerability: State of the Art in Relation to Families and Children

Patricia MacElveen-Hoehn, R.N., Ph.D., and Sandra J. Eyres, R.N., Ph.D.

The purpose of this presentation is to review the concepts of social support and vulnerable families and children, propose a theoretical model on coping and adaptation, and ascertain any significant implications for the delivery of health care services and future research.

The review of the literature indicates that major problems persist in the classification, conceptualization, empirical investigation, and clinical application of social support due to a lack of clarity regarding the definition of social support and how it works. Related perspectives such as bonding, child development, and child rearing also reaffirm the need for and the utilization of social support. High-risk factors, such as low maternal age, poverty, single parenthood, and long-term health problems, increase the vulnerability of families and children. This literature strongly suggests that the interactions of adults and children with supportive members of their social networks are important in the development of essential cognitive and social skills, as well as for the promotion of security and comfort. Supports from individuals, families, and groups also are associated with more successful adaptation and favorable outcomes.

Despite numerous articles and research projects, however, questions concerning how social support works to assist vulnerable children and families remain. Seven factors are proposed as a theoretical model to identify threatening situations and coping difficulties so that appropriate support can be provided. These factors are surprise, experience, confusion, perceived effectiveness, perceived allies, perceived uniqueness of threat, and overload. Additional testing is required for this model so that a more meaningful investigation and utilization of social support can be established. Additional research also is indicated to determine the specific types of support needed in the presence of certain factors, network style preferences, the supply and demand for support over the life span, and cultural aspects of coping and support processes. The position that appropriate social support will promote mastery and self-determination has significant implications for health professionals.

INTRODUCTION

Social support has a great fascination for many of us because of our overlapping interests in peoples' health under certain circumstances, such as job loss (Gore, 1978), or complications of pregnancy (Nuckolls, Cassel, & Kaplan, 1972). For others interested in the study of growth and development, the concept of social support represents a broader perspective than has been used historically. A different approach is when social scientists converge to collaborate in efforts to address social support as it relates to a defined problem. For social scientists, that problem is the special population of infants and families who are identified as sharing some factor which makes them more vulnerable than others in similar situations. The focus of this conference was to discuss the status of social support research in relation to these special populations.

Examples will be drawn selectively from the available literature to illustrate the origins of social support and the movement towards an appreciation of its complexity of meanings. Related concepts, such as attachment and social ecology, will be discussed to demonstrate the range from micro analyses to more middle range analyses that appear appropriate to the concept of social support.

Next, there will be an exploration of the utilization of a model of coping and adaptation as a way to integrate social support into a theoretical framework. Within that framework, a beginning typology of factors which increase the threat of coping problems will be presented, with examples from vulnerable groups which are the subject of concern. Finally, comments will be provided on issues which will need to be considered in future efforts.

VULNERABILITY

Vulnerable infants and their families are those who, because of specific factors, are more likely to experience undesirable outcomes in their lives. Several factors associated with mothers at risk for serious perinatal problems are: young or late age for childbearing, limited education, poverty, four or more closely spaced children, single parenthood, potential for genetic disorders, drug abuse, chronic illness, complications in a minor's pregnancy, or other health problems. The term, vulnerable infants, is defined here by the following factors: prematurity; low birth weight; presence of abnormalities, congenital anomalies, or disabilities; critical illness; and failure to thrive. When infants and children have a life-threatening illness, chronic disease, or handicapping conditions, they and their families may be at risk for long periods of time due to the numerous demanding challenges and problems. The death of a child is probably one of the most difficult experiences for most families to master. The deprived social ecology of isolated families with disturbed dynamics and of high-risk neighborhoods fosters unsanctioned opportunities for battering, abuse, and neglect of infants and children (Hymovich & Chamberlain, 1980; Garbarino & Sherman, 1980; Sawin, Hawkins, Walker, & Penticuff, 1980).

SOCIAL SUPPORT

Perhaps because of the ubiquity of social support in our personal lives and in society at large, the study of social support is especially difficult. Many empirical investigations have used the term, social support, with little clarification, no definition, and numerous untested assumptions. Efforts at fitting the concept of social support into a theoretical framework are rare. Thus far, no consensus on meaning has been achieved. This question of definition is crucial to such issues as: conceptualization; measurement and levels of analysis for empirical studies; potential implications for the development of social and health policy; and the use of social support in informed clinical interventions with individuals, families, and communities.

The origins of social network concepts can be traced to the seminal work of Cooley (1902) on primary groups and the looking-glass self, Mead's social self (1934), Simmel's (1908) separate analyses of social configurations and the relationships of social integration to national rates of suicide, and the introduction of sociometric analysis by Moreno (1934). The subsequent evolution of the concept and the use of network concepts have been summarized elsewhere (Gottlieb, 1981), including the debate about whether the study of social support systems is likely to be more efficient if pursued within the paradigm of social network analysis (Wellman, 1981). Another theme stimulating the study of social support during the last decade is its interaction with concepts of stress and mental and physical health outcomes.

More recent spatial and temporal expansions in the perspectives concerning social support are reflected in the emergence of social ecology (e.g., Cochran & Brassard, 1979) and the consideration of social support as a life-span issue (Antonucci, 1976; Kahn & Antonucci, 1980; Baltes, 1978; Knudtson, 1976).

REVIEW OF THE LITERATURE
Definition of Social Support

House (1981) defines social support as interpersonal transactions involving at least one of the following: emotional concern, information, appraisal, and instrumental aid. These four categories tend to include most of the descriptive terms used by others as illustrated in the following examples:

1. *Emotional concerns.* Liking, love, empathy, affect (House, 1981; Kahn & Antonucci, 1980); expressive relations, security (Dean & Lin, 1977); acceptance of feelings (Barrera, 1981; Hamburg & Killilea, 1979); attachment, intimacy (Weiss, 1974; Barrera, 1981; Dean & Lin, 1977; Kahn & Antonucci, 1980); confiding relationship with reciprocity (Surtees, 1980); approval, esteem, succorance (Kaplan, Cassel, & Gore, 1977); genuine

respect, admiration (Kahn & Antonucci, 1980; Porrett, 1979); and empathetic understanding (Porrett, 1979).

2. *Information (or messages about).* Being cared for, loved, esteemed, valued, a member of a network of communications and mutual obligation (Cobb, 1976); affirmation and agreement of rightness, appropriateness of an act or statement (Kahn & Antonucci, 1980); uniqueness as a person, feedback validation (Dean & Lin, 1977; Caplan, 1974); advice, feedback, guidance (Tolsdorf, 1976; Barrera, 1981; Weiss, 1974); the environment (Cassel, 1974; House, 1981; Kahn & Antonucci, 1980); and clarification of expectations (Kaplan, Cassel, & Gore, 1977).

3. *Appraisal.* Information for evaluation of self (House, 1981); validation of identity (Caplan, 1974); promotion of competence (Caplan, 1974); and reassurance of worth (Weiss, 1974).

4. *Instrumental aid.* Material goods and services (House, 1981); things, money, time, entitlements (Barrera, 1981; Kahn & Antonucci, 1980); assistance in attaining goals, sharing tasks, dealing with demands (Barrera, 1981; Caplan, 1974; Tolsdorf, 1976); and reliable alliance, assistance (Weiss, 1974).

Two remaining "relational" functions identified by Weiss (1974) that did not seem to fit easily into House's categories were social integration and the opportunity for nurturing. Barrera's (1981) social participation, which includes interactions for fun and relaxation and diversion from demanding conditions, also was difficult to categorize.

Other Perspectives on Social Support

Bonding. The literature on attachment from a human development perspective has focused primarily on early mother-infant bonding. Findings of interest are those suggesting that the security of the attachment is associated with toddlers' increasing competency in exploring, problem solving, and the development of positive peer interactions (Bowlby, 1969, 1973; Lieberman, 1977; Easterbrooks & Lamb, 1979; Arend, Gove, & Sroufe, 1979; Waters, Wippman, & Sroufe, 1979). Henderson and associates (1978) related the dynamics of early attachments disrupted by loss (Bowlby, 1969, 1973), with adult needs for intimate supportive relationships (Weiss, 1974) and the identification of four factors associated with working-class women being at risk for depression (Brown, Bhrolchain, & Harris, 1975). These risk factors are: 1) loss of a mother before age 11, 2) lack of an intimate relationship (husband/boyfriend), 3) unemployment, and 4) three or more children under age 14 at home. The relationship between significant early loss and the other three factors is intriguing. Clinically, the presence of unresolved grief of the early loss of a parent or sibling is frequently associated with depression, anxiety, and somatization. The three latter factors all have implications for social isolation and the lack of opportunities for supportive relationships.

Social ecology. Reviews indicating that the prevailing construct of attachment has limitations led to the proposal of a social network approach as a more promising way to study the development of social relationships (Weinraub, Brooks, & Lewis, 1977). These researchers urged that the study of children's relationships occurs within the context of their social network which varies along historical and cultural dimensions.

Cochran and Brassard (1979), who credit Bronfenbrenner as the architect of an ecology of human development, have described a model to assess the social ecology of the parent and child and its possible effects on child development. Using a network analysis framework, they follow influences of the parents' personal social network both directly to the child or mediated through the parent. Developmental processes that are related to the network include direct cognitive and social stimulation, emotional and material support, access to opportunities for active participation in the parents' networks, observational models of adults outside the home, and sanctions for behavior. Parents exchange emotional and material assistance with members of their networks, who in turn provide other role models of parenting behaviors and who may influence child rearing behavior through control and sanction. Cochran and Brassard (1979) cite the important observation by Parke and Collmer (1975) that abusive parents who were abused by their own parents are most often isolated and do not have access to other patterns of child rearing behavior from their social network. Therefore, they repeat the only parenting behaviors they know and abuse their own children.

Cochran and Brassard (1979) emphasize the process in mastering skills related to reciprocity at different stages in the child's development both through observation and interaction with network members. They identified five social developmental areas related to network variables in a review of the literature. These include attachment, independence behavior, experience with social roles, child rearing attitudes and behaviors, and the continuous development of the self-concept. Cognitive abilities which may be affected by members of the social network are perceptual differentiation, task completions, representational thinking, and cognitive receptivity.

In reality, of course, the influences and effects of the network can range from positive to negative; i.e., the presence of a network is not a social panacea. In contrast to the aspects of a basically positive social ecology, as described previously, are the consequences for parent-child relationships which are found in the socially impoverished environments of socially isolated families and families living in high-risk neighborhoods. In both cases the essential elements of support systems are unavailable. The parent-child relationship is deprived of nurturance, feedback, enduring supportive relationships, and protective behaviors. Garbarino and Sherman (1980) define these conditions as "the human ecology of child maltreatment" where violence and abuse are common. The authors point out, however, that there is no correlation between the risk score of a neighborhood and socioeconomic or demographic factors. Stack (1974) vividly describes the ongoing exchanges of all manners of social, material, and financial supports in a poor, urban, black community. Creativity and ingenuity characterize the strategies employed within that network of people as they struggled daily to survive.

It has been proposed that in order for the environment to be abundant in social supplies, the balance between the needs and resources in peoples' lives must form the ability to share with and care about others in the neighborhood (Collins & Pancoast, 1976). Natural helping networks are predicated on the residents of a neighborhood having community patterns of interaction, shared values, norms of reciprocity, and general caring about children and adults in the neighborhood. Natural helping networks are potent sources of social support (Collins & Pancoast, 1976).

Social support and child rearing. Having a first baby is a common challenge in life. The transition to parenthood can be especially difficult for some couples due to the requirements of infant care, the couple becoming a family (dyad to triad), changes in many facets of the couples' relationship, financial responsibilities, and relating to relatives and others in the new role of mother or father. Often one or both parents lack information about normal growth and development, have limited experience with babies, and are unprepared for parenthood. Many new parents are unaware of the spectrum of feelings associated with becoming a parent, and many believe that their feelings of ambivalence and conflict about parenthood are unusual and not how other parents feel. Thus, the transition to parenthood is likely to be more comfortable for new parents who are in a network where they have contact with others sharing the same experience.

Some couples may change their social network, emphasizing relationships with other new parents, and perhaps deemphasizing relationships with individuals who are not interested in or tolerant of their new interests and role changes. This alteration of the network also occurs in response to such events as the loss of a spouse, a job change, or a move to a new location. Knowledge of the impact of these events on the availability of resources is limited. So, too, is an understanding of changes in the social network related to movement through individual developmental phases and family life cycle stages.

Some parents seem to derive great benefit from groups where there are opportunities for sharing common experiences and feelings. Group members can also receive and give information about child development and parenting skills (Kagey, Vivace, & Lutz, 1981; Sweeny & Davis, 1979).

Wandersman and associates (1980) reported that certain relationships were most important for postpartum adjustment. The parenting group was a significant support for the father, the social network a significant support for the mother, and groups seemed to be useful to new parents, but they did not have a measurable effect on postpartum marital adjustment.

Norr and associates (1980) found that multiparous women were not any different from primiparas in the experiences surrounding birth. Multiparas frequently received less support from their husbands and others, and contrary to expectations they were not better informed than primiparas.

The immediate family has significant supportive functions. Brandt (1980) clarifies the family as a source of support using Weiss' "relational" functions of attachments, social integration, opportunity for nurturance, reassurance of worth, reliable alliance, and guidance. Brandt (1980) cited numerous studies demonstrating the more positive outcomes for various members of the family when adequate support is available to foster the individual's growth and development and mediate life stress. The interaction of the husband and wife was related to maternal competencies, and, therefore, it was beneficial to the infant. Brandt (1980) also described the family as part of its community and identified factors affecting the community as supportive or nonsupportive to families.

Additional Considerations

We have attempted thus far to illustrate a few facets of the social support concept within selected contexts of child development, parenthood, and the neighborhood or community. Interactions with supportive members of the social network can provide a wide variety of psychosocial resources, information about the self and the environment, positive appraisal of the self, and reliable instrumental and material assistance. We suggest further that the interactions within the network promote the development of cognitive and social skills in both children and adults, and these interactions are part of the supportive functions of the social environment. Within this social support network context, the infant arrives, grows, and develops, acquiring the essential skills necessary to love, learn, work, and play.

It is necessary to review the supports for infants and families when risk factors are identified. For example, low income, black adolescent mothers constitute a group who are at risk for numerous psychological, social, and health problems. Studies show, however, that some of these mothers can successfully negotiate the difficult transition to motherhood, despite the problems posed by their adolescence (Furstenberg & Crawford, 1978; Mercer, 1980; Zuckerman, Winsmore, & Alprit, 1979). Success is usually defined by such factors as their abilities to take on the maternal role, to enjoy their babies, to continue their schooling, and to continue to mature in their relationships with others. Support was the key to whether these adolescent mothers experienced success, or were traumatized, unable to care for their infants or themselves, or experienced other long-term effects from the interruption of their education. A number of supports were identified. The adolescent was permitted to live at home; thus room and board were provided. Grandmothers helped with child care tasks and provided information about mothering, but they did not undermine their daughter's sense of competence or her identity as the infant's mother. These grandmothers provided essential material and psychosocial assistance. Other family members helped with babysitting and participated in interactions which were affirming to the adolescent mother. A positive relationship with her boyfriend and/or the infant's father was an important source of affection and affirmation. Peers were rarely a significant source of support for these adolescents during pregnancy or after the birth of their infants.

Another study used a multimethod approach to assess social support and the adjustment of adolescents to pregnancy, and efforts were made to measure socially supportive behaviors, support satisfaction and need, social network indices, negative life events, receipt of natural helping behaviors, and symptomology (Barrera, 1981). Findings indicated that the best predictor of psychosocial symptoms, especially depression, was dissatisfaction with the support received. The size of the supportive network seemed to buffer the impact of negative life events, and those adolescents experiencing the most stress also received the most amount of supportive actions. All measures of social support, however, did not relate to adjustment.

Adolescent mothers reportedly tend to have special needs for orientation to the future, skills for effective decision making, sensitization to needs of their infants, and the reinforcement of positive maternal behaviors (Levenson, Atkinson, Hale, & Hollrer, 1978). Educational programs not only provide information, but the support of shared experiences within a group that reduces the sense of aloneness. Health services and day care for the infants may be included in comprehensive programs (Tankson, 1976). These programs focus upon supporting the continued growth and development of the adolescents and the enhancement of their skills and emotional capacities to mother their infants. Such interventions also attempt to reduce repeated pregnancies and behaviors which severely limit educational achievement, job attainment, and other material opportunities for optimal development.

Women who attempt to provide for all the family needs as a single parent represent a financially impoverished group, struggling to deal with the multiple demands on their time, energy, and emotional resources. When mothers lack a satisfying, intimate relationship with a spouse or partner, there often is a significant deficit in their social environment. The importance of such a relationship is associated with protection against the effects of high life stress, better feelings about being an effective and competent parent, and being more responsive to their children's needs (Barnard & Eyres, 1977; Crnic, Greenberg, Ragozin, Robinson, & Busharn, 1981; Longfellow, Zelkowitz, Saunders, &

Belle, 1979). Single mothers who can request and receive help from family and friends are found to have more positive patterns of interaction with their children and more effective parenting behaviors (Hetherington, Cox, & Cox, 1978). When a satisfying intimate relationship is absent, women may be more vulnerable, not only because of the effect of isolation, but also because of the effects of adversive, intrusive, demanding contacts with others, especially relatives, who add to the drain on their emotional resources. Mothers with low income who live in the inner city may be trapped within a nonsupportive network from which they are unable to extract themselves and which is associated with increased depression (Longfellow, et al., 1979). Wahler (1980) described insular mothers as those who are not isolated necessarily but whose contacts with others are primarily negative, adversive, and demanding. Mother-child problems appeared to reflect the interpersonal problems of the mother with adults outside the home. Mothers were able to successfully complete a parent training program, but their ability to sustain the changes in mother-child interactions appeared to depend on the quality of their daily interactions with other adults.

The literature addressing the relationship between the stress of life changes and the development of physical and psychological problems and the role of social support has been plagued by definitional, conceptual, and methodological problems (Dohrenwend & Dohrenwend, 1978). Many questions have been raised about the direct or indirect effects of social support on health (House, 1981); the relationship of locus of control and sensation seeking to social support (Sarason, Johnson, & Sugel, 1978); structural characteristics of social networks and social support (Wellman, 1981); and conceptual analysis including the temporal, psychological, and social situation for both the meaning of events and responses to them (Eckenrode & Gore, 1981).

SUPPORTIVE RESOURCES

How people use supportive resources may be a function of personal network style, i.e., whether they operate basically in affiliative, associative, or restrictive networks (MacElveen, 1978). Consider the stress of such life events as the birth of a baby with congenital heart disease, a diagnosis of cystic fibrosis, the loss of a remission in a child with leukemia, or the confirmation of a developmental disability. Where do families subject to intermittent crises, chronic sorrow, or system overload from care and treatment demands find the energy to sustain their social networks? How do these families remain in contact with network members, groups, clubs, and other organizations? How do they maintain the norm of reciprocity in the exchange of various supportive behaviors and instrumental assistance over long periods of time? How does perceived or assigned stigma affect opportunities for social support? Many families dealing with long-term health problems do become socially isolated. Social participation is often one of the first uses of time and energy that is omitted. Withdrawal from social interaction outside the family may be one-sided or mutual. Some families can transcend misfortune or major long-term health problems. Many give up or exhaust supportive relationships with friends and neighbors during times when their need for support may be very great.

Support groups are a comforting resource to many people who find themselves in a situation which is not a well understood experience by members of their own personal network. Attitudes, knowledge, and required skills may be lacking. Effective support for the specific needs generated by the situation and for the specific internal responses that are common under the circumstances may be unavailable. Special groups may be necessary, for example, to address the needs of parents with neonates in intensive care, premature infants, children with physical handicaps or developmental disabilities, and children with life-threatening illnesses and long-term chronic conditions. Additionally, experienced parents may be necessary to deal with new parents on a one-to-one basis. These kinds of supportive opportunities can reduce feelings of uniqueness, provide information and understanding from a parent's perspective, and promote relationships which allow for freer expressions of feelings which are sometimes not possible with persons who have not experienced the situation. The recognition of sharing the same problems, communicating about them, and problem solving in the group foster the emergence of a group identity which may address research, economic, or political issues. This mobilization to action reduces feelings of helplessness and hopelessness. For example, parents of developmentally disabled children use their groups and organizations to pressure for legislation and education programs.

A MODEL OF SUPPORT: THE THEORETICAL FRAMEWORK

A common theme throughout the recent literature on social support is the need for a model of support. LaRocco, House, and French (1980, p. 214) state:

> ...it is time to stop simply "proving" that social support is related to stress
> and strain and to begin to consider the mediating factors or mechanisms
> through which social support functions....In other words, what is needed is
> a model of support, grounded in a theoretical framework, that allows one
> not only to predict the effects of support, but to understand how it works
> the way it does.

In order to assist vulnerable children and families, the timely question is-- how does social support work? Pursuing this question will provide more precise information on the nature of social support and, therefore, may provide a more orderly approach to the problems of measurement.

The remainder of this paper will examine a few potential answers to the question of how social support works, but the investigation is not intended to be exhaustive or fully developed.

While research which uses the concept of social support may be thought of as a body of literature in and of itself, it is also necessary to examine and incorporate other relevant aspects of the literature. Social support is generally considered to be helpful in assisting individuals buffer the negative effects of their environment, leading to an investigation of the literature on coping and adaptation.

The Lazarus Model

There are a variety of formulations on how people respond to signals from their environment, but few are general in that they consider a range of responses. In the area of parent and child health, this is critical because we are dealing with a multiplicity of outcomes: affective (as in postpartal depression), behavioral (as in malparenting), and physiological (as in complications of pregnancy and delivery). One of the exceptions to the lack of generality is the work of Lazarus and his colleagues (Lazarus, 1974; Lazarus, Averill, & Opton, 1974; Lazarus, 1975; Folkman, Schaefer, & Lazarus, 1979). While their formulations have not reached the predictive stage, there are several concepts central to the Lazarus model which should be examined.

1. *Cognitive appraisal.* Upon receiving a stimulus from the environment, it is cognitively evaluated for its significance to the individual's well-being and for the individual's potential for mastery. The result of the "primary appraisal" relevant to the significance to the individual's well-being can be 1) benign, 2) positive, 3) challenging, or 4) threatening. The result that occurs depends on the individual's beliefs and expectations about the stimulus and its consequences.

   In the "secondary appraisal," the individual considers the kind of adaptive action required and the kind and strength of resources he has for meeting the challenge. This appraisal determines the amount of threat posed by the stimulus.

2. *Emotion* results from the cognitive appraisal and consists of subjective affect, behavioral impulses, and physiological changes.

3. *Self-regulation of emotion.* Individuals work to avoid an uncomfortable emotional state. In the Lazarus terminology, this is also called self-management or coping. There are several major types of coping or managing:

   a. Direct action. The individual uses cognitive reappraisal to obtain more feedback about his own reactions and the cues in the environment, and he works toward altering or mastering the situation posed by the stimulus.

   b. Palliation. This strategy is used when direct action is perceived as having too high a cost or is considered an impossible option. It includes defenses such as denial or selective attention deployment, taking tranquilizers or alcohol, and using relaxation techniques.

c. Anticipatory coping. This type of coping also occurs in response to signs of potential future threat. Individuals prepare by gaining information or resources so as to alleviate or avoid stress.

The research of the Lazarus group supports the process described previously in that experimentally manipulating cognitive appraisal produced different emotional responses as indexed by physiological indicators. When viewers of a potentially upsetting film were primed with a description which denied the reality of the bloody events in the film, or were encouraged to view them in a detached objective manner, they were less aroused than subjects in the control group who were offered no suggestion for the cognitive appraisal (Lazarus & Alfert, 1964).

White's Classification of Coping Behavior

The personal aspects of coping are further enriched by White's (1974) classification of coping behavior deduced from observing animals and young children. He proposes three basic strategies:

1. *Securing adequate information.* Individuals seek the amount or rate of information that is useful in clearly guiding their actions. They will not know what to do if there is too little information. On the other hand, if there is too much, they will withdraw to escape the confusing overload. Information can be obtained in a variety of ways including reading and talking to others. White also suggests that information can be useful in an immediate situation or can be stored to prepare for future action.

2. *The effort to maintain internal organization.* This includes enhancing and maintaining self-esteem and a sense of self-competence. White contends that we strive toward an inner assurance that we can do the things necessary for a satisfactory life.

3. *Maintaining autonomy.* Organisms like having options and preserving an acceptable level of freedom. We believe this goal of adaptation has been given too little attention in the social support work to date.

Learned Helplessness

Other potentially pertinent literature can be used as examples of the process of building a stronger theoretical base for the phenomenon social support. Learned helplessness as described by Seligman (1975) is the expectation that outcomes are not affected by one's own actions, and this expectation results from past experiences of ineffectiveness. In this condition, the individual is not motivated to initiate voluntary responses because he believes they would be futile. The individual is influenced cognitively in that he does not learn that his responses can be effective, and a depressed affect results from realizing his ineffectiveness.

Recently, attribution theory was used to reformulate the theory of learned helplessness (Abramson, Garber, & Seligman, 1980). In the attributional approach, when people perceive themselves to be helpless, they wonder *why* they are helpless; i.e., they make causal attributions about their perceived ineffectiveness. Three dimensions have been proposed along which causal attributions are made, but only personal-universal, or internal-external, will be considered. At the personal-internal end of the continuum, the person believes that only he is ineffective; others are effective in influencing outcomes through their actions. At the universal or external extreme, the person believes that not only he but also everyone else is helpless; i.e., something about the situation or in the environment prevents effective action by any comparable others. Low self-esteem is much more likely to result for those who perceive only themselves as ineffective or helpless, those at the personal or internal end of the continuum.

The idea of learned helplessness is easily related to the previously discussed coping framework through the concept of appraisal; i.e., the evaluation of the probability of successfully dealing with a situation presented by the environment and the corresponding emotional responses are likely to be influenced by beliefs about past successes or failures. The more unique the individual feels about his helplessness, the more profound may be the consequences for feeling inadequate and vulnerable.

CLASSIFICATION OF RISK FACTORS

It is necessary to consider who is at high risk of feeling threatened or of having problems with coping in relation to the concepts presented in the Lazarus model, by White's classification of coping behavior, and through the aspects of learned helplessness. A beginning classification is proposed in Table 1. These risk factors are probably not mutually exclusive; nor is it likely that they are exhaustive. Their purpose is to demonstrate that it is possible to derive potential indicators of vulnerability based on the types of conceptualizations considered in this paper, and that these factors are amenable to empirical testing and are relevant to parent and child health.

Surprise

The factor of surprise requires rapid appraisal without prior rehearsal. Although not all findings are consistent, there has been work which suggests that adaptation to unexpected deaths is more difficult than when death is predictable (Parkes, 1975; Bowlby, 1980). It is difficult to prepare for some events because they are by their nature unexpected. Other situations can be anticipated more readily, but some individuals are better prepared than others.

Table 1
Beginning Classification of Risk Factors for
Perception of Threat and Coping Problems

| Risk Factor | Risk of Threat and Coping Problems | |
	High Risk	Low Risk
Surprise	Situation unexpected.	Situation anticipated or viewed as a possibility.
Experience	Challenge new. Unprepared. No previous experience or anticipatory preparation.	Previous experience relevant to situation. Gained needed knowledge beforehand.
Confusion	Trouble interpreting information and cues regarding the situation.	Understands the "language" of the environment.
Perceived effectiveness	Has "failed" before in similar situation. Low on self-esteem and mastery.	Sense of mastery for similar situations.
Perceived allies	Feels alone. Perceives no present or potential allies to assist.	Part of network of mutual obligation.
Perceived uniqueness of threat	Feels singled out and different in the situation.	Knows others are or have been in same situation.
Overload	Multiple simultaneous situations drawing on coping resources.	Few events which require coping.

Experience

Prior experience or anticipatory coping can assist when the event does occur. For example, there is more uncertainty on the part of parents as to what the demands are and whether they will successfully meet them with the first child than with the subsequent ones. Some parents prepare ahead of time and better than other parents for the first labor and delivery experience and for caring for the new baby.

Confusion

Threat can be magnified by confusion about the cues coming from the environment, their meaning, and, therefore, about how to respond appropriately. This confusion and its effect on health was discussed by John Cassel years ago in the early stages of the literature on social support (Cassel, 1974). Confusion can arise from being transplanted to unfamiliar surroundings and from a lack of cultural familiarity with the content and expectations of social exchange. Currently, the factor of confusion must be having an effect on the parents who adopt children from other countries. One has only to talk to the adoptive parents of these children to clearly get the message that they encounter many threats to their being "good parents." It is also apparent that the adopted children have as great a challenge in feeling secure in their strange surrounding and knowing what is expected of them.

Perceived Effectiveness

Previous failure or perceived past events as a personal failure can also lead to a high perception of threat and a feeling of helplessness. In the parent-child health area, this is perhaps best exemplified by parents who have experienced a previous sudden infant death. They are especially vulnerable as they anticipate the care and responsibility for a second infant.

Perceived Allies

Since secondary appraisal of available resources to assist the individual determines the degree of threat, those who assess themselves as having to manage alone are likely to perceive greater threat. This factor typifies single parents who bear the many challenges of child rearing by themselves.

Perceived Uniqueness of Threat

It is not clear how the perceived uniqueness of a threat creates discomfort, but the importance of this factor is attested to by the desirable effects of self-help groups. Those who have experienced an event, such as the loss of a child, find comfort in knowing that other parents in similar situations have experienced comparable feelings and symptoms.

Overload

Life presents individuals with varying amounts of stimuli with which to deal. The component of overload due to the finite amount of coping resources has been documented in the extensive research on the relationship between life changes and illness.

The specification and testing of risk factors such as these are necessary steps in moving toward a clinical utilization of the research on social support; i.e., they provide a base to assess the particular types of support which are lacking, thereby suggesting the most appropriate support to be provided. For example, for the parents who lose a child and are experiencing their feelings as unique, the necessary intervention would be to introduce them to other parents who have lost a child or refer them to a group such as Compassionate Friends.

SOCIAL SUPPORT AND THE COPING PROCESS

In the Lazarus conceptualization, there is little emphasis placed on how other individuals can assist in the coping process, but some possibilities are quite evident. For example, in regard to appraisal, other individuals can assist in validly evaluating the significance of the stimulus or potential threat. These persons can be perceived as available and willing to complement or stand in as resources and enable the individual to meet his need for action. They can assist in promoting the individual's sense of mastery, and they can encourage and provide cues in the reappraisal process. These supportive persons can assist in taking direct action to manipulate the environment, or they can anticipate the future and encourage the individual to prepare for it.

None of these concepts are incompatible with the literature on social support. For example, Cobb's (1976, pp. 300-301) often-quoted definition of social support substantiates the need for persons who provide social support--Social support is " . . . information that one is cared for and loved; that one is valued and esteemed; and that one belongs to a network of mutual obligation."

The question that remains to be answered in terms that can explain health-related outcomes is--what good does it do a person to be loved, valued, and in network of mutual obligation? Based on an examination of the concepts in this paper, the good probably comes from an increased sense of self-worth and mastery and from being valued enough that others are likely to assist in the manner discussed, as well as the fact that a mutually obliged network provides greater accessibility or perceived accessibility to allies to assist.

In the research to date, social support has usually been measured subjectively, i.e., by the subject's report of how positive the efforts of others are on his behalf (House, 1981). While this practice can be justifiably questioned, the fact remains that perceived supportiveness is what has been empirically related to health states. This would indicate that any theoretical attempts to better explain how social support works should consider the perceptual or cognitive link.

The logic of an approach such as the one proposed in this paper is also supported by the theme of the "buffering" effects of social support (LaRocco, et al., 1980); i.e., social support often explains significant differences in health outcomes only under conditions of high stress. This indicates the relevance of an individual's coping process and the potential roles of social support.

RESEARCH CONSIDERATIONS

The framework to study social support and vulnerable families which has been described in this paper requires additional, extensive descriptive work. For example, how well do social scientists understand the stimuli in typical situations and the elements of potential threat for parents and children? It is impossible to view any situation as presenting a single environmental stimulus. Stimuli occur in sets, or patterns, for example, the situation of bringing home a new baby. In our research we have been developing a method to describe the concerns mothers and fathers have in this situation. It has been found that parents are willing and even eager to tell investigators what worries them, and some patterns of most frequent concerns have been identified. These findings may provide helpful directions for planning supportive activities to alleviate the threatening aspects of the situation as parents view them. In the past, the health care system has attempted to prepare parents-to-be and to try to help them over the initiation period, but the point is how well does the preparation and the help correspond to what the parents actually perceive to be their difficulties. The same questions could be asked of the many situation where professionals want to assist families. The final answers will depend on descriptive work done from the family's perspective.

There are also many potential benefits to be gained from experimental trials suggested by a framework such as the one proposed in this paper. In addition to finding ways to help vulnerable individuals more effectively, it would help to test proposed models and their causative relationships. Here the work of Jean Johnson and associates (1978) is exemplary. They prepare patients for the sensory experiences they will have during hospital procedures using experimental designs. Those who are so prepared and know what to expect tend to have more positive outcomes following the procedure. The findings are not always simple and straightforward; however, they are cumulative. Their replications lend credence to the principle that people do better when they know what to expect. Information from professionals is supportive, anxiety is reduced, and patients feel more in control and better able to master the situation.

Closer to our own field of interest, preparation for childbirth and its relationship to better mental health states are now being conceptualized in terms of women's sense of mastery in the situation (Humenick & Bugen, 1981). We believe that the key to future gains rests not only in experimenting as to whether preparation for childbirth makes a difference in mental health outcomes, but also as to whether preparation increases mastery and mastery contributes to mental health. It is time to identify and measure potential intervening variables through which the social environment assists individuals in potentially stressful situations. The intervening variables need to be derived from some explanatory process if cumulative progress is to occur.

In this paper, we have focused more on future research concerning social support by professional care personnel than from environmental networks. This is partly because in the effort to assist families, it is logical to have professional care personnel behaving in the most supportive ways possible.

As Cassel (1974) pointed out and as behavioral scientists are well aware, the social environment is a source of both threat and support. Because professionals deal with families in difficult circumstances, it becomes very easy to be more representative of a threat than a support. For example, this situation might occur when a professional provides information too fast or in language that is confusing rather than supportive. Assumptions also might be threatening if professionals failed to assess the background of the family members for their mastery, both past and present. It is easy for professionals to overlook evaluating the availability of natural social supports which people can use as resources.

THE FUTURE

We would like to close with some cautionary notes as we look toward the future. Social support is a very complex construct which, for all its intuitive appeal, we are only beginning to understand. Currently, we are making numerous assumptions which have not been empirically tested. Among the complexities which require attention is the tendency for people to prefer different types of networks and to interact with them in different styles (MacElveen, 1978). Additionally, we use different parts of our networks for support depending on the aspect of our lives which is involved (Hirsch, 1980). As House stated, we need to understand better the answers to *"who give what to whom regarding which problems"* (1981, p. 22). Overlying these issues are the longitudinal factors that influence the supply and demand of support over the life span (Kahn & Antonucci, 1980). Cultural context is also another large and important dimension in understanding individual coping and the processes which support it.

It is fascinating to ponder the potential implications of understanding and implementing social support in formal care systems. If we and others (House, 1981; Dill & Feld, 1982) are correct, the logical outcome will be promoting mastery and self-determination, "empowering" the potentially vulnerable. This, by definition, will be at odds with many current practices designed for efficient control and prescriptive compliance.

Helping efforts by health care systems may not be completely beneficial. Assistance which is nonproductive may be overprotective; and support may be considered an image of inadequacy, or it may generate assymetrical or nonreciprocal relationships (DiMatteo & Hays, 1981). The need for future attention to the role of promoting autonomy and independence as a definitional part of social support is evident.

All of these issues are important for progress in studying social support. The most critical, however, is the need to explore and develop theoretical frameworks.

CRITIQUE
Toni C. Antonucci, Ph.D.

The recent attention paid to the concept of social support and its role in physical and mental health is extremely gratifying. It is now widely accepted that interpersonal relationships and specifically social support have an important and direct effect on the health of the individual. But as Drs. MacElveen-Hoehn and Eyres have appropriately stressed, it is now incumbent upon us to move past this recognition point and begin to understand how social support works.

I would like to begin by saying that I am pleased to be a part of this conference and I am particularly happy to be offering a critique on this first paper. It seems to me that there is an implied challenge to delivering the first paper in a roundtable conference such as this. The authors faced the task of surveying the field, reviewing the literature, directing our attention to the problems still remaining to be solved, and pointing us in the direction of solving those problems. Drs. MacElveen-Hoehn and Eyres have certainly met that challenge. They have also resolved the problem of addressing a multifaceted audience at this conference, consisting of theoreticians, researchers, and clinicians (sometimes all within the same person) by addressing their comments to the multiple issues raised by each of these perspectives. In short, they have provided the diverse interests among us with theoretical, experimental, and practical information. I have tried to continue this three-tiered approach in my remarks.

It is an exciting and challenging task to be in the position of commenting on a "state of the art" paper. I have addressed myself not only to the specific issues raised in our first paper, but I have also addressed the broader issues raised by Drs. MacElveen-Hoehn and Eyres in a more general manner. I have used this opportunity to attempt to both integrate these considerations and to extend them to include what have been considered diverse areas. I have been somewhat expansive in my efforts, i.e., sometimes making what others might consider unwarranted leaps from theory to data and then back to theory. I hope you will bear with me in exploring these proposed linkages.

THEORY

At the theoretical level, I agree with Drs. MacElveen-Hoehn and Eyres that it is important to consider the possibility of direct and indirect effects of social support, i.e., social support as a main effect or buffer. Although it is not clearly understood how social support works, our understanding of the conceptualizations of the different effects seems straightforward. In the case of main or direct effect, social support is hypothesized to affect well-being directly. A frequently cited study by Lowenthal and Haven (1968), for example, found that elderly people who have a confidant report higher levels of well-being than people who do not. An analogous finding might be that families with supportive networks will have infants with higher well-being who are more likely to develop normally.

Some argue that social support reduces the effect of objective stress on sub-jective stress, thereby reducing the negative impact that stress would have on well-being (House, 1981). Still others argue that the existence of social sup-port buffers or insulates the individual from the objective stress (Jackson, 1980). This minimizes the effect of objective stress upon the subjective stress experienced by the individual. The effect would be no decrease or less of a decrease in well-being resulting from that stress and perhaps no discernible effects of social support (Jackson, 1980). Examples of the former buffering effect might include the young pregnant teen who experiences the stresses of the situation, but is helped through this difficult time by a supportive social network. The stress, therefore, might cause a minimum negative impact on the teenager's well-being. In the latter type of buffering, the family of a han-dicapped child might be faced with the objective stress of caring for a depen-dent and needy child. This stress might never be subjectively experienced and have no effect on perceived well-being; thus, no impact on the social support network would be found. The objective stress of caring for the handicapped child might be prevented from being translated into a subjective stress through a myriad of supportive behaviors exhibited by the support network, in this case, network members who help provide care for the handicapped child. In short, there are a variety of ways in which social support might affect well-being when a family is faced with a vulnerable infant.

I think these differences are important theoretically. However, an additional problem continues to be present. Are there factors which both decrease the likelihood of social support being available and concomitantly increase the likelihood that vulnerability exists or stress will occur? I believe that the answer to this question is most probably yes. For example, the reason teenagers become pregnant might be a lifetime of poor or negative social support.

RESEARCH

The next question to ask, as Drs. MacElveen-Hoehn and Eyres so clearly in-dicated, is — what are these factors?

To consider this question, I believe it makes sense to examine the evidence that has accumulated over the past several years. In this regard, this first paper has been very helpful in highlighting a variety of areas that seem divergent and yet may actually have an impact upon our understanding of social support. Consider Drs. MacElveen-Hoehn and Eyres' inclusion of the literature in the areas of attachment, competency, self-concept, negative outcomes such as child abuse and parent maltreatment, stress and life changes, coping, and a recognition of the importance of a life span framework. I must confess that I, too, tend to believe that if we are to understand the etiology of social support, we must investigate many facets of the literature. Social support is a complicated concept, and its implications are far reaching.

I have focused on the very useful framework Drs. MacElveen-Hoehn and Eyres have suggested with the above content areas in mind. They have integrated several converging lines of research to offer a potential answer to the question of how social support works. Their model considers seven risk factors. These are surprise, experience, confusion, perceived effectiveness, perceived allies, perceived uniqueness of threat, and overload. The model relies heavily upon the individual's perception of the situation. Some might see this as a methodological flaw, but I disagree since satisfaction with network is highly correlated with positive outcomes such as health. It is also apparent that it is the individual's perception of the situation, accurate or not, which determines the effect of a support network. I would concede, however, that understanding how the individual arrived at that perception is a very critical question. The framework offered by Drs. MacElveen-Hoehn and Eyres, therefore, had intuitive appeal to me. I believe that it will be useful to consider the risk factors they cited and then determine, based on one's knowledge of the individual, whether he or she should be considered high or low risk.

In fact, the model reminded me of recent work being conducted by a variety of researchers on the importance of predictability, understanding, and control. I would like to offer these concepts as potentially helpful in extending the MacElveen-Hoehn and Eyres' framework. Predictability, or the ability to forecast periods of stress and safety, has been shown to be an important factor in coping. Schultz and Hanusa (1980) report that familiarizing an individual with scheduling improves the individual's ability to adapt to an institution. Sears (1981) notes that ability to predict an event improves adaptability to it. The work of Johnson and associates (1978), cited by MacElveen-Hoehn and Eyres, prepared individuals for hospital procedures by familiarizing them with the sensory experiences they would have, and it confirms this point. Essentially, by providing people with greater predictability, they were able to produce more positive outcomes. Several of the risk factors mentioned by MacElveen-Hoehn and Eyres seem related to predictability, including surprise and experience.

A second factor said to enhance coping is understanding. Although not necessarily related to predictability or control, understanding can affect coping. As already noted by MacElveen-Hoehn and Eyres, Lazarus and Alfert (1964) discuss the importance of "cognitive appraisals." Shelly Taylor (1982), for example, has found that many victims of breast cancer experience the need to understand the disease, its causes, and prognosis. Again people seem to cope better if they feel they understand the processes at work.

Understanding appears to be directly related to the risk factor of confusion. Finally, the notion of control seems to permeate all the risk factors; i.e., one who feels in control is more likely to assume that there are people upon whom he or she might call in times of need or overload. Certainly this might be considered a form of control. Several notable studies have been reported which indicate the importance of control. As noted by MacElveen-Hoehn and Eyres, Seligman (1975) uses this concept to define learned helplessness. Additionally, Langer and Rodin (1976) demonstrated the effect of perceived control over a small portion of the environment on adaptation to institutionalization of an older sample. In short, I believe the research which has been conducted and is yet to be conducted surrounding the concepts of predictability, understanding, and control has much to offer to facilitate our understanding of the classification of risk factors outlined by Drs. MacElveen-Hoehn and Eyres.

In our search to understand, I believe we must continue to ask questions. For example, how will repeated experiences of predictability, understanding, and control affect the individual? I propose that the answer to this question is involved in the complex construct of self-esteem. The adult who has been continually exposed to these experiences will be positively affected. A life time of experiences accumulate and substantially contribute to how individuals view themselves. These experiences are perceived as related abilities.

Is there any relationship among the experiences of predictability, understanding, and control and social support? I suggest that there is. Consider the following simplified interpretation. The individual who is surrounded by an environment that is predictable, understandable, and controllable is surrounded by a supportive environment. The proposed relationship among these variables can be related to the example of infant development and attachment. We are beginning to recognize that the mother-infant attachment or their social bond is an important foundation for competence with regard to both social and cognitive skills in the older child. Such diverse researchers as Ainsworth, Blehar, Waters, & Wall (1978); Gewirtz (1972); Lewis, Goldberg, & Campbell (1969); and Watson (1972) have argued that one of the crucial variables operating in the mother-child relationship is contingency. I suggest that the infant is being taught that the world is predictable, understandable, and controllable. Securely attached or appropriately bonded infants become competent children and later competent adults. As competent adults they seek and develop a social support network that will maintain these contingency factors of predictability, understandability, and control. Assuming that self-esteem is a dynamic concept, these experiences continually enhance one's feelings of self-esteem.

Of course, the opposite scenario could be described, perhaps the family who will have the most difficulty coping with a vulnerable infant. For this family, contingent interactions will be unfamiliar, and experiences will have been perceived on the whole to be neither predictable, understandable, nor controllable. The individual family member's resultant self-esteem will be low, and the support network is not likely to have been a very positve influence. I recognize that these links may seem somewhat tenuous, but I believe that consideration of these factors within a life span framework will help extend our understanding of how social support operates and how it develops. Each of these concepts can be examined separately in systematic research endeavors. In addition, there are clear implications of these ideas for practical application.

PRACTICAL APPLICATION

If the hypothesized relationships described previously are valid, the next question to be asked is: how can this new understanding be useful? With regard to the notion of contingency, I believe that both infants and adults can be trained in contingencies. Although perhaps not evident from the brief previous discussion, the reason the contingency experience is important for infants is that they "learn the rules of the game" (Watson, 1972). They learn that if they cry, for example, mom will attend to them, and concomitantly if mom does call them, she expect them to attend to her. A continuous build up of these experiences leads children to have a working knowledge of how to affect the environment and how one will be affected by it. Thus, the older child who has had a positive, supposedly contingent relationship with the mother will later know rules to be applied when interacting with peers.

This concept is an intuitive conclusion, but I propose that the same principles are operating when the individual becomes an adult. I offer as corroborating evidence the fact that adults appear to be both more satisfied with and more positively influenced by supportive relationships which are reciprocal. Reciprocity is defined as supports which are exchanged. Support networks which are reciprocal indicate that the individual provides others with support and also is provided with support from others (Wentowski, 1981; Satarioano, Minkler, & Langhauser, 1981; Kahn & Antonucci, 1980).

If contingency and reciprocity are indeed both important to the development and functioning of social support, training and intervention could be implemented for at risk populations. Using the framework Drs. MacElveen-Hoehn and Eyres provided, individuals exposed to risk factors who are at high risk could be provided with an intervention program designed to maximize their experiences of understanding, predictability, and control. They would then be encouraged to seek out similar reciprocal relations.

Infants and their parents also could be exposed to training programs designed to provide maximal contingency experiences. Experimental research has already established that infants can learn contingencies in a laboratory setting (Ramey & Watson, 1972; Millar, 1972). The contingency training of vulnerable infants by their parents may represent a signifcant intervention for both the infants and their parents.

CONCLUSION

I strongly agree with Drs. MacElveen-Hoehn and Eyres that we must now turn our attention to the question--what makes social support work? I think their integration of the social support literature with the coping literature is both innovative and exciting. In my comments I have tried to extend their framework for understanding the underlying mechanisms of social support both at the research and practical level. I hope this somewhat expansive integration has provided a stimulating and useful springboard for future research and practice.

DISCUSSION

M. Cranley: Social support is now being provided in the context of a profesional service, and there is a fee for service. I wonder if you have any comments about how in a therapeutic relationship between a nurse and a client you could build in reciprocity to make the client feel better about receiving service, apart from just paying for it?

T. Antonucci: Your comments remind me of an article awhile back about support from formal sources (Cobb & Erbe, 1978). The authors argue that you need to provide support during times of crisis, but that if you maintain that supportive relationship past that crisis, you are doing both the patient and yourself a disservice. The patient is building a dependency or a lack of reciprocity. One should ask why a physician would maintain a one-sided relationship of providing support at such a critical level for the patient. Physicians should be developing personal reciprocal support relationships. So that is one level of the comment. At the classical level of intervention, I would say that it is really our job to teach people to develop reciprocal relationships somewhere. I don't consider fee-for-service reciprocity, and by that I mean, patients don't own you because they paid you. I guess you could look at it that way, but it's not the same kind of reciprocity that seems to work. However, it is true that people who can't pay frequently feel bad about that, and this has been known to interfere with the physician-patient relationship. One way to arrange for reciprocity is to have the reciprocity going from the provider to the recipients and then to a third party who needs a service the recipient can render. I have this grand fantasy where you set up a scheme of interlocking support systems. People with mutual needs are interconnected, such as grandparents and older lonely people babysitting for single parent families. If you can develop relationships, I think in most communities there are people who have needs that complement each other. If you can set up these relationships, I think you're doing a big service. So I guess the answer consists of two points: 1) don't let the formal relationship get out of hand, last too long, or be too dependent; and 2) try to get the recipient to provide a service or be a support to other people.

P. MacElveen-Hoehn: I think that we are not really clear yet on the difference between a contractual relationship, which is usually what our professional relationship is and a supportive relationship, which may be something that is less formal. I'm not sure we can talk about both relationships simultaneously without defining the difference. I certainly have been surprised because I have had various people over time list the important people in their lives, from whom they would be expecting to get support, and I have yet to have people list their physician or the nurses that they interact with in the health care system.

Prof vs personal

J. Norbeck: I have had the same experience with patients regarding the social support network. One of the categories that we ask people to list is health care providers. For the most part, people did not list health care providers but there are some exceptions. People who are coming in for oncology care, for example, develop a special relationship with the nurse they see during these frequent visits, and in certain of these cases, a special relationship develops which is really different from the role description of the oncology nurse. In that case the nurse is listed or another health care provider, but it certainly is an exception.

P. Brandt: I would like to focus on another approach in our search to understand social support. I think one can have high self-esteem and feel like a competent person, but other factors can make a big difference in whether you obtain social support or not. For example, I may have less experience with certain problems and not be able to ask for help when I need it. I would like us to broaden our approach in thinking about what social support means, because support can be affected by situational factors which interact with personality attributes such as communication skills or extroverted behavior. I look at attachment and competence as being more of a psychoanalytic or personality development approach, but our understanding of social support also will be enhanced by studying how ecological and behavioral views of human behavior interact to influence one's social support.

S. Eyres: I don't know if it's so much a different theory being brought to bear that's the answer, or whether we need to get a little more multifaceted regarding the context which we are using to define social support. For example, it is still possible to think in the terms that Toni Antonucci has drawn for us about the youngster learning to believe that things are controllable and predictable, and, therefore, going on to have a positive view of himself and be more effective. I think concurrently that the person, no matter what age, is going to be affected by things within the situation as you have suggested.

There was a recent chapter by Wrubel, Benner, and Lazarus (1981) on this subject. I believe that we have to get more complex with this whole business of social support before we can make it manageable to study. And I think we need to start thinking about different aspects of the situation: the individual, the environment, what has happened to trigger the event, and the whole set of circumstances in which the event is happening. Maybe that is what you are calling an ecological view.

P. Brandt: That is part of what I was getting at; there are multiple interacting factors which impact whether a person has support available and/or can actualize support when needed.

S. Eyres: I think part of our task is to bring theories and bodies of literature together, but I think the biggest task we have, and Toni Antonucci was alluding to this, is synthesizing and drawing from the body of knowledge we gather. And I think that when we do that, we may not recognize it as a certain kind of theory any longer. I would hope it will be a new synthesis.

K. Barnard: I find myself about to relate to you something I never thought I would find myself saying today, but Toni Antonucci's remarks about predictability, understandability, and control led me to the experiment we've done with premature infants, in which we provided rocking and heartbeat experiences to them (Barnard & Bee, 1981). For one of the experimental groups, rocking and heartbeat stimulation was based on their activity patterns. When they were inactive for 90 seconds, it resumed, but they could not turn it on again for 45 minutes. The stimulus was contingent upon their inactivity, but they also had a descrimination learning task in which they had to learn when they could cause it to resume. These tasks involve learning prediction and control. Now, the fascinating result about this group was that those infants at 2 years of age had an IQ on the Bayley Infant Scales 33 points higher than the control group. D. Magyary, P. Brandt, and I, along with some others, are planning a follow-up of these children at school age. If this set of stimulus conditions gave a schema for learning about predictability, control, and temporal relationships, perhaps this one paradigm continues to provide them with a schema to transfer to other analyses of situations. I have been constantly impressed with one of the items that is so important in terms of health teaching which is in line with Jean Johnson's (1978) work; i.e., by helping people understand what they might experience, how to predict what is going to happen when they have surgery and become unconscious, or the whole basis of how we orient children to hospitalization, are concepts really based on preparing them to be able to anticipate. I think predictability is an extremely important concept, and I agree with S. Eyres that we may, in fact, be moving toward a major reformulation of how social relationships and learning interface.

L. Cronenwett: I agree with Patti Brandt, but I still think we need evidence that social support encompasses more than some larger factor like social competence. When I read the papers for this conference, I was struck with the fact that either the results or the references indicated that social support was correlated with problem solving skills, a successful marital relationship, fetal attachment, all things which represent the same sort of ability, i.e., the ability to either commit or receive from other human beings. So at this point, I am still waiting for some evidence that there is something else besides the social competence factor that evolves, possibly from the time you are young until you are an adult. Indeed, there may be moments when you do not have the kind of support you need, for example, if your child dies of SIDS and you do not know anyone else whose child died of SIDS. There might be those moments, but a person with social competence may be able to immediately obtain the support that is needed, e.g., by contacting others who have this situation.

P. Brandt: I think your comments are excellent. A global social competence factor appears to be an important variable in the correlation data obtained in social support studies. However, the explained variance between social support and variables such as the marital relationship is generally found to be about 25-30%. We don't have information about the remaining unexplained variance of 70-75%. Would it be important to assess specific abilities and personality styles within selected situations? For example, is it necessary to know the person's communication skills, problem solving ability, past experience in similar situations, self-esteem, and interactive styles (extroversion versus introversion) in order to explain the level of social support obtained? And, would the outcome differ if the situation was different, or if the person had physical and/or mental health difficulties?

T. Antonucci: I think that we probably need to develop a whole other set of classifications about this aspect. One set should be developed at the individual level, and some of the examples I was giving were at the individual level and in terms of individual development. I also want to consider the person who lives in an environment where the support networks are noncontingent or are not helpful for whatever reasons, negative support, etc., and this person has had a lifetime of that experience. That is one problem we need to deal with and solve--how do these persons modify their life experiences to the point where they can have a more positive adjustment?

The other consideration is the person who is generally pretty competent, is fairly good at establishing contingent relationships, and has a network of people who are similarly contingent. What happens when this person is confronted with a situation that is very different from all the other kinds of situations previously encountered? Illness and the sudden infant death syndrome are good examples. A person who is suddenly confronted with problems or crises like these, which are discordant from their life experiences, is very different from a person who has a series of life experiences that are noncontingent. Both types of individuals require different sets of questions to determine how these people differ.

M. Rose: I would also like to speak to the area of predictability of the environment. In my own research on coping behaviors, one of the things I measured was what I call precoping behaviors, which are exploratory information-seeking behaviors (Rose, 1972). Children generally spend a lot of time doing them, but in comparing behaviors between home and hospital, precoping behaviors increased significantly in the hospital. While I certainly support the efforts made in preparing children for hospitalization, one of the things that happened during hospitalization was that the number of times the child was allowed to move from precoping to coping behaviors without being interfered with in any way decreased significantly in the hospital. There were a lot more episodes where children were interrupted in the preparatory cycle and were not allowed to handle the situation themselves. Also, the things they looked at in the hospital were often very mundane things which are never included in preparation for hospitalization, such as looking in the trash can, at the babies, and a whole number of other items. So I think sometimes social support is not always interacting, but instead is allowing children, and probably adults, to proceed at their own rate and to be sensitive when they need help and when they need to be allowed to proceed at their rate.

K. Pridham: I have a question about the concept of hope and how it may relate to issues that Drs. Antonucci and MacElveen-Hoehn were discussing. How does that concept relate to the notion of contingency, if at all?

T. Antonucci: How does hope relate to contingency? I do not know if they are different, but it certainly seems to me that unless you believe in contingencies, that is not true either. I was going to say the unless you believe in contingencies, why would you have hope? But, I think they are different because you can come to hope from two different perspectives. One is the control ability-contingency perspective where you can control it, change it, and, therefore, you should be hopeful. The other perspective is faith or something like that where someone is going to come and do it for you--providence, fate, or destiny, and that does not require any control.

P. MacElveen-Hoehn: I think the area of hope does encourage some very interesting questions, and I'm not sure what hope itself implies, possibly some mastery potential. We also have to recognize that hope is as dynamic as social support is, in that the projection of hope often changes over time in a situation. What was an original hope may, with increasing feedback in the situation, be shifted to something with a greater possibility of being mastered. I am more familiar with that in terms of hope in relation to terminal illness. Whereas in the beginning when the first symptoms occur, the hope always is, "This isn't anything serious." When the diagnosis is that it is malignant, then the hope changes to, "Well, certainly this can be handled, can be treated." And then when it is treated, the patient shifts again to the hope, "They got it all." I think we have to appreaciate that hope does vary due to changes in the situation and feedback from the environment.

S. Eyres: One would hope that if the supports were working in a non-life-threatening situation, that the hope would improve and that there would be more hope if the supports are working.

N. Jackson: Or, if not more hope, that the hope won't be false hope. One of my favorite authors, C.P. Snow (1972) talks about false hope as being one of the greatest tragedies in life, and hope that can be realized should be the kind of hope that is consistent with information from the environment.

P. MacElveen-Hoehn: Would we then assume that false hope or unreasonable kinds of hope are really maladaptive coping, i.e., is this disfunctional for the individual?

N. Jackson: I think that really depends on the individual. If we consider the kind of person that C.P. Snow writes about or I consider the kind of person that I think of myself as being, it would be maladaptive. It is not consistent with the kind of life I want to live, but I can acknowledge that there may be kinds of people for whom false hope may be essential. And there may be times that I will encounter in my life when I, too, will need some false hope.

REFERENCES

Abramson, L., Garber, J., & Seligman, M. (1980). Learned helplessness in humans: An attributional analysis. In J. Garber, & E.P. Scligman (Eds.), *Human helplessness: Theories and applications.* New York: Academic Press.

Ainsworth, M.D.S., Blehar, M.C., Waters, E., & Wall, S. (1978). *Patterns of attachment: A psychological study of the strange situation.* Hillsdale, NJ: Lawrence Erlbaum.

Antonucci, T. (1976). Attachment: A life span concept. *Human Development, 19,* 135-142.

Arend, R., Gove, F.L., & Sroufe, L.A. (1979). Continuity of individual adaptation from infancy to kindergarten: A predictive study of ego resiliency and curiosity in preschoolers. *Child Development, 50,* 950-959.

Baltes, P.B. (Ed.). (1978). *Life-span development and behavior* (Vol. 1). New York: Academic Press.

Barnard, K.E., & Bee, H. (1981). *Premature infant refocus.* (Final Report, Grant #MC-R-530348, Maternal & Child Health & Crippled Children's Services, Bureau of Community Health Services, HSA, PHS, DHHS.) Seattle, WA: University of Washington.

Barnard, K.E., & Eyres, S. (1977). *Child health assessment. Part II: Results of the first twelve months of life.* Seattle, WA: University of Washington Press.

Barrera, M. (1981). Social support in adjustment of pregnant adolescents: Assessment issues. In B. Gottlieb (Ed.), *Social networks and social support.* Beverly Hills: Sage Publications.

Bowlby, J. (1969). *Attachment and loss, Vol. I: Attachment.* London: Hogarth Press.

Bowlby, J. (1973). *Attachment and loss, Vol. II: Separation: Anxiety and anger.* London: Hogarth Press.

Bowlby, J. (1980). *Attachment and loss, Vol. III: Loss.* New York: Basic Books.

Brandt, P.A. (1980). Social support and life change during early family development. In P. Chinn & K.B. Leonard (Eds.), *Practice in pediatric nursing*. St. Louis: C.V. Mosby.

Brown, G., Bhrolchain, M., & Harris, T. (1975). Social class and psychiatric disturbance among women in an urban population. *Sociology, 9,* 225-254.

Caplan, G. (1974). *Support systems and community mental health*. New York: Behavioral Publications.

Cassel, J. (1974). Psychosocial processes and "stress": Theoretical formulation. *International Journal of Health Services, 4*(3), 471-482.

Cobb, S. (1976). Social support as a moderator of life stress. *Psychosomatic Medicine, 38,* 300-314.

Cobb, S., & Erbe, C. (1978, November). Social support for the cancer patient. *FORUM on Medicine,* 24-29.

Cochran, M.M., & Brassard, J.A. (1979). Child development and personal social networks. *Child Development, 50,* 601-616.

Collins, A., & Pancoast, D. (1976). *Natural helping networks*. Washington, DC: National Association of Social Workers.

Cooley, R. (1902). *Human nature and social order*. New York: Scribner.

Crnic, K.A., Greenberg, M.T., Ragozin, A.S., Robinson, N.M., & Busharn, R. (1981). *The effects of stress and social support on maternal attitudes and the mother-infant relationship*. Paper presented at the Society for Research in Child Development in Boston.

Dean, A., & Lin, N. (1977). The stress-buffering role of social support. *Journal of Nervous and Mental Disorders, 65,* 403-416.

Dill, D., & Feld, E. (1982). The challenge of coping. In D. Belle (Ed.), *Lives in stress*. Beverly Hills: Sage Publications.

DiMatteo, M.R., & Hays, R. (1981). Social support and serious illness. In B.H. Gottlieb (Ed.), *Social networks and social support*. Beverly Hills: Sage Publications.

Dohrenwend, B.S., & Dohrenwend, B.P. (1978). Some issues in research on stressful life events. *Journal of Nervous and Mental Disease, 166,* 7-15.

Easterbrooks, M.A., & Lamb, M.E. (1979). The relationship between quality of infant-mother attachment and infant competence in initial encounters with peers. *Child Development, 50,* 380-387.

Eckenrode, J., & Gore, S. (1981). Stressful events and social supports: The significance of context. In B.H. Gottlieb (Ed.), *Social network and social support*. Beverly Hills: Sage Publications.

Folkman, S., Schaefer, C., Lazarus, R. (1979). Cognitive processes as mediators of stress and coping. In V. Hamilton, & D. Warburton (Eds.), *Human stress and cognition: An information processing approach*. New York: John Wiley & Sons.

Furstenberg, F.F., & Crawford, A.G. (1978). Family support: Helping teenage mothers to cope. *Family Planning Perspective, 10*(6), 322-333.

Garbarino, J., & Sherman, D. (1980). High risk neighborhoods and high risk families: The human ecology of child maltreatment. *Child Development, 51,* 188-198.

Gewirtz, J.L. (1972). *Attachment and dependency*. Washington, DC: V.H. Winston.

Gore, S. (1978). The effect of social support in moderating the health consequences of unemployment. *Journal of Health and Social Behavior, 19,* 157-165.

Gottlieb, B.H. (Ed.). (1981). *Social networks and social support*. Beverly Hills: Sage Publications.

Hamburg, B.A., & Killilea, M. (1979). Relation of social support, stress, illness, and use of health services. *The Surgeon General's report on health promotion and disease prevention*. (No. 017-001-00417-1). Washington, DC: Government Printing Office.

Henderson, S., Duncan-Jones, P., McAvery, H., & Ritchie, K. (1978). The patient's primary group. *British Journal of Psychiatry, 132,* 74-86.

Hetherington, E.M., Cox, M., & Cox, R. (1978). The aftermath of divorce. In J. Stevens & M. Matthews (Eds.), *Mother-child father-child relationships.* Washington, DC: National Association for the Education of Young Children.

Hirsch, B.J. (1980). Natural support systems and coping with major life changes. *American Journal of Community Psychology, 8*(2), 159-172.

House, J.S. (1981). *Work stress and social support.* Reading, MA: Addison-Wesley.

Hymovich, D., & Chamberlain, R.W. (1980). *Child and family development.* New York: McGraw-Hill.

Humenick, S., & Bugen, L. (1981). Correlates of parent-infant interaction: An exploratory study. In R.P. Lederman & B. Raff (Eds.). *Perinatal parental behavior: Nursing research and implications for newborn health.* March of Dimes *Birth Defects: Original Article Series, XVII* (6), New York: Alan R. Liss.

Jackson, J.S. (1980). *Addendum to grant application: Three generation life cycle analysis of black aging.* Ann Arbor, MI: (Author) University of Michigan, Institutes for Social Research.

Johnson, J., Fuller, S., Endress, M., & Rice, V. (1978). Altering patient's responses to surgery: An extension and replication. *Research in Nursing and Health, 1*(3), 111-121.

Kagey, R.J., Vivace, J., & Lutz, W. (1981). Mental health primary prevention: The role of parent mental support groups. *American Journal of Public Health, 71*(2), 166-167.

Kahn, R., & Antonucci, T. (1980). Convoys over the life course: Attachment, roles, and social support. In M. Blum (Ed.), *Life-span development and behavior* Vol. 3. New York: Academic Press.

Kaplan, B.H., Cassel, J.C., & Gore, S. (1977). Social support and health. *Medical Care, 15* (Suppl.), 47-58.

Knudtson, F.W. (1976). Life-span attachment: Complexities, questions, considerations. *Human Development, 19,* 182-196.

Langer, E., & Rodin, J. (1976). The effects of choice and enhanced personal responsibility for the aged: A field experiment in an institutional setting. *Journal of Personality and Social Psychology, 34,* 191-198.

LaRocco, J., House, J., & French, J. (1980). Social support, occupational stress and health. *Journal of Health and Social Behavior, 21*(3), 202-218.

Lazarus, R. (1974). Psychological stress and coping in adaptation and illness. *International Journal of Psychiatry in Medicine, 5*(4), 321-333.

Lazarus, R. (1975). The self-regulation of emotion. In L. Levi (Ed.), *Emotions: Their parameters and measurement.* New York: Raven Press.

Lazarus, R., & Alfert, E. (1964). Short-circuiting of threat by experimentally altering cognitive appraisal. *Journal of Abnormal and Social Psychology, 69*(2), 195-205.

Lazarus, R., Averill, J., & Opton, E. (1974). The psychology of coping: Issues of research and assessment. In G. Coelho, D. Hamburg, & J. Adams (Eds.), *Coping and adaptation.* New York: Basic Books.

Levenson, P., Atkinson, B., Hale, J., & Hollrer, M. (1978). Adolescent parent education: A maturational model. *Child Psychiatry and Human Development, 9*(2), 104-117.

Lewis, M., Goldberg, S., & Campbell, H. (1969). A developmental study of information processing within the first three years of life: Response decrement to a redundant signal. *Society of Research in Child Development Monograph, 34*(9), Serial No. 133.

Lieberman, A.F. (1977). Preschoolers' competence with a peer: Relations with attachment and peer experiences. *Child Development, 48,* 1277-1287.

Longfellow, C., Zelkowitz, P., Saunders, E., & Belle, D. (1979). *The role of support in moderating the effects of stress and depression.* Paper presented at The Society for Research in Child Development, San Francisco.

Lowenthal, M.F., & Haven, C. (1968). Interaction and adaptation: Intimacy as a critical variable. *American Sociological Review, 33,* 20-30.

MacElveen, P. (1978). Social networks. In D. Longo & R. Williams (Eds.), *Clinical practice in psychosocial nursing.* New York: Appleton-Century-Crofts.

Mead, G.H. (1934). *Mind, self and society.* Chicago: University of Chicago Press.

Mercer, R.T. (1980). Teenaged motherhood: Part I--The teenage mother's news and responses; Part II--How the infants fared. *Journal of Obstetric and Gynecologic and Neonatal Nursing, 9*(1), 16-27.

Millar, W.S. (1972). The study of operant conditioning under delayed reinforcement in early infancy. *Society of Research in Child Development, 37*(2), Series 147.

Moreno, J.L. (1934). Who shall survive? *Nervous and Mental Disease Monograph Series,* No. 58.

Norr, K.L., Block, C.K., Charles, A.G., & Meyermy, S. (1980). The second time around: Parity and the birth experience. *Journal of Obstetrical, Gynecologic and Neonatal Nursing, 9,* 30-36.

Nuckolls, K., Cassel, J., & Kaplan, B. (1972). Psychosocial assets, life crisis and the prognosis of pregnancy. *American Journal of Epidemiology, 95,* 43-44.

Parke, R.D., & Collmer, C.W. (1975). Child abuse: An interdisciplinary analysis. In E.M. Hetherington (Ed.), *Review of child development research* (Vol. 5). Chicago: University of Chicago Press.

Parkes, C.M. (1975). Determinants of outcome following bereavement. *Omega, 6*(4), 303-323.

Porrett, D. (1979). Social support in crisis: Quantity or quality? *Social Science and Medicine, 13,* 715-721.

Ramey, C.T., & Watson, J.S. (1972). Nonsocial reinforcement of infants' vocalizations. *Developmental Psychology, 6,* 538.

Rose, M.H. (1972). The effects of hospitalization on the coping behavior of children. In M. Batey (Ed.), *Communicating nursing research: The many sources of nursing knowledge.* Boulder, CO: Western Interstate Commission for Higher Education.

Sarason, I., Johnson, J., & Sugel, J. (1978). Assessing the impact of life changes: Development of the life experiences survey. *Journal of Consultation and Clinical Psychology, 46,* 932-946.

Satariano, W.A., Minkler, M.A., & Langhauser, C. (1981). *Supportive exchange: A missing link in the study of social networks and health status in the elderly.* Paper presented at the Gerontological Society of America, Toronto.

Sawin, D.B., Hawkins, R.C., Walker, L.O., & Penticuff, J.H. (Eds.). (1980). *Exceptional infant Vol. 4: Psychosocial risks in infant environment transactions.* New York: Brunner/Mazel.

Schulz, R., & Hanusa, B.H. (1980). Experimental social gerontology: A social psychological perspective. *Journal of Social Issues, 36*(2), 30-46.

Sears, D.O. (1981). Life-stage effects on attitude change, especially among the elderly. In S.B. Kiesler, J.N. Morgan, & V.K. Oppenheimer (Eds.), *Aging: Social change.* New York: Academic Press.

Seligman, M. (1975). *Helplessness.* San Francisco: W.H. Freeman.

Simmel, G. (1950). *Soziologne.* Leipzig: Duncker and Humblot, 1908. *[The sociology of George Simmel]* (K. H. Wolff, trans.). New York: Glencoe Free Press.

Snow, C.P. (1972). *Strangers and brothers.* New York: Scribner's.

Stack, C. (1974). *All our kin: Strategies for survival in a black community.* New York: Harper & Row.

Surtees, P.G. (1980). Social support, residual adversity and depressive outcome. *Social Psychiatry, 15,* 71-80.

Sweeny, S.L., & Davis, F.B. (1979). Transitions to parenthood: A group experience. *Maternal-Child Nursing Journal, 8,* 59-64.

Tankson, E.A. (1976). The adolescent parent: One approach to teaching child care and giving support. *Journal of Obstetric and Gynecologic and Neonatal Nursing, 5*(3), 9-15.

Taylor, S. (1982, April). *Adjustment to threatening events: A theory of cognitive adaptation.* Presentation at the Katz-Newcomb Lecture, The University of Michigan.

Tolsdorf, C.C. (1976). Social networks, support and coping. *Family Process, 15,* 407-417.

Wahler, R.G. (1980). The insular mother: Her problems in parent-child treatment. *Journal of Applied Behavior Analysis, 2*(13), 207-219.

Wandersman, L., Wandersman, A., & Kahn, S. (1980). Social support in the transition to parenthood. *Journal of Community Psychology, 8,* 332-342.

Waters, E., Wippman, J., & Sroufe, L.A. (1979). Attachment, positive effect and competence in the peer group: Two studies in constant validation. *Child Development, 50,* 827-829.

Watson, J.S. (1972). Smiling, cooing and "the game." *Merrill-Palmer Quarterly, 82,* 323-341.

Weinraub, M., Brooks, J., & Lewis, M. (1977). The social network: A reconsideration of the concept of attachment. *Human Development, 20,* 31-47.

Weiss, R.S. (1974). The provisions of social relationships. In Z. Rubin (Ed.), *Doing unto others.* Englewood Cliffs, NJ: Prentice-Hall.

Wellman, B. (1981). Applying network analysis to the study of support. In B.H. Gottlieb (Ed.), *Social networks and social support.* Beverly Hills: Sage Publications.

Wentowski, G.J. (1981). Reciprocity and the coping strategies of older people: Cultural dimensions of network building. *The Gerontologist, 21*(6), 600-609.

White, R. (1974). Strategies of adaptation: An attempt at systematic description. In G. Coelho, D. Hamburg, & J. Adams (Eds.), *Coping and adaptation.* New York: Basic Books.

Wrubel, J., Benner, P., & Lazarus, R. (1981). Social competence from the perspective of stress and coping. In J. Wine & M. Smye (Eds.), *Social competence.* New York: Guilford Press.

Zuckerman, B., Winsmore, G., & Alprit, J.J. (1979). A study of attitude and support systems of inner city adolescent mothers. *Journal of Pediatrics, 95*(1), 122-125.

The Norbeck Social Support Questionnaire

Jane S. Norbeck, R.N., D.N.Sc.

The purpose of this paper is to summarize the development and testing of the Norbeck Social Support Questionnaire (NSSQ) and to discuss several issues that have arisen in recent use of the instrument.

The NSSQ is a self-administered questionnaire that measures multiple dimensions of social support. Three functional properties--affect, affirmation, and aid--from Kahn's (1979) definition of social support are measured. The network properties of size, stability (duration of relationships), and accessibility (frequency of contact) are also measured, as well as changes in the convoy or support system due to losses of relationships. Nine categories are used to determine sources of support. Graduate students of nursing (N = 130) were used as subjects for several studies to test reliability and validity, and employed adults (N = 136) were used for additional validity testing and to provide normative data.

Reliability was established through analysis of internal consistency and test-retest measures taken a week apart. Very high levels of internal consistency and test-retest reliability were found for the functional and network properties, and medium levels for the loss items. At a 7-month retesting, medium levels of stability were found, and the instrument was sensitive to changes in the network composition over time. Although the network composition changed, the overall level of functional support remained stable.

Validity of the NSSQ was tested in relation to response bias and concurrent, construct, and predictive validity. The results indicated that the instrument is free from the response bias of social desirability. Medium levels of concurrent validity were shown with two other social support instruments. Construct validity was demonstrated by significant associations between NSSQ measures and two interpersonal constructs expected to be related to social support, while no significant relationships were found between the NSSQ measures and an unrelated interpersonal construct. Predictive validity was tested by examining the hypothesis that social support serves as a buffer for life stress. Among the functional properties, the interaction of aid and life stress accounted for 13.2% of the variance in negative mood. Of the network properties, duration of relationships had significant main and interaction effects, accounting together for 19.3% of the variance in negative mood.

Normative data from a sample of employed adults provide means and standard deviations for each subscale and variable of the NSSQ, as well as descriptive data about sources of support.

Issues arising from current usage of the NSSQ concern various approaches to handling scores from the instrument in data analysis, use of the instrument with special populations, and general versus situation-specific support.

INTRODUCTION

The Norbeck Social Support Questionnaire (NSSQ) was developed in 1980 as a research instrument which could provide scores for multiple dimensions of social support. These scores are based on respondents' ratings of members in their social support networks. Testing to establish the psychometric properties of the instrument was conducted with two colleagues from the University of California, San Francisco: Dr. Ada Lindsey and Dr. Virginia Carrieri, (Norbeck, Lindsey, & Carrieri, 1981; 1983). Since the complete reports of the psychometric testing are available, this paper will summarize these findings and present some additional issues on the use of this instrument.

THE NSSQ

Although there are similarities in the conceptualization of social support among the various definitions that have been proposed, consensus has not been reached in the field about what constitutes social support or how it should be measured. Most definitions depict multiple dimensions or components of social support, and these components can be regarded as comprising two general types of support: psychological support (e.g., affiliation, affirmation, or emotional support) and tangible support (e.g., direct aid). When psychometrically sound instruments have been developed to put these various components into operation, the question of what comprises social support can be determined empirically.

Thus, the instruments developed at this point in the social support field can be regarded as first-generation instruments. The results from the use of these instruments can provide a sound basis for more definitive and refined instruments in the future. This basis will be richer to the extent that the various first-generation instruments represent diverse conceptual components and diverse measurement strategies, so it is particularly appropriate that the two instruments presented at this roundtable differ both conceptually and in format.

The NSSQ was developed from the definition of social support and the concept of convoy described by Robert Kahn and Toni Antonucci (Kahn, 1979; Kahn & Antonucci, 1980). Using this definition, social support consists of three components: affect, affirmation, and aid, and it occurs through supportive interpersonal transactions within the person's social network or convoy. The convoy describes a set of relationships that develop and change over time and form the more or less stable group of persons on whom the individual relies for support and those who rely on the individual for support. Concepts from social network research are used to describe structural characteristics of the convoy.

The NSSQ has questions to measure functional properties of social support (affect, affirmation, and aid); structural or network properties of the convoy (number in the network, duration of relationships, and frequency of contact); and changes in the convoy due to losses of relationships. These questions are presented in Table 1.

Table 1
Questions and Subscales of the Norbeck Social Support Questionnaire

Subscale		Questions
Affect	1.	How much does this person make you feel liked or loved?
Affect	2.	How much does this person make you feel respected or admired?
Affirmation	3.	How much can you confide in this person?
Affirmation	4.	How much does this person agree with or support your actions or thoughts?
Aid (short term)	5.	If you needed to borrow $10, a ride to the doctor, or some other immediate help, how much could this person usually help?
Aid (long term)	6.	If your were confined to bed for several weeks, how much could this person help you?
Duration of Relationships	7.	How long have you known this person?
Frequency of Contact	8.	How frequently do you usually have contact with this person (phone calls, visits, or letters)?
Recent Losses	9.	During the past year, have you lost any important relationships due to moving, a job change, divorce or separation, death, or some other reason?
Losses (quantity)	9a.	Please indication the number of persons from each category who are no longer available to you.
Losses (quality)	9b.	Overall, how much of your support was provided by these people who are no longer available to you?

Note. A five-point Likert scale is provided for questions 1-8 and 9b. Questions 9a and 9b are to be answered only if the respondent answered question 9 affirmatively. The categories in 9a are: spouse or partner; family members or relatives; friends; work or school associates; neighbors; health care providers; counselor or therapist; minister, priest, or rabbi, and other.

The format of the NSSQ was designed to obtain detailed information from respondents in a manner which would not be confusing or difficult to complete. It can be self-administered in about 10 minutes (range 5-20 minutes). The respondent is first asked to "List each significant person in your life on the right. Consider all the persons who provide personal support for you or who are important to you. Use only first names or initials and then indicate the relationship, as in the following example." Nine categories are presented in a list to assist the respondents to think of people who may be appropriate to include in their network list. These categories are: spouse or partner; family members or relatives; friends; work or school associates; neighbors; health care providers; counselor or therapist; minister, priest, or rabbi; and other. In scoring the NSSQ, these nine categories are used to describe the composition of the network. The amount of support available from various sources (e.g., friends versus relatives) can also be determined.

Questions 1-8 (see Table 1) are then presented on a series of half-pages which are visually aligned with the network list. For each question, the respondent rates the individual members on the network list on a 5-point Likert scale. In scoring the NSSQ, these ratings are totaled to provide a score for each question. Thus, the support scores are based on rating for actual network members rather than global perceptions of what support is available.

After the psychometric testing was completed on the initial version of the NSSQ, minor revisions were made, and the revised version was typeset and printed. The actual content of the questions was not changed from the initial version, but three changes in format and instructions were made:

1. The number of spaces provided for respondents to list their network members was increased from 20 to 24.
2. An additional instruction was added to the first page: "You do not have to use all 24 spaces. Use as many spaces as you have important persons in your life."
3. The wording of question 9b was changed to obtain the *number* of persons from each category who are no longer available to the respondent, rather than merely the categories from which losses occurred.

The changes in format necessitated corresponding changes in scoring and coding the data from the NSSQ, and a revised scoring instruction manual was developed.[1]

Reliability and Validity

The psychometric testing that has been completed on the NSSQ is summarized in Table 2. Demographic characteristics of the three subject groups that were used in these studies are presented in Table 3.

[1]Copies of the revised NSSQ and scoring instructions are available from Jane S. Norbeck.

Table 2
Psychometric Testing of the NSSQ

	Subject Group[a]	N
Reliability		
Internal Consistency	I	75
Test-Retest (1 week interval)	I	67
Stability versus Sensitivity		
(7 months' interval)	I	44
Validity		
Response Bias	I	75
Concurrent Validity		
1. Social Support Questionnaire[b]	I	42
2. Personal Resource Questionnaire[c]	II	55
Construct Validity	III	131
Predictive Validity	II	53
Normative Data		
Employed Adults (male and female)	III	136
Pooled Data from Other Investigators		varies

[a]Group composition: I and II are graduate students in nursing, and III is composed of employed adults. See Table 3 for demographic characteristics.

[b]Developed by Cohen and Lazarus (Schaefer, Coyne, & Lazarus, 1981).

[c]From Brandt and Weinert (1981).

Table 3
Demographic Characteristics of Subject Groups

	Group[a]		
	I	II	III
Number in Group	75	55	136
Sex: Male	1	0	47
Female	74	55	89
Age: Mean	30.3	32.9	35.8
Range	23-51	23-59	22-67
Education: Mean	16.4	16.4	15.9
Range	14-20	15-22	10-22
Ethnic Group: Asian	3%	4%	11%
Black	0	2%	4%
Caucasian	92%	87%	71%
Hispanic	1%	4%	4%
Native American	0	2%	6%
Other	4%	2%	4%
Marital Status: Single	43%	40%	46%
Married	37%	38%	42%
Divorced or separated	20%	20%	10%
Widowed	0	2%	2%

[a]Group composition: I and II are graduate students in nursing, and III is composed of employed adults.

Internal consistency. The internal consistency of the items and subscales of the NSSQ was found to be very high. The correlation between the two affect items was .97, between the two affirmation items .96, and between the two aid items .89. The affect and affirmation items were also highly correlated (.95 to .98), but the aid items seemed to represent a more distinct component because the correlations between the aid items and the affect or affirmation items were lower (.72 to .78).

These three functional subscales were also highly related to the three network subscales of number in the network, duration of relationships, and frequency of contact. The correlations among the network subscales and affect and affirmation ranged from .88 to .97, and the correlations between the network subscales and aid ranged from .69 to .80. The correlations among the three network subscales ranged from .88 to .96. None of the loss items were significantly related to any functional or network subscale, but among the loss items the correlations ranged from .54 to .68.

Test-retest reliability. A 1-week interval was selected to test stability to minimize carry-over effects from too short of an interval and to minimize measuring actual changes in social support that might occur over a longer time. The 1-week test-retest reliability for the functional and network properties ranged from .85 to .92, and the correlations for the loss items ranged from .71 to .83. Thus, the instrument was judged to have high test-retest reliability.

Stability versus sensitivity. In contrast to the 1-week interval, a 7-month follow-up testing revealed lower, but significant, test-retest correlations ranging from .58 to .78. There were significant differences between the first testing and the 7-month follow-up testing on two subscales: number in the network, and duration of relationships. When sources of support were examined, three categories had changed significantly during the 7-month interval which appeared to reflect actual changes in these students' networks upon attending graduate school. Support from neighbors had increased, support from family and relatives had decreased, and new friends had been substituted for friends who had been dropped from the initial network list.

Although changes had occurred in the composition of the network for this group of students during their first year in graduate school, the overall level of functional support available to them had not changed significantly. Thus, it appears that the amount of support available was stable over time because this group of students had substituted new network members for those who were no longer available. The significant differences which occurred at the 7-month follow-up reflect the sensitivity of the instrument to changes in network structure over time.

Response bias. To study the possibility of a response bias based on the reporting of socially desirable answers rather than honest self-reports, the

NSSQ was administered in conjunction with the Marlowe-Crowne Test of Social Desirability (Crowne & Marlowe, 1960).[2] None of the items from the NSSQ were significantly related to the social desirability measure; thus, by this criterion, the instrument was judged to be relatively free from the social desirability response bias.

Concurrent validity. Concurrent validity was tested with two different measures of social support. One subject group completed the NSSQ and the Social Support Questionnaire (SSQ) developed by Cohen and Lazarus (Schaefer et al., 1981). The two instruments measure different, but related, subscales. Affirmation was significantly related to the SSQ measure of informational support (.33); affect was significantly related to the SSQ measure of emotional support (.51); but aid was not related to the SSQ measure of tangible support. Tangible support, however, had very low reported internal consistency (.31) and may not be a reliable measure of aid. The SSQ measure of emotional support was also significantly related to affirmation (.56), aid (.44), and a composite score of the three network subscales (.53).

Another subject group completed the NSSQ and the Personal Resource Questionnaire (PRQ) developed by Brandt and Weinert (1981). Medium levels of association (.35 to .41) between the three functional components of the NSSQ and the two parts of the PRQ were found; and lower, but significant, levels of association between most of the network properties of the NSSQ and the PRQ were established (.31 to .32).

Construct validity. Construct validity was tested by administering the Fundamental Interpersonal Relations Orientation (FIRO-B) developed by Schutz (1978) to subjects who also completed the NSSQ. Two of the FIRO-B constructs (need for inclusion and need for affection) were expected to be related to social support, and one FIRO-B construct (need for control) was expected to be unrelated. As predicted, need for inclusion and need for affection were significantly related to all the NSSQ functional subscales (.18 to .27) and to most of the network subscales (.17 to .23). None of the correlations between NSSQ subscales and need for control were significant. The small-to-moderate correlations indicate that a person's interpersonal needs are related to their self-reports of the amount of social support available to them. This would only be true with populations that had adequate social support; in other cases, the discrepancy between a person's need for inclusion or affection and their social support might indicate inadequate social support.

[2]To avoid repetition of information presented in the NSSQ articles, the psychometric properties of instruments used in validating the NSSQ will not be described in this paper. Only instruments with previously established reliability and validity were selected for use in validating the NSSQ.

Predictive validity. Testing of predictive validity was based on the theoretical model that social support buffers life stress (Cassel, 1976; Cobb, 1976, Dean & Lin, 1977). Life stress and social support were measured as predictor variables for the outcome variable of negative mood.

Life stress was measured with a life events questionnaire that followed the format developed by Sarason (Sarason, Johnson, & Siegel, 1978) and included additional items of relevance for female respondents established by Norbeck (in press). In Sarason's format, preestablished weights or stress units for life events are not used; instead the respondent rates the desirability and impact of life events that have occurred during the past year. Impact scores from the events regarded as bad events by the respondent comprise the negative life events score, i.e., life stress.

The negative mood score from the Profile of Mood States (McNair, Lorr & Droppleman, 1971) was used as the outcome variable. In a hierarchical multiple regression analysis, life stress was entered first, followed by each of the functional subscales (affect, affirmation, and aid) entered separately, and finally an interaction term for the product of each social support subscale and life stress was entered. The overall R^2 for the model was .351. Life stress had a strong main effect on negative mood and accounted for 16.1% of the variance. None of the functional subscales had significant main effects, but the interaction of life stress and aid was significant and accounted for 13.2% of the variance.

The network subscales (number in the network, duration of relationships, and frequency of contact) were analyzed in a similar manner in a separate multiple regression. The overall R^2 was .361. In addition to the same main effect already found for life stress, one network subscale, duration of relationships, had a significant main effect which accounted for 11.7% of the variance. The interaction of life stress and duration of relationships was also significant and accounted for 7.6% of the variance.

The amount of variance accounted for by the social support subscales and their interactions with life stress was 19.0% for the functional subscales and 20.0% for the network subscales. This effect size is similar to that reported by Wilcox (1981).

Normative data. Because most of the testing of the NSSQ was done with students, and primarily female respondents, it was important to administer the instrument to a more general population to begin to establish normative data. Staff level employees from a large university medical center were considered representative of a sample of employed adults. In every NSSQ subscale, males had slightly lower scores than females, but none of the differences were significant so scores were collapsed on sex for all subsequent analyses.

In addition to means and standard deviations for each subscale (e.g., the mean number listed in the network was 12 persons, and the standard deviation was 5.5), descriptive data for each of the 9 sources of support categories are available. For this sample the category of friends comprised 43.7% of the network, followed by the category of family or relatives (35.9%). These two categories also accounted for the highest amount of functional support and frequency of contact.

The normative data base will be greatly expanded through data sharing from investigators who are currently using the NSSQ. Both clinical and nonclinical populations of diverse cultural groups will be represented.

ISSUES IN HANDLING SCORES FROM THE NSSQ

Two aspects or features of the NSSQ scores affect data analysis, and investigators have to make decisions about how to handle the data. One issue is whether to combine subscales into a component variable score or use the subscales scores separately. For example, affect, affirmation, and aid can be combined into a Total Functional Support score; while number in the network, duration of relationships, and frequency of contact can be combined into a Total Network Properties score; and the three loss items can be combined into Total Loss score. The second issue is related to the format of the NSSQ in which respondents rate the network members that they have listed. Because the same individuals and the same number of individuals are rated by a given respondent for each question, the scores for that respondent will necessarily be highly related. Various approaches to these two issues will be discussed.

Subscale Versus Component Variable Scores

This data handling issue was examined with the data described in the section on predictive validity. Multiple regression analyses were done on the outcome measure of negative mood with the predictor variables of life stress and social support entered hierarchically. Social support was entered either in the form of subscales or as a composite score for the functional components, and both subscales and the composite score were used for the network property components.

Because the subscales (affect, affirmation, aid; or number, duration, frequency) within the NSSQ are so highly intercorrelated, they were entered hierarchically. In the multiple regression, life stress was entered first, followed by NSSQ subscales (or composite variable), and finally interaction terms (life stress multiplied by social support).

The amount of variance accounted for by the social support scales and their interactions with life stress was 19.0% for the functional subscales (affect, affirmation, aid) and 20.0% for the network subscales (number, duration, frequency). When the composite score for functional support (Total Functional) was substituted for the separate subscales in another multiple regression analysis, the entire effect for functional support and its interaction with life stress was only 1.9%, compared to 19.0% for the subscale entered separately.

Similarly, when the composite score for the network subscales (Total Network) was substituted for the three subscales, only 1.2% of the variance was accounted for, compared to 20.0% for the subscales entered separately. Thus, even though the subscales are high intercorrelated, they carry distinct information that was lost in combining them into a composite variable. This finding suggests that the subscales in this instrument should not be combined into a total score if the social support effect is primarily from a single subscale or its interaction term. Other investigators have been successful in using a composite score when more than one subscale was related to the outcome measure.

Number Listed in the Network as a Score of Artifact in Other Subscales

The format of the NSSQ creates large scores for each subscale for subjects who have listed more persons on their network list than for subjects who have only listed a few persons, regardless of the quality of support. Hypothetically, a person who listed only 6 persons and rated each of them with the highest rating (5) would have a score of 30. Another person might have listed 15 persons but rated them very low (2), also creating a score of 30.

Two approaches exist to compensate for this potential problem. First, the subscales can simply be averaged by dividing each score by the number in the network. This average score corrects for the number listed, but at the expense of losing information about the size of the network, as well as differential amounts of support from various areas of the network.

A second approach solves these problems, but requires a hierarchical multiple regression (or discriminant analysis) approach to the data. If the number in the network is entered prior to the subscales (affect, affirmation, aid) or composite variable (Total Functional), the effect of size of the network is removed from the remaining scores, but its effect on outcome is still taken into account. This approach also can be used for the network property subscales or the composite score.

USE WITH SPECIAL POPULATIONS

Although the NSSQ was designed to be self-administered, with certain populations researchers have found either a guided self-administration or an interview administration to be preferable. As with any written instrument, a certain level of proficiency in reading and writing is required. Some respondents need assistance in understanding the instructions and can then proceed to complete the instrument unassisted.

Most of the use of the NSSQ has been self-administered. Guided self-administration, however, has been used with elderly respondents (Nichols, in progress), and an interview conducted in sign language has been used with a deaf population (Magilvy, 1982).

When the NSSQ is administered in an interview, it is helpful to provide the respondent with cards that display the appropriate Likert scale for each question. As the interviewer proceeds down the network list, the respondent can refer to the scale in responding to the question for each person listed.

MEASUREMENT CHOICES

In the development of any instrument, the measurement strategy is based on a number of choices which characterize and also limit what and how the instrument measures. It is important to make these characteristics explicit because they may affect results as much as conceptual qualities of the instrument.

The NSSQ measures perceived support rather than actual support, general support rather than situation-specific support, and it is based on rating of actual network members rather than on global reactions to questions. It should be noted that only the issue of general versus situation-specific support has been studied in relation to the NSSQ.

In terms of the selection of content, the NSSQ measures both functional qualities of social support and certain, but not all, network characteristics. Important network characteristics that are not measured by the NSSQ are density or connectedness of the network and the multidimensionality or multiplexity of relationships. The notion of reciprocity of support is only indirectly, and incompletely, included in the NSSQ through the following instructions to the respondent for selecting individuals for the network list: "Consider all the persons who provide personal support for you *or who are important to you*" *[italics added]*. Finally, the issue of conflicted versus conflict-free support (Cronewett, 1982) is not addressed directly in the NSSQ; however, the respondent can rate individuals on the network list variably on different functional questions (e.g., high on aid, but low on affirmation).

General Versus Situation-Specific Support

Helmrath and Steinitz (1978) presented an interesting case study of seven couples who had experienced the death of an infant shortly after birth. Although these were middle class, educated couples who had good relationships with family members and friends, they were essentially isolated in their grief. Their external support system failed to provide support for this particular unexpected crisis. For anticipated and more normative events, however, individuals can seek out people with the experience or values necessary to provide support. The shift ina couple's friendship patterns after the birth of a first child, for example, results in a network with a higher proportion of couples with children and a greater availability of mutual support for parenting.

Kahn (1979) holds that a certain level of support is needed on a day-to-day basis to promote individual well-being and adequate performance in major social roles. Additional support, often of greater intensity or specificity, may be needed to cope with life's transitions, acute stressors, or chronic stressors (Norbeck, 1981). Thus, both general ongoing support and situation-specific support are needed at times.

In a study of 69 married and single, low-income mothers of preschool children, both the NSSQ and a 5-item situation-specific questionnaire were used to measure social support (Norbeck, in preparation). The situation-specific items were derived from previous interviews with single mothers. The revised life events questionnaire described earlier (Norbeck, in press) was also administered as a predictor variable, and the outcome variable was the positive symptom distress index from the Brief Symptom Inventory (Derogatis, 1977).

The overall R^2 for the hierarchical multiple regression analysis was .313. Main effects from life stress accounted for 8.8% of the variance; main effects from the NSSQ subscales 7.6%; and main effects from the situation-specific social support measure 8.0%. The interaction of life stress and the NSSQ subscales accounted for 3.7% of the variance, and the interaction of life stress and the situation-specific measure was 3.3%. Thus, each social support measure and its interaction with life stress accounted for 11.3% of the variance in psychiatric symptoms.

These findings suggest that the NSSQ best serves as a general measure of social support, but greater predictive power for clinical or special populations may be attained by using the NSSQ or another general measure as a background measure, supplemented by a situation-specific measure. McKenna (1982) has adapted the NSSQ to measure both general and situation-specific support in her work with battered women. After administering the NSSQ, three additional questions are incorporated in the format of the network list. Does this person [on the network list] know about the battering? If so, what was the person's response? Was that response helpful or not helpful?

CONCLUSION

The NSSQ is a brief, easily administered instrument that has been shown to meet basic criteria for reliability and validity. The ultimate criterion for the utility of an instrument is its predictive validity. Initial evidence reviewed in this paper shows favorable results in stress-buffering effects for some of the subscales of the NSSQ. Preliminary reports from other investigators using the NSSQ suggest that different constructs emerge as significant for different clinical populations. If this is so, then the NSSQ may be useful in identifying specific social support needs of individuals coping with various specific situation or illnesses.

Research has documented that social support is a relevant variable for many health and adjustment outcomes in coping with stress (Gore, 1978; Norbeck & Tilden, in press; Pearlin, Lieberman, Menaghan, & Mullan, 1981; Wilcox, 1981). Now the more complex question articulated by Mitchell and Trickett (1980, p. 28) must be addressed-·"What types of social networks [or social support] are most useful for which individuals in terms of what particular issues under what environmental conditions?"

As suggested, certain components of social support that are salient for one clinical population may be irrevelant for another. Such findings are the necessary empirical grounding for planning effective intervention. Nurse investigators have begun reporting studies of the social support needs of specific populations, such as patients undergoing maintenance hemodialysis (Dimond, 1979), the elderly (Fuller & Larson, 1980), and chronic schizophrenics (Turner, 1979). These important initial studies each used a different approach to measure social support. Now with the development and validation of social support instruments, it finally will be possible to compare results across studies. This advance constitutes the immediate contribution these first-generation social support instruments are making to the field.

Evaluation of the Personal Resource Questionnaire: A Social Support Measure

Clarann Weinert, S.C., R.N., Ph.D.

The purpose of this study was to further the psychometric evaluation of the Personal Resource Questionnaire (PRQ). The PRQ was developed to measure social support as a multidimensional construct.

The PRQ is a two part measure of social support. Part 1 consists of life situations in which one might be expected to need some assistance. It provides descriptive information about the person's resources, whether or not they have experienced the situation in the past 6 months, and their satisfaction with these resources. Part 2 contains a 25-item Likert scale that measures the respondents' level of perceived social support. The questionnaire can be self-administered, requires approximately 10 minutes to complete, and is easily scored for use with various statistical techniques.

Based on data generated by the author and on three additional data sets provided by collaborating researchers, psychometric properties of the PRQ were investigated. There was sound evidence to rule out the explanation that the respondents' answers on the PRQ reflect a reporting simply of socially desirable answers. There were no significant differences between the scores for women and the scores for men on either Part 1 or Part 2 of the PRQ. Evidence was provided to substantiate criterion-related validity. Part 2 of the PRQ was predictive of dyadic consensus. Likewise, initial validation of construct validity was evident. Part 2 of the PRQ is correlated with mental health indicators. Yet, the analyses indicate that there is reason to believe that the PRQ is not simply another way of measuring the construct of depression and anxiety. Consistently strong estimates of reliability, determined by the use of Cronbach's alpha, were obtained indicating a high level of internal consistency for the PRQ-Part 2.

This report of the early psychometric evaluation of the PRQ can provide researchers with information which can guide their use of this social support measure. There are now some established base line profiles of responses for comparisons. The validity and reliability of the PRQ are sufficiently established so as to permit the continued use of the tool with some level of confidence in interpreting the results.

INTRODUCTION

In recent years researchers from health related and social science disciplines have focused attention on the study of social forces in the environment that contribute to the maintenance and promotion of health. A central theme emerging in this work is the idea that the "human climate" plays a significant role in the maintenance of individuals' health and in the nature of their responses to stressors. MacElveen (1978) noted it appears that one vital aspect of the human experience, particularly important for achieving and sustaining high levels of functioning and life satisfaction, is being connected or linked to other "supportive" people.

A review of the literature indicates that despite the impressive amount of empirical research conducted to date on social support, this body of knowledge has major limitations. Norbeck, Lindsey, and Carrieri (1981), for example, argue that there is a lack of conceptual agreement on what social support is and how it functions to protect health or buffer the effects of stressors. In addition, study designs have inadequately measured the multidimensional aspects of social support and the failure of many of these research efforts to build on cumulative findings has resulted in relatively few attempts to expand the underlying explanatory models. "Social support has been measured differently from study to study, usually by questionnaires or instruments that have not been tested for reliability or validity" (Norbeck et al., 1981, p. 264). House (1981) states that if we are to see and capitalize on the potential scientific and practical uses of the concept of social support, first we must know what it is, how to measure it, and how it operates.

In this paper, a multidimensional conceptualization of social suport is discussed and a description and evaluation of an instrument designed as a more comprehensive measure of social support are presented. The development of this instrument, referred to as the Personal Resource Questionnaire (PRQ), its potential usefulness, and a psychometric evaluation are also discussed.

SOCIAL SUPPORT

All of us have an intuitive sense of what constitutes social support. We know people whom we regard as "supportive," from whom we receive support, and to whom we often give support. The term, social support, is used frequently, as though there was a common agreement on its definition; yet, this is clearly not the case. Social support has been defined both in terms of information (Cassel, 1974b; Cobb, 1976) and in terms of the exchange of material goods, services, emotional comfort, intimacy, assistance, and problem solving (Brown, Bhrolchain, Ni, & Harris, 1975; Caplan, 1974; Finlayson, 1976; MacElveen, 1978; Tolsdorf, 1976). Social support is implied by the availability of a spouse or confidant, close ties with friends, and having relatives nearby. Kahn and Antonucci (1980) identified three distinct perspectives on social support: functional, emotional, and appraisal support. They defined social support as interpersonal transactions that include one or more of the following key elements: affect, affirmation, and aid. All of these definitions are instructive and suggest that social support is not a unidimensional concept, but rather one that includes a range of phenomena.

Likewise, the functions of social support in relation to health are not clearly understood. Various alternative hypotheses have been suggested: social support has a direct effect on health, social support interacts with the level of stress in its impact on health, social support is a mediating factor which stimulates the development of coping strategies and promotes mastery over health related behavior, and the lack of social support exacerbates the impact of stressful life events on health (Hamburg & Killilea, 1979). Thoits (1982) noted several serious problems with the empirical literature regarding social support. One problem that she cites is that the direct effects of the events upon support and the interaction (buffering) effect of the events with social support have been confounded. Thoits also noted that the relationship among events, support, and mental health indicators has not been clarified theoretically. Thus, the possibility that support itself is an etiological factor has been overlooked.

To understand these mechanisms or to evaluate these alternative hypotheses, a unifying framework is needed together with common measures of social support and research designs to clarify the causal relationships among stress, social support, and various health indicators. There also is the possibility that social support operates differentially across various population subgroups (Gore, 1978; Lin, Simeone, Ensel, & Kuo, 1979; Hirsch, 1980), and this possibility must be examined empirically using common methods across groups. Bloom (1982) noted that in some situational contexts, social support may even be a "nonsupport" for the attainment of desired goals.

Sarason and his associates (1983) have indicated that as reasonable as an emphasis on the importance of social support appears to be, the task of empirically demonstrating the effects of social support has barely begun. One of the most serious barriers to objective research has been the lack of a reliable, general, and easily administered index of social support. The tools that have been developed have serious limitations and restrictions in applicability. Some instruments (Miller & Ingham, 1976; Medalie & Goldbourt, 1976; Brim, 1974; Renne, 1974) are not conceptually based, nor do they tap the multidimensional aspects of social support. Other instruments (Henderson, 1980) are comprehensive, but complex, and they require a research design that includes intensive interviews by highly skilled, well-trained interviewers. Furthermore, many instruments are situationally focused or bound and assess little more than the size and density of a person's social network.

A major source of conceptual confusion has been the lack of distinction between social network characteristics and the kinds of exchanges (supports) which are involved in relations with persons in one's network. A social network represents the person's structural links with others, and the term, social support, refers to the meaning or content of these relationships. This distinction is useful in the search for a conceptual definition of social support, and it leads in the direction of considering what functions are served by human relationships.

The work of Robert Weiss (1969, 1974) corresponds well with this line of thinking. He has identified five major categories of relational functions believed to be necessary for well-being. In addition, he has linked these findings with threats to well-being or conditions which prevent the adequate fulfillment of these relational functions. Based on Weiss' five dimensions of social relationships, social support has been defined in this paper in a comprehensive fashion as composed of the following dimensions: provision of attachment for intimacy; social integration, i.e., being an integral part of a group; opportunity for nurturant behavior; reassurance of worth as an individual and in role accomplishments; and availability of informational, emotional, and material help. These five dimensions of social support can be available from sources within the family system or external to it. Thus, social support can come from informal sources such as a spouse, family members, a confidant, or kin; or it may come from more formal sources such as professional care providers, agencies, self-help groups, and other social organizations.

THE PERSONAL RESOURCE QUESTIONNAIRE

The Personal Resource Questionnaire (PRQ) was developed to measure social support as a multidimensional construct. A detailed account of the tool, its development, validity (content, face, and predictive), and reliability (internal consistency) is presented in an article by Brandt and Weinert (1981). Briefly, the PRQ is a two-part index or set of measures of social support. Part 1 consists of life situations in which one might be expected to need some assistance, and it provides descriptive information concerning the person's resources, whether or not they have experienced the situation in the past 6 months, and their satisfaction with the help received from their resources. Part 2 contains a 25-item Likert scale, developed according to Weiss' (1969, 1974) relational dimensions, that measures a respondent's perceived level of social support. A 5-item Self-Help Ideology Scale developed at Harvard University by Belle (1980) was appended to the PRQ to estimate the ideological stance of an individual toward self-help and to assess how this stance affects the need for social support. The PRQ can be self-administered, requires approximately 10 minutes to complete, and is easily coded for statistical analysis.

Psychometric Evaluation

During the development of the PRQ, several procedures were utilized to establish the validity of the tool. Face validity was established using input from nurse researchers with experience in the area of social support to validate the adequacy of the content. Feedback from graduate-prepared individuals with health or social science backgrounds and from adults in the general community were used to establish face validity and to assure that the tool was understandable and easy to complete.

The initial psychometric evaluation was based on data from Weinert's (1981) doctoral dissertation research. This research investigated the relationships among three sets of variables: the stress of long-term illness, the level of social support of the "well" spouse, and the level of functioning of the family. The sample was composed of 149 white, middlescent (ages 30-50), middle class families in which one of the marital partners had multiple sclerosis.

Predictive validity was tested using two criteria available in this study: a measure of family functioning developed by Pless and Satterwhite (1973), and two subscales from the Marital Adjustment Scale (Spanier, 1976) — dyadic satisfaction and dyadic consensus. The validity coefficients ranged from .21 to .23 for Part 1 and from .30 to .44 for Part 2 (see Table 1).

Based on Nunnally's (1978) position, that it is reasonable to expect only modest correlations when evaluating the worth of predictor tests, the validity coefficients obtained for the PRQ-Part 2 indicated a predictive function for family functioning and marital adjustment.

Table 1
Predictive Validity Coefficients

Criteria	Predictor Scores	
	PRQ-Part 1	PRQ-Part 2
Dyadic Consensus	.23*	.30**
Dyadic Satisfaction	.23*	.41**
Family Functioning Index	.21*	.44**

N = 149
*p<.004
**p<.001

Note. Adapted from "The PRQ — A Support Measure" by P. Brandt and C. Weinert, *Nursing Research*, 1981, *30*(5), 277-280. Copyright 1981 by the American Journal of Nursing Co. Reprinted by permission.

The initial testing for construct validity of Part 2 indicated statistically significant correlations between the Self-Help Ideology Scale and three of the five dimensional scales: intimacy (r = -.25), assistance (r = -.23), and social integration (r = -.14). While these results indicate that the relationship is in the expected direction, the strength of the correlations warranted only guarded conclusions.

The final criterion used in this initial evaluation related to the distinctiveness of the subscales in the PRQ-Part 2. Moderate intercorrelations (.58 to .62) for the subscales of intimacy, social integration, worth, and assistance or guidance suggested that there was some overlap of these four scales. Relatively low correlations (.26 to .38) between the nurturance scale and the other four subscales were obtained. Given the fairly strong internal consistency coefficient (α .77) for the nurturance scale, the lower correlations (.26 to .38) probably are not due to poor reliability of the scale. These results more likely indicate that nurturance is an independent dimension (see Table 2).

In this initial psychometric evaluation, reliability estimates were also computed. Using Cronbach's alpha for PRQ-Part 2, an internal consistency reliability coefficient of α = .89 was obtained. The reliability coefficients for the dimensional subscales ranged from α = .61 to α = .77 (see Table 3). This early psychometric evaluation indicated that the PRQ had respectable measurement properties.

Table 2
Correlation Matrix for Dimensional Subscales of the PRQ

Dimensional Subscales	Correlations			
	SI	N	W	A
Intimacy (I)	.59*	.26*	.61*	.62*
Social Integration (SI)		.26*	.62*	.63*
Nurturance (N)			.39*	.38*
Worth (W)				.59*
Assistance (A)				

N = 149
*p<.001

Note. Adapted from "The PRQ — A Support Measure" by P. Brandt and C. Weinert, *Nursing Research,* 1981, 30(5), 277-280. Copyright 1981 by the American Journal of Nursing Co. Reprinted by permission.

Table 3
Internal Consistency for PRQ-Part 2

Scales	Reliability Coefficients
Total PRQ-Part 2	.89
Subscales	
Intimacy	.75
Social Integration	.61
Nurturance	.77
Worth	.70
Assistance	.75

Note. Adapted from "The PRQ — A Support Measure" by P. Brandt and C. Weinert, *Nursing Research,* 1981, *30*(5), 277-280. Copyright 1981 by the American Journal of Nursing Co. Reprinted by permission.

Personal Resource Questionnaire: Modifications

After the PRQ had been used in the dissertation research of both Brandt (1981) and Weinert (1981) and in several other research projects conducted by nurse researchers who had requested the use of the PRQ, modifications were considered. The Nursing Research Emphasis (NRE) Research Team at the School of Nursing at the University of Washington had selected the PRQ as the primary social support tool to be used in each of the six NRE projects. Based on collaboration with the NRE members and the initial performance of the tool, minor modifications were made. The revisions of PRQ-Part 1 included modifications in the resource options; wording, format, and sequencing of questions to improve readability; and the exclusion of the confidant question (Lowenthal & Haven, 1968). To establish the adequacy of the domain of concerns of the eight life situations, an additional question was included. The respondents were asked what has been the greatest concern or problem for them in the past 6 months. As in the other eight life situations, resources were indicated, as well as the satisfaction with the help received for these problem situations. There were virtually no modifications of PRQ-Part 2. However, the Self-Help Ideology Scale that had been appended initially to the PRQ was excluded. The psychometric properties of the Self-Help Ideology Scale did not warrant continued use of this scale. While the modified PRQ is currently being used in several research projects, data are not available at this time. Thus, the discussion in this paper is based on data obtained using the original form of the PRQ.

RESULTS

When researchers requested to use the PRQ, agreements were reached in order to provide access to their data to facilitate further psychometric evaluation of the questionnaire. It was anticipated that the input from these various collaborating researchers would further test predictive and construct validity; help to assess sex, age, socioeconomic, social desirability, and other systematic biases; and also establish base line response patterns across various groups of respondents. At the time of this writing three data sets, in addition to Weinert's, were available for analysis.

Iversen (1981) explored the relationships among life changes, social support, and illness in an aging population. This sample consisted of 120 elderly persons, mean age of 68 years, primarily caucasian, middle class, who were alumni of the University of Washington. Murtaugh (1982) investigated the relationship between social support and depression in a group of 77 low-income mothers. The mean age of this sample was 28 years, and the majority of respondents were caucasian, with slightly more than a high school education, and an average income of $6,900. The respondents in Murtaugh's study were enrolled in the WIC or Child Health Clinic programs in King County, Washington. The PRQ also was used in doctoral dissertation rescarch by Lobo (1982) who studied couples attending prenatal classes. These 94 couples were highly educated, middle class, caucasians, who were expecting their first child. In Weinert's study (1981) of families living with a long-term illness, only the "well" spouses were given the PRQ. This sample was composed of intact families in which one of the marital partners had multiple sclerosis; the marital partners were 30-50 years of age; and they lived in the states of Washington, Alaska, or Oregon. This sample followed the characteristic demographic profile of multiple sclerosis and was composed primarily of better educated, middle class, caucasians. Each of these four data sets was examined for its potential contributions to the further psychometric testing of the PRQ. While some of these data sets were appropriate for only minor contributions, each set provided additional information on the "behavior" of the PRQ.

PRQ-Part 1

In the development and initial evaluation of a measurement instrument, it is important to identify base line response patterns across various groups of respondents. In Part 1 of the PRQ, eight life situations were presented in which an individual might need assistance. A list of potential social support sources, e.g., spouse, relative, etc., was provided, and the respondents were asked to indicate the sources available to them for each situation. The number of resources indicated were summed across situations, with a possible range of 0-72. The respondent then indicated if the situation had occurred in the past 3-4 months, and if so, to what degree on a five-point scale was satisfaction

Table 4
Mean Scores on PRQ-Part 1 and Part 2

Samples	PRQ-Part 2		PRQ-Part 1	
	Mean	SD	Mean	SD
Iversen (N = 120)	17.2	10.1	125.4	25.8
Weinert (N = 149)	20.2	10.1	129.2	25.9
Murtaugh (N = 77)	18.8	7.8	134.4	24.9
Lobo (N = 188)	—	—	140.4	17.9

SD = standard deviation.

Note. Adapted from "The PRQ — A Support Measure" by P. Brandt and C. Weinert, *Nursing Research,* 1981, *30*(5), 277-280. Copyright 1981 by the American Journal of Nursing Co. Reprinted by permission.

felt with the assistance received. Across situations, the satisfaction scores could range from 1-40.

The PRQ-Part 1 was not administered by Lobo (1982). The total number of resources from the other three studies ranged from 17.2 (Iversen, 1981) to 20.2 (Weinert, 1981). The differences among scores was not statistically significant (see Table 4).

Table 5 contains the average frequency with which each source of social support was indicated as a resource by those in the samples. As is evident from these frequencies, the spouse was consistently indicated as a source of support. In Weinert's (1981) sample, the spouse was indicated in almost five out of eight of the various life situations presented on the PRQ-Part 1. In Murtaugh's (1982) study, the women turned to relatives or friends in over four of the eight situations and less often to their spouses. This can be explained partially by the fact that over 40% of the women in this sample were divorced, separated, or never married. By design, the respondents in Weinert's (1981) sample were married, and over 80% of the persons in Iversen's (1981) study were married. As anticipated, the least frequently used resources were agencies and books. Overall, these results indicate that given these eight life situations, the average number of resources available to individuals in fairly stressful circumstances is relatively consistent across the three samples.

Table 5
Frequency of Resources Selected in PRQ-Part 1

Resource	Iversen[a]		Weinert[b]		Murtaugh[c]	
	Mean	SD	Mean	SD	Mean	SD
No One	.6	1.2	.3	1.1	—	—
Spouse	4.2	2.8	4.9	2.6	3.9	3.2
Child	2.9	2.7	2.6	2.7	.6	1.1
Relative	1.9	2.5	3.0	2.8	4.8	2.5
Professional	2.0	1.9	2.0	2.1	1.5	1.8
Agency	.3	.8	.6	1.5	.5	1.2
Friend	2.5	2.4	3.6	2.6	4.6	2.7
Spiritual Advisor	1.0	1.7	1.6	2.5	1.0	2.0
Books	.7	1.1	.7	1.4	.6	1.2
Prayer	1.1	1.9	2.1	2.8	1.5	2.5

SD = standard deviation.
[a]N = 120
[b]N = 149
[c]N = 77

The average number of these eight life situations actually experienced by the respondents in the past 3-4 months was 1.3 for Iversen (1981), 3.2 for Weinert (1981), and 4.5 for Murtaugh (1982). The respondents in Murtaugh's (1982) sample experienced more of the particular life situations in the PRQ-Part 1 than those persons in the other two samples. One possible explanation is that this reflects their generally less stable life circumstances. The participants in Murtaugh's study were young women responsible for small children. Many of these women did not have the consistent support of the stable marital or partner relationship, and most of them currently were living at poverty income levels.

The average satisfaction score was calculated based on the satisfaction levels only for those situations which actually had been experienced. Thus, these scores should not be interpreted as general satisfaction with the total number of resources in PRQ-Part 1. The elderly persons in Iversen's (1981) study tended to indicate a higher level of satisfaction with the help they received with their problems (see Table 6). On a 5-point rating scale for satisfaction, the mean score of 4.7 indicates a very high level of satisfaction with help received for the life situations they experienced in the past 3-4 months.

PRQ-Part 2

The PRQ-Part 2 contains 25 items, each using a 7-point Likert response scale to indicate the respondent's level of perceived social support. The possible range of total scores for the PRQ-Part 2 is 25-175. The mean scores ranged from 125.4 for Iversen (1981) to 140.4 for Lobo (1982) (see Table 4). The level of perceived social support for the elderly population (Iversen) was significant-

Table 6
Average Satisfaction Scores for PRQ-Part 1

Samples	Situations Experienced		Average Satisfaction	
	Mean	SD	Mean	SD
Iversen (N = 120)	1.3	1.4	4.7	2.1
Weinert (N = 149)	1.3	1.4	3.7	1.1
Murtaugh (N = 77)	4.1	1.8	3.7	.7

SD = standard deviation.

ly lower than the scores of any of the other three groups of respondents. Likewise, the Lobo sample was statistically higher than any of the other groups. Caution should be exercised in interpreting the meaning of these comparisons. The design of Lobo's study called for both the husband and wife to complete the PRQ; thus, there is some degree of nonindependence which cannot be statistically controlled in this analysis.

Relationships Between PRQ-Part 1 and Part 2 Scores

Many of the existing social support instruments are actually measures of the size of the network or available resource pool, and they are used as indicators of social support. The conceptual leap from size (number of resources) to content (social support) is often made. One of the intents of the PRQ was to bridge this conceptual gap. The total scale for the PRQ-Part 1 roughly indicates the size of the resource pool, while the PRQ-Part 2 measures the multidimensional construct of social support. When Part 1 and Part 2 were correlated for each of the study samples, only moderate correlations were obtained (Iverson .40, $p < .001$), (Weinert, .41, $p < .001$), and (Murtaugh, .43, $p < .001$). These correlations are in the expected direction. However, their magnitude does not support the notion that a simple quantification of the available resource pool is an adequate measure of the level of social support.

It could be argued that satisfaction with help received might be highly correlated with one's perception of social support and the number of resources available. The correlations between the average satisfaction with Part 1 and Part 2 are displayed in Table 7. These correlations are moderate except for the correlation between average satisfaction and PRQ-Part 2 in Weinert's study (.51, $p < .001$). These results do not indicate a consistent pattern of strong relationships between satisfaction with help received and either the number of resources available or one's overall perception of social support. The findings by Weinert (1981) do give some indication that there is a relationship between one's satisfaction with help received and the level of perceived social

Table 7
Correlation between Average Satisfaction and
Total PRQ-Part 1 and Total PRQ-Part 2

PRQ	Average Satisfaction		
	Iversen	Weinert	Murtaugh
Part 1	.26**	.35***	.19*
Part 2	.20*	.51***	.33**

*p<.05
**p<.01
***p<.001

support. Yet, the direction of this relationship is not clear. Likewise, the inconsistent pattern across the study population indicates that caution should be exercised in interpreting these findings. Further empirical investigation is necessary to assess the relationship between satisfaction with help received and the perception of the level of social support.

Validity

Systematic response biases. In establishing the validity of a psychosocial instrument, it is important to rule out the explanation that a respondent's answers reflect a reporting simply of the socially "desirable" answers, rather than honest self-reports. Murtaugh (1982) administered a short version of the Marlowe-Crowne Social Desirability Scale (Strahan & Gerbasi, 1972). A high correlation between the two scales would indicate that the participants had answered the questions on the PRQ in a socially desirable manner. A correlation of - .06 (n.s.) was obtained, indicating no social desirability response bias.

When evaluating a measurement tool, it is also necessary to investigate response patterns that may be systematically associated with particular sample characteristics, e.g., gender or age. It should be noted that because of various limitations some data sets could not be tested for certain response biases. For example, because virtually all respondents were caucasian in each of the four studies reported here, variation in response on the PRQ according to respondents' race could not be examined. A difference to means test (t-test) was used for the analysis involving sample characteristics.

Of the available data sets, Weinert's (1981) respondents represented the most normal age distribution of adults. In her sample there were no significant differences between the scores of men and the scores of women on either Part 1 or Part 2 of the PRQ. Likewise, no significant difference was obtained for either part of the PRQ when comparing those who were less than 40 years old with those who were older than 40. However, when the scores for the more extreme age group (Iversen, 1981) were examined, there was a significant difference between those who were less than 68 years old and those older than 68. On Part 1 the "less than 68 year old" group scored higher on the total number of resources (mean 19.1) than the "over 68 year old" group (mean 14.4). The younger group had a mean of 128.7 on Part 2, while the mean for the older group was 120.7. The differences between both sets of scores were not highly significant ($p < .10$). These outcomes are not surprising since it would be anticipated that persons in their seventies and above have most likely lost family and friends. Thus, they may not see themselves as having as many resources to turn to or as having readily available sources of social support according to the definition and measurement techniques used.

In earlier research Weinert (1982) investigated the direct and indirect effects of age on dyadic satisfaction and dyadic consensus in her sample of couples living with long-term health problems. The direct effect of age had a positive impact on marital adjustment. When the indirect effects were explored, it was found that age reduced the effects of social support and that along with the stress of illness the overall positive effect of age was diminished but not completely overridden. The social environment and issues of social support for the elderly warrant extensive investigation. The PRQ must be tested further using the full age spectrum to make definite statements about the effects of age on the available resource pool and on the level of perceived social support.

The effect of education on the PRQ scores could be partially investigated in both Weinert's (1981) and Lobo's (1982) data sets and tentative conclusions drawn. When Weinert's sample was divided into two education levels: persons with a high school degree or less education ($\overline{X} = 121.7$, SD = 39.2), and those with more than high school education ($\overline{X} = 133.0$, SD = 19.2); a significant difference ($p < .05$) on the PRQ-Part 2 was obtained. That is, persons with more education perceived themselves as having more social support than those with less education. No significant differences on this variable were obtained in Lobo's sample. Clearly, the effects of education must be assessed using more sensitive statistical procedures and with a more normal distribution of education levels.

Reported income is a problematic indicator of actual income and one that tends to be the most difficult demographic variable to measure. In the data sets available, the variability in reported income was not adequate enough for an accurate evaluation of its impact.

Criterion-related validity. Criterion-related validity, sometimes referred to as predictive validity, "is at issue when the research aim is to use an instrument to estimate some important form of behavior that is external to the measuring instrument itself, the latter being referred to as the criterion" (Nunnally, 1978, p. 87). "The operational indicators of the degree of correspondence between the test and the criterion are usually estimated by the size of their correlation" (Carmines & Zeller, 1979, p. 17). Lobo (1982) administered the Dyadic Consensus Scale from Spanier's Marital Adjustment Scale (1976) to the couples in her study. There was a significant correlation between the PRQ-Part 2 and the Dyadic Consensus (61, p < .001). As reported earlier in this paper, Weinert (1981) obtained a correlation of .30 (p < .001) between the PRQ-Part 2 and the Dyadic Consensus Scale scores. According to Nunnally (1978), it is reasonable to expect only modest correlations when evaluating the worth of predictor tests. Based on Nunnally's standards, there is evidence from both sets of data (Lobo and Weinert) to substantiate criterion-related validity for the PRQ-Part 2 in relation to one aspect of marital adjustment, that is, the degree of dyadic consensus.

Construct validity. Construct validity is central to the measurement of abstract theoretical concepts and "is concerned with the extent to which a particular measure relates to other measures consistent with theoretically derived hypotheses concerning the concepts (constructs) being measured" (Carmines & Zeller, 1979, p. 22). According to Carmines and Zeller (1979), construct validity is not established by confirming a single prediction on different occasions or confirming many predictions in a single study. Construct validation requires a pattern of consistent findings involving different researchers using different theoretical structures across a number of different studies. For the theoretical construct of social support, it is necessary to evaluate the PRQ in relation to mental health measures in order to establish construct validity.

Extensive consideration and research effort have been focused on the relationship of social support with various aspects of mental health. The works of Henderson (1974, 1977), Caplan (1964), Weiss (1974), Dean and Lin (1977), Brown, Bhrolchain, Ni, and Harris, (1975), and House (1981), to cite a few examples, indicate a relationship between the level of social support and neurosis, depression, anxiety, and other mental health problems. Yet, it is reasonable to hold that the theoretical construct of social support is not the same construct as depression, anxiety, etc. It is expected that the correlation of anxiety and depression with the PRQ will be negative in the low-to-moderate range. Thus, in a bivariate analysis, it is predicted that higher scores on perceived social support (PRQ-Part 2) will be associated with low levels of anxiety and depression. If high positive correlations (.8 or .9) were obtained between the PRQ and the mental health status measures, one would question whether an estimate of similar constructs had been obtained.

Murtaugh's (1982) data set provides an initial validation of construct validity for the PRQ measure of social support. Along with the PRQ, she administered Zung's Self-Rating Depression Scale (1974). This scale addresses the most commonly found characteristics of depression: pervasive affect disturbances, physiological disturbances, psychomotor disturbances, and psychological disturbances. Correlations in the expected direction and magnitude were obtained between Part 1 of the PRQ and Zung's Scale (-.20, p < .05) and between Part 2 of the PRQ and the Zung Scale (-.42, p<.001). The correlations were in the direction and of the magnitude that provide some validation of construct validity; i.e., there is a relationship between the construct of social support and depression. Yet, the PRQ and the Zung Depression Scale are not measuring the same construct.

Further validation of construct validity was obtained by Norbeck, Lindsey, and Carrieri (1982). Their sample was composed of 55 female graduate students in a master's program in nursing, 87% of whom were caucasian, with a mean age of 32.9 years, and 4.4 years of education beyond high school. During testing of the Norbeck Social Support Questionnaire (Norbeck, Lindsey, & Carrieri, 1981), other tests were administered: the PRQ, the State and Trait Anxiety Scale (Speilberger, Gorsuch, & Lushene, 1970), and the Profile of Mood States (POMS) (McNair, Lorr, Droppleman, 1971). The State and Trait Anxiety Scales measure self-reported levels of anxiety. The POMS is an adjective rating scale that measures six identifiable mood states: anxiety, depression, anger, vigor, fatigue, and confusion. The correlations of the PRQ with the measures of anxiety and moods states are presented in Table 8.

In the study by Murtaugh (1982) of low-income mothers and in the study of graduate students by Norbeck and her colleagues (1981), there are some encouraging results concerning the construct validity of the PRQ-Part 2. As indicated previously, it is not reasonable to assume that the PRQ-Part 1 results can be easily interpreted. The PRQ-Part 1 simply is a count of the number of resources available and not an index or scale of social support. The results of the PRQ-Part 1 have been included here primarily for their comparison value with the findings for the PRQ-Part 2. The Part 2 results, however, merit much closer attention. The results reported previously substantiate the prediction that Part 2 is correlated with mental health indicators. Based on the strength of these correlations, there is reason to believe that it is not simply

Table 8
Correlations Matrix for Anxiety and Mood Scales
with PRQ-Part 1 and PRQ-Part 2

	PRQ-Part 1	PRQ-Part 2
State Anxiety	-.37*	-.42***
Trait Anxiety	-.22	-.47***
POMS	-.10	-.46***

*p<.05
**p<.01
***p<.001

another way of measuring the constructs of depression and anxiety. Additional empirical work to further assess construct validity of the PRQ-Part 2 as a measure of social support is currently in progress.

Distinctiveness of the subscales in the PRQ-Part 2. As reported by Brandt and Weinert (1981), the initial testing of the distinctiveness of the subscales in the PRQ-Part 2 produced moderate intercorrelations for the four subscales: intimacy, social integration, worth, and assistance (ranging from .58 to .62 p <.001). However, low correlations were obtained for the nurturance subscale with the other four subscales (ranging from .26 to .38, p <.001). This same trend is evident in three additional data sets (see Table 9). These results provide further evidence that nurturance may be an independent scale. Theoretically, nurturance is distinct from the other four dimensions. The nurturance subscale items were designed to measure the support a person provides to younger people; whereas the intimacy, social integration, worth, and assistance subscales measure support received from others. These results sug-

Table 9
Correlation Matrices for Dimensional Subscales of the PRQ-Part 2

Dimensional Subscales	Correlations				
	Iversen (N = 120)				
	I	SI	N	W	A
Intimacy (I)		.61**	.42**	.57**	.64**
Social Integration (SI)			.59**	.73**	.60**
Nurturance (N)				.67**	.53**
Worth (W)					.55**
	Murtaugh (N = 77)				
	I	SI	N	W	A
Intimacy		.64**	.27*	.64**	.70*
Social Integration			.43**	.74**	.65**
Nurturance				.53**	.42**
Worth					.65**
	Lobo (N = 188)				
	I	SI	N	W	A
Intimacy		.52**	.37**	.61**	.63**
Social Integration			.36**	.67**	.50**
Nurturance				.39**	.34**
Worth					.59**

*p <.01
**p <.001
A = assistance

gest that further testing should include the use of factor analysis as a means of empirically examining the distinctiveness of these theoretically defined dimensions or subscales.

Reliability

Reliability concerns the extent to which an experiment, test, or any measuring procedure yields the same results on repeated trials. There are four standard methods for estimating reliability of empirical measures: test-retest, alternate forms, split halves, and internal consistency (Carmines & Zeller, 1979). According to Nunnally (1978), internal consistency (coefficient alpha) should be assessed before other types of reliability estimates are employed. Using Cronbach's alpha, internal consistency reliability coefficients for the total PRQ-Part 2 and each of the dimensions for each of the four available data sets were obtained (see Table 10). These alphas for the total PRQ-Part 2 ranged from .88 for Lobo (1982) to .90 for Iversen (1981). The lowest alpha was .59 (Iversen) for the subscale of social integration. While there is some variation in these reliability coefficients among samples, the magnitude of the alphas imply a fairly high level of internal consistency.

SUMMARY OF THE PSYCHOMETRIC EVALUATION OF THE PRQ

The PRQ is in the early stages of psychometric testing. The conclusions, based on the analysis of the four available data sets, should be interpreted accordingly.

Table 10
Internal Consistency for PRQ-Part 2 for Each of the Four Data Sets
Reliability Coefficients

Scales	Iversen[a]	Weinert[b]	Murtaugh[c]	Lobo[d]
Total PRQ-Part 2	.90	.89	.90	.88
Subscales				
Intimacy	.67	.75	.66	.70
Social Integration	.59	.61	.76	.70
Nurturance	.80	.77	.79	.68
Worth	.66	.70	.90	.73
Assistance	.70	.75	.69	.69

[a]N = 120
[b]N = 149
[c]N = 77
[d]N = 188

In regards to the validity of the PRQ there is sound evidence, from Murtaugh's (1982) study, to rule out the explanation that the respondents' answers on the PRQ reflect a reporting simply of the socially desirable answers. The limitations of the four available data sets have been clearly stated. Due to these limitations, it was not possible to get substantial evidence to rule out response patterns that may be systematically associated with particular sample characteristics, e.g., age, education, and socioeconomic status. One exception was that in Weinert's sample of middlescent adults (1981), there were no significant differences between the scores of men and the scores of women for either Part 1 or Part 2 of the PRQ.

Both Lobo's (1982) study and this study provide evidence to substantiate criterion-related validity for the PRQ-Part 2. Significant correlations were obtained between the PRQ-Part 2 and the criterion, dyadic consensus, indicating that the level of perceived social support was predictive of one aspect of marital adjustment, i.e., dyadic consensus.

Initial validation of construct validity was evident in both Murtaugh's (1982) data set and in the work by Norbeck and her colleagues (1981). For Part 2 of the PRQ, the results of the analysis substantiate the prediction that the PRQ is correlated with mental health indicators. There is also reason to believe that the PRQ is not simply another way of measuring the constructs of depression and anxiety.

Consistently strong estimates of reliability, determined by the use of Cronbach's alpha, were obtained. These results indicate that PRQ-Part 2 has a fairly high level of internal consistency.

Additional empirical investigation is needed to further establish the validity and reliability of the PRQ. The report of the early psychometric evaluation can provide researchers with information about the PRQ which can guide their use of this social support measure. Likewise, there are now some established base line profiles of responses for comparisons. The validity and reliability of the PRQ are sufficiently established so as to permit the continued use of the tool with some level of confidence in interpreting the results.

PSYCHOMETRIC TESTING IN PROGRESS

The contributions to the development of the PRQ through collaboration with other researchers are substantial and highly valued. However, there are certain essential aspects of the psychometric evaluation that these studies cannot adequately address. These include providing an estimate of reliability (test-retest method) and establishing validity (social desirability bias and construct validity). To begin to establish parameters for a normative data base, Brandt and Weinert are conducting the next phase of psychometric evaluation with a well, middlescent group of respondents. A list of alumni from the University of Washington with undergraduate degrees in the behavioral sciences provided a population for the selection of a random sample of 100-150 adults. The respondents are men and women between the ages of 30 and 37. This phase of testing includes the use of the test-retest method to establish reliability of the PRQ. The two administrations of the PRQ (4 weeks apart) will also provide a means of evaluating the short-term stability of the construct of social support as measured by Part 1 and Part 2 of the PRQ.

One of the major aspects of construct validity consists of determining the extent to which observables tend to measure the same thing, several different things, or many different things. Other researchers have found that their measures of social support correlate with psychiatric symptomology and personality characteristics (Lin et al., 1979; Sarason et al., 1983). It is essential to establish that the PRQ is measuring something other than mental health or personality characteristics. To further assess this aspect of construct validity, three established personality and mental health measures — the Beck Depression Inventory (Beck, 1972); the State Trait Anxiety Inventory, 1968 (Speilberger et al., 1970); and the Eysenck Personality Inventory, 1963 (Eysenck & Eysenck, 1968) — are being administered along with the PRQ.

To further rule out the possibility that the respondents' answers simply reflect socially desirable responses rather than honest self-reports, the short form of the Marlowe-Crowne Social Desirability Scale is also being administered in our follow-up study.

This phase of psychometric testing, along with the previous testing, and the contributions made by our colleagues will provide a solid base from which to evaluate the PRQ and from which to make further modifications. It is anticipated that this phase of testing will substantiate the earlier findings of positive psychometric properties.

Research Goals

There are two goals for these research efforts. One goal is to establish a sound research instrument that can be used in interdisciplinary research. A valid and reliable instrument with a strong theoretical basis, such as the PRQ, is essential if valid conclusions are to be drawn concerning the impact of social support in mitigating the consequences of both acute and long-term illness. Research is also needed concerning the role of social support in the maintenance of good health and in the establishment of environments which promote health. A second goal involves developing the PRQ for clinical application. After adequate testing, the tool will be adapted for use in nursing diagnosis, planning, and intervention. A valid and reliable instrument, that is convenient to use and applicable to populations with varying demographic profiles, would be valuable in assisting nurses and other health professionals. Such an instrument could be used to assess the level of support available within the client system, as well as to facilitate the identification and recommended use of resources available to the client. In addition, the PRQ may be useful in evaluating various nursing intervention and social support programs for clients.

Empirical research relevant to the first goal is well under way, and the results are very encouraging. Thus far, the second goal has only received minimal attention. Norbeck (1981) has noted that a large portion of the social support research has explored the relationships between social support and health or other adjustment outcomes. She also notes that while these relationships imply that interventions for persons with inadequate social support might reduce their risk for certain negative outcomes, serious gaps in knowledge exist that limit our information concerning appropriate intervention mechanisms and their potential impact on outcomes. Norbeck also sets forth a comprehensive model of the elements and the relationships that must be studied in order to incorporate the research on social support into nursing practice. This model provides a blueprint which needs to be seriously considered as the PRQ is prepared for clinical application.

CRITIQUE*
Nancy Ewald Jackson, Ph.D.

Drs. Norbeck and Weinert have provided much useful new information about the social support measures that they have developed. Their papers also reflect many of the important issues in the study of social support. This critique will focus on the ways in which the PRQ and the NSSQ seem to be similar to and different from one another. Some subjective remarks will be included about my perceptions of the strengths and weaknesses of each instrument. I will also provide more general remarks about how social support is being studied these days and how I think it should be studied.

THE PRQ AND NSSQ: SIMILARITIES AND DIFFERENCES

Perhaps the most striking and most important similarity between the two instruments described by Weinert and Norbeck is that the authors share a conviction that the study of social support will benefit from the repeated use of measures that can be administered in a wide range of contexts by many different investigators. Drs. Norbeck, Brandt, and Weinert have devoted a great deal of time and talent to the development of such instruments, and they are also doing everything they can to facilitate the use of their questionnaires by other investigators. The openness and generosity with which these researchers have worked is in the best tradition of scholarship, and the benefits of this approach are evident in the variety of studies using the NSSQ and PRQ that Drs. Norbeck and Weinert have summarized in their papers.

*Preparation of this paper was supported by a Nursing Research Emphasis Grant No. R21-NU00820 from the Division of Nursing to the University of Washington School of Nursing.

The PRQ and the NSSQ also have several substantive attributes in common. Both originate in theoretical perspectives in which social support is defined as a perceived rather than an objective phenomenon and as a multidimensional rather than a unidimensional one (Kahn & Antonucci, 1980; Weiss, 1974). In both respects, the authors of the PRQ and the NSSQ have chosen positions that are widely advocated in the field (e.g., Cohen & Hoberman, in press; Hirsch, 1980; Sarason et al., 1983). In choosing this approach, however, Norbeck, Weinert, and their colleagues have encountered the problems of validating a construct that exists in the mind of the individual and that must be defined in terms of psychometrically and functionally distinct subscales. More work will need to be done before the difficulties involved in getting a grasp on this kind of concept are fully overcome.

While the NSSQ and PRQ are similar at the most general level, the differences between the two instruments are also striking. One obvious difference is in the hypothesized aspects of social support measured by the two instruments: affect, affirmation, and tangible aid in the NSSQ; and intimacy, social integration, worth, assistance, and nurturance in the PRQ. I think, however, that this may be the least important difference between the two instruments. Except for the nurturance subscale of the PRQ, which measures the perception of support given rather than received, the content of the items suggests that the instruments are covering much the same aspects of support.

To me, the more important differences between the two measures are the result of what may be thought of as their placement at different points on a continuum from description of network structure and function to the individual's personal synthesis of whatever information goes into creating a perception of support. The format and scoring of the NSSQ, as Norbeck has used it, emphasize the number of people in the respondent's network who are potential sources of support. Part 1 of the PRQ also focuses on types of people who are perceived as potentially supportive, but the number of network members checked influences only one subscore, which is intended as a point of reference rather than a measure of social support per se. Part 2 of the PRQ focuses on the respondent's feelings without any reference to specific individuals.

Each emphasis has both advantages and disadvantages. The strength of the intrapsychic, highly synthesized orientation of Part 2 of the PRQ is that the content of the measure has a high degree of face validity as an index of something that is hypothesized to buffer the effects of life stress. It is easy to imagine feelings of the sort measured by Part 2 of the PRQ affecting mental or physical health. As Dr. Weinert has mentioned, the difficulty is that this measure is so close in content and form to common measures of the concepts one is trying to predict that there is reason to worry that the social support measure may be contaminated by physical health, depression, anxiety, or other psychosocial factors. Do those who lack, or fail to perceive, social support become depressed? Do those who are depressed perceive themselves, realistically or not, as lacking in social support? Or is there some third variable that influences both perceived support and depression and accounts for a spurious association between the two measures?

The NSSQ may be better protected against this kind of contamination because of its more structured format and heavier emphasis on relatively more objective information about network size. It is possible, nonetheless, that the ratings given to each individual tested on the NSSQ for the number of people listed as important may be just as susceptible as the PRQ responses to contamination from the psychosocial outcomes one hopes to predict from measures of social support. This issue must be resolved empirically.

A more immediate problem with the NSSQ is the complexity of the functional subscales. This problem could easily be remedied by rescoring the NSSQ as suggested by Dr. Norbeck to obtain average rather than total scores and by looking at other data available from the questionnaire, such as the extent to which ratings on the affect, affirmation, and aid subscales vary across network members. In general, rescoring of the NSSQ could yield more useful information about relationships within and between subscales than is available from analyses based on the standard scoring system.

With the standard NSSQ scoring system, one does not know to what extent the variance in the affect, affirmation, and aid subscale scores is attributable to average rating per network member as opposed to number of network members listed. Dr. Norbeck has commented that respondents rarely list a network member without also giving the individual a relatively high rating on at least some of the six rating items. If number of listings is the major source of variance, then the figures Dr. Norbeck has reported for internal consistency of her three functional subscales are not valid. Since the same network list is used for all items, items and subscales are forced to be intercorrelated.

It would also be useful to know the extent to which the associations of NSSQ functional subscale scores with health outcomes are attributable to average rating per network member or number of members listed. There is other evidence suggesting that network size per se, or even number of potential sources of support, are relatively poor predictors of some psychosocial outcomes (Sarason et al., 1983; Weinert, 1982). Thus it is possible that average ratings on the NSSQ, if they have enough variance, might predict as well or better than the composite rating x number scores Dr. Norbeck has used. This question could be resolved by reanalyzing existing data.

GENERAL EVALUATION

Both of these instruments are valuable contributions to the field, but they are so different in style and structure that I suspect they will appeal to different groups of investigators. As a cognitive psychologist, I tend to think of interesting phenomena as being located within the mind of an individual. Thus I find Part 2 of the PRQ attractive. I am also attracted by the fact that the structure of the PRQ is more amenable to traditional approaches for evaluating a measure than the NSSQ is in its standard form. Nonetheless, I can easily imagine research or clinical settings in which I would prefer to use the NSSQ. This instrument is a highly efficient device for gathering a large amount of information about specific people in the respondent's network. Thus, it is potentially very useful in any clinical or research setting in which one wants to know about a person's social milieu and how individuals in it are perceived. The NSSQ provides social network data that are simply not available from the PRQ, and the instrument can be used as a flexible data base rather than a standard, fixed, form questionnaire.

Both the PRQ and the NSSQ have some power to predict various psychosocial outcomes. As reported by Drs. Norbeck and Weinert, the variance accounted for by these measures, alone or in interactions with life stress, falls in the range of 10-20%. Given the complexity of the prediction problems involved, these relatively small effects are probably inevitable and should not be dismissed as uninteresting. Based on their predictive powers, these measures are certainly worthy of further study and use.

On the other hand, I am disturbed by the modest amount and erratic pattern of convergence among the several measures of social support used in the studies reported by Drs. Norbeck and Weinert. Subscales and summary scores from the NSSQ, PRQ, and the Cohen and Lazarus SSQ had only 10-28% common variance in samples of nursing graduate students Dr. Norbeck mentioned. One hopes that greater degrees of convergence among measures will be reported in future studies of more diverse populations and that analyses of the content and structure of each measure will facilitate specific predictions regarding patterns of correlation. For example, one would expect the number of support sources marked in Part 1 of the PRQ to be strongly related to the number of network members listed in the NSSQ and the average satisfaction score on Part 1 of the PRQ to be related to the average rating per network member on the NSSQ. Similarly, I share Dr. Weinert's puzzlement at the modest and erratic correlations found among the three PRQ subscores (number of resources, average satisfaction, and perceived support) in the three samples for which these data are available. One would hope to find consistently high correlations between satisfaction and perceived support.

Validation of a construct requires confirmation of a full matrix of specific predictions about both convergence and divergence among measures. Without data indicating convergence among measures of social support, one cannot use the moderate correlations between social support and outcome measures as evidence that social support is a separate construct, such as the Murtaugh (1982) data reported by Dr. Weinert.

The discrimination ability of the functional components of social support that these instruments were designed to measure is another critical issue that has not yet been adequately addressed. All but one of the subscales of the PRQ show a considerable degree of overlap, as do the three functional subscales of the NSSQ. Demonstrating that these subscales have some useful unique variance will do much to validate the conceptualizations of social support underlying the design of these instruments. Can affect, for example, be separated from affirmation to a sufficient degree to permit a hypothesis that one or the other dimension will predict well-being in particular populations in particular contexts? If not, the definition of social support as composed of these distinct dimensions will have no credibility or utility. The regression analyses reported by Dr. Norbeck, which suggest that her three functional subscales work better as separate predictors than as a composite, are a step in the right direction. However these findings need to be confirmed in further research. One investigator who seems to be having some success in tackling this problem in Sheldon Cohen (Cohen & Hoberman, in press).

Cohen's CHISEL-2 (Cohen & Hoberman, in press) is a brief questionnaire similar to Part 2 of the PRQ, but with some items expressed more concretely. This scale was designed for use with college students, but Cohen has also developed a version for use with a community sample. Scale items were chosen to measure tangible aid, appraisal support, self-esteem support, and belongingness. Cohen has had more success than Drs. Norbeck, Brandt, or Weinert in developing independent and differentially predictive subscales. Given the similarity between the CHISEL-2 and the PRQ, it would be very interesting to test the extent to which scores on these instruments relate to one another.

ISSUES IN THE STUDY OF SOCIAL SUPPORT
Persistent Problems

To a great extent, the problems Drs. Weinert and Norbeck have faced in developing and evaluating their social support measures are the problems of the field as a whole.

The empirical and theoretical literature on social support has been reviewed repeatedly during the past decade (e.g., Cobb, 1976; Heller, 1979; Mueller, 1980). When I read these reviews, I am struck by the extent to which they all make a convincing argument for the importance of social support as a correlate of well-being and provide coherent syntheses of the various theoretical perspectives on the field. These are also clear signs of progress in some areas. If one looks at the older reviews, the importance of instruments such as the PRQ and NSSQ is dramatically evident. We have come a long way from the need to make inferences about social support based on variables such as marital status. On the other hand, reviews of the empirical findings in the field do not yet show much progress toward verification of any particular model of the structure and function of social support. We seem to be stuck at the level of first-generation conceptualizations. In order to move forward, we need to address three kinds of problems: the poor quality of much of the data in the field, the lack of a strong tradition of theory development and theory testing, and failure to capitalize on the potential of a greater variety of research designs.

Reviewers and theorists have not yet had very good data to work from in building and testing models of social support. Much of the empirical literature has been published in articles that include only sketchy, and often suspect, reports of data analyses and results. Some findings of impressive magnitude may be artifacts of the use of multivariate analytic techniques with small sample sizes. A reviewer of the social support literature also may be concerned about the reliability of simple bivariate effects in some studies. Most the analyses reported involve the Pearson r. In inspecting the data on which these correlation coefficients have been computed, one often notices that the distribution of one or more measures is very strongly skewed. This is detectable when the scale limits or the range of scores for each measure is given with the mean and SD, and one SD above or below the mean substantially exceeds the range of scores in that direction. There may be only one or two individuals in a sample whose extremely high or low scores on a predictor or outcome measure are entirely responsible for a reported small sample r. In such cases the reliability of the association is seriously in doubt (Jacobsen, 1981).

The comprehensiveness, clarity, and reliability of data from studies of social support are of particular concern to the reviewer because progress in the field must be based on a systematic comparison of effect sizes across populations, contexts, and outcome and social support measures. I hope that in their negotiations with journal editors, future writers in this field will insist firmly on the need to include the fullest possible data summaries in their publications. The field will also show more rapid progress if investigators are able to get enough funding to permit work with the large samples needed for this kind of research.

A comprehensive and reliable data base, however, is only one of the requirements for a constructive, heuristic synthesis of the literature. We need to remember to keep moving back and forth between data and the conceptualizations or theories that guided their generation. For example, what does it mean for Weiss' (1974) theory that nurturance is more distinct than the other aspects of social support he hypothesized? Should nurturance still be considered part of social support, or is it a separate construct? What criteria would one use in making this decision? Similarly, if investigators repeatedly find that tangible or instrumental aid scores surpass more affective-expressive components of support in predicting psychosocial outcomes, does this mean that the effective aspect of such aid is practical rather than interpersonal? Also, what do Dr. Norbeck's findings and those of other researchers, inspired by Kahn and Antonucci's (1980) explanatory framework of the hypothetical determinants and effects of convoy properties, contribute to the refinement of this intriguing conceptualization into a true causal model? To the extent that the answer to questions like these is, "Well, the data don't directly bear on the theory," something is wrong. Studies need to be better designed as explicit tests of the available theories, and theories need to be specified more fully so that the appropriate tests are apparent.

In considering the available conceptualizations and data in the social support field, one quickly becomes aware of the need for readily disconfirmable theories of social support. I am reminded of Sir Francis Bacon's maxim, "Truth emerges more readily from error than from confusion." We need less confusion and more good, clear error.

One aspect of the social support literature stands out as an example of good hypothesizing and hypothesis testing. Several theorists have proposed that social support should function as a buffer rather than as a simple effect in the prediction of health outcomes. In other words, maximal effects of social support should be detectable only under conditions of high situational stress or life change. Although the data are not consistent across all studies, this hypothesis has been supported in several different contexts (Cohen & Hoberman, in press; Crockenberg, 1981; Sarason et al., 1983; and Dr. Norbeck's presentation). These data provide some of the most provocative evidence regarding how social support works. Similarly, specific and testable predictions should be equally useful in the investigation of possible roles of different aspects of support in different contexts; relationships between past, current, and anticipated network structure and perceived support; the role of individual social skills in the generation of a supportive network; and so on.

SUGGESTIONS FOR FUTURE RESEARCH

Progress in the study of social support will be greatly facilitated by more explicit theorizing and better attention to the theoretical implications of research results. Future research, however, will also need to be somewhat different from the studies that typify current research in the field. The literature to date has been excessively dominated by cross-sectional correlational studies of relationships between social support and some outcome variable. Too little attention has been paid to the concurrent and developmentally prior structural and experiential variables that might account for the perception of social support. Without knowing what causes social support, we cannot know what it is. These antecedent "anchors" are especially important because it is unlikely that social support will ever prove to be an extremely powerful predictor of health outcomes. The concept of intelligence survived for many years without

Table 1
Potential Contributions from Different Kinds of Research
to Understand the Nature and Function of Social Support

Kind of Study	Purpose
Correlational	
— With support as an outcome variable related to environmental characteristics, personal history, and personal attributes	To define support in terms of a coherent pattern of observable antecedents.
— Longitudinal	To "disambiguate" the direction of cause and effect relationships between social support and health outcomes and/or social support and its environmental and personal correlates.
Experimental	To confirm the causal nature of observed correlations between social support and various outcomes.
	To isolate aspects of experience that are responsible for the perception of support and/or for health outcomes mediated by this perception.
	To provide guidelines for cost-effective interventions.

any consensus on its experiential antecedents or processing components because intelligence test scores are relatively strong predictors (r's $\cong$ .5 to .6) of school performance. Intelligence, therefore, was definable as that which predicts school learning. It is not much of a definition, but it helps. Given correlations of less than .3 to approximately .45 between social support and health outcomes and the broad array of outcomes that social support may moderate, a definition even partly in terms of outcome is not likely to have much use. We need to know where social support comes from and what its working parts are like in order to get much further than we are now.

Two kinds of studies, which complement one another, are likely to tell us what we need to know (see Table 1).

The first type, correlational research, is similar to the work that has been done already, but should be more comprehensive and explicitly analytical. Measures such as the NSSQ and PRQ, for example, could be part of studies in which network properties and individual and subgroup characteristics are related to the perception of various aspects of social support in the context of different kinds of life challenges. The work of Hirsch (1980), though it has some serious limitations, has something of the flavor of what I am suggesting. By treating perceived social support as an outcome rather than a predictor in some studies, it may be possible to develop complex models that account for virtually all the explainable variance in social support. At that point, we will be much more confident of what social support is.

Longitudinal developmental studies should be particularly useful in determining the process by which the perception of support emerges. Even short-term longitudinal studies would be helpful in disentangling the cause-effect relationship between perceived support and psychosocial outcomes.

A second kind of research that is much needed is experimental or quasi-experimental intervention research. There is an unfortunate tendency among some nurse scientists to reserve experimentation for the final stage of research in any area. This makes sense if the intervention one contemplates is the administration of a potentially dangerous treatment to human subjects. There is no general reason, however, to think of experimentation as being necessarily the last step in a program of research. Experiments can be used at any stage of research to confirm theoretically important correlational findings; to demonstrate that hypothesized causal relationships actually do, or do not, exist; and to isolate those aspects of an event or situation that are actually responsible for an effect. The recent literature in cognitive psychology provides excellent guidelines for combining correlational and experimental studies to generate understanding a complex intrapsychic concept (Butterfield, Siladi, & Belmont, 1980).

Experimental studies are especially important to nurse scientists interested in social support because the ultimate goal of such research is not prediction, but remediation. A measure of social support that predicts well-being effectively, but does so for unknown reasons, does not provide guidelines for appropriate treatment.

Current texts and articles on program evaluation, like the cognitive psychology literature, provide guidelines for doing experiments that will yield findings with both theoretical and practical relevance. One can conceive, for example, perceived social support as a mediating process in an intervention such as an environmental modification, instructional program, or other treatment designed to affect some health outcome. Imagine that one has access to individuals such as parents of infants with developmental disabilities. These parents are expected to be at high risk for some negative outcome such as depression, an effect that might be reduced by improving social support. Subgroups of parents could be given experimental treatments, including access to a support group of parents in similar circumstances, access to tangible aid such as housekeeping and child care assistance, counseling of the extended family or friends regarding the concerns and needs of these parents, or training of social skills that the parents can use in eliciting support from family and friends (see Table 2).

Table 2
**Plan for a Hypothetical Experiment to Evaluate Social
Factors Contributing to Depression in Parents of Infants with
Developmental Disabilities and to Determine the Role of
Perceived Support in Mediating Treatment Effects**

Treatment	Mediating Process	Desired Outcome
Support group for parents		
Tangible aid for parents	More support perceived ?	Less depression
Counsel extended to family and friends regarding parents' needs		
Teach parents social skills for eliciting support		
No treatment (This group is not essential to the design)		

In evaluating the effects of such interventions, it is important to know whether the treatment affects the outcome of interest (e.g., depression) and whether this effect is indeed mediated by an intervening effect on perceived social support.

If a treatment works, and if its effect can be accounted for by a change in perceived social support, one has gained basic knowledge about the nature of social support, as well as immediately useful information about how to help a population of interest. For example, a finding that providing tangible aid resulted in less depression for the treatment group than a no-treatment or other control group would have different implications if the difference in depression levels was mediated by a group difference in level of perceived support than if the effect on depression occurred without any effect on the supposed mediator. In the latter case, one would conclude that tangible aid is helpful in averting or alleviating depression, but that benefits are not the result of change in the perception of support.

Interactions between the characteristics of subjects and the efficacy of different experimental treatments can also help clarify the nature of hypothesized causal relationships. One might predict, for example, that training in social skills would affect skill level, perception of support, and level of depression only for those subjects who were initially rated low in social skills. Training should have no effect where a deficit does not exist. If social skills training was equally effective for high and low skill subjects, one would wonder whether the effect might be due to some extraneous feature of the training, such as the opportunity for interaction with classmates in the training program. A well-designed experiment yields data that facilitate the identification of critical elements in an intervention so that eventual large-scale applications of the intervention will be cost effective.

The theoretical and long-term, practical usefulness of experimental intervention research is not limited to situations of immediate practical significance. Relatively economical interventions in contrived or trivial settings could be very useful in addressing such issues as the relationships among network characteristics, dimensions of perceived support, and well-being. For example, individuals facing various types of minor challenges might be placed in settings that are high or low in availability of tangible aid, affirmation, intimacy, or whatever. One might predict that the efficacy of the various interventions would be greater or less for certain kinds of challenges and certain kinds of people. The social psychological literature contains many examples of this kind of study. Although the results of experiments conducted in artificial settings must be confirmed in more realistic contexts, the history of research in the behavioral sciences supports the potential usefulness of such studies. The test for whether experimental research is appropriate should not be the level of knowledge in the field or the appropriateness of a large-scale intervention at that point, but simply whether there is some experimental design that will provide an efficient means for furthering an understanding of the phenomenon of interest.

CONCLUSION

In closing, I would like to thank Drs. Norbeck, Weinert, and Brandt for giving us such useful instruments to employ in our continued pursuit of the elusive nature of social support. We still have a long way to go before we can expect to understand this concept well enough to be able to manipulate it effectively. A conference like this one, however, has provided an excellent opportunity for us to work together on some of the rigorous problem definition and problem solving that the field needs.

DISCUSSION

F. Montes: May I say something as a spectator? Raising money is a special situation, and I want to tell you that these presentations have provided me, as a lay person, with a kind of social support that I need to help provide tangible aid through the March of Dimes to help fund research and education. This is a form of reciprocity that was alluded to earlier in the presentation.

J. Fawcett: I would like to respond to Dr. Jackson's comment about journal editors and more data. There has to be a balance between too much data and too little data submitted as part of a research report. It is not unusual for manuscripts submitted to *Nursing Research* to include tables with 100 or more correlation coefficients, or 10 or 20 t tests. In most cases, only a few of the statistics reach significance. There are some very serious problems in interpreting these results. Experiment-wise error must be considered. The theoretical reason for so many statistical tests also must be considered. In many instances, the tests were done more as a "fishing expedition" than as tests of theoretically supported hypotheses.

I think we could agree with Dr. Jackson's point that it is important for the reader to know that many statistical tests were carried out and that just a few reached the required level of significance, but I would add that the reader should also know the reasons why so many tests were conducted.

S. Feetham: From critiquing many proposals — over 40 in the last few months — one of the things I think is even more fundamental to the analysis question is the need for a conceptual framework that is consistent with a multivariate design and subsequently multivariate analysis. In many of the proposals I reviewed, what is lacking is the initial conceptualization that is supportive of multivariate research. I'm hearing repeatedly at this conference that such a framework is needed. In the few instances when a conceptual framework might exist, the analysis may fall down by falling back into univariate analysis, which, again, is less powerful. The efforts must go all the way back to the very beginning conceptualization; that is where we need to give more attention.

M. Cranley: I have a question for Clarann Weinert. How were the life situations selected that were included in Part 1?

C. Weinert: What we attempted to do was to look at possible situations that would cover the gamut of short-term and long-term situations and try to have domains that were pretty inclusive. One of the things that we did in the revision of the PRQ was to see how inclusive domains were by asking an open ended question on Item 9. This item reads, "Have there been any major concerns or problems that you've had in the last year?" and if so, "Who did you go to for help?" We do not have any data back to tell us whether or not those eight situations cover the possible gamut in a global sense, but we did try to test this out.

P. Brandt: As I recall, after reviewing the literature that was available on support at that time, we decided to develop a tool that would be applicable across populations and health problems rather than one applicable only to parents, for example, of children with chronic conditions. Therefore, we decided to sample acute and long-term problem situations which would be relevant to the person as well as to family members.

S. Eyres: I wonder if you would enlarge a little bit on one suggestion you had for using social support as the outcome — the dependent variable — if you don't know what to measure as the dependent variable for social support? I'm not clear as to what you mean.

N. Jackson: I think that one has to do this in many stages, and the operational definitions that we have of social support, as in the two questionnaires we have just been discussing, would strike me as perfectly reasonable first approximations. The point is to measure social support in whatever rough and ready way is available and look at the extent to which the perception of support can be explained by the person's social skills, the extent to which the convoy is stable and disrupted, and the kind of life challenge he/she is experiencing at the time. If one could develop a model through repeated hypothesizing and testing that would account for all the variance in either a unidimensional or multidimensional construct of social support, then, one would have the feeling that this is social support. If one coupled that with concurrent programs of research relating social support to outcomes, then, using those two things together would narrow down the definition of that central link. Almost all of the models use social support as a link in the middle between some personal and environmental characteristics and some outcome related to health. Yet, in a lot of the research, social support is out at the end. It's the first thing in the hypothesized causal chain that is being measured. Fortunately, this is not true of all the literature, and certainly not true of all of the papers for this conference. There are a number of people who are looking at antecedents, and both the PRQ and the NSSQ are very useful in that respect because they do provide some information about the individual's social network, which is one of the things one would certainly want to look at in terms of what causes the feeling of social support.

S. Eyres: So what you are suggesting then is a kind of a program of research that's mapped out to get at these different aspects?

N. Jackson: Very definitely. It's not the sort of thing that can be done in one quick study.

S. Eyres: No, I didn't mean one quick study, but I meant there has to be some orchestration between those different things that you were discussing.

N. Jackson: Yes.

K. Barnard: Dr. Jackson has proposed with her diagram the need to move into looking at more causal explanations and experimental models. I think this point is appropriate to consider concerning social support research. We need to raise questions for experimentation, manipulate certain forms of social support, and observe what happens within different groups. There's an excellent article written by Craig Ramey and associates (1981) in a book on the psychological development of preterm infants (Friedman & Sigman, 1981). Ramey, in giving a theoretical base for looking at early intervention with children, outlines the need to look at different attributes of the individual in relation to different situations. This is an approach that could be considered a model we need in the area of social support.

L. Cronenwett: Dr. Norbeck, when you asked questions such as, "How much does this person make you feel liked or loved?" did you think you gained more information using a Likert type response scale with "not at all" being one level and four possible responses for the "yes" category, versus just requesting a dichotomous "yes" or "no" response? In other words, do you think you're getting some statement about quantity or quality that you wouldn't get with a dichotomous response?

J. Norbeck: Particularly in the tangible support items, you see a full range of scores, so you would lose information by using a dichotomy. For the emotional support items, there is less spread of scores. Most subjects rate their network members at the two highest levels for emotional support, but there are cases when an individual is rated very low (a score of 1 which indicates no support).

In terms of the mathematical answer to your question, I really don't know how much the range would make a difference, i.e., what you gain or lose by ranking on a five-point, three-point, or a two-point scale. However, it is rare that subjects use the lowest score, so a dichotomy might not work with this questionnaire.

The ratings of level of support on the NSSQ are influenced by the format and instructions. Subjects are first asked to make a list of supportive persons in their life. It is unlikely that a nonsupportive person's name is going to be on the network list in the first place. This is equally true for the emotional kinds of support on the NSSQ.

S. Humenick: Are you saying then that people do not respond by listing supporters whom they view as providing tangible aid but not emotional support? In other words, if these situations exist, they are unreported in answer to your questionnaire.

J. Norbeck: In the extreme sense, that's true. If the person is on the network list, usually they're getting ratings of around four and five, although occasionally there are individuals who will get lower scores. But the place where the scores drop is in the aid items. The general trend on the scores is that the highest mean score is for two affect items. Slightly lower scores are given to the two affirmation items, and then the aid items receive an even lower score.

S. Humenick: I think that is interesting, because in the real world I would suppose there are instances where people provide tangible aid without emotional support. Thus, apparently when individuals respond to your questionnaire, they are thinking of support as affective support.

J. Norbeck: That appears to be the case.

L. Cronenwett: The way Dr. Mercer asked her question about support, she received a higher percentage of tangible aid answers. I think Dr. Mercer worded her question, "Who helped you and what was the most helpful," or something like that, and this elicited high tangible aid responses, while both Dr. Norbeck and I obtained lower perceived access to tangible aid and higher in the socioeconomic categories. These differences demonstrate how you get different responses by the questions you ask.

R. Mercer: Tangible aid may be the easiest type of support to discuss. Also, in response to Dr. Humenick, tangible aid was provided without perceived emotional support. Subjects more often responded to the question, "In what way was this person helpful," with answers such as, "Changing his diaper, feeding," or "Help with household chores," whereas, "Telling me that I was a good mother" or "Understanding my feelings" didn't come up nearly as often.

L. Cronenwett: We don't think about comparison support as help. If someone says, "Did she help you?" what immediately comes to mind, I think, is tangible help. You don't think, "Oh my friend, she was there for me to compare stories with, I was helped by seeing that, and because she was a good mother, I was a good mother." You don't think of that kind of support immediately when someone says, "How were they helped?"

S. Eyres: What would happen in approaching the measurements of social support if one started an instrument like Dr. Norbeck's and had them list people with whom they had the most contact, who were part of their normal everyday world, and then had them rate whether they gave them positive or negative things?

K. Barnard: Well, Henderson did use that approach, and that's what he asked. As I remember his scale, he asked for the amount of contact that individuals had with other individuals, and whether this was a positive or negative contact (Henderson, Duncan-Jones, McAuley, & Ritchie, 1978). He did not ask specifically if there was other aid, and he found, of course, that positive contact was associated with less mental health disturbance.

S. Eyres: Maybe part of our problem in studying social support is that we're only looking for the good that comes from the transaction with other people in the environment. The early conceptualizations of what the social environment does for us definitely talks about conflict that can come from those people who are also giving tangible aid, such as helping with the baby (Cassel, 1974).

P. MacElveen-Hoehn: We know from the work of Belle and her colleagues (1979) at Harvard that frequent interactions with people can lead to greater stress and depression. This was true when those interactions were demands for assistance, problem solving, or emotional support since the low income, urban mothers in that study were often already overburdened by the demands in their lives and the limitations of resources available to them. Wahler (1980) found that mothers were unable to continue newly learned parenting behaviors when the social interactions in their daily lives were adversive, conflictual, or highly demanding. Thus, we see two examples where mother-child interaction was negatively affected by contact with others which was counterproductive to the mother's mental health or maintenance of positive parenting behaviors. We would all agree I think that interaction does not guarantee support; interaction can even be an additional demand or drain on scarce resources.

By definition, support means positive input or help in some way. When we say negative support, that is a contradiction in terms. We need some kind of word to describe interactions which are meant to be supportive but which are experienced as nonhelpful, e.g., overprotective or nonunderstanding.

T. Antonucci: I think this issue about negative support versus the use of another term comes up frequently in the study of social support. It's like development. It's easy to talk about development in infants and kids, but what do you talk about when people are 50-70 or 70-90? Do you call that development? We need to rethink the assumed directionality of these terms. Why does it always have to be positive? Why can't it be negative? We have collected some data concerning negative support as well as positive support, and negative support accounts for the most variance. We use the kind of close and important approach that Dr. Norbeck uses, and that gives you a bias in and of itself. If you start with questions that ask about what people do for you, you get one set of people. If you ask who's close and important, you may get another set of people. People who are close and important to you or who do things for you can still get on your nerves or demand too much of you. In our study (Kahn & Antonucci, 1979), the comparison of a voluminous amount of positive support measures with a much fewer number of negative support measures indicates that the latter account for a higher proportion of the variance in outcome measures such as well-being, life satisfaction, and quality of life. Clearly this notion of negative support, whether we use this label or another, is critically important to an individual in their assessment of their social network.

P. MacElveen-Hoehn: There is also a generalization about a person being "supportive," that implies a person is qualified and available for all circumstances. We know this is not true. Somebody can provide support for a mother going back to work, but not for her leaving her husband; or give positive feedback for being a good cook, but give potent negative appraisals of how she is raising the children. There is still a lot of ambiguity and confusion around what support is as well as how it works.

L. Cronenwett: Or a network structure that could be very good in one situation, but negative in another?

S. Feetham: A way that we handle that issue is in our instrumentation by using the Porter format (Porter, 1962; Roberts & Feetham, 1982; Feetham & Humenick, 1982) which asks: how much is there now, how much should there be, and how important is this to you. Using this format, you get their perception of the amount and then the differentiation of how much should there be of that. Subtracting "how much is there" from "how much should there be" provides a discrepancy score which is another way of perhaps controlling for some of the issues about which you are talking.

REFERENCES

Beck, A.T. (1972). *Depression: Causes and treatments.* Philadelphia: University of Pennsylvania Press.

Belle, D. (1979). *Lives in stress: A context for depression.* Cambridge, MA: Harvard Graduate School of Education.

Belle, D. (1980). *Stress and families.* Unpublished research project proposal, Harvard University.

Bloom, J. (1982). Social support systems and cancer: A conceptual view. In J. Cohen (Ed.), *Psychosocial aspects of cancer.* New York: Raven Press.

Brandt, P. (1981). *Relationship of mothers' negative life experiences and social support to the restrictive discipline and environmental stimulation of her developmentally disabled child.* Unpublished doctoral dissertation, University of Washington.

Brandt, P.A., & Weinert, C. (1981). The PRQ — A social support measure. *Nursing Research, 30*(5), 277-280.

Brim, J. (1974). Social network correlates of avowed happiness. *Journal of Nervous and Mental Disease, 58,* 432-439.

Brown, G., Bhrolchain, M., Ni, M., & Harris, T. (1975). Social class and psychiatric disturbances among women in an urban population. *Sociology, 9,* 225-254.

Butterfield, E.C., Siladi, D., & Belmont, J.M. (1980). Validating theories of intelligence. In H. Reese & L. P. Lipsitt (Eds.), *Advances in child development and child behavior* (Vol. 15). New York: Academic Press.

Caplan, G. (1964). *Principles of preventive psychiatry.* London: Travisiock Publications.

Caplan, G. (1974). *Support systems and community mental health.* New York: Behavioral Publications.

Carmines, E., & Zeller, R. (1979). *Reliability and validity assessment.* Beverly Hills: Sage Publications.

Cassel, J. (1974a). An epidemiological perspective of psychosocial factors in disease etiology. *American Journal of Public Health, 64,* 1040-1043.

Cassel, J. (1974b). Psychosocial processes and stress: Theoretical formulations. *International Journal of Health Services, 4*(3), 471-482.

Cassel, J. (1976). The contribution of the social environment to host resistance. *American Journal of Epidemiology, 104,* 107-123.

Cobb, S. (1976). Social support as a moderator of life stress. *Psychosomatic Medicine, 38*(5), 300-314.

Cohen, S., & Hoberman, H.M. (in press). *Positive events and social supports as buffers of life change stress.*

Crockenberg, S. (1981). Infant irritability, mother responsiveness, and social support influences on the security of infant-mother attachment. *Child Development, 52,* 857-865.

Cronenwett, L.R. (1982). *Parent assessment project questionnaire.* Unpublished research material, University of Michigan.

Crowne, D.P., & Marlowe, D. (1960). A new scale of social desirability independent of psychopathology. *Journal of Counseling Psychology, 24,* 349-354.

Dean, A., & Lin, N. (1977). The stress-buffering role of social support: Problems and prospects for systematic investigation. *Journal of Nervous and Mental Disease, 165,* 403-417.

Derogatis, L.R. (1977). *SCL-90 administration, scoring and procedures manual,* (Rev. version). Baltimore: Johns Hopkins University School of Medicine.

Dimond, M. (1979). Social support and adaptation to chronic illness: The case of maintenance hemodialysis. *Research in Nursing and Health, 2,* 101-108.

Eysenck, H., & Eysenck, S. (1968). *Eysenck personality inventory.* San Diego: Educational and Industrial Testing Service.

Finlayson, A. (1976). Social networks. *Social Science and Medicine, 27,* 287-291.

Friedman, S.L., & Sigman, M. (Eds.). (1981). *Preterm birth and psychological development.* New York: Academic Press.

Fuller, S.S., & Larson, S.B. (1980). Life events, emotional support, and health of older people. *Research in Nursing and Health, 3,* 81-89.

Gore, S. (1978). The effect of social support in moderating the health consequences of unemployment. *Journal of Health and Social Behavior, 19,* 157-165.

Hamburg, B.A., & Killilea, M. (1979). Relation of social support, stress, illness, and use of health services. *Healthy people: The Surgeon General's report on health promotion and disease prevention.* (No. 017-001-00417-1). Washington, DC: Government Printing Office.

Heller, K. (1979). The effects of social support: Prevention and treatment implications. In A. P. Goldstein & F. H. Kanfer (Eds.), *Maximizing treatment gains: Transfer enhancement in psychotherapy.* New York: Academic Press.

Helmrath, T.A., & Steinitz, E.M. (1978). Death of an infant: Parental grieving and failure of social support. *Journal of Family Practice, 6,* 785-790.

Henderson, S. (1974). Care-electing behavior in man. *Journal of Nervous Disease, 159,* 172-181.

Henderson, S. (1977). The social network, support and neurosis. *The British Journal of Psychiatry, 131,* 185-191.

Henderson, S. (1980). A development in social psychiatry: The systematic study of social bonds. *Journal of Nervous and Mental Disease, 168,* 63-69.

Henderson, S., Duncan-Jones, P., McAuley, H., & Ritchie, K. (1978). The patient's primary group. *British Journal of Psychiatry, 132,* 74-86.

Hirsch, B. (1980). Natural support systems and coping with major life changes. *American Journal of Community Psychology, 8,* 159-172.

House, J. (1981). *Work stress and social support.* Reading, MA: Addison-Wesley.

Iversen, C. (1981). *An exploratory study of the relationships among presence and perception of life change, social support and illness in an aging population.* Unpublished master's thesis, University of Washington.

Jacobsen, B.S. (1981). Know thy data. *Nursing Research, 30,* 254-255.

Kahn, R.L. (1979). Aging and social support. In M.W. Riley (Ed.), *Aging from birth to death: Interdisciplinary perspective.* Boulder, CO: Westview Press.

Kahn, R.L., & Antonucci, T.C. (1979). *Social support of the elderly: Family/friends/professionals.* Proposal funded by National Institute on Aging, HHS, No. AGO 1632.

Kahn, R.L., & Antonucci, T.C. (1980). Convoys over the life course: Attachment, roles, and social support. In P.B. Baltes & O.C. Brim, Jr. (Eds.), *Life-span development and behavior* (Vol. 3). New York: Academic Press.

Lin, N., Simeone, R., Ensel, W., & Kuo, W. (1979). Social support, stressful life events, and illness: A model and an empirical test. *Journal of Health and Social Behavior, 20*(2), 108-119.

Lobo, M. (1982). *Mother's and father's perception of family resources and their adaptation to parenthood.* Unpublished doctoral dissertation, University of Washington.

Lowenthal, M., & Haven, C. (1968). Interaction and adaptation: Intimacy as a critical variable. *American Sociological Review, 33,* 20-30.

MacElveen, P. (1978). Social networks. In D. Longo & R. Williams (Eds.), *Clinical practice in psychosocial nursing: Assessment and intervention.* New York: Appleton-Century-Crofts.

Magilvy, K. (1982). *Deaf and hearing-impaired older women: Influences on quality of life.* Unpublished doctoral dissertation. University of Colorado.

McKenna, L.S. (1982). *Social network, social support and the psychological adaptation of battered women.* Unpublished dissertation proposal, University of California, San Francisco.

McNair, D.M., Lorr, M., & Droppleman, L.F. (1971). *POMS manual for profile of mood states.* San Diego, CA: Educational and Industrial Testing Service.

Medalie, J., & Goldbourt, U. (1976). Angina pectoris among 10,000 men: Psychosocial and other risk factors as evidenced by a multi-variant analysis of a five year incidence study. *American Journal of Medicine, 60,* 910-921.

Miller, P., & Ingham, J. (1976). Friends, confidants, and symptoms. *Social Psychiatry, 11,* 51-58.

Mitchell, R.E., & Trickett, E.J. (1980). Social networks as mediators of social support: An analysis of the effects and determinants of social networks. *Community Mental Health Journal, 16,* 27-44.

Mueller, D.P. (1980). Social networks: A promising direction for research on the relationship of the social environment to psychiatric disorder. *Social Science and Medicine, 14A,* 147-161.

Murtaugh, J. (1982). *A descriptive study of social support and depression in low income women.* Unpublished master's thesis, University of Washington.

Nichols, E.G. (research in progress). *Relationship between age, life experience, perception of dialysis, social support and life satisfaction.*

Norbeck, J.S. (1981). Social support: A model for clinical research and application. *Advances in Nursing Science, 3*(4), 43-59.

Norbeck, J.S. (in press). Modification of life events questionnaires for use with female respondents. *Research in Nursing and Health.*

Norbeck, J.S. (in progress). General and situation-specific social support needs of mothers of young children.

Norbeck, J.S., Lindsey, A.M., & Carrieri, V.L. (1981). The development of an instrument to measure social support. *Nursing Research, 30*(5), 264-269.

Norbeck, J.S., Lindsey, A.M., & Carrieri, V.L. (1982, June). Personal communication.

Norbeck, J.S., Lindsey, A.M., & Carrieri, V.L. (1983). Further development of the Norbeck Social Support Questionnaire: Normative data and validity testing. *Nursing Research, 32*(1), 4-9.

Norbeck, J.S., & Tilden, V.P. (in press). Life stress, social support, and emotional disequilibrium in complications of pregnancy: A prospective, multivariate study. *Journal of Health and Social Behavior.*

Nunnally, J. (1978). *Psychometric theory.* San Francisco: McGraw-Hill.

Pearlin, L.I., Lieberman, M.A., Menaghan, E.G., & Mullan, J.T. (1981). The stress process. *Journal of Health and Social Behavior, 22,* 337-356.

Pless, J., & Satterwhite, B. (1973). A measure of family functioning and its application. *Social Science and Medicine, 7,* 613-621.

Porter, L.W. (1963). Job attitudes in management: Part 2, Perceived importance of need as a function of job level. *Journal of Applied Psychology, 47*(2), 141-148.

Ramey, C.T., Zeskind, P.S., & Hunter, R. (1981). Biomedical and psychosocial interventions for preterm infants. In S.L. Friedman & M. Sigman (Eds.), *Preterm birth and psychological development.* New York: Academic Press.

Renne, J. (1974). Measurement of social health in a general population survey. *Social Service Research, 3,* 25-44.

Sarason, I.G., Johnson, J.H., & Siegel, J.M. (1978). Assessing the impact of life changes: Development of the Life Experiences Survey. *Journal of Consulting and Clinical Psychology, 46,* 932-946.

Sarason, I.G., Levine, H.G., Basham, R.B., & Sarason, B.R. (1983). Assessing social support: The social support questionnaire. *Journal of Personality and Social Psychology, 44,* 127-139.

Schaefer, C., Coyne, J. C., & Lazarus, R. (1981). The health related functions of social support. *Journal of Behavioral Medicine, 4,* 381-406.

Schutz, W. (1978). *FIRO awareness scales manual.* Palo Alto, CA: Consulting Psychologists Press.

Spanier, G. (1976). Measuring dyadic adjustment: New scales for assessing the quality of marriage and family dyads. *Journal of Marriage and Family, 38,* 15-28.

Speilberger, C., Gorsuch, R., & Lushene, R. (1970). *STAI manual for the state-trait anxiety inventory.* Palo Alto, CA: Consulting Psychologists Press.

Strahan, R., & Gerbasi, K. (1972). Short homogeneous versions of the Marlowe-Crowne social desirability scale. *Journal of Clinical Psychology, 28,* 191-193.

Thoits, P. (1982). Conceptual, methodological, and theoretical problems in studying social support as a buffer against life stress. *Journal of Health and Social Behavior, 23*(2), 145-159.

Tolsdorf, C. (1976). Social networks, support, and coping. *Family Process, 15*(4), 407-417.

Turner, S.L. (1979). Disability among schizophrenics in rural community: Services and social support. *Research in Nursing and Health, 2,* 151-161.

Wahler, R.G. (1980). The insular mother: Her problems in parent child treatment. *Journal of Applied Behavioral Analysis, 2*(13), 207-219.

Weinert, C. (1981). *Long-term illness, social support, and family functioning.* Unpublished doctoral dissertation, University of Washington.

Weinert, C. (1982, April). *Social support: Influence on middlescent families living with long-term illness.* Paper presented at the Pacific Sociological Association Meetings, San Diego, CA.

Weiss, R. (1969). The fund of sociality. *Trans-Action, 6*(9), 36-43.

Weiss, R. (1974). The provisions of social relationship. In D. Rubin (Ed.), *Doing unto others.* Englewood Cliffs, NJ: Prentice-Hall.

Wilcox, B.L. (1981). Social support, life stress, and psychological adjustment: A test of the buffering hypothesis. *American Journal of Community Psychology, 9,* 371-386.

Zung, W. (1974). The measurement of affects: Depression and anxiety. In P. Pinchot (Ed.), *Psychological measurement in psychopharmacology.* Paris: Karger.

Social Support as a Factor in the Development of Parents' Attachment to Their Unborn

Mecca S. Cranley, R.N., Ph.D.

Two studies are discussed which have investigated the association between aspects of social support and parents' attachment to their unborn children. The first study involved interviews of 30 women in the third trimester of pregnancy and utilized a broad conceptualization of social support measured by a questionnaire developed for the study. Overall social support was positively associated with the woman's attachment to her fetus; support from health care professionals was more highly correlated with attachment (.74) than was support from family and friends (.25). The second study utilized questionnaires from 326 couples to investigate the relationship between fetal attachment and satisfaction with the marital relationship. Results revealed a positive association between marital relationship and attachment to the fetus for both men and women. Implications for further research are discussed.

There appears to be consensus in the literature that the 9 months of gestation are not just for the physical development of the fetus. Equally dynamic is the development of the woman into a mother. Integral to that development is an elaborate consideration, or reconsideration, of the woman's own identity, the identity of her developing fetus, and perhaps most importantly, of the relationship between herself and her fetus. It is this relationship, defined as maternal-fetal attachment, which is the subject of this paper.

Although the preponderance of research on mothers' attachment to their infants has concentrated on the period immediately following birth, there is growing evidence that this process of attachment has its beginnings during pregnancy (Leifer, 1977; Carter-Jessup, 1981; Cranley, 1981a, 1981b). A number of factors have been postulated to influence the development of this prenatal involvement with the fetus. One of the most frequently mentioned factors is social support.

SOCIAL SUPPORT

Antonovsky (1974, p. 253) has noted that ties to others are a significant "resistance resource."

> On the simplest level, a person who has someone who cares for him is likely to more adequately resolve tension than one who does not. Even without employing the resources of others, simply knowing that these are available increases one's strength.

Gongla (1976) presented a conceptualization of coping with stress from a systems perspective. In her paper she stated that the major criterion for judging the effectiveness of coping, viz., preserving the character or integrity of the system, can be considered from three different levels: physiological, psychological, and social. In discussing the social levels, the notion of belonging to and being able to draw upon a group was cited as one of the factors which facilitate coping. Feelings of isolation or abandonment have been found to contribute significantly to psychiatric patients' definition of an event as stressful, as well as to their ability to cope with the crisis (Dressler, Donovan, & Geller, 1976).

Of greater interest to the issue of antepartal attachment, Nuckolls, Cassel, and Kaplan (1972) studied 170 pregnant women in an attempt to discover a relationship between life crisis and complications of pregnancy. In addition to obtaining life change scores, they measured "psychosocial assets." This latter variable included five components, three of which were concerned with support structures: marital duration and happiness; relationship with extended family; and community adjustment, friendship patterns, and support. The remaining two components related to the individual (e.g., self-esteem, perception of health, loneliness, adaptability) and definition of the pregnancy. Results of the study indicated that when there was a high life change score, the psychosocial asset score was significant in predicting complications of pregnancy. Stated another way, women with high life change scores *and* high psychosocial asset scores had only one-third the complication rate of those women with low asset scores. Thus, it would appear that the psychosocial assets, a large component of which was the support component, offset the effects of high life change scores.

Rubin (1975) discussed the importance of support from significant others in the context of the tasks of pregnancy. Ensuring the acceptance of the child by significant others is one of the tasks enumerated by Rubin (p. 146):

> No one task of pregnancy is more important than another, but this one of security in acceptance seems to be the keystone of successful pregnancy. The fact that women who are pregnant are most concerned with this aspect in the first trimester, and again early in the third trimester, seems to indicate that security in acceptance is a condition necessary to produce and sustain the energy for all other tasks.

The central theme appears to be that the woman must be given to in order to be able to give. This implies a person or persons in her environment who are available and willing to give, whether the giving is of advice, material things, or moral support.

Approaching the problem from the negative perspective, Kempe (1976) and Gray, Cutler, Dean, and Kempe (1979) cited the lack of a social support structure during pregnancy as a high-risk factor, associated with subsequent child abuse and neglect. Thus, it appears that a social support network is necessary before the attachment process can begin.

Before proceeding, it is necessary to establish a definition of social support. Although a variety of authors have defined social support, the most commonly cited one was developed by Cobb (1976). Cobb conceived social support as information (versus goods and services) that the individual possessess which leads her to believe she is loved and cared for, esteemed and valued, and belongs to a network of communication and mutual obligation. This information is communicated in intimate relationships of mutual trust and in interactions with the public in work, social, and wider community settings. It includes knowledge about the availability of goods and services upon which she may draw as a member of the network.

SOCIAL SUPPORT STUDIES

Two studies are discussed in this paper which have used Cobb's definition of social support in the investigation of the association between social support and parents' attachments to their unborn children. The first study involved women during the third trimester of their pregnancies, and it examined social support in a broad conceptualization. The second study focused specifically on the dyadic relationship between the parents of the fetus as a unique form of social support.

Study I: Maternal-Fetal Attachment and Social Support

This study involved home interviews of 30 women during the third trimester of their pregnancies (Cranley, 1981b). These women were predominantly from working class families, and there were a few professionals. The modal educational level was high school graduation. Eight were expecting their first child, 15 their second, and 7 their third or a later child. All women delivered normal infants at term.

Instrument. During the interview the women completed the Fetal Attachment Scale (Cranley, 1981a) and responded to questions about their social support system. The Fetal Attachment Scale is a 24-item Likert-type scale composed of 5 subscales representing different, but related, facets of antepartal attachment behavior. The subscales are Roletaking, Differentiation of Self from the Fetus, Giving of Self, Attributing Characteristics to the Fetus, and Interaction with the Fetus. Men and women respond to these subscales in a similar pattern, although women have significantly higher scores on all subscales than do their partners (Cranley, 1981a, 1981b, 1982). The pattern of response for both men and women is characterized by lower scores on those subscales which require a more intense interpersonal relationship with the fetus, viz., Attributing Characteristics to the Fetus and Interaction with the Fetus.

The questions concerning social support were based on two underlying assumptions. The first assumption was that the nature of social support will differ according to age and developmental stage of the individual and the circumstances in which the woman finds herself. The second assumption was that both intrafamilial and extrafamilial or community resources can contribute support and that this support is additive. This assumption was addressed by McCubbin when he wrote, "The family is called upon . . . to actively employ coping behaviors within the family system and in relationship to the community," and these coping behaviors include the "procurement of social support from the community, interpersonal relationships and extended family" (1979, p. 243).

With these assumptions in mind, the development of a measure of social support for pregnant women was undertaken. Questions were phrased to elicit information about the extent to which women perceived themselves to participate in a network that provided the following components of social support:*

1. Someone to provide help, advice, or information relative to the pregnancy.
2. Someone to provide help, advice, or information relative to other things besides the pregnancy.
3. Relationship with her mother. (Deutsch, 1945; Caplan, 1961; and others have described the importance of the pregnant woman's relationship with her own mother.)
4. Intimate relationship with someone who cares for her and shares her interest in the pregnancy.
5. Contact with others in a similar situation, specifically other pregnant women.
6. Contact with health care professionals.

Health care professionals were specifically included because it is a basic professional philosophy among health care providers that it is important to provide emotional or psychological support to the patient as well as physical care. A woman may perceive herself to be receiving support from the health care community if she believes she is receiving high quality care and if she believes the professionals are concerned about her as an individual. For this reason, questions were included pertaining to available support from the health care community.

*The components and two subsequent paragraphs were added after the conference.

A major omission from this measure was specific reference to financial resources, although needing a loan of money was given as one of the examples when asking the question about whom the woman could call on for help with things other than the pregnancy.

A social support score was obtained by summing the scores on all items. During data analysis two subscales were identified: one which measured support from family and friends (FFSUP), and the second which measured support from health care professionals (HCSUP). The coefficient of reliability (Cronbach's alpha) for the entire scale was .64, while that for the Family and Friends subscale was .62, and for the Health Care Support .77.

Results. The range of social support scales for this sample of pregnant women was 38-60 from a possible range of 10-65. The mean score was 50.1 (SD = 5.7). Scores on the Family and Friends subscale ranged from 15-30 (possible range 4-35) with a mean of 20.5 (SD = 4.1). A particularly interesting finding was the degree to which these women were involved in extended family networks; 60% lived within a few minutes of their mothers, and another 10% lived within a half day's drive. In indicating whom they would call on for help or advice, only one woman did not include family members. She specifically stated, "Well, I couldn't put any of my sisters down (on the list). I always have to help them." One woman whose parents and parents-in-law both resided out of state listed several friends she would call on for help. Then she said, "Well, it depends on the kind of help I needed. If it was really important — something big — I would call my father or my husband's father, or our mothers, too."

Scores on the Health Care Support subscale were high, with a range of 16-30 (possible range of 6-30) and a mean of 25.6 (SD = 2.8). The score of 16 was 6 points below the next lowest score, so that 29 of the scores ranged from 22-30. The subject scoring 16 had many subjective symptoms throughout her pregnancy and believed her obstetrician regarded her as a "crock." Her dissatisfaction prompted her to seek consultation independently with a second obstetrician. She did, however, return to her original physician for the completion of her care. The majority of women spontaneously spoke of their physicians in positive terms, and almost all listed him as the first person they would call on for advice about their pregnancies. A trusting, nonquestioning relationship seemed to prevail, not at all unlike the stereotypical relationship between a pregnant woman and her physician. However, an incidental finding of this study was a tendency toward lowered perception of medical support as the education of women increased (r = -.32, p<.05). Contacts with nurses were limited to the office nurses employed by the physicians. These nurses had traditional office functions of escorting the woman to the examination room and taking her weight, blood pressure, and urine sample. Interaction was almost exclusively social.

Some degree of skepticism may be warranted in evaluating the health care support scores. The subjects entered the study through their physicians' cooperation, and all were aware that the investigator was a nurse. The location of the mean so near the upper end of the range suggests that there may have been a tendency toward wanting to make a socially acceptable or even flattering response. Furthermore, during the interviews, several women complained about how busy the physician was and the difficulties they had getting questions answered; yet these same women scored very high on the Health Care Support scale. One woman stated it wasn't until half way through her second pregnancy with the same physician that he remembered her name; yet she responded "strongly agree" to the statement "I feel like the doctors and nurses care about me as a person." Subjects were least likely to agree with the statement, "Someone always explains the reasons for the care I receive so that I understand it."

Relationship to fetal attachment. The correlation coefficient for the total Social Support Scale with maternal-fetal attachment was .51 (significance = .002). The subscales, Family and Friend Support and Health Care Support, were then correlated separately revealing correlation coefficients of .25 and .74, respectively. Both subscales were most highly associated with behaviors in the Roletaking and Differentiation of Self subscales of the Fetal Attachment Scale, although the Health Care Support subscale was almost as highly correlated with the Interaction with the Fetus and Attributing Characteristics to the Fetus scales as well.

Partial correlations were computed to rule out any influence of age or parity on the association between social support and maternal-fetal attachment. The results were as follows: controlling for age only, partial r = .50; controlling for parity only, partial r = .52; and controlling for both age and parity, partial r = .49. All partial correlations were significant at alpha levels less than .01.

Interviews with the subjects revealed that support took a variety of forms. One common form was the increased nurturance which the women accepted from those around them. This support included fellow employees who were described as protecting them from certain tasks, especially those involving lifting, and encouraging them to rest and "take it easy." Husbands were most often mentioned in this respect, as they did things for their wives in the form of household chores and shopping, as well as monitoring their diets and activities. These were activities the men either did not do at all when their wives were not pregnant or which they had performed to a much lesser extent. Although no quantitative measures were taken, it was the impression of the author that only a few of these families might be described as approaching egalitarianism. The more common pattern was the division of labor according to traditional sex roles. For example, most families made arrangements for a female relative or friend to care for the house and older children and cook while the mother was in the hospital.

Another source of nurturance was the subject's own mother. Several women had daily contact with their mothers because their mothers either lived next door or cared for an older child while the women worked. All of those who did not have such a reason for early daily contact, however, reported an increased frequency of contact with their mothers, particularly late in pregnancy. This group included those women whose mothers lived out of state, whom they telephoned more frequently. All subjects reported that this increased frequency was initiated by their mothers, not by themselves.

The women sought information and reassurance about themselves and their pregnancies from several sources. As mentioned before, almost all named their physician as a person they would ask for advice about their pregnancies. Others named were their own mothers, older sisters, or women friends who had already had children or who were nurses. Apart from the physicians who were all men, no male friends or family members, including husbands, were mentioned as being able to provide any help specific to the pregnancy. For this sample of women, it would appear that childbearing was definitely "woman's work." This was in spite of the fact that over half of the men attended childbirth classes and all but six were in the delivery room at the time of birth. (Fathers were not present for two of the vaginal deliveries and four of the cesarean births.)

Because of the striking relationship between the support of health care professionals and fetal attachment ($r = .74$), this area warrants further exploration to discover more precisely which behaviors or attitudes of health professionals are most supportive. Such information may help clinicians to increase their effectiveness in promoting the health of childbearing families. It is possible, however, that participation in an antepartal care program regardless of its quality may give the woman sufficient confidence in her own well-being and the health of the fetus to free her to form an attachment, or perhaps women who are more attached to their unborn are more likely to seek health supervision during pregnancy. Clearly further study is indicated to answer these intriquing questions.

The support of family and friends (FFSUP) had less of an association with attachment to the fetus. Since this finding appears to be in conflict with the literature (Rubin, 1975), it is proposed that the fault may be partially due to the scale that was developed to operationalize this concept. Further efforts to measure this variable should include a means of quantifying the quality as well as the amount of support. For example, women whose mothers were deceased automatically received lower scores even though they may have had a highly satisfactory support system without their mothers.

Other findings. A negative relationship between age and the Family and Friend Support subscale of social support was observed ($r = .35$, significance $= .02$). The 7 subjects who were 30 years of age or older were then examined to see if there were any similar reasons why they received lower social support scores. Of those who had low social support scores and whose scores were below the mean of the Fetal Attachment Scale, one woman, who was having her fifth child, reported she did not ask anyone for advice about her pregnancy but felt she could "figure it out for myself if I think long enough." Although she maintained regular contact with her parents and 10 living siblings, they all lived out of state, and she specifically excluded them as being helpful saying she always had to help them. This woman was gregarious, included a long list of friends she could call on for various kinds of help, and in general, appeared to have a good support network for her own needs. The remaining two women were primigravidas. One of their mothers was deceased; the other mother lived out of state. Neither had any friends who were recently or currently pregnant. Both listed only the physician as a source of help or advice about their pregnancies. One gave as her reason, "I don't like to get the old wives' tales." Both were career women who had been married for several years and had purposefully delayed childbearing until, as they neared their thirtieth birthday, they decided it was, in one woman's terms, "now or never." Both of these women rated their pregnancies as "moderately stressful" because of their ages.

The correlation between maternal age and the Health Care Support subscale was nonsignificant.

Study II: Fetal Attachment and Couples' Dyadic Relationship

This study utilized questionnaires to investigate the relationship between marital relationships and fetal attachment (Cranley, 1982). Rubin (1975) has suggested that a major developmental task for pregnant women is to insure acceptance of the expectant child by those significant to her, in particular her family. A man, on the other hand, is more likely to invest in or become attached to a child when he has a high paternity confidence; i.e., he knows the child his mate bears is his own (Daly & Wilson, 1980). In addition, the man is dependent on a relationship with the pregnant woman in order to vicariously experience the fetus. Cobb cited the dyadic relationship as an important component of social support where information about being loved and cared for is transmitted in "intimate situations involving mutual trust" (1976, p. 301). These factors suggest the importance of the marital, or similar dyadic, relationship during pregnancy for the development of attachment to the fetus.

Procedure. To investigate the association between attachment to the fetus and marital relationship, data were collected from 326 couples in 6 Wisconsin communities. Questionnaires were distributed in antepartal health care and childbirth education settings, completed by the couples, and returned anonymously in business reply envelopes provided for that purpose.

Each questionnaire consisted of the appropriate Maternal or Paternal Fetal Attachment Scale and the Spanier Dyadic Adjustment Scale (Spanier, 1976). In addition to the usual demographic data, information about gestational age of the fetus was also collected.

Spanier's (1976) Dyadic Adjustment Scale was designed to assess the quality of a marriage or similar dyad. Spanier defined marital adjustment as a process "the outcome of which is determined by the degree of . . . dyadic satisfaction, dyadic cohesion, consensus on matters of importance to dyadic functioning" and affectional expression (1976, p. 17). These four factors define the subscales of the measurement scale. Spanier reported a reliability coefficient of .96 using Cronbach's alpha. In the present study a reliability of .81 was obtained.

Findings. The 326 couples who responded were predominantly middle class; the majority were Hollingshead's class III defined as skilled craftsmen, clerical, and sales workers (Hollingshead, 1975). On the average the fathers were about 1½ years older than the mothers and had approximately 1 more year of education. The women were from 8-42 weeks' pregnant, and the average gestational age was 29 weeks. Forty-four percent, or 145 women, were 20 weeks' gestation or less. Fifty-six percent were expecting their first child, 30% their second.

As hypothesized, marital relationship was positively associated with attachment to the fetus for both women and men (women, r = .32, p = .000; men, r = .30, p = .000). For men marital relationship was most highly correlated with the Giving of Self subscale (r = .30, p = .000) and was not at all correlated with the Differentiation of Self subscale. Perhaps this is not surprising since the fetus is never "a part of" the man in the same way as it is of the mother, residing as it does within her body. For women there were very similar correlations between marital relationship and all of the subscales.

The four parts of Spanier's (1976) Dyadic Adjustment Scale were analyzed separately and individually correlated with the Fetal Attachment Scale (FAS) and its subscales. Information about sexual relationships during pregnancy has led to the speculation that the affectional subscale would reflect higher scores earlier in pregnancy. Also, since it is this portion of the Spanier which appears to deal the most with the issue of intimacy, it was hypothesized that this subscale might be more highly correlated with the FAS. However, neither of these speculations was supported by the data. Scores on all four Spanier subscales were consistent between the first and second halves of gestation and all were similarly correlated with the FAS.

In order to investigate the possible influence of the stage of the pregnancy on the marital relationship, the sample was divided at 20 weeks' gestational age, the time by which virtually all women have recognized fetal movement. There were 145 couples ≤ 20 weeks and 181 couples > 20 weeks. No differences were found in the couples' appraisal of their marital adjustment between those in the first half of pregnancy and those in the second half (F = .003, p = .96). Although this cross-sectional investigation is less convincing than longitudinal data, it does suggest that the stages of pregnancy with their differing physical and psychological characteristics do not appreciably alter the marital relationship.

However, the stage of pregnancy did influence the scores on the Fetal Attachment Scale (see Figure 1). Although the pattern of responses to the subscales remained similar (scores on the subscales of Roletaking, Differentiation of Self, and Giving of Self were higher than scores on the subscales of Attributing Characteristics to the Fetus and Interaction), the actual scores tended to be higher when measured during the last half of pregnancy. Significant increases occurred on the subscales of Differentiation of Self, Attributing Characteristics to the Fetus, and Interaction. These subscales measure behaviors which require more familiarity and interaction with the fetus which may come only with time and after fetal movement is recognized.

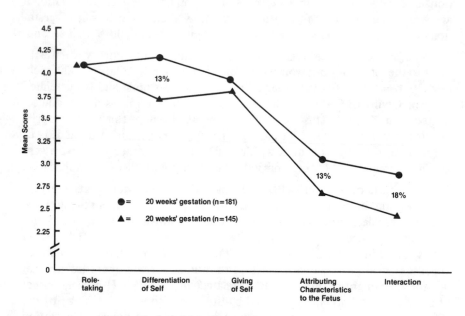

Figure 1. Responses of parents to the Fetal Attachment Scale by gestational age.

CONCLUSION

The findings of the two investigations described here support the association between social support and the development of attachment to the unborn child. At this time, however, the data are still quite global and do not suggest ways to assess a family's or woman's support system in order to prescribe interventions with any precision. It is necessary to look with more discrimination at the various types and sources of social support to determine if any are more critical than others in the development of a relationship with the fetus. Further efforts are needed to determine whether or not there is a hierarchy of importance to the types of support (e.g., financial support more important than emotional support) and to the sources of support (e.g., husband's support more necessary than that of extended family, or a family's support more critical than peer support). In addition, the use of a general measure of social support which would permit comparison with nonpregnant populations would be useful to determine how different or similar fetal attachment is in comparison to other human relationships.

CRITIQUE
Mary Ann Curry, R.N., D.N.Sc.

Dr. Cranley's research is extremely important as it examines the potential relationship between antepartum parental-fetal attachment and social support. The implications of this research are considerable if one agrees with Cobb (1976) that social support begins in utero and also with the conceptualization of Kahn and Antonucci (1980) that the early dyadic interaction between infants and their primary caregivers forms the basis for all future relationships and hence the ability to acquire social support. Based on these hypotheses, it would follow that a critical period for intervention has been identified if social support is found to influence a parent's ability to attach to his/her infant, and this attachment in turn influences the development of the infant's ability to establish healthy relationships and later social support.

Facilitating the development of attachment during pregnancy makes sense. The maturational crisis of pregnancy and resultant ego function disequilibrium provides the potential for women to be more open to growth and change during this time (Tilden, 1980). Further, the temporal dimension of pregnancy allows for change over time. Unlike the brief period immediately following birth, which has been both intensively studied and manipulated to facilitate attachment, pregnancy offers time to carefully influence the development of an individual's attachment to the fetus.

As was clearly explicated in the framework of these studies, social support is a conceptually logical variable to study concerning its relationship to antepartum attachment. Further, because Nuckoll's work (Nuckoll, Cassel, & Kaplan, 1972) indicates that social support may also mediate the effects of life stress on the outcome of pregnancy, the importance of studying social support during pregnancy is evident. Finally, since social support is a phenomenon that is clearly within the domain of nursing practice, this research is highly significant to nursing practice.

Each of the studies presented in Dr. Cranley's paper will be critiqued individually. Comments regarding the future study and use of social support conclude this paper.

STUDY I: MATERNAL-FETAL ATTACHMENT AND SOCIAL SUPPORT

The assumptions underlying the construction of the questions used in the first study were logically derived from previous research and theory. Although it was unclear what specific questions were asked[1], the dimensions tapped with the questions were based on the study's assumptions and the literature which encompassed availability of help from family, friends, and health professionals; the woman's relationship with her mother; and the existence of close or intimate relationships. More detailed information regarding the actual questions and the scale construction would have been very helpful. For example, what was the range of responses to the open-ended questions regarding extent of social network? What probes, if any, were used? What specific questions were used in constructing the scales, and how many questions were in each scale?

The total scores indicate that this sample had good social support. The mean score of 50.1 on a scale ranging from 38-60 with a standard deviation of 5.7 indicates that scores were distributed over the high end of the scale. The raw data presented in tables or histograms would have permitted more interpretation of the data.

While the scores on the Family and Friends subscale were much more variable than the Health Care subscale scores, it appeared that most women in the study enjoyed good support from family and friends. However, since support from both family and friends were collapsed into one scale and 60% of the sample lived within a few minutes of their mothers, it would have been surprising if scores had been low. The author commented on the high degree of involvement with extended family networks, which also would have had a positive influence on the scores, but one wonders how this can be generalized to other geographic areas and/or populations. The literature and clinical experience suggest that many childbearing families do not enjoy this same degree of family support.

---

[1]Sample questions from the Maternal-Fetal Attachment Scale and additional details on this study have been published (Cranley, 1981b), and Dr. Cranley's presentation was revised after the conference to include additional information.

The location of the mean near the upper end of the Health Care Support subscale suggests a tendency toward making socially acceptable responses as the author suggests. The finding that women with high educational levels had lower perceptions of health care support makes intuitive sense if one reasons that women with higher educations may also have more knowledge and concomitantly, higher expectations. It would be fascinating to compare perceptions of health care support provided by nurse midwives and nurse practitioners.

The high correlation between social support and maternal-fetal attachment was not surprising. However, the proportionately greater variance contributed by the Health Care Support scale of .74 compared to the Family and Friend Support subscale of .25 was very surprising. One possible explanation is the scale used to measure perceived support from family and friends wasn't sensitive enough. It had the lowest reliability coefficient, and as the author described, if the woman's mother was dead, she automatically received a lower score. Without additional data it is impossible to determine how much variance other persons contributed to the subscale.

There is a much more difficult conceptual and methodological issue, however; i.e., to what extent does the woman's history of being nurtured contribute to her current perception of being nurtured by family and friends? For example, to what extent does the woman's past relationship with her mother and past and current conflicts influence her current perceptions? The psychoanalytic theories of the psychology of pregnancy certainly suggest that this may be a significant influence, particularly if there are unresolved conflicts (Benedek, 1956; Bibring, 1959, 1961; Deutsch, 1945). Similarly, Lumley's data (1982) which found an association between a history of family nurturing experiences and early antepartum fetal attachment supports the potential influence of this factor.

The high levels of association between the Family and Friends subscale and the Roletaking and Differentiation of Self subscales of the Fetal Attachment Scale are not surprising given the rather well defined societal role of pregnant women in our culture. This was supported by the interview data which found that increased nurturance was identified as a common form of social support. The injunctions to "take it easy" which were interpreted as support, quite likely also reinforced the pregnant role status. Brandt and Weinert (1981) found that nurturance emerged as an independent scale on their social support measure, and the perception of nurturance as a form of social support during pregnancy certainly merits further study.

Another issue to consider is — to what extent do social, economic, and cultural factors influence the ability of family and friends to provide support during pregnancy? For example, what are the effects of unemployment on a husband's ability to nurture his pregnant wife? Likewise, how nurturing can friends and co-workers be if they are concerned with their own basic needs?

Health Care Support

The very high correlation coefficient (.74) between the Health Care Support subscale and the Fetal Attachment Scale supports the emerging theory that health providers can have a significant impact on the development of attachment. Most of the studies reported in the literature support this theory, including the Guatemalan study of the influence of *doula* support during labor and subsequent attachment (Sosa, Kennell, & Klaus, et al., 1980) and Stainton's study (1981) of the impact of nursing care on the postpartum development of maternal attachment. Dr. Cranley's study suggests that the development of attachment may also be significantly influenced by health providers during the antepartal period.

The subscale constructs of the Fetal Attachment Scale are actually very well suited for intervention by health providers, and perhaps explain the high correlations. The routine antepartum visit which includes the assessment of fetal heart tones, fetal growth, palpation of the fetus, and focus on the fetus as a separate entity could certainly influence a woman's differentiation of self, attribution of characteristics to the fetus, and interaction with the fetus. Rather weak, but supportive evidence for this is found in Carter-Jessup's study (1981) which suggested that postpartum attachment can be influenced by teaching pregnant women to interact with their fetus during pregnancy. The possibility that the "routine" prenatal procedures can influence attachment, even when delivered in the uninvolved manner described by some of the sample subjects, certainly needs further study and clarification.

Other aspects of the relationship between the support of health care professionals and fetal attachment also warrants futher study. As the author suggests, we need to discover which behaviors and attitudes are perceived as most supportive. If, as this study suggests, physicians who don't even remember their client's name can influence attachment, what is the potential impact of a nurse midwife or nurse practitioner, who not only remembers the client's name, but also incorporates teaching and psychosocial care into the health care provided during pregnancy?

The author speculates that participation in prenatal care may, in and of itself, be sufficient reassurance to allow a woman to feel free to form an attachment to her infant. This is not an unlikely proposition; the assurance of safe passage during pregnancy and birth is a basic need of all pregnant women. If this should be the case, then what about the thousands of pregnant women in this country right now who do not have access to prenatal care? How free are women in our society today to form an affectional relationship with their infant when their basic needs for health care and possibly food, clothing, and shelter are unmet? I would strongly urge that each of us within our own disciplines, and as members of society, address this critical issue as well.

STUDY II: FETAL ATTACHMENT AND COUPLES' DYADIC RELATIONSHIP

The second study investigated the influence of a specific aspect of social support — the effect of the marital relationship on the development of antepartum attachment. This is a logical and important variable to study because there is evidence that a woman's perception of her husband's support is related to subsequent maternal behavior (Curry, 1979; Westbrook, 1978). A conceptual issue that has not been systematically addressed, however, is whether there are intrapsychic and/or intrapersonal factors within the woman that would influence her choice of mate and, hence, not only influence her perceptions of his support, but also the type of support that he is able to give. Again, the issue of the origin of social support — the potential that early human experiences influence a person's ability to form and maintain supportive relationships — emerges as a critical conceptual issue.

Methodology

Several methodological concerns will be presented before discussing the study's findings. A major methodological concern is the instrument used to measure marital or dyadic adjustment. While it is one of the best tools available at the present time, the questions invite socially acceptable responses. Thus, the tool's precision is questionable. This may be the reason why no differences in adjustment were found between couples during the first or second half of their pregnancies. However, using the same instrument, Tomlinson and Irvin (in preparation) also found very little variance in prenatal scores. They were able to predict divorce 4 years after the birth of the child with much more highly variable scores obtained 4 months after delivery.

Another methodological issue concerns the sample. A large amount of data was collapsed without reference to whether or not differences were found on either instrument in terms of parity, attendance at childbirth classes, or socioeconomic differences. Finally, the method of data collection poses a severe threat to validity. If the couples were able to complete the questionnaires at home, it is highly conceivable that they may have discussed the tools and even collaborated when completing them.

Results

The findings are definitely dramatic. In this sample with these measures, marital relationship was highly correlated with antepartum fetal attachment. Information regarding the range, mean, and standard deviations of the scores for men and women on both scales and the correlation between subscales of each instrument would permit more interpretation and speculation. The finding that the Giving of Self subscale was most highly correlated with attachment for men certainly suggests possibilities for further study and intervention. The higher subscale scores would be expected on the Differentiation of Self, Attributing Characteristics to the Fetus, and Interaction with Fetus in the second half of pregnancy after quickening had occurred.

This study suggests several areas for further study. Is length of marriage related to marital adjustment and/or fetal attachment? Would more sensitive qualitative data gathered during antepartal interviews yield a different understanding of marital adjustment during pregnancy? Who, if anyone, provides a similar support to pregnant women without partners? How does that support influence her attachment? In other words, can a pregnant woman without a partner receive support from her mother or friend which will have a similar influence on attachment?

CONCLUSION

Certain advances are necessary to bring the knowledge of social support to a level for professional practice. The importance of discovering more about the origins of social support, and in particular the intrapersonal components, appears critical. Dr. Barnard has addressed this when she said, "We need to know how clients learn to interact, trust, and depend on others" (1981, p. 286).

We also need to operationally define and test constructs used to define social support and to identify and test interventions for practice. How independent or interdependent are the constructs? Do they form a hierarchy, and if so, does it change as a result of life situations and individual coping and adaptation styles?

Likewise, I agree with Dr. Cranley that we need to determine if a hierarchy of social support exists within the context of pregnancy, and in particular in the facilitation of parental-fetal attachment. Further, how would social, cultural, economic, and religious factors influence such a hierarchy?

As stated earlier, we need to identify and test interventions for practice. While this may conceptually "put the cart before the horse" in terms of refining the concept of social support, it could be complementary work. Facilitating antepartum attachment with social support can serve as an example. First, the constructs salient to the individual woman and family would need to be identified. For example, does this woman perceive a need for intimacy, nurturance, or social integration? Following this, different interventions could be tested. Referral to parent education classes may influence the size of the network, as well as provide an opportunity for social integration. Social support provided by the nurse could provide confirmation of love and value, as well as provide the opportunity for an especially vulnerable woman to learn to trust and depend on another human being. Finally, referral of the couple for counseling may strengthen the dyadic relationship, thereby increasing a sense of mutual obligation.

The last need is to develop simple, sensitive, assessment measurements. Ideally, they would also provide some ranking or priority list of needed social support that could be used to guide practice interventions, but this is not to suggest that the measures developed thus far are discredited. The suggestion is made so that this very important variable can be systematically evaluated by the practicing professional.

DISCUSSION

L. Walker: My first comment is about your positive statements about caregivers. It reminds me of personal experience I had with a friend 2 months before his marriage totally fell apart. He voluntarily commented to me that the relationship had never been better. In retrospect, it seemed to me that his comment was surprising. I have tried to interpret that comment, and I wonder if positive comments sometimes are made even if things are not going well because you are already committed. The pregnancy and physician may be similar to an airplane trip when you are at the point of no return. You know you've made your down payment, and you've got to go through with it. When incidents occur, denial may be the most adaptive response to make, and so it may only be afterwards that some real issues arise which were related to the actual management of labor but were denied earlier.

I love the neonatal period, and all my research has been done in that area, but I realize unfortunately that is a pretty limited perspective. So much happens during pregnancy. I would have liked more information in Dr. Cranley's presentation, i.e., a little bit more precise, theoretical development; a few more specific hypotheses about how that social support is working; a little bit more development on what the nature of attachment is prenatally; and specifically how the relationship might relate to prenatal attachment. Specifically, I've found the work of Bibring and associates (1961) useful in tying together psychological adaptation across pregnancy and the period following birth. Through a somewhat dialectic process, mothers move between fusion with the child and individuation. Attachment, in contrast, bespeaks a more static phenomenon. Yet, we well know that a mother has to adapt her relationship with the infant as development transforms the dependent newborn into a mobile, curious toddler. In the light of the infant's development, attachment would be expressed and perhaps experienced by mothers in corresponding new ways.

T. Antonucci: I agree with you, and I think it is important to add this information. Let's face it; the research on attachment is based on very tenuous, clinical judgments, e.g., the Ainsworth-Strange situation. You go through an eight-episode procedure which involves a mother and stranger entering a room where the child is according to a pre-set protocol. But when you get right down to it, that A, B, C classification is a clinical judgment. There are a lot of items coded: number of looks, number of vocalizations, etc., but the bottom line is clinical judgment. There is a lot of work to be done yet in terms of quantifying what we all accept at the clinical and conceptual levels.

R. Mercer: Bibring's (1965) work also mentions the importance of the woman resolving conflicts with her mother and moving from a mother-daughter to a peer relationship as she assumes a parent-child relationship with her own child. It would seem that most of the mothers in Dr. Cranley's work had ready access to their mothers for this kind of intrapsychic work. Their relationships must have been good, or it seems that they were good. Ballou (1978), more recently, has also looked at the woman's resolution of conflicts with her mother from a psychoanalytic framework. She observed that the mate was very critical in helping the woman resolve this conflict. It seems that, indeed, the mate and the mother are both very important in helping the woman reach the point of being able to take in and be dependent during labor, delivery, and early postpartum before she takes over the independent functions of mothering.

T. Antonucci: I was really intrigued by that finding about mothers and their pregnant daughters. I can't believe that all those mothers living near their daughters have had these great relationships throughout their lifetimes. This may be more personal projection here, but I really think that during pregnancy mothers and daughters tend to ignore their differences. I would like to see some more research done in this area, not necessarily in the psychoanalytic framework, but just generally, on how and what these dynamics are.

P. MacElveen-Hoehn: I'd like to respond to that, Tony. I think that there is some comparison between Abernathy's (1973) study, again in terms of the relationships pregnant women have with their mothers, and that of Belle (1982) in the Harvard study. Abernathy found very positive outcomes in the relationship between mother and daughter, while Belle found greater depression among the women who had close contact with their mothers. The major difference between these studies appears to be socioeconomic in that Belle studied ghetto mothers and Abernathy had a very middle class sample. The question may be whether or not educated middle class women have some choices about the kind of contact they have with their mothers. The ghetto women in the Belle study were trapped within a network that they couldn't get out of, and their mothers may have been a burden instead of a support.

T. Antonucci: You point to something I have become aware of in a somewhat different context. I have recently been reviewing the literature on social support among adults and find that there are consistent class differences. People of lower socioeconomic status are more likely to have homogeneous networks consisting primarily of family. People of higher socioeconomic status are more likely to have networks that consist of both family and friends. If one thinks about the lives of people in different socioeconomic groups, this difference can almost be considered a life style difference. People of lower socioeconomic status tend to remain closely tied to family almost to the exclusion of friends. Higher socioeconomic status people are more likely to maintain relationships with both family and friends.

Bengtson's research on generations suggests that relationships with family are often based on a sense of obligation, whereas relationships with friends are more often considered optional (Bengtson & Cutler, 1976). Using this reasoning, one might expect that relationships with friends are likely to have a more positive impact than relationships with family if both are present. But a lack of positive relationships with family might have a more negative impact than a lack of relationships with friends because an obligation is not being met. For example, if you have a couple of adult children in the neighborhood and they never show up for anything, elderly parents are likely to feel bad about it; but if the children visit on a regular basis, the parents may feel like "they're supposed to." On the other hand, if friends visit the parents, this is a source of particular satisfaction for them because their friends don't have to; it is *not* an obligation.

K. Barnard: Elizabeth Hutchins (1978) for her dissertation in anthropology at the University of Washington did an ethnographic study of both women who delivered term and preterm babies. I have always been fascinated that one of her unpublished findings was that mothers who delivered preterm babies were often closely knit to their family of origin and had fewer supports from outside of their family of origin. This appears to be related to what we've alluded to — that the constriction of that close initial tie has not allowed them, for whatever reason, to move beyond.

Another point I wanted to make is that since pregnancy is a common event for all subjects, this could be influencing relationships and thus, reducing the variance. This is commonly seen anytime a subject receives a treatment. Bloom (1966) indicates that anytime a standard condition prevails, the variability is reduced in that sample. I would suggest that perhaps the reduced variability you see is because of the pregnancy.

J. Fawcett: I would like to support Dr. Barnard's comment about reduced variability. Almost all of the data I have ever obtained from any tool used with pregnant families reveals a restricted range. Because of this reduced variability, it is not possible to obtain high correlations.

For example, in one of my studies of family experiences during pregnancy, I hypothesized that identification would account for similarities in spouses' body image changes during pregnancy and the postpartum (Fawcett, 1978). This hypothesis was not supported, even though the spouses' body image changes were similar. The lack of support for the hypothesis was due to the restricted range of spouses' strength of identification scores. Other research has found similar restrictions in the range of scores for married couples who were not pregnant. I also hypothesized that marital adjustment might account for body image similarities. Again, the findings were the same. Lack of support for this hypothesis apparently was due to the restricted range of the Dyadic Adjustment Scale (DAS) scores (Spanier, 1976). I administered the DAS at the twelfth postpartal month; so it appears that restricted ranges occur not only during pregnancy, but later on as well.

An interesting aspect of this problem would be to determine just when, if ever, the range of scores for identification and marital adjustment is more variable. I asked my study subjects if they would have answered the DAS items differently at other times in their marriage. Most people said they would have answered differently in the early months or years of marriage. One husband even said, "Absolutely, in the first part of our marriage, because my wife was having an extramarital affair." His wife agreed, saying, "I was having an extramarital affair early in our marriage. Yes, I would have answered these questions differently at that time."

Perhaps a longitudinal study mapping changes in identification and marital adjustment from early marriage through pregnancy to the later years of marriage would be helpful. At least it would give us some information about the stability of restricted ranges. Another interesting aspect of the problem is the study subjects per se. It may be that only those couples who have good marriages or who identify strongly volunteer to be in pregnancy studies. This certainly seems to be the case in my studies. I suspect this methodological problem is always going to be a problem in pregnancy studies that use volunteers.

R. Mercer: Robrecht (1981) interviewed fathers at 1 year postpartum, and her qualitative data suggest that the man looks at the relationship somewhat differently from his perspective and expectations. The fathers had expected their sex life to change during pregnancy and the first 2 months postpartum, along with the emotional lability and mood changes. However, all had expected the sexual relationship and marital relationship as a whole to be back as it was prepregnancy by 4-6 months or 8 months. At 1 year, they were very displeased that things still were not the same as before.

L. Cronenwett: I agree with Dr. Fawcett. One couple in our study after responding to Spanier's Dyadic Adjustment Scale wrote, "You know, if I didn't feel positive about my marriage, I wouldn't be having this baby." It's as if they are saying, "Why are you even asking me; of course, my marriage is satisfactory, or I wouldn't be having a baby." I agree that there may be class differences, however. In our first nonanalytical look at the videotapes of our postpartum support groups, we are questioning the findings of the LaRossas (1981) which indicates that when the baby comes, marital roles become less egalitarian and more traditional. We were expecting to find that, but based on the anecdotal remarks of working class couples in our groups, it does seem these working class couples are becoming more egalitarian. It's the opposite in middle-class marriages. They may have been very egalitarian, but after the baby, since the wife is at home, she is expected to do more traditional things. We are finding that divergence, and I wonder if anyone else is finding this.

P. MacElveen-Hoehn: Were those working class women planning to return to work after the baby was born?

L. Cronenwett: Well, yes, but not right after childbirth. But yes, many of our sample mothers are returning to work at some point.

P. MacElveen-Hoehn: I'm wondering whether the need for two incomes precludes the traditional sex role preference of the mothers staying at home and the father being the provider. In order for the mother to return to work earlier, perhaps the working class father agrees to be helpful in ways that are new behaviors for him.

L. Cronenwett: These videotapes were made about 2 months postpartum. Almost none of the women were back to work yet. We'll have data on the timing and effect of their return to work eventually. So far, these impressions are just anecdotal, but it is something we should examine, especially with Dr. Cranley also saying the working class men were doing more.

S. Humenick: I don't have any data on lower class clients, but I have some data on upper class women that are not published yet. Prior to the birth, during the pregnancy, both the men and the women were asked questions about their intent to interact with their babies. It was very clear that the mothers expected to interact with the babies more than the fathers did. However, after birth the mothers' reported interaction was much higher than they expected, and the fathers' reported interaction was much lower than they expected. We are calling this interaction pattern a branching effect. Upper class couples probably plan to be more egalitarian than lower class couples, but there seems to be a definite division of labor taking place after birth.

K. Barnard: I'd like to go back to Lorraine Walker's statement about denial. It seems to me that it does raise a question in dealing with pregnant couples. I also think the concept of denial needs to be tested. Should we probe about the conflicts that couples are having, or is it more protective to encourage their denial of the problem? I think that we simply don't know, and it is a real conflict when you are dealing with these women prenatally as to what direction to take, because clearly there are two paths and we don't really know which one to follow.

L. Walker: I was at a case conference meeting in a philosophy course, and the psychotherapists were discussing this issue. They actually had a videotape of a couple who apparently seemed to be blocking and showing denial. The couple would talk about how they never could stand other people's children when they were toddlers, but that they felt they could really accept their baby. All the clinicians were just sitting there feeling really upset. In this case, the denial was about the change that would follow after the pregnancy. Then the issue arose — should you attempt to change that level of coping during that period, i.e., during the pregnancy when they seem to be very much locked into denial? I am not sure; I don't know how to answer that question. The clinicians agreed that until couples were ready to really deal with the issue, clinicians should remain available, but not confront them about the use of that denial mechanism at that point. I thought this was a very interesting and hard decision.

K. Barnard: In the study of supportive therapy during pregnancy, Shereshefsky and Yarrow (1973) report that when women who previously had conflict with their mothers but were motivated during pregnancy to reestablish the relationship, often they were rebuffed by their mother. On the other hand, in many instances where the mother-daughter relationship was poor, when the husband became the intermediary for his wife and protected her, their relationship improved. These examples illustrate the problems of dealing with interpersonal conflict during pregnancy. Perhaps it is best to deemphasize resolution of interpersonal conflicts during pregnancy unless the client strongly initiates the process.

T. Antonucci: I would agree that this is the question, and I think that unless there is some question of terminating the pregnancy, you really have no right to intervene if there is denial. I feel very certain there is a relationship between a person's psychological state during pregnancy and the outcome of the pregnancy. Professionals should not interfere with a couple's denial; denial may be a good coping mechanism. If they can deny until after the baby is born, that might serve an adaptive purpose for that particular couple.

R. Lederman: There are some data to support your position. In terms of the purposes of denial and its function for adaptation, one of the earliest studies I know of on this was done by Peter Wolff and associates (1964) where they measured cortisol levels of the parents of children who were dying of cancer. They were studying coping and defense mechanisms, and one of the functional defense mechanisms was denial. Parents expressing denial had lower plasma cortisol levels. Now, if we were to take that — with some imagination — and transfer it to what we currently know about emotions and hormonal levels and their possible influence on adaptation to pregnancy and progress in labor, you would be very wary about actions which could affect catecholamine and cortisol levels. Denial could be functional.

I have discussed this dilemma to some extent with clinicians, and I can share some of my own thoughts with you. There are instances when denial is strong, e.g., when there are serious questions about the marital relationship or adequacy as a mother. There already may be fears that motherhood will not be a rewarding experience, that it may well be a decompensating experience. There are women with such concerns, and their doubts are strong. If a woman tells you, "I can't face that possibility now; it's too threatening," it would be dangerous in my opinion to intervene. I think this is also the opinion of others. The other advice from clinicians, however, is that while it would be dangerous to try to proceed at a rate that would be uncomfortable for the mother, it would be very good to establish a relationship of trust so that when the woman is ready — now, at some later point in the pregnancy, or in early parenthood

— she would be able to confront her doubts and receive the help she needs.

I have been very interested in the woman's relationship with the husband, as well as her relationship with the mother, and in the accurate assessment of these relationships. Depending on the measurement technique, one should probably expect to find a constricted range of scores for the quality of the marital relationship in a first pregnancy.

I think there is more variation reported by women during second and subsequent pregnancies. In a first pregnancy, we have discovered there is a reevaluation of the whole marital relationship, and the pregnancy is viewed as confirming the permanence of the marriage (Lederman, in press). It is also threatening for the pregnant woman to anticipate what might eventually happen if the marriage is not perceived as good; the woman fears for her own survival and who will take care of her and her child. These questions have a high priority in a pregnant woman's mind. We have found a tendency toward camouflaging or evasiveness and denial of a poor relationship, unless it's very, very poor, and then it is difficult to conceal.

If you only ask the woman general questions about her marital relationship and how she is getting along with her husband, etc., you are likely to get the same kind of glib answers. The point is to know what to ask, and we have become sensitive only by experience in terms of what to ask. One of the questions to ask is whether there are any changes in her relationship now that she is pregnant. There are certain changes that are warranted; the woman cannot do the same things as well as she did before. She may not be able to do all the cooking, shopping, and cleaning that she had been doing, or she may not be able to perform other customary activities, even if it has been an egalitarian relationship. Generally, the woman and her husband recognize that she can't quite do all that she did before, that she needs some form of assistance. Therefore, an important question to ask is, "Has there been any change in the way your husband relates to you?" When the woman says that there is no change, that is the first clue. I'm not saying it is the answer, but it is a clue that there is an unresponsive, unsensitive relationship.

Another good key to the quality of the marital relationship is the couple's sensitivity in dealing with the changes that are implied in sexual relationships during pregnancy. Invariably, and in general, the woman's interest declines, although I am being very, very general now, and the husband's interest remains similar to his previous level, usually moderate to high. How do they reconcile these differences? Is it done verbally or nonverbally? How sensitive are they in meeting each other's needs, and what steps do they take? This is the second good clue to the couple's marital relationship. These are just two examples for obtaining a better idea of the marital relationship. If you do not ask these kinds of questions, I suspect you are going to get answers that reflect a narrow range of high adaptation, and you're not going to be able to utilize the data in correlational studies. This is unfortunate, considering the importance of the marital relationship for family life.

There is also a difference between the reporting that occurs during pregnancy and the more candid reports made postpartally. There's enough evidence to suggest that the marital relationship is even more significant during the postpartum period versus the prenatal period as regards adaptation. In fact, the literature almost uniformly reports that the marital relationship is very important in the postpartum period (Shereshefsky & Yarrow, 1973; Lederman, et al., 1981; Russell, 1974). Why, then, is the literature ambivalent about the prenatal period? Well, I think it is due to a paucity in the methods of evaluation and also possibly because the baby is not on the scene yet, has not intervened, and hasn't made his/her demands known.

Ballou (1978) and Deutscher (1970) indicate that the marital relationship can ameliorate other poor relationships, and perhaps even create confidence in the parenting role when the woman's relationship with her mother is poor. Deutscher has even indicated that couples have to learn to parent each other before they can learn to parent a child. In other words, both partners are alone with their own doubts and concerns about the changes that are occurring and the new, critical, life roles that they're about to assume.

Nurses have so much extensive and exclusive contact with expectant couples that they could be the stimulus for couples to develop sensitivities to each other's needs. This knowledge could be used to ultimately develop sensitivity for the needs of the child by teaching parents to become aware of what these needs are. One can't assume that they always know what they are. Expectant parents need help. The nurse can help by asking if certain situations have arisen yet, and how they're going to cope with them. This is a form of anticipatory guidance. Some suggestion and interpretation about behavior can be provided. Such inquiry and discussion helps parents to focus their thoughts. Although it is unknown whether this will help, it is worth trying these methods of intervention which have proven worthwhile in the past.

REFERENCES

Abernathy, V. (1973). Social network and response to maternal role. *International Journal of Sociology and the Family, 3,* 86-92.

Antonovsky, A. (1974). Conceptual and methodological problems in the study of resistance resources and stressful life events. In B.S. Dohrenwend & B.P. Dohrenwend (Eds.), *Stressful life events: Their nature and effects.* New York: John Wileysons.

Ballou, J.W. (1978). *The psychology of pregnancy.* Lexington, MA: Lexington Books, D.C. Heath.

Barnard, K. Closing. (1981). In R.P. Lederman and B.S. Raff (Eds.), *Perinatal parental behavior. Nursing research and implications for newborn health.* March of Dimes *Birth Defects: Original Article Series, 17*(6), 285-288. New York: Alan R. Liss.

Belle, D. (1982). *Lives in stress: Women and depression.* Beverly Hills, CA: Sage.

Benedek, T. (1956). The psychobiological aspects of mothering. *American Journal of Orthopsychiatry, 26,* 272-278.

Bengtson, V.L., & Cutler, W.E. (1976). Generations and intergenerational relations: Perspectives on age groups and social change. In R.H. Benstock & E. Shanas (Eds.), *Handbook of aging and the social sciences.* New York: Van Nostrand.

Bibring, G. (1959). Some considerations of the psychological process in pregnancy. *The Psychoanalytic Study of the Child, 14,* 113-121.

Bibring, G.I. (1965). Some specific psychological tasks in pregnancy and motherhood. *1st international congress of psychosomatic medicine and childbirth. Paris, 8-12, July 1962.* Paris: Gauthier-Villars.

Bibring, G., Dwyer, T., Huntington, D., & Vallenstein, A. (1961). A study of the psychological processes in pregnancy and of the earliest mother-child relationship. *Psychoanalytic Study of the Child, 16,* 9-24.

Bloom, B.S. (1966). *Stability and change in human characteristics.* New York: John Wileysons.

Brandt, P., & Weinert, C. (1981). The PRQ-A social support system. *Nursing Research, 30,* 277-280.

Caplan, G. (1961). *An approach to community mental health.* New York: Grune & Stratton.

Carter-Jessup, L. (1981). Promoting maternal attachment through prenatal intervention. *MCN, The American Journal of Maternal-Child Nursing, 6,* 107-112.

Cobb, S. (1976). Social support as a moderator of life stress. *Psychosomatic Medicine, 38,* 300-314.

Cranley, M.S. (1981a). Development of a tool to measure maternal-fetal attachment. *Nursing Research, 30,* 281-284.

Cranley, M.S. (1981b). Roots of attachment: The relationship of parents with their unborn. In R.P. Lederman & B.S. Raff (Eds.), *Perinatal parental behavior: Nursing research and implications for newborn health,* March of Dimes *Birth Defects: Original Article Series, 17*(6), 59-83.

Cranley, M.S. (1982). *Parents' relationship with their unborn: The influence of marital satisfaction and perceived stress.* Paper presented at Midwest Nursing Research Society, Columbus, Ohio.

Curry, M.A. (1979). *The effect of skin-to-skin contact between mother and infant during the first hour following delivery on the mother's maternal attachment behavior.* Unpublished doctoral dissertation, University of California, San Francisco.

Daly, M., & Wilson, M. (1980). Discriminative parental solicitude: A biological perspective. *Journal of Marriage and the Family, 42,* 277-288.

Deutsch, H. (1945). *The psychology of women: A psychoanalytic interpretation.* (Vol. II). New York: Grune & Stratton.

Deutscher, M. (1970). Brief family therapy in the course of first pregnancy: A clinical note. *Contemporary Psychoanalysis, 21*-35.

Dressler, D.M., Donovan, J.M., & Geller, R.A. (1976). Life stress and emotional crisis: The idiosyncratic interpretations of life events. *Comprehensive Psychiatry, 17,* 549-557.

Fawcett, J. (1978). Body image and the pregnant couple. *MCN, The American Journal of Maternal Child Nursing, 3,* 227-233.

Gongla, P.A. (1976). Effective coping with stress. *Case Western Reserve Journal of Sociology, 8,* 51-80.

Gray, J.D., Cutler, C. A., Dean, J. G., & Kempe, C. H. (1979). Prediction and prevention of child abuse. *Seminars in Perinatology, 3,* 85-90.

Hollingshead, A.B. (1975). *Four factor index of social status.* New Haven, CT: Author.

Hutchins, E.A. (1978). *Sociocultural and other factors related to premature termination of pregnancy.* Unpublished dissertation, University of Washington.

Kahn, R.L., & Antonucci, T.C. (1980). Convoys over the life course: Attachment, roles and social support. In P.B. Baltes and O.C. Brim, Jr. (Eds.), *Life Span Development and Behavior* (Vol. 3). New York: Academic Press.

Kempe, C.H. (1976). Approaches to preventing child abuse: The health visitor concept. *American Journal of Disabilities in Children, 130,* 841-847.

LaRossa, R., & LaRossa, M. (1981). *Transition to parenthood: How infants change families.* Beverly Hills, CA: Sage.

Lederman, R.P. (in press). *Psychosocial adaptation to pregnancy.*

Lederman, E., Lederman, R.P., Work, B.A., Jr., & McCann, D.S. (1981). Maternal psychological and physiologic correlates of fetal-newborn health status. *American Journal of Obstetrics and Gynecology, 139,* 956-958.

Leifer, M. (1977). Psychological changes accompanying pregnancy and motherhood. *Genetic Psychology Monographs, 95,* 55-96.

Lumley, J. (1982). Attitudes to the fetus among primigravidae. *Australian Paediatric Journal, 18,* 106-109.

McCubbin, H.J. (1979). Integrating coping behavior in family stress theory. *Journal of Marriage and the Family, 41,* 237-244.

Nuckolls, K.B., Cassel, J., & Kaplan, B.H. (1972). Psychosocial assets, life crisis and the prognosis of pregnancy. *American Journal of Epidemiology, 95,* 431-441.

Robrecht, L.C. (1981). *The first year of fatherhood: Fathers' perspectives on the transition to fatherhood.* Unpublished master's thesis, University of California, San Francisco.

Rubin, R. (1975). Maternal tasks in pregnancy. *Maternal and Child Nursing Journal, 4,* 143-153.

Russell, C.S. (1974). Transition to parenthood: Problems and gratifications. *Journal of Marriage and the Family, 36,* 294-301.

Shereshefsky, P.M., & Yarrow, L.J. (1973). *Psychological aspects of first pregnancy and early postnatal adaptation.* New York: Raven Press.

Sosa, R., Kennell, J., Klaus, M., et al. (1980). The effect of a supportive companion on perinatal problems, length of labor, and mother-infant interaction. *New England Journal of Medicine, 303,* 597-600.

Spanier, G.B. (1976). Measuring dyadic adjustment: New scales for assessing the quality of marriage and similar dyads. *Journal of Marriage and the Family, 38,* 15-28.

Stainton, M.C. (1981). *Parent-infant interaction: Putting theory into nursing practice.* Calgary, Alberta: The University of Calgary.

Tilden, V. (1980). A developmental conceptual framework for the maturational crisis of pregnancy. *Western Journal of Nursing Research, 2,* 667-679.

Tomlinson, T., & Irvin, B. *Family adaptation patterns four years after the birth of the first child.* (Manuscript in preparation at the OHSU School of Nursing, 3181 Sam Jackson Park Road, Portland, Oregon 97201.)

Westbrook, M. (1978). The reactions to childbearing and early maternal experience of women with differing marital relationships. *British Journal Medical Psychology, 51,* 191-199.

Wolff, C.T., Friedman, S.B., Hofer, M.A., & Mason, J.W. (1964). Relationship between psychological defenses and mean urinary 17-hydroxycoricosteroid excretion rates: I. A predictive study of parents of fatally ill children. *Psychosomatic Medicine, 26,* 576-591.

Information Needs and Problem Solving Behavior of Parents of Infants

Karen F. Pridham, R.N., Ph.D., FAAN

Two approaches were used to investigate the problems or issues that parents of infants encounter: the study of circumstances that are naturally recognized by the parent as an issue, and the study of simulated problems concerning commonly occurring infant care issues. A paradigm of problem solving behavior was used to formulate the component of a descriptive study for the purpose of examining the problem solving behavior of mothers during their infants' first 3 months. Mothers who participated in both studies were married or living with a partner, were 17 years or older, and had healthy infants.

The objective of the first study was to capture in the mothers' own terms their specification and description of the issues on which they were working and the nature of the infant care task, including the types of help mothers used and the stressors and supports they experienced. Logs were used by 62 mothers (38 primiparae and 24 multiparae) for 90 days after their infants' births to record these issues, types of help, stressors, and supports. Predetermined categories were used to code the data. The type of help used varied significantly by category of issue. Books were used most frequently for issues of growth and development and baby care, and they were used more often than all types of clinicians combined for these types of issues. For over one-third of issues, no help of any type was used. Multiparae and primiparae did not differ significantly in the total number of issues reported, nor in the frequency with which help was used.

This study was supported by DHHS Grant ROl-NU-00606 from the Nursing Research Branch, Division of Nursing, DHHS, the University of Wisconsin-Madison, School of Nursing, and the Department of Family Medicine and Practice.

The author is indebted to Marc F. Hansen, M.D., for his valuable contributions to this paper and to the study from which the paper was derived.

This paper was revised after the conference in response to some of the comments noted in the Critique presented by L.O. Walker.

The objective of the second study was to examine the types of goals and decision making rules that mothers applied to two simulated infant care problems: one concerning the amount of the feeding, and the second concerning noncontingent crying. Four simulated problem exercises were presented to 22 mothers (14 primiparae and 8 multiparae), using a telephone interview in the infants' first 3 months. The results of the study revealed that mothers gave a variety of names to the same problem. The types of goals that mothers identified varied by type of problem. More mothers cited competence as a goal for the crying than the feeding problem. More mothers were able to state the decision rule they had used for naming the problem than for choice of action to solve the problem (implementing). Almost as many multiparae as primiparae could not state a rule for their decisions about actions to take, whereas only primiparae could not state a rule for their decision about the name of the problem. The most frequently used decision rule for both the naming and implementing phases of problem solving was a type of rule that was related to some empirical condition. Primiparae tended to cite sources external to themselves (most often the infant's grandparent) for rules for both naming and implementing decisions to a greater extent than multiparae.

Despite the involvement of nurses and physicians in the problem solving that parents do concerning their newborns and very young infants, little is known from systematic study about the character of either the problems which parents encounter on a day-to-day basis or the processes which they use to deal with these problems. The kinds of problems that parents identify, however, as well as the processes which they use to solve problems are likely to reflect their views of their world, and thus affect the decisions they make and their actions in relation to child rearing (Barnard & Eyres, 1979; Nisbett & Ross, 1980). This paper deals with the problems or issues which parents formulate and the processes which they use to deal with these problems in terms of two types of approaches: the study of circumstances, perhaps recurring, that are naturally recognized by a parent as constituting a problem or issue and that are dealt with either independently or with some type of assistance; and the study of simulated problems concerning infant care issues that are assumed to be common and that are presented to the parent as if they were actually occurring for the purpose of demonstrating processes of naming and solving a problem. A paradigm of problem solving behavior is used to organize and develop the issues concerning problem solving that are highlighted in regard to the two types of approaches.

PROBLEM SOLVING

Problem solving is one method of adaptation. Adaptation is the process of dealing with present or anticipated stressors and/or changes in functioning that are initiated by stressors (Pridham, Hansen, & Conrad, 1978). Problem solving is a goal-directed process, which may be described in terms of phases; i.e., individuals or groups may be observed to follow steps as they move from identifying a problem to implementing solutions to assessing their outcomes (Boyd, 1969; Klein & Hill, 1979; Pridham & Hansen, 1980). Each problem solving phase has its characteristic information to be obtained, decisions to be made, and actions to be taken. Each phase also includes an evaluation of the decisions made and actions taken which may be used as feedback to guide the problem solving process. For example, if a mother decides that her infant is hungry—the action is to name the circumstance "hunger"—she may or may not have used available and relevant information that supports the accuracy of naming.

A problem solving model specified by Boyd (1969) for educational settings was developed and further specified for clinical settings by Pridham, Hansen, and Conrad (1977, 1979). The paradigm they developed includes seven major phases, not all of which necessarily occur with every problem. Furthermore, although there is a logic and an expected order to the sequencing of the phases, in actual practice, phases may occur in some other order. In addition, the process may have an iterative character to it, and problem solvers may return to phases previously negotiated. Klein and Hill (1979, p. 552) referred to the features or variables associated with the phases of problem solving as "phasing rationality."

The process of problem solving begins when the individual problem solver attends to a specific stressor in the ongoing process of scanning, or evaluating, one's own state and functioning. The active process of scanning is intentional and deliberate. When scanning is passive, the individual's attention is considered captured and focused on an issue by a sense of existing or anticipated discomfort or challenge (Neisser, 1976). Other phases of the problem solving process are summarized as follows (Pridham, Hansen, & Conrad, 1977, 1979):

1. Formulating. Exploring an issue of concern, including specifying and naming it, and perhaps examining the significance of the problem.
2. Appraising. Determining the importance or feasibility of working on the problem, and whether or not those involved in the problem are ready and willing to work on it.
3. Developing readiness and willingness to problem solve. Work that is directed toward developing readiness and commitment when the problem is viewed as important to solve, but those involved with the problem are not ready or willing to do so.
4. Planning. Deciding about the division of labor and the mechanics of problem solving. Who will do the problem solving and when? What strategies or techniques will be used? What issues will be dealt with, and in what order?
5. Implementing. Putting solutions into effect.
6. Evaluating. Establishing whether or not the problem was solved adequately and effectively, and perhaps whether the right problem was addressed.

Other individuals may be involved in decision making for any or all of the phases of the process.

The character and quantity of events and conditions that are perceived as stressors by an individual compete for the problem solver's resources of time and energy. The influence of these stressors on problem solving behavior is likely to be conditioned by the character and amount of supports, both specific and nonspecific to the problem, that problem solvers perceive themselves to have. Supports may have protective, buffering, or strengthening functions in the presence of stressors (Cassel, 1974; Kaplan, Cassel, & Gore, 1977; Nuckolls, Cassel, & Kaplan, 1972). Furthermore, in the absence of, or with a low sense of support, the effects of stressors may be exacerbated (Gore, 1978).

The problem solving paradigm was used to formulate the components of an ongoing, descriptive study for the purpose of examining the problem solving behavior of mothers during their babies' first 3 months in regard to two types of problems: naturally occurring and recognized problems, and problems that simulate naturally occurring problems (Pridham, Hansen, Heighway, & Bradley, 1980). Problems that occurred during the course of infant feeding (e.g., the infant stops sucking the nipple sooner than expected, or falls asleep during feeding) were also examined in the study, but they are not discussed in this paper. The families that participated in this study, on the whole, have received obstetric or pediatric care or both from the three teaching practices of the University of Wisconsin Department of Family Medicine and Practice in the Madison area. Mothers eligible to participate in this study during enrollment periods who used these clinics are married or living with a partner in a stable relationship, are 17 years of age or older, reside within a radius of 30 miles of Madison, and have healthy infants. Sample characteristics, methods, and procedures are described in relation to the specific study that was done for each of the two types of problems.

PROBLEMS NATURALLY RECOGNIZED BY PARENTS

It is important for clinicians to have a knowledge of the problems or issues which parents naturally recognize and determine as problems by themselves in the course of the day's activities. First, this set of problems is most likely to accurately describe the "problem space" or the parent's internal representation of the task regarding the infant (Newell & Simon, 1972). Second, clinicians who offer anticipatory care need to work with a sense of this "problem space" if the information and guidance they offer are to be perceived by parents as being supportive of their problem solving efforts.

The anticipatory guidance that is traditionally offered to parents of infants, either during the perinatal period or in the context of well baby care, often relies on assumptions about the types of conditions, events, and circumstances that will constitute problems for parents (Pridham, Hansen, & Conrad, 1977). There are limited systematic investigations of the question, "What, in a clinically useful sense, is a problem for parents of infants?" One source of the available inventories or typologies of the problems or issues that parents identify as concerns is the surveys that have been made of the content of office visits or telephone calls that parents make to clinicians (Hercules & Charney, 1969; Sumner & Fritsch, 1977; Sonnen, 1980). These surveys have made a valuable contribution toward understanding the problems that parents experience. However, the surveys are limited to issues that parents identified as problems which they believed deserved a clinician's attention, and the lists of problems which resulted may be biased by what clinicians accepted or were perceived by parents to accept. Furthermore, parents may formulate types of problems that are never brought to a clinician's attention. Several investigators inventoried the concerns that parents of infants identified outside the context of clinical encounters (Adams, 1963; Cibulka & Price, 1978; Gruis, 1977; Robertson, 1961). Although the work of these investigators is useful in specifying areas of concern for parents of infants, the scope of the issues regarding the infant and infant care that were examined is limited either by the focus of the interview questions or the predetermined items of concern. What was needed was a means of capturing in parents' own terms their specification and descriptions of the problems or issues on which they were working and the nature of the infant care task.

Study

For the study of the problems or issues relating to the infants by the mothers, Pridham, Hansen, Bradley, & Heighway (1982) used logs which were kept by 62 mothers of newborns (38 primiparae and 25 multiparae) for 90 days after their infants' births. These mothers ranged in age from 17-43 years (mean age = 26.7 years, SD = 4.3). The mean years of education was 15.03 (SD = 2.5). The mean socioeconomic status score, using the Hollingshead Four Factor Index (1975) was 48.4 (SD = 13.8), a score that is typical of minor professionals (e.g., grade school teachers and vocational counselors), technical workers, and people with medium sized businesses.

Method

Mothers logged issues about the infant and infant care, as well as types of help used, if any, on a daily basis. Approximately 9,800 issues were identified. In addition, mothers recorded circumstances that made the day more difficult and circumstances that made the day better. For purposes of analysis, we called the former stressors and the latter supports. A system of classification that captured in the mothers' own terms the character of the infant care task was developed by using mothers' own language to structure the categories of the issues on which they were working, the stressors, and the supports.

Results

The 700 + category labels for issues regarding the infant and infant care, which preserved the mothers' language, were collapsed into the following 7 major categories:

1. Growth and development. Questions about the adequacy of infant development, as well as comments about developmental accomplishments.
2. Issues of temperament. Organized in terms of the nine characteristics of behavior, including regularity and adaptability, identified by Thomas and Chess (1977). In order for an issue to be labeled as one of these characteristics, the parent must clearly be discussing the infant's style of behavior.
3. Infant care issues. Ongoing and recurring events of day-to-day life with an infant, including feeding, managing sleep, elimination, and bathing.
4. Parenting. Feelings and attitudes related to being a parent and to the effects of an infant on personal and family life in general.
5. Special events. Both anticipated and unanticipated events, including such issues as taking the infant out, leaving the infant with someone, and health care encounters.
6. Illness. Trauma, physical and physiological issues (diarrhea), and concerns about health status in general.
7. Behavior. Descriptions of day-to-day behavior, as well as references to crying and to habits such as use of a pacifier.

For five of these major categories (growth and development, infant care, parenting, special events, and illness), the number of issues identified varied significantly with time, although, on the whole, the number of issues decreased as the infant grew older. Issues of infant care dropped between the first and second months and then remained stable in frequency [$F(2,116) = 11.36$, $p < .001$]. Issues regarding illness dropped consistently across the 3 months [$F(2,116) = 16.38$, $p < .001$]. Within the first month, issues relating to both parenting and special events were significantly more frequent than in the second and third months for parenting, [$F(2,116) = 12.08$, $p < .001$], and for special events, [$F(2,116) = 4.51$, $p = .01$]. Issues concerning growth and development were highest in the second month [$F(2,116) = 3.53$, $p = .03$]. Issues related to infant temperament generally increased over the 3 months, whereas issues referring to infant behavior (primarily crying) decreased on the whole. However, the effect of time was not significant for the frequency with which issues of temperament or behavior were mentioned.

Overall, mothers reported about as many supports as stressors in each month

of the study. Stressors and supports included references to the following:
1. Self. Related to the mother's own feelings and physical status.
2. Responsibilities and tasks. Accomplished in relationship to home, family members, neighbors, and work.
3. Resources. Help from individuals and the availability of services, knowledge, and skills.
4. Activities. Nonroutine functions, such as visits with friends and relatives, recreation, and social events.
5. Behaviors. Actions by someone else, including family members and friends and acts of affection and affirmation.
6. Conditions. Environmental states, including how busy the parent is and the extent to which the day's activities go smoothly.
7. Events. Unusual or very infrequent occurrences, such as a move to a new home or a death in the family.

Too much or too little help, for example, was identified by mothers as a stressor, while enough help was identified as a support. Having "too much to do" was identified as a stressor, whereas "having one less thing to do" was identified by mothers as a support.

The percentage of all identified issues for which help was sought dropped from 35% in the first 2-week period to 22% in the second 2-week period and decreased to 13% and 12% in the second and third months. The type of help used for each category of issue is shown in Table 1. When help was sought, it was for illness almost 42% of the time, and then from the family physician most frequently. The husband or partner was most frequently the source of help for issues of temperament, parenting, and special events, and tied with books and other printed materials as a source of help for the issue of infant behavior. Books were used most frequently for issues of growth and development, temperament, and infant care, and they were used more often than the primary care nurse clinician and other clinicians (primarily other nurses, including nursery nurses and community health nurses) combined. Type of help used varied significantly by category of issue [Kruskal-Wallis one-way analysis of variance, X^2 (6) = 31.96, p < .001].

It is interesting to note that of the 744 categories of issues identified by mothers at least once, 492 (about 66%) were not associated with use of clinician help. For over one-third of the issues (37%), no help of any type was used. Issues for which either no clinician help or no help at all were used were located in all seven of the major categories of issues.

Multiparae and primiparae did not differ significantly in the total number of issues reported; the groups had a mean of 156 (SD = 65.0) and 150.6 (SD = 60.2) issues, respectively. Although primiparae sought help about 1.5 times as frequently as multiparae, the difference between means for the two groups was not significant [t (60) = 1.38, p > .05 two tailed].

Table 1
Frequency Distribution of Type of Help Used by Mothers for Each Category of Issue (N = 62)

Type of Help Used	Growth and Development	Temperament	Infant Care	Parenting	Special Events	Illness	Behavior
	No.	No.	No.	No.	No.	No.	No.
1. Husband/Partner	46 (.22)[a]	24 (.36)	113 (.16)	31 (.31)	50 (.31)	97 (.09)	61 (.29)
2. Grandparent	13 (.06)	10 (.15)	50 (.07)	7 (.07)	23 (.14)	76 (.07)	19 (.09)
3. Other Relative	2 (.009)	0	30 (.04)	5 (.05)	10 (.06)	21 (.02)	10 (.05)
4. Friend/Neighbor	5 (.02)	3 (.05)	47 (.07)	4 (.04)	12 (.08)	53 (.05)	20 (.09)
5. Primary Family Physician	30 (.14)	4 (.06)	90 (.13)	13 (.13)	29 (.18)	291 (.28)	13 (.06)
6. Primary Nurse Clinician	25 (.12)	2 (.03)	83 (.12)	11 (.11)	7 (.04)	127 (.12)	14 (.06)
7. Other Clinician	13 (.06)	3 (.05)	86 (.12)	8 (.08)	9 (.06)	122 (.12)	13 (.06)
8. Books	71 (.34)	19 (.29)	178 (.28)	16 (.16)	13 (.08)	223 (.22)	61 (.29)
9. Other	6 (.03)	1 (.01)	15 (.02)	4 (.04)	6 (.04)	13 (.01)	2 (.009)
Total	211 (.999)	66 (1.00)	692 (.99)	99 (.99)	159 (.99)	1,023 (.98)	213 (.999)

[a] The numbers in parentheses are the proportions of the column total.

Summary

In summary, the changes in frequency with which the various types of issues are reported over time may indicate a change in saliency for several of the categories of issues for mothers. The drop in concerns related to illness may point out the parents' sense of their infants' vulnerability in the neonatal period. Furthermore, to an increasing extent over the course of the 3 months, mothers relied on their own resources to deal with issues concerning their infant. The majority of categories of issues that mothers had on their minds at least once were never brought to a clinician's attention, indicating the possibility of a large component of parental problems of which clinicians are unaware. Mothers selected the type of help used on the basis of the type of issue. One of the tasks that remains to be done is to examine the subcategories of issues, phrased in parents' own language, in order to identify the types of issues for which clinicians' help was more frequently used. Multiparae and primiparae were less different than expected, both in terms of extent to which issues concerning the infant were identified, and in the use of help.

SIMULATED PROBLEM SOLVING

A description of problems that a parent naturally recognizes concerning an infant is a logical starting point for clinical anticipatory care. However, a knowledge of the types of goals and decision making rules that parents use for problem solving their infant care tasks is necessary to plan appropriate anticipatory care. Skill in problem solving is determined both by an individual's store of knowledge and its structure (problem representation), as well as by the rules, procedures, or heuristics, that operate on that knowledge (the processes of problem solving) (Greeno, 1980). A parent's goals in relation to naturally recognized problems concerning the infant are likely to condition for the parent the meaning of the phenomena that are involved and specify the direction that the problem solving will take (Fingarette, 1963; Miller, Pribram & Galanter, 1960; Neisser, 1976). Furthermore, a parent is likely to apply some criteria or rules, more or less explicit and more or less based in data, to name a problem and to determine action to solve it (Newell & Simon, 1972). To the extent that goals and decision making rules can be expressed verbally or be ascertained by others, goals and rules are part of a parent's cognitive equipment that may be developed and modified through interaction with others (Piaget & Inhelder, 1969). However, at the present time, knowledge of the types of goals and decision making rules that parents apply for the solving of naturally recognized problems is lacking.

Studies of problem solving behavior, on the whole, have used some form of process tracing that requires subjects to think aloud while dealing with a problem or to make a verbal report of processes used after the task is completed (Shulman & Elstein, 1975). Furthermore, as a consequence of the variability that is likely to exist and the difficulty that sometimes occurs in making all the pertinent information known to a problem solver in a real setting, the problems that are used in studies of problem solving are often simulated (Elstein, Shulman, & Sprafka, 1978; Norman & Feightner, 1981). Simulations are based on the assumptions that: the decisions made by individuals in solving a simulated problem are similar to those they would make when working on an actual problem, and subjects are able and willing to verbalize their thought processes. The criteria that Ericsson and Simon (1980) stipulated for predicting the accuracy of verbal reports include the problem solver thinking aloud, use of specific and well-timed probes, and ensuring that problem solvers are not required to restructure the information provided but only have to report information to which they had directly attended.

In recent years, the bulk of the studies of problem solving behavior have concerned the problem solving that clinicians or teachers do (Dincher & Stidger, 1976; Elstein, Shulman, & Sprafka, 1978; Elstein & Bordage, 1979; Hammond, Kelly, Schneider, & Vancini, 1966a, 1966b; Hammond, Kelly, Castellan, Schneider, & Vancini, 1966; Hammond, Kelly, Schneider, & Vancini, 1967; Holzemer, Schleuterman, Farrand, & Miller, 1981; Kassirer & Gorry, 1978; McLaughlin, Carr, & Delucci, 1981; Shavelson & Stern, 1981). Few precedents exist for the study of the problem solving processes employed by lay persons.

The problems with which clinicians concern themselves are analogous to problems naturally recognized by parents to the extent that the nature of the problem is not self-evident, but must be formulated. However, problem solving in a clinical setting is different from a mother's experience of dealing with naturally recognized problems in several respects. The environment in a clinical setting is dedicated to problem solving, the application of a formally learned process, the expectation that observational and other types of empirical data will be used, and the availability of specific and well-designed tools with which to collect data. Nevertheless, studies of clinical problem solving provide a model for the investigation of problem solving of naturally recognized problems by parents. Wolkenheim's (1982) study focused specifically on the scanning behavior of nurses in role played situations. Elstein, Shulman, and Sprafka (1978) used several types of simulation methods to examine the diagnostic phase of physicians' problem solving, including components such as acquisition of information or cues, generation of hypotheses, interpretation of cues, and evaluation of hypotheses.

Studies of problem solving in educational settings may also provide insights for the investigation of the problem solving that parents of infants do. Shavelson and Stern (1981) discussed the bases of teachers' selection of data and inferences involved in the naming of problems.

Problem Solving Processes

Several investigators have examined problem solving processes that lay people used, either for the process as a whole or for component parts. Goldfried and D'Zurilla (1969) used a cognitive role playing situation to examine the problem solving competence of freshmen entering college. Subjects were presented with a written description of the situation and asked to imagine themselves in it, and then in writing to describe in detail their responses (feelings, thoughts, immediate actions, and plans). Spivack, Platt, and Shure (1976) presented verbal descriptions of situations involving interpersonal problems to children, adolescents, and adults. They asked subjects about interpersonal causes of the problem (formulating), the means by which the problem could be addressed (planning), the sequence of steps that the individual would apply to solve the problem (implementing), and the expected consequences of actions taken (evaluating). In addition, they examined the capacity of subjects to identify potential interpersonal problems that were implicit in a set of circumstances (scanning).

Chao (1979), as a participant-observer for 11 mothers of infants, studied three cognitive processes (orienting, evaluating, and delineating) involved in forming concepts about the infant and about the mother herself as mother. Evaneshko and Bauwens (1976), using an anthropological perspective and focusing on the formulating phase of problem solving, examined the rules that lay people used for classifying events as a medical emergency. Capon and Kuhn (1979) investigated the means used by adult female shoppers in a supermarket to determine which of two comparable items was the better buy. Sonnen (1980) used the paradigm of problem solving behavior formulated by Pridham, Hansen, and Conrad (1977, 1978) to classify the phase of the problem solving—either formulating, planning, or evaluating—with which parents requested help by telephone to a pediatric clinic.

Tversky and Kahneman (1974) described several heuristics, or strategies, for identifying problems that are commonly used by lay problem solvers in situations of uncertainty. These heuristics include the "availability hypothesis" (the frequency or likelihood of personally experienced events is used as a basis for identifying a problem) and the "representativeness hypothesis" (the decision as to whether or not some event belongs to a specific class of events is made on the basis of relatively simple resemblance or criteria of goodness of fit). Nisbett and Ross (1980) postulated that knowledge structures, including beliefs or theories, or propositions about the characteristics of objects, and schematic notions of events and persons also are used in formulating or naming. Furthermore, assessments of representativeness are often derived from an individual's theories of the types of events and characteristics or attributes that occur together or in relation to each other. Benner (1982), in studies of the problem solving behavior of graduate nurses, concluded that the performance of highly experienced nurse experts, unlike that of novices, was guided by maxims. These maxims have the characteristics of the type of theories or professional knowledge that Nisbett and Ross (1980) described. The availability and representativeness types of heuristics, theories, and maxims all function to deal with ambiguous information and to supplement the information that is given with much data that are assumed. A question that needed investigation was whether or not mothers use heuristics and maxims as rules to guide their decision making concerning infant care issues.

Study

This study, therefore, addressed the following questions in order to provide a basis for anticipatory care and to relate characteristics of problem solving to health outcomes:

1. What kind of names do mothers give situations involving an unexpected, discrepant, or noncontingent event?
2. What kind of goals and decision making rules do mothers have concerning naturally recognized problems which are presented in a simulated format?
3. How do types of goals and rules vary with the type of problem?
4. How do other people, including clinicians, function in relation to mothers' decision making rules? Are clinicians a source of rules to any extent?
5. How do multiparae and primiparae differ in goals and decision making rules? Can multiparae be assumed to be experts and primiparae novices?

Method

The initial study of maternal problem solving of simulated problems concerning infant care included 22 mothers (14 primiparae and 8 multiparae). Additional subjects are currently being enrolled in order to obtain a larger sample. The mothers' mean age was 27 years (SD = 5.3), and mothers averaged 2.8 years of education beyond high school (SD = 2.6). The mean socioeconomic status score, using the Hollingshead Four Factor Index (1975) was approximately 44 (SD = 13.9), a score that is representative of people who are minor professional (e.g., grade school or vocational counselors), technical workers, or who have medium sized businesses.

The content of the simulated problem exercises was developed through two phases of pilot tests. In the first phase, pilot subjects identified an infant care problem that had been an issue for them within the previous 4 days, and then were guided by the interviewer in recalling the processes of problem solving they had used for as many of the seven phases of problem solving that were relevant. This phase of the pilot testing demonstrated that the mothers who were interviewed could think about and report the thinking that they had done in response to the interview questions. For the most part, the remainder of the interview questions requested descriptions and explanations of concrete experiences. The next phase of the development of the simulated problem exercise involved pilot testing three "standardized" problems that conceivably were experienced by most mothers of infants within the first 3 months.

Two problems were subsequently chosen for the simulation exercise on the basis of the literature and a review of the log data obtained in pilot testing. Each problem involved only one parameter of difficulty: decreased amount (for bottle feeders) or length (for breast feeders) of the infant's feeding, or the example of unexplained (noncontingent) crying. Adams (1963) learned that the mothers whom she interviewed were most interested in the amount of intake needed by the baby and ways to tell when the infant had had enough to eat. Sumner and Fritsch (1977) learned by monitoring parents' telephone calls to clinicians in the infants' first 6 weeks that the highest percentage of calls were about feeding, with questions about crying and colic next highest in frequency. Klaus and Kennell (1976, pp. 54-55) questioned mothers about noncontingent crying in order to examine the differences between mothers who had extended contact with their babies after birth and those who had not by asking, "When the baby cries and has been fed and the diapers are dry, what do you do?"

Although the information concerning the problem situation that was given to the mothers was fixed in amount and standard in presentation, the simulated problem used in this study varied from the "standard" fixed simulation in at least one respect. In order to increase the parent's sense of the reality of the problem situation as well as to make it possible to examine the scanning phases of the parent's problem solving, each mother was asked to imagine the situation as if it were occurring that day for her and her infant. The interview began with a request that the mother describe how the day had gone, including things that she had noticed and expected about the baby that were pertinent with one of the problem situations as follows:

1. Decreased amount/length of feeding. The next time that you feed your baby, your infant stops nursing after about 4 minutes on one breast (or a time that is shorter than the mother has specified as the minimum length of the feeding). Your baby is awake, but just not interested in nursing any longer on this or the other breast. You do all of the things that you usually do for a feeding.

   For bottle feeding mothers, the situation specified an amount of formula taken by the baby that was about half the amount that the parent, earlier in the interview, had stated that the baby usually took at a feeding.

2. Unexplained (noncontingent) crying. You have given the baby his/her next feeding. The feeding goes fine, and you are satisfied with it as a feeding. An hour later, the baby starts to fuss, fusses momentarily, then starts to cry, and now is crying steadily.

For both situations, the parent was informed that, other than feeding or crying behavior, "the baby seems just like he/she has been before this event occurred." Following the presentation of the problem situation, the mother was guided by the interviewer's structured questions through six of the problem solving phases, excluding "developing readiness and willingness to problem solve." If mothers identified several hypotheses about what was going on, they were asked to select the most likely one as the name of the problem. The selected hypothesis, or firm diagnosis, that the mother had made was used as the basis for subsequent questions, including the following:

1. Goal(s) regarding the problem situation. Given that (name parent had given situation) is occurring, what would you like things to be like? What would you want to have happen?

2. Decision making rule(s) for naming the problem (formulating).

    a. You said (name the parent has given the situation or issue) was the most likely thing to be happening. How did you decide that this was happening?

    b. It sounds as if you might be using some rule or principle to decide what is going on here. Would you state this rule or principle?[1]

    c. How did you happen to know or learn this rule or principle?

3. Decision making rule(s) for actions that would be taken (implementing).

    a. How was it that you decided (actions that mother had identified) are the things that you would do?

    b. It sounds as if you might be using some rule or principle in order to decide what to do. Would you state this rule or principle?

    c. How did you happen to know or learn this rule or principle?

Each of the problem exercises was presented twice, on an alternate basis. The schedule of problem exercises is shown in Table 2. All problem exercises were done on the telephone and taped.

Table 2
Schedule of Administration of the Simulated Problem Exercise

Problem	Description	Infant's Age (Days)
1	Decreased amount/length of feeding	10-14
2	Unexplained (noncontingent) crying	22-28
3	Decreased amount/length of feeding	50-56
4	Unexplained (noncontingent) crying	78-84

[1]A rule or principle could be specified either in terms of a report of one's concrete experience or in terms of an abstraction from one's experience.
In the latter case, formal thinking is demonstrated (Inhelder & Piaget, 1958, pp. 339-342).

Coding categories for open-ended questions were derived from the pilot tests of the simulated exercise as well as from the literature. Responses were coded very soon after the interview using the tape recording of the interview to complete the written notes. One of every set of four interviews was coded by another interviewer to check intercoder agreement. The mean percentage of agreement for coding examined throughout the study, including missed cases, was 74.36% (SD = 5.88; range 62.87%-85.71%).

For purposes of analysis, the data for the two administrations of each of the two types of problems (feeding and crying) were combined. The responses for the four simulated problems were combined when logical to do so, making cell size large enough for chi square tests of the effects of parity on the category distributions, using the Minitab package of statistical programs (Ryan, Joiner, & Ryan, 1980). Differences in specific category frequencies by type of problem (feeding, crying) and by parity (primipara or multipara) were tested by collapsing cell frequencies for all other categories and using the chi square test for a 2 x 2 table.

Results

Mothers attributed a varity of meanings to the circumstances that were presented, both for the feeding and crying problems. The frequencies of the names given the problems are shown in Tables 3 and 4. For each problem, most of the 44 instances of naming referred to the infant rather than to external conditions. Only in very few instances did mothers state that they would make nothing of the situation. A little more than one-third of the naming responses to the feeding situation focused on the infant's lack of hunger or a manifestation of the infant's present feeding pattern. For each of the two problems, discomfort was one of the more frequently named responses (about 23% and 39% for the feeding and crying problems, respectively), and illness was named in about 9% of the responses for each type of problem.

The types of goals—what mothers wanted things to be like, or what they wanted to happen—that mothers reported most frequently concerned resolution of the problem situation itself, i.e., wanting the baby to feed, to stop crying, or to go back to sleep (see Table 5). The type of goal identified varied by type of problem. In particular, for the feeding problem, 25% of the goals reported referred to an outcome, other than resolution of the immediate problem, that was focused on the interests of the infant as a person; e.g., "the baby not feeling pressured to do something she didn't want to do." This category of goal, however, was identified only about 7% of the time for the crying problem, X^2 (1) = 5.44, p < .02. Approximately 16% of the responses for the feeding problem referred to outcomes focused on the mother herself, e.g., the baby going to sleep so mother could get some sleep. For the crying problem, however, only about 2% of the responses were concerned with these

Table 3
Names Given Feeding Problems

Problem Name	Frequency[a]	Percent
Baby isn't hungry.	12	27.27
Event is a manifestation of the baby's feeding pattern.	4	9.09
Baby is ill. Something is wrong with baby.	4	9.09
Baby has a discomfort.	10	22.72
Baby's state is an issue (e.g., sleepy, tired).	3	6.81
Baby wants attention, to be held, to play.	5	11.36
External conditions are the problem (environment or mother's skill).	2	4.54
There is no issue. Nothing is going on.	4	9.09
Total	44	99.97

[a]Responses for each of the two administrations of the simulated problem are combined for the 22 mothers.

Table 4
Names Given Crying Problems

Problem Name	Frequency[a]	Percent
Baby is hungry.	5	11.36
Baby is ill.	4	9.09
Baby has a discomfort.	17	38.63
Baby's state is an issue.	5	11.36
Baby wants attention, to be held, to play.	7	15.90
Baby is angry, frustrated, feels insecure.	4	9.09
External conditions are the problem (environment or mother's skill).	1	2.27
There is no issue. Nothing is going on.	1	2.27
Total	44	99.97

[a]Responses for each of the two administrations of the simulated problem are combined for the 22 mothers.

types of goals, X^2 (1) = 4.95, p<.05. Furthermore, for the crying problem, about one-third of the responses concerned goals related to the mother's possession of adequate knowledge, skills, or resources to deal with the problem, whereas only about 9% of the responses for the feeding problem dealt with this type of goal, X^2 (1) = 9.32, p<.005. Multiparae and primiparae did not differ significantly in types of goals identified, X^2 (5) = 1.23, p>.05.

The responses of the request to state the decision rule used for naming indicated that a variety of rules were used (see Table 6). The most frequent type of decision rule for naming both feeding and crying problems was the representativeness hypothesis. For example, one mother stated, "If babies don't eat, they are probably not hungry, unless they show other signs of a problem," e.g., have fever or are fussy. Some interesting differences are noted between the frequency distributions for the feeding and crying problems, although they are not statistically significant. Mothers stated rules related to observing and reflecting on observations as methods of naming somewhat more frequently for the feeding problem than the crying problem, X^2 (1) = 0.98, p>.05. This type of rule took the form, "I watch for more than one thing to decide what is going on. I try to watch the whole picture." The availability hypothesis was also used slightly more frequently for feeding than crying problems, X^2 (1) = 0.52, p>.05. The use of this type of rule was manifested by the following statement, "What is going on is more likely to be a common problem than something extraordinary." This mother had indicated that she and her baby had an experience with the feeding problem as stated, and she

Table 5
Type of Goals Stated in Relation to Feeding and Crying Problems

Reference of Goal	Feeding		Crying	
	No.[a]	Percent	No.[a]	Percent
Resolution of immediate problem (resuming feeding/stopping crying).	18	40.90	20	45.45
Outcome (other than problem resolution) focused on baby.	11	25.00	3	6.81
Outcome focused on mother.	7	15.90	1	2.27
Ambiguous outcome focused on either baby or mother, or both.	2	4.54	3	6.81
Mother's possession of adequate knowledge, skill, resources.	4	9.09	16	36.36
Goal not identified.	2	4.54	1	2.27
Total	44	99.97	44	99.97

[a]Responses for each of the two administrations of each type of problem (feeding and crying) were combined for 22 mothers.

had named it: "The baby had an upset stomach from gas." An equivalent number of responses for the feeding and the crying problem expressed the self-evidence of the name, including the statement of an experience without specifying its character or another indication that a rule was unnecessary. A few responses for both types of problems were in the form of a proposition or belief, either about problems in general (e.g., "Something that happens more than once is a problem"), or about the specific problem (e.g., "A baby might not be hungry at all times"). There were a greater number of statements to the effect that there was no rule, or that a rule could not be stated about crying problems, although the difference was not significant, $X^2 (1) = 1.09$, $p > .05$.

The distribution of frequencies of the types of decision rules for naming differed significantly for multiparae and primiparae, $X^2 (6) = 21.04$, $p < .05$ (see Table 7). Only primiparae (about 20%) claimed that there was no rule, or that they could not name a rule. Four primiparae stated "no rule" for naming two of the four problems. Furthermore, primiparae were more likely than

Table 6
Type of Decision Rule Used for Naming Feeding and Crying Problems

Decision Rule	Feeding		Crying	
	No.[a]	Percent	No.[a]	Percent
Rule related to observing and reflecting on data.	8	18.18	5	11.36
Rule related to the frequency, familiarity of the problem (availability hypothesis).	6	13.63	4	9.09
Proposition/belief about problems in general and not specific to this problem or its particular type.	2	4.54	0	—
Representativeness hypothesis (If this, then I think that . . .).	12	27.27	19	43.18
Proposition/belief related to this specific type of problem.	5	11.36	2	4.54
No rule is needed. The name is self-evident (known from experience, common sense).	7	15.90	7	15.90
"There is no rule." Can't state rule.	4	9.09	7	15.90
Total	44	99.97	44	99.97

[a]Responses for each of the two administrations of each type of problem (feeding and crying) were combined for 22 mothers.

Table 7
Type of Decision Rule Used for Naming Four Simulated Problems by Parity

Decision Rule	Multipara (N = 8)		Primipara (N = 14)	
	No.[a]	Percent	No.[a]	Percent
Rule related to observing and reflecting on data.	2	6.25	11	19.64
Rule related to the frequency, familiarity of the problem (availability hypothesis).	7	21.87	3	5.35
Proposition/belief about problems in general and not specific to this problem.	0	—	2	3.57
Representativeness hypothesis (If this, then I think that . .).	10	31.25	21	37.50
Proposition/belief related to this specific type of problem.	4	12.50	3	5.35
No rule is needed. The name is self-evident (known from experience, common sense).	9	28.12	5	8.92
"There is no rule." Can't state rule.	0	—	11	19.64
Total	32	99.99	56	99.97

[a]Responses for each of the four simulated problems, including two feeding and two crying problems, are combined.

multiparae to use a rule related to observing and reflecting as methods of naming, X^2 (1) = 2.90, $0.10 < p > .05$. On the other hand, multiparae were more likely to claim that no rule was needed because the name was self-evident, or that an unspecified experience was the basis of naming, X^2 (1) = 5.61, $p < .025$.

Four types of sources of the decision rule for naming were identified: empirical data; external sources, including printed material and other people; derivation of the rule from a widely applicable philosophy; and intuition/common sense. The most frequently cited source of rules was experience (approximately 34% for feeding and 52% for crying). External sources were cited equally as often (about 16% of responses) for the feeding and crying problems (see Table 8). The external source cited most often was the infant's grandparent, maternal or paternal. In only one case, for one of the crying problems, was a nurse identified as the source of the rule. Multiparae tended to identify an empirical basis (experience or observation) for the decision rule to a greater extent than primiparae (about 53% compared to 37%), but the difference was not significant, X^2 (1) = 2.03, $p > .05$. Primiparae used external sources about 23% of the time compared to about 9% of the time for multiparae, again with a nonsignificant difference, $X^2 (1) = 2.62$, $p > .05$ (see Table 9).

Table 8
Source of the Decision Rule for Naming for Feeding and Crying Problems

Source of Decision Rule	Feeding		Crying	
	No.[a]	Percent	No.[a]	Percent
Experience/observation (empirical basis).	15	34.09	23	52.27
External source.	9	20.44	7	15.90
Derivation from a widely applicable philosophy.	4	9.09	1	2.27
Intuition/common sense	4	9.09	1	2.27
No response. Decision rule not stated.	12	27.27	12	27.27
Total	44	99.98	44	99.98

[a]Responses for each of the two administrations of each type of problem (feeding and crying) are combined for 22 mothers.

Table 9
Source of the Decision Rule for Naming
by Parity for Four Simulated Problems

Source of Decision Rule	Multipara		Primipara	
	No.[a]	Percent	No.[a]	Percent
Experience/observation (empirical basis).	17	53.12	21	37.50
External source.	3	9.37	13	23.20
Derivation from a widely applicable philosophy.	1	3.12	4	7.14
Intuition/common sense	2	6.25	3	5.35
No response. Decision rule not stated.	9	28.12	15	26.78
Total	32	99.98	56	99.97

[a]Responses for each of four simulated problems, including two feeding and two crying problems, are combined.

The types of rules stated for implementing decisions, or deciding the type of action to take, were similar in character to the rules stated for naming. Furthermore, the distribution of frequencies of type of decision rule for implementing is relatively similar for the feeding and crying problems, other than for the use of a general strategy relying on nonspecific experiences (see Table 10). This type of rule was stated more frequently for the crying problem, $X^2(1) = 1.82$, p $>.05$, and it is exemplified by the statements: "I used experience to decide. I do what has worked in the past. I use the trial and error method." At least one-fourth of the responses for both types of problems claimed that a rule could not be stated for the decision about actions to take, a higher percent than for a rule for naming the problem. The distribution of the frequencies of rule types was similar for parity groupings (see Table 11). Multiparae, as well as primiparae, indicated that they could not state a rule for their decisions about actions to take (32.15% and 25.00% respectively), $X^2 (1) = 0.68$, p $>.05$. Eight of the 22 mothers could not state a rule for implementing for at least two of the four problems, one of whom had been unable to state a decision rule for naming twice, and another of whom was unable to state an implementing rule for each of the four problems.

Table 10
Type of Decision Rule for Implementing
for Feeding and Crying Problems

Source of Decision Rule	Feeding		Crying	
	No.[a]	Percent	No.[a]	Percent
Observe behavior. Reflect.	3	6.81	2	4.54
Rule related specifically to the stated problem (representativeness hypothesis).	11	25.00	10	22.72
Use the most obvious, available action (availability hypothesis).	4	9.09	32	6.81
General strategy relying on (nonspecific) experience.	6	13.63	11	25.00
What to do is self-evident. Use common sense.	5	11.36	6	13.63
Action is not needed, since problem is not significant.	2	4.54	1	2.27
Decision rule not stated. Can't state rule.	13	29.54	11	25.00
Total	44	99.97	44	99.97

[a]Responses for each of the two administrations of each type of problem (feeding and crying) are combined for the 22 mothers.

Table 11
Type of Decision Rule for Implementing by Parity
for the Total Set of Four Problems

Source of Decision Rule	Multipara (N = 8)		Primipara (N = 14)	
	No.[a]	Percent	No.[a]	Percent
Observe behavior. Reflect.	0	—	5	8.62
Rule related specifically to the stated problem (representativeness hypothesis).	8	25.00	13	23.22
Use the most obvious, available action (availability hypothesis).	1	3.12	6	10.71
General strategy relying on (nonspecific) experience.	7	21.87	10	17.85
What to do is self-evident. Use common sense.	5	15.62	6	10.71
Action is not needed, since problem is not significant.	1	3.12	2	3.57
Decision rule not stated. Can't state rule.	10	31.25	14	25.00
Total	32	99.98	56	99.98

[a]Responses for each of the four simulated problems, including two feeding and two crying problems, are combined.

The sources of the decision rule for implementing were much the same for the feeding and crying problems (see Table 12). Empirical data (experience/observation) were most frequent, followed by external sources. The distribution of frequencies for multiparae and primiparae did not differ significantly, $X^2 (4) = 3.15$, p > .05 (see Table 13). However, it is interesting that only primiparae named an external source of the decision rule concerning actions for feeding problems, whereas both primiparae and multiparae named external sources for crying problems (about 21% and 25% of the responses, respectively). Reading was the external source in over 50% of the cases (10 out of the 17 responses for the two types of problems, combined). Doctors were the only clinicians named as sources, and then only twice. Again, the most frequently identified persons named as external sources of the decision rule for implementing were maternal and paternal grandparents.

Summary

The variety of names that mothers gave the same data highlights a factor in the process of naming, i.e., the importance of the context in which a problem is perceived to occur. Furthermore, the mother's goals vis-a-vis the prob-

Table 12
Source of the Decision Rule for Implementing
for Feeding and Crying Problems

Source of Decision Rule	Feeding		Crying	
	No.[a]	Percent	No.[a]	Percent
Experience/observation (empirical basis).	22	50.00	18	40.90
External source.	7	15.90	10	22.72
Don't know. No response.	2	4.54	4	9.08
No rule identified.	13	29.54	12	27.27
Total	44	99.98	44	99.97

[a]Responses for each of the two administrations of each type of problem (feeding and crying) are combined for the 22 mothers.

Table 13
Source of the Decision Rule for Implementing
by Parity for Four Simulated Problems

Source of Decision Rule	Multipara		Primipara	
	No.[a]	Percent	No.[a]	Percent
Experience/observation (empirical basis).	17	53.12	23	41.07
External source.	4	12.50	13	23.21
Don't know. No response.	1	3.12	5	8.92
No decision rule identified.	10	31.25	15	26.78
Total	32	99.99	56	99.98

[a]Responses for each of four simulated problems, including two feeding and two crying responses, are combined.

lem were not always simply one of the baby resuming feeding or stopping crying, but sometimes they concerned the interests of the infant as a person or the mother's own comfort and needs. The types of goals that mothers identified demonstrated the difference that type of problem might make, since concern about competence was significantly greater for crying in contrast to feeding problems.

The extent to which mothers stated a decision rule varied with both the problem solving process involved (formulating or implementing) and parity. More mothers stated a decision rule for the naming in contrast to the implementing phase of the problem solving process. For naming, only primiparae could not state a decision rule, whereas multiparae and primiparae did not differ significantly on decision rules for implementing. Perhaps for some mothers, the name of the problem automatically specifies the action to be taken, and as a consequence, there is no need to make an independent decision about action.

The more frequent indications by multiparae that the name of the problem was self-evident suggest a feature of the expert status as described by Benner (1982); i.e., it is not possible to obtain from an expert the component processes or elements of her thinking. However, multiparae were not any more likely than primiparae to indicate self-evidence as the type of decision rule for choice of actions to deal with the problem (implementing). The frequency with which goals concerning competence were stated for the crying problem suggests: the achievement of expert status may vary from problem to problem, and an infant's crying may pose a special challenge to problem solving skills.

The representativeness response, on the whole, was the most frequently used type of decision rule for both naming and implementing. It states a rule that is more specifically related to an empirical observation or condition than any other type of rule that was used. However, its proportionate use varied with the phase of the problem solving process involved. For naming, the next most frequent response was, "self-evident," whereas for implementing, especially for crying problems, the use of a general strategy that relied on nonspecific experience, including the use of trial and error was the second most frequent response after the representative response. Whether the data that the mothers noted and related to a known class of events/conditions was salient data and comprehensive enough of the conditions that needed to be observed in order to exclude false positives is another issue. Tversky and Kahneman (1974), as well as Nisbett and Ross (1980), discussed the limitations and the advantages of the use of heuristics and theories for purposes of decision making. However, it may be more difficult for a mother to develop a theory or propositional knowledge concerning actions to take, given a specific event or condition, than it is to develop a theory concerning the name of a problem when she is given specific observations. Perhaps the type of knowledge structure that many mothers applied to determine what to do was what Nisbett and Ross (1980) refer to as a schema. A schema is not expressed in propositional terms, but refers to a mental structure having a dynamic or relational aspect. The mothers who used the trial and error strategy, for example, may have applied a schema that assumed, given a specific condition, no one action or sequence of actions was likely to resolve it. The extent to which the various types of decision rules influence the outcomes of problem solving is an area that remains to be investigated.

Primiparae tended to cite external sources for both naming and implementing rules to a greater extent than multiparae, indicating a greater recognized and acknowledged dependency on others. The extent to which grandparents were identified as the external source suggests a relatively prominent role in the decision making of mothers that does not necessarily rely on proximity, and a relatively minor role for clinicians.

CONCLUSION

This paper addressed the formulation of naturally recognized problems by parents and their problem solving of simulated problems, including naming the problem and specifying goals and decision rules used. Furthermore, the types of help that mothers used to deal with the naturally recognized problems and the external sources of the mothers' decision rules for naming and implementing simulated problems were discussed. Clinical implications of the study of the naturally recognized problems include the potential usefulness of a means of describing mothers' problems as well as the type of help they are likely to seek and use, given specific types of problems.

Although the size of the sample used for the study of simulated problem solving was small and only two types of problems were examined, findings indicate that aspects of mothers' problem solving could be related to concepts that are available in the literature on problem solving by lay people. Furthermore, the data suggest that processes of naming and implementing varied with type of problem and parity. In addition, the processes used to problem solve may vary by the problem solving phase that is involved. The variety of types of names, goals, and decision rules which mothers cited for the simulated problems also supports efforts to find a clinically useful means of exploring with a mother her problem solving processes in relation to specific types of problems.

The extent to which any specific type of name, goal, or decision rule influences outcomes remains to be examined, and this aspect is the next item for investigation. Other questions for systematic study include the consistency with which decision rules are used from one episode of a problem to another, as well as across types of problems, and how decision rules are likely to be learned. Furthermore, the extent to which clinicians are potential sources of decision rules, of whatever type, is another issue. This issue may be related to the extent to which decision rules may be didactically taught or only learned through demonstration and modeling with concurrent commentary or explanations.

CRITIQUE*

Lorraine O. Walker, R.N., Ed.D.

The following critique was prepared for the original presentation by Dr. Pridham at the roundtable. Subsequent to the critique, Dr. Pridham revised the paper addressing several areas presented in the original critique. A comparison of the published paper and this critique will be helpful to the reader to reinforce how the concerns presented in the critique can be addressed and add substance and clarity to the presentation of research. Such efforts will strengthen nursing research and facilitate the development of nursing knowledge.

> The birth of the first child can be both a source of stress and an event to test the family's coping strategies. That is, the baby can cause certain stresses arising from lack of sleep, tiredness, less time for self and spouse, and feelings of overwhelming responsibility and being tied down. At the same time though, the baby can provide a sense of fulfillment, new meaning in life and can strengthen the bond between husband and wife, thus contributing to a sense of family cohesiveness (Miller & Sollie, 1980, p. 464).

Specifically, new mothers have found the following items bothersome: worry about personal appearance since the baby, physical tiredness and fatigue, the baby interrupting sleep and rest, worry about loss of figure, and feeling edgy or emotionally upset (Russell, 1974). The addition of an infant to the family, thus, has physical and emotional implications for parents in addition to social ones.

Within this larger context of transition to parenthood, Dr. Pridham and her associates have adopted a paradigm of problem solving behavior to explore naturally recognized and simulated problems faced by parents on a day-to-day basis. They note, "Problem solving is one method of adaptation. Adaptation is the process of dealing with present or anticipated stressors and/or changes in functioning that are initiated by stressors" (Pridham, Hansen, & Conrad, 1978). This work has opened the way to understanding a much neglected topic in parent-infant research—the cognitions of parents in coping with the day-to-day realities of parenthood.

This critique will focus first on the conceptual foundations of the research in this area and then on methodological dimensions. Next, the paper will consider issues pertinent to applying knowledge of parental needs, resources, and decision making to practice.

*I wish to express my appreciation to Ira Iscoe, Director of the Institute of Human Development and Family Studies, The University of Texas, for his assistance in the beginning stages of this paper, and to Mira Lessick, doctoral student at The University of Texas, for her assistance in informational retrieval during preparation of this manuscript.

CONCEPTUAL FRAMEWORK

Turning first to the conceptual framework of parental problem solving, the following questions arise. What is the relationship between issues or problems which parents face on a day-to-day basis and the concept of stressors? How, if at all, do problems or issues faced by parents relate to Lazarus' notion of "hassles" (Lazarus, 1981)? Reaching a bit more clarity on the concepts in use and their interrelationships would advance the conceptual bases for research in this area.

Second, while problem solving may be described as a cognitive activity in response to stress, impairment in cognitive processes can occur in response to stress. According to Caplan (1981, p. 415), under stress, "the individual's orderly process of externally oriented instrumental ego functioning is upset; this happens precisely when it is important for him to be operating at his maximum effectiveness so that he can grapple with his problems." To be clinically useful, a problem solving paradigm may well need to be expanded to deal with how parents maintain cognitive functions under the day-to-day stresses of parenting. In this line, Caplan's (1981) recent explication of how social support facilitates effective coping seems relevant. For example, Caplan argues that social support reduces arousal level so that cognitive approaches may be engaged.

The third conceptual difficulty in the study of parental problem solving lies in the need for a model to link parental information needs, resources, and decision making to health related outcomes. Works moving in this direction include that of Norbeck (1981), Cronenwett and Kunst-Wilson (1981), and Kahn and Antonucci (1980). Representing the overall model linking parental needs, resources, and decision making to health related outcomes, of course, is primarily a theoretical issue, not a methodological one. Theoretical assumptions, however, undergird choices of design and method (Hinshaw, 1979a, 1979b). Thus, a weak theory base can ultimately limit the extrapolations possible from a given experiment or descriptive study.

METHODOLOGY AND FINDINGS

The second focus of this critique is on the specific research methods and findings reported by Dr. Pridham.

In the first study of naturally recognized problems, Dr. Pridham notes that the existing literature is limited in its representation of the problems of new parents and that what is needed is a means of capturing in parents' own terms their personal definitions of problems. Using logs completed by mothers over 91 days, issues related to their babies and infant care, as well as stressors and supports, were obtained. In combing through a very large and presumably rich data set, seven categories of naturally recognized problems were identified. The categories were development, infant care, parenting, special events, illness, temperament, and behavior. Having found myself eagerly awaiting some insights into the unique problems of parents unspoiled by the biases of professionals and researchers, I was disappointed to find the end products labeled and categorized in old, familiar terms.

When one inspects the data provided from the first study, however, some important information about the resources used by new mothers may be gleaned. When one inspects the data in Table 1, two resources emerge as both predominant and consistent resources to new mothers: husband/partner and books. The husband/partner was the resource used for managing 20% or more (22-36%) of the problems in the categories of growth and development, temperament, parenting, special events, and behavior. In turn, books were used as a resource in managing 20% more (22-34%) of the problems in the categories of growth and development, temperament, infant care, illness, and behavior. These findings are intriguing in that a survey I completed of adoptive parents showed a quite similar pattern (Walker, 1976). Excluding concerns related to adoption where the social worker was the major resource, spouses and books were found to be the predominant and most widespread resources reported in dealing with problems. My conclusion from these findings is that one new way in which nurses might assist new parents with problems is by entering the world of publishing. With the knowledge available from Dr. Pridham's study of naturally recognized problems, the structure for nurse-authored publications has been identified. An apparently rich market awaits to be tapped by nurses with knowledge of development, parenting, and related topics.

In order to specify the task of clinical anticipatory care of new parents, the second study in the presentation explored the types of goals and decision making rules that parents use for problem solving infant care tasks, the extent to which these goals and decision making rules could be expressed verbally or ascertained by others, and if the goals and rules are part of a parent's cognitive equipment that may be developed and modified through interaction with others. Because such knowledge is currently lacking, this study involved simulated problem solving exercises conducted with 22 mothers (14 primiparae and 8 multiparae) on 4 occasions. Using tape recorded telephone interviews, mothers progressed through standardized sequences of questions pertinent to their goals, rules for problem naming, and rules for actions to be taken in relation to simulated feeding and crying episodes of their babies. Salient socioeconomic characteristics of mothers who participated in the simulated exercises are provided, and detailed information is given about the interview protocols.

My critique of the research methods and findings will focus on three areas. First, about two-thirds of the statistical tests of significance reported in the body of the paper are nonsignificant. The data patterns associated with these nonsignificant statistical results, however, are discussed in as much, if not more, detail as findings which were statistically significant. While I recognize the preliminary nature of this research, I believe that adoption of a criterion for statistical significance of findings which deviates from conventional ones needs to be explicitly addressed and justified. Perhaps inferential statistics were not relevant to this study.

My second methodological critique of the simulated problem solving exercises is that reliance on quantitative methods for summarizing interview data puts the reader out of touch with the texture of mothers' goals and rules in problem solving through feeding and crying episode problems. The numbers in a sense mask much of the meaning that mothers apply to the feeding and crying episodes. Transmitting more of the mothers' actual problem solving operations by using case study examples as an adjunct to quantitative evidence would perhaps give clinicians and researchers more insight into maternal reasoning processes.

Third, the study indicates that 8 of the 22 mothers could not state a rule for at least 2 of the 4 problems, one of whom had been unable to state a decision rule for naming twice, and another of whom was unable to state an implementing rule for each of the 4 problems. This raises a number of questions. Did these mothers differ in any way from others who could articulate such rules? Are the parental goals and rules employed in solving infant care problems related to patterns of mother-infant interaction, child-development outcomes, or the overall richness and sensitivity of the environment available to the infant? These questions will no doubt be addressed in further research.

IMPLICATIONS FOR PRACTICE

The final section of this paper is directed at moving social support research into practice. In focusing on practice, I reviewed the following American Nurses' Association (1981) statement on nursing research:

> Nursing research develops knowledge about health and the promotion of health over the full lifespan, care of persons with health problems and disabilities, and nursing actions to enhance the ability of individuals to respond effectively to actual and potential health problems.

Within the confines of this statement, I then formulated the following questions. How can a knowledge of new parents' information needs, resources to help them, and their decision making be:

1. applied within the context of promotion of health over the lifespan, as well as in the care of persons with health problems and disabilities?
2. used to design nursing actions to enhance the ability of individuals to respond effectively to actual or potential health problems?

The following responses, by no means, will be final answers to these questions, but they will stimulate further investigations.

Primarily, extensive literature supports the proposition that social support may moderate the effects of stress on individuals' well-being (e.g., see Cobb, 1976; Caplan, 1981). Individuals with high stress who experience high levels of social support manifest less illness, disability, and maladaptation than those with comparable stress but low social support. I believe that within the health and helping professions, social support is often seen as the psychosocial analog of the polio vaccine, the magic bullet for primary prevention. Less commonly, critics argue that alternate interpretations of social support research must be considered, weighed, and tested (Heller, 1979). The question has been raised as to whether social support is a concomitant rather than a determinant of response to stress (Heller, 1979). I ask, is individual competence—the ability to get one's needs met through social resources—what really underlies the association between social support and reduced morbidity incidence? Is the relationship between social support and competence indeed a reciprocal one? Despite a burgeoning literature on social support (Mitchell & Trickett, 1980; Gottlieb, 1981), these and other questions can only be provisionally answered. Increasingly, however, the concepts of mastery and competence in response to stress are hypothesized as adjuncts to and/or mutually influential in effective responses to stressful events (Mitchell & Trickett, 1980; Caplan, 1981; Cowen, 1977; Mitchell, 1982; Adler, 1982; Iscoe, 1974; Buehler & Hogan, 1980). Dr. Pridham's work, therefore, may be seen as part of a larger descriptive body of literature on the concept of parental competence (Abernethy, 1973; Belsky, Robins, & Gamble, in press).

According to Iscoe (1982), executive competence (the skill to use resources in instrumental ways (Ausubel & Sullivan, 1970; Berzonsky, 1978) and a rich social network (which increases the options available to an individual) are central ingredients in primary preventive efforts as well as in dealing with existing health related problems. In the context of families with young children, parental executive competence and rich social resources seem particularly relevant to children at high risk for health problems because of social, psychological, or medical reasons. Knowledge of parents' information needs, resources to help them, and their decision making provides dimensions for assessing the quality of parental executive competence and available social support in these cases.

NURSING INTERVENTIONS

Nursing interventions can be planned to enhance the ability of individuals to respond effectively to actual or potential health problems. Depending upon whether one operates from a disease conception or developmental conception of intervention, however, the nature and goal of the interventions will vary accordingly (Danish, Smyer, & Nowak, 1980). Within a disease framework, intervention approaches before, during, or after a stressful event correspond to the notions of primary prevention, secondary prevention, and remedial services. In a developmental perspective, however, interventions before, during, and after stressful life events parallel enhancement, support groups, and counseling approaches (see Danish, Smyer, & Nowak, 1980, for a fuller development of this classification of interventions). Thus, interventions relevant to parents of young infants may take many potential forms, not just one. Primary prevention, for example, might focus on reducing the incidence of psychopathology in families with young children, while enhancement might focus on promoting growth and change within beginning families. Consistent with the distinction between disease-oriented versus developmental-oriented interventions, Caplan (1961, p. vii) defined primary prevention as "processes involved in reducing the risk that people in the community will fall ill with mental disorders."

While my intent here is not to develop a proposal for the types of interventions that nurses might pursue, I do wish to underscore the wide range of ways in which nurse researchers might choose to define research of nursing interventions with families of young children. I also wish to share my concern over a general "descriptive-itis" syndrome in nursing research, i.e., the reluctance to accomplish research concerning intervention in contrast to descriptive research. There is an assumption that clinical nursing research is on the upswing and that descriptive studies of nurses and nursing students are no longer planned, but I think that may be at least partially untrue. In a recent survey of research articles published in 1981 in *Nursing Research, Western Journal of Nursing Research,* and *Research in Nursing and Health,* only 9% of the 104 articles reviewed dealt with interventions in contrast to 25% which dealt with nurses or nursing students (Walker, 1982). When I conducted an informal poll of nurse faculty as to what the ideal proportion of articles aimed specifically at nursing interventions should be, the consensus was 40%. Within those 3 journals, then, there was a 31% deficit in the area of research on intervention. While nurse researchers may argue that there is not yet enough descriptive information on specific intervention areas, I submit that intervention is only partially based on descriptive research. Gathering large amounts of descriptive information does not necessarily provide information on means of intervention. In the meantime, clinicians dealing with patients on a day-to-day basis must intervene with clients without benefit of research supporting these interventions. I suggest that much nursing impact on health care may be lost in hesitating to research intervention.

INTERVENTION PROGRAMS

A brief summary of intervention programs which are potentially relevant to the health of infants and their parents is relevant for nursing concerns regarding parental competence and social support for families, even though most of these programs have not been conducted by nurses. Table 1 summarizes information about the programs, and this information was obtained by computerized literature searches and other means. The intent was to represent types of programs rather than provide an exhaustive list of these programs. The information in Table 1 has limitations because the literature about these programs was not always specific, and the actual focus of the programs and their interventions may not coincide exactly with my inferences about them. An attempt was made, however, to accurately describe the features of the programs. As an inspection of program foci indicates, the programs included both disease and developmental orientations to intervention. The programs further varied from therapeutic work with psychotic mothers to a drop-in center for any parent in the community. Of particular relevance to the consideration of competence and social support is Powell's (1980) report of a program aimed at interpersonal dimensions of establishing and maintaining social networks, but details about this intervention program were particularly sketchy, thus limiting further commentary.

In closing, I believe I have not completely answered the two questions I set out to consider, but I hope that I have given some direction as to how nurses might respond effectively to them. I also want to thank Dr. Karen Pridham for her pioneering work in the field of parental problem solving. It was a challenge to respond to her provocative paper.

DISCUSSION

T. Antonucci: I have a question about your table in the critique. Could you give us a sense of what the size of these studies are? What was the total population for each study?

L. Walker: In most cases I didn't have a lot of that information available. I think they vary a great deal. What I wanted to do in the critique was simply to just communicate some of the rough information. Some of these studies are relatively small groups; I would say about 30. Some of them are larger than that certainly. I think one of the most difficult things in using this method for retrieving the information is that often a lot specifics of the program are simply not given. Some of the programs are ongoing right now, and are going to be doing evaluative research on the program impact, but the researchers may not know what the true population will be at this time.

T. Antonucci: By this method of retrieval, you mean computer search?

L. Walker: Yes. Other ways of getting at this information, to be more exhaustive and complete, include contacting project directors for updated project overviews of known projects and retrieving data on current funded projects through the Smithsonian Science Information Exchange. Since my purpose in the critique was to illustrate new ways in which nurses might think about intervention, easy access to source material was my primary concern.

The advantage of the table in the critique is that these studies were published references, and if you wanted to read about them, you could look up the articles and read them.

Table 1

Intervention Programs for Families with Young Children

Source	Population	Intervention	Program Focus
Tyler & Kogan, 1977	Handicapped preschool children and their parents	Behavioral instructional sessions to enrich mother-child repertoire and decrease negative behaviors	Remedial
Funderburk, Richardson, & Johnson, 1977	Parents immediately following birth of a Down syndrome infant	Early intensive counseling and instruction	Secondary prevention
Walcer & Slaughter, 1979	Low income minority mothers	Discussion groups to enhance ego development	Enhancement?
McGuire & Gottlieb, 1979	Lower-middle class, first time parents with infants approximately 1 year of age	Parent discussion groups	Supportive and primary prevention
Powell, 1980	White, low-income parents with infants under 6 months	Interpersonal dimensions of establishing and maintaining a social network	Primary prevention
Vaughn, Huntington, Samuels, Bilmes, & Shapiro, 1975	Any interested parent in the community	Parent Drop-in Center providing guest speakers, discussion, study groups	Supportive and primary prevention
Nover, Williams, & Ward, 1981	Psychotic mothers or mothers with personality impairment and their infants and families	Comprehensive approach including therapeutic work with infants and parents, outreach infant day care center	Remedial and secondary prevention
Wandersman, Wandersman, & Kahn, 1980	White, middle-class couples who had attended prepared childbirth classes	Postpartum parenting groups with discussion and written material	Supportive and primary prevention
Leifer, Spiker, Roth, Morrison, & Leventhal-Belfer, 1982	Low-income disturbed family infant units with infants under 1 year	Focus on improving parent-infant interaction, parental competence, infant development, and family supports with psychodynamic, ecological, systems, and transactional perspectives	Remedial and secondary prevention

N. Jackson: I would like to return for a moment to Dr. Pridham's second study, because I think she may be at the beginning of something that in the long run will prove to be very useful to nursing. The use of the simulated problem solving technique is one that seems to me to be potentially very helpful because people who have used this technique in other situations have found that by analyzing the performance of experts in the problem solving situation, they can then develop guidelines for training novices to perform equally well. But at this point in Karen's research she has both an advantage and a problem. The advantage is that the data are sorting out nicely and that there is variance on a number of components of the problem solving process. People aren't all doing the same thing. The problem is that the comparison at this point is between primiparae and multiparae, and I think it may be premature to assume that multiparae are experts. Exactly what constitutes an expert? For example, the children of primiparae are expected to perform better on some cognitive tasks. I hope that you'll be able at some point in your research to obtain some independent assessment of how the children are developing, then reexamine the parents' response in that simulated problem solving situation, and find out which parents were performing like experts on the basis of their child's progress.

J. Fawcett: The question of the expert may be answered in part by the study being conducted by Lorraine Tulman, a doctoral student at the University of Pennsylvania School of Nursing. Tulman is comparing the way mothers and nursing students move through the sequence of touch (from finger tip touch to full embrace) with the newborn. Previous experience with babies will be controlled, of course.

I would also like to comment on Lorraine Walker's findings regarding what is published in journals. *Nursing Research* has an 85-90% rejection rate, not because of priorities in topics, but rather because many studies are theoretically and methodologically flawed and because many of those that are not severely flawed are very poorly written.

K. Barnard: I'd like to move on to the topic of who provides support. I think that the findings in Dr. Pridham's work are interesting in terms of support provided by fathers and books. We've finished a study about nursing intervention during the first 3 months of life (Barnard, 1982). We had three models. One was a highly individualistic model based on assessment, where the nurse was free to do whatever she felt was necessary. This model involved the development of a therapeutic personal relationship between the nurse and the mother. The second was an information model where the nurse used a structured protocol to instruct the mother about her infant's behavior. The third was a more broadly based family health model. When we looked at outcomes of mothers and infants at 3 and 10 months, we essentially found no differences in terms of which model was used, except for a group of families we called multiproblems.

One interesting finding relates to the topic under discussion; perhaps you can help us figure out what the data mean. At 6 months we sent the mothers a questionnaire, partly to get information, but also to keep track of them. We asked them to check on a list of topics which ones had been discussed by the nurse. Meanwhile the nurses filled out a nursing log reporting what they did on each contact. From that nursing log, we coded what the nurse reported. You've seen data from part of the log in the paper our group has presented at this conference. On the topic of birth control, for example, data from the nurses' logs showed similar nurse coverage of birth control, yet 90% of the mothers in the individualized model reported that the nurse talked to them about birth control, whereas only 30% of the mothers indicated that this had been discussed in the other two groups. This raises a question for me—what makes a person link up the information given with the person giving it? In other words, why is it that fathers were attributed with giving this information to the mother? Why weren't the nurse clinicians credited?

It seems to me there is another dimension here, one affected by the person's interpersonal relationships. It, therefore, might be important to consider this relationship when a person identifies sources of information. On one hand, I could say that it really doesn't matter who they say gives them information, but on the other hand, I think it represents an interesting phenomenon.

J. Fawcett: Kishi's study is one that examined the type of interaction between health care provider and client recall of information in well-baby clinics (Kishi, 1981). Flander's Interaction Analysis System was used to code the health care provider (nurse or pediatrician) and client's (the baby's mother) interaction. The results of the study indicated that recall was related to the amount of information given rather than to the type of interaction. More specifically, recall was lower when only a little information or a great deal of information was given. The findings suggest there may be a critical amount of information associated with enhanced client recall of that information. Perhaps that is what is occurring in Dr. Barnard's study. In other words, perhaps the different programs are structured so that certain amounts of information are provided during each interaction, and that the program with the critical amount of information is the one where the mother's recall is enhanced.

G. Anderson: Twice today it has occurred to me that books may be an important source of support for parents. Books could be read at the parents' own learning pace and when they were feeling receptive. Parents may not be able to take in all the information that is given verbally, even if they are feeling receptive, because it may be given too fast. However, they can reread the books when necessary. These may be additional reasons why nurses should start writing more books of this sort.

B. Bishop: I want to follow up on Gene Anderson's comment. As a practicing nurse, I wasn't surprised at that number at all, not that there is a relationship necessarily. I remember the team I was working with spent an enormous amount of time going through materials to recommend to people who had a 12th grade education, a 9th grade education, a 6th grade education, or for those who could hardly read and write. The experience that really surprised me when working with the young or with those persons who had short attention spans was that if you handed them just one of the instruction sheets at a time, they would read it all. Then they would keep all of them and put them together in a loose leaf notebook and share it with all their friends and neighbors. Also, they were able to refer back to these resources themselves. However, I don't necessarily think there is a correlation between these resources and the fact that the health care provider told patients about it. But evaluating learning materials is one activity where you spend a lot of time so that when a problem arises, even if there's no professional readily available to answer questions, the client will have some initial information on hand.

G. Crawford: I want to ask Dr. Pridham about the first study. You said that you looked at things that made the day better or helped and indicated that these were supports. You gave us a few examples of what some of those supports were. I wonder if you could share some more information with us about the items or persons you identified in that study as support. Could you comment how these items or persons fit into the definitions of support that we have been discussing?

K. Pridham: I think that's a good question. We retained the language that the parents used so that the most proximal categories maintained their designations. There is a hierarchy of categories. Obviously we had to reduce the data for some purposes in order to answer some kinds of questions, but we were able to identify and code the major categories with a fair amount of reliability.

Our problem with coding the open-ended data was primarily miscodes concerning the issue. People identified issues related to themselves as factors that helped and made the day better, e.g., "I slept all night last night." Tasks or responsibilities that were identified as supports included long entries such as, "I went to the office to finish up some work." As was the case for all of the categories, resources were identified either as stressors or supports. The lack of help with the baby, or an older child, or some other kind of tangible aid which was not provided showed up as a stressor. In the support column, mothers might state, "My mother cooked supper last night, and my husband took the older child out for a walk. My friend gave me a car seat."

There were some issues of direct aid in the category of resources. The opportunity to have lunch with a friend and going out to a fast food place to eat were the kinds of remarks that were often made about things that made the day better, and we coded them in that broad category of activities and plans. Behavior includes issues of affect and affirmation. Women remarked, "Somebody complimented me on the way I looked. Susan, the older child, cooperated today."

There was also a category of labeled conditions. The remark, "The weather was terrible," was said often, and primarily identified as a stressor. Infrequently occurring or unusual events like a death in the family, the neighbor's trailer house burned, somebody had an auto accident, and very unusual events were coded as stressors. Events that mothers identified as supports included, "Husband accepted into graduate school," "Baby had her 4 weeks' birthday today," and "Christmas today."

REFERENCES

Abernethy, V.D. (1973). Social network and response to the maternal role. *International Journal of Sociology of the Family, 3,* 86-92.

Adams, M. (1963). Early concerns of primigravidae mothers regarding infant care activities. *Nursing Research, 12*(2), 72-77.

Adler, P.T. (1982). An analysis of the concept of competence in individuals and social systems. *Community Mental Health Journal, 18*(2), 34-45.

American Nurses' Association. (1981). *Research priorities for the 1980's.* Kansas City, MO: Author.

Ausubel, D.P., & Sullivan, E.V. (1970). *Theory and problems of child development* (2nd ed.). New York: Grune & Stratton.

Barnard, K.E. (1979, July—1982, June). *Models of newborn nursing.* Project funded by the Division of Nursing, Public Health Service, Grant R01 NU-00719-03.

Barnard, K.E., & Eyres, S.J. (Eds.). (1979). *Child health assessment, Part 2: The first year of life.* (DHEW pub. No. HRA 79-25). Washington, DC: Superintendent of Documents.

Belsky, J., Robins, E., & Gamble, W. (in press). The determinants of parental competence: Toward a contextual theory. In M. Lewis & L. Rosenblum (Eds.), *Social connections: Beyond the dyad.*

Benner, P. (1982). From novice to expert. *American Journal of Nursing, 82*(3), 402-407.

Berzonsky, M.D. (1978). Ausubel's satellization theory: Application to some research on adolescents. *Adolescence, 13,* 167-180.

Boyd, R.D. (1969). *The relationship between the molar and molecular models.* Unpublished manuscript, University of Wisconsin-Madison, Department of Continuing and Vocational Education, School of Education.

Buehler, C.A., & Hogan, M.J. (1980). Managerial behavior and stress in families headed by divorced women: A proposed framework. *Family Relations, 29,* 525-532.

Caplan, G. (1961). *An approach to community mental health.* New York: Grune & Stratton.

Caplan, G. (1981). Mastery of stress: Psychosocial aspects. *American Journal of Psychiatry, 138,* 413-420.

Capon, N., & Kuhn, D. (1979). Logical reasoning in the supermarket: Adult females' use of a proportional reasoning strategy in an everyday context. *Developmental Psychology, 15*(4), 450-457.

Cassel, J. (1974). Psychosocial processes and "stress": Theoretical formulation. *International Journal of Health Services, 4*(3), 471-481.

Chao, Y.M. (1979). Cognitive operations during maternal role enactment. *Maternal Child Nursing Journal, 8,* 211-274.

Cibulka, N.J., & Price, E.A. (1978). *Concerns of new parents during the early postpartum period.* Unpublished master's thesis, University of Wisconsin-Madison.

Cobb, S. (1976). Social support as a moderator of life stress. *Psychosomatic Medicine, 38,* 300-314.

Cowen, E.L. (1977). Baby-steps toward primary prevention. *American Journal of Community Psychology, 5,* 1-22.

Cronenwett, L.R., & Kunst-Wilson, W. (1981). Stress, social support, and the transition to fatherhood. *Nursing Research, 30,* 196-201.

Danish, S.S., Smyer, M.A., & Nowak, C.A. (1980). Developmental intervention: Enhancing life-event processes. In P.B. Baltes & O.G. Brim (Eds.), *Life-span development and behavior* (Vol. 3). New York: Academic Press.

Dincher, J.R., & Stidger, S.L. (1976). Evaluation of a written simulation format for clinical nursing judgment. *Nursing Research, 25,* 280-285.

Elstein, A.S., & Bordage, G. (1979). Psychology of clinical reasoning. In G.C. Stone, F. Cohen, N.E. Adler, & Associates (Eds.), *Health psychology: A handbook.* San Francisco: Jossey-Bass.

Elstein, A.S., Shulman, L.S., & Sprafka, S.A. (1978). *Medical problem solving: An analysis of clinical reasoning.* Cambridge: Harvard University Press.

Ericsson, K., & Simon, H.A. (1980). Verbal reports as data. *Psychological Review, 87,* 215-251.

Evanshko, V., & Bauwens, E. (1976). Cognitive analysis and decision-making in medical emergencies. In M. Leninger (Ed.), *Transcultural health care issues and conditions: Health care dimensions.* Philadelphia: F.A. Davis.

Fingarette, H. (1963). *The self in transformation.* New York: Harper Torchbooks.

Funderburk, S., Richardson, K., & Johnson, J. (1977). The adaptation of parents: Postpartum crisis counseling (letter). *Pediatrics, 60,* 383.

Goldfried, M.R., & D'Zurilla, T.J. (1969). A behavioral-analytic model for assessing competence. In C.D. Spielberger (Ed.), *Current topics in clinical and community psychology* (Vol. 1). New York: Academic Press.

Gore, S. (1978). The effect of social support in moderating the health consequences of unemployment. *Journal of Health and Social Behavior, 19(2),* 157-165.

Gottlieb, B.H. (Ed.). (1981). *Social networks and social support.* Beverly Hills, CA: Sage.

Greeno, J.G. (1980). Trends in the theory of knowledge for problem solving. In D.T. Tuma & F. Reif (Eds.), *Problem solving and education: Issues in teaching and research.* Hillsdale, NJ: Lawrence Erlbaum Associates.

Gruis, M. (1977). Beyond maternicity: Postpartum concerns of mothers. *MCN: American Journal of Maternal Child Nursing, 2,* 182-188.

Hammond, K.R., Kelly, K.J., Castellan, N.J., Schneider, R.J., & Vancini, M. (1966). Clinical inference in nursing: Use of information-seeking strategies by nurses. *Nursing Research, 15(4),* 330-336.

Hammond, K.R., Kelly, K.J., Schneider, R.J., & Vancini, M. (1966a). Clinical inference in nursing: Analyzing cognitive tasks representative of nursing problems. *Nursing Research, 15(2),* 134-138.

Hammond, K.R., Kelly, K.J., Schneider, R.J., & Vancini, M. (1966b). Clinical inference in nursing: Information units used. *Nursing Research, 15(3),* 236-243.

Hammond, K.R., Kelly, K.J., Schneider, R.J., & Vancini, M. (1967). Clinical inference in nursing: Revising judgments. *Nursing Research, 16(1),* 38-45.

Heller, K. (1979). The effects of social support: Prevention and treatment implications. In A.P. Goldstein & F.H. Kanfer (Eds.), *Maximizing treatment gains.* New York: Academic Press.

Hercules, C., & Charney, E. (1969). Availability and attentiveness: Are these compatible in pediatric practice? *Clinical Pediatrics, 8(7),* 381-388.

Hinshaw, A.S. (1979a). Planning for logical consistency among three research structures. *Western Journal of Nursing Research, 1,* 250-253.

Hinshaw, A.S. (1979b). Theoretical substruction: An assessment process. *Western Journal of Nursing Research, 1,* 319-324.

Hollingshead, A.B. (1975). *Four-factor index of social status.* Unpublished manuscript, Yale University.

Holzemer, W.L., Schleutermann, J.A., Farrand, L.L., & Miller, A.G. (1981). A validation study: Simulations as a measure of nurse practitioners' problem-solving skills. *Nursing Research, 30*(3), 139-144.

Inhelder, B., & Piaget, J. (1958). *The growth of logical thinking from childhood to adolescence.* New York: Basic Books.

Iscoe, I. (1974). Community psychology and competent community. *American Psychologist, 29,* 607-613.

Iscoe, I. (1982, September). Personal communication.

Kahn, R.L., & Antonucci, T.C. (1980). Convoys over the life course: Attachment, roles, and social support. In P.B. Baltes & O.G. Brim (Eds.), *Life-span development and behavior* (Vol. 3). New York: Academic Press.

Kaplan, B.H., & Cassel, J.C., & Gore, S. (1977). Social support and health. *Medical Care, 15*(5), 47-58.

Kassirer, J.P., & Gorry, G.A. (1978). Clinical problem solving: A behavioral analysis. *Annals of Internal Medicine, 89,* 245-255.

Kishi, K.I. (1981). *Communication patterns between health care provider and client and recall of health information.* Doctoral dissertation, University of Pennsylvania.

Klaus, M.H., & Kennell, J.H. (1976). *Maternal-infant bonding.* St. Louis: C.V. Mosby.

Klein, D.M., & Hill, R. (1979). Determinants of family problem-solving effectiveness. In W.R. Burr, R. Hill, F.I. Nye, & I.L. Reiss (Eds.), *Contemporary theories about the family: Research-based theories* (Vol. 1). New York: The Free Press.

Lazarus, R.S. (1981). Little hassles can be hazardous to health. *Psychology Today, 15,* 58-62.

Leifer, M., Spiker, D., Roth, C.H., Morrison, M., & Leventhal-Belfer, L. (1982, March). *Parent-infant development service: Clinical research of parent-infant interaction.* Symposium presented at the International Conference on Infant Studies, Austin, TX.

McGuire, J.C., & Gottlief, B.H. (1979). Social support groups among new parents: An experimental study in primary prevention. *Journal of Clinical Child Psychology, 8,* 111-116.

McLaughlin, F.E., Carr, J.W., & Delucchi, K.L. (1981). Measurement properties of clinical simulation tests: Hypertension and chronic obstructive pulmonary disease. *Nursing Research, 30*(1), 5-9.

Miller, G.A., Pribram, K.H., & Galanter, E. (1960). *Plans and structure of behavior.* New York: Holt, Rinehart & Winston.

Miller, B.C., & Sollie, D.L. (1980). Normal stresses during the transition to parenthood. *Family Relations Journal of Applied Family & Child Studies, 29*(4), 459-465.

Mitchell, R.E. (1982). Social networks and psychiatric clients: The personal and environmental context. *American Journal of Community Psychology, 10,* 387-401.

Mitchell, R.E., & Trickett, E.J. (1980). Task force report: Social networks as mediators of social support. *Community Mental Health Journal, 16*(1), 27-44.

Neisser, U. (1976). *Cognition and reality: Principles and implications of cognitive psychology.* San Francisco: W.H. Freeman.

Newell, A., & Simon, H.A. (1972). *Human problem solving.* Englewood Cliffs, NJ: Prentice-Hall.

Nisbett, R., & Ross, L. (1980). *Human inference: Strategies and shortcomings of social judgment.* Englewood Cliffs, NJ: Prentice-Hall.

Norbeck, J.S. (1981). Social support: A model for clinical research and application. *Advances in Nursing Science, 3*(4), 43-59.

Norman, G.R., & Feightner, J.W. (1981). A comparison of behavior on simulated patients and patient management problems. *Medical Education, 15,* 26-32.

Nover, R.A., Williams, D.W., & Ward, D.B. (1981). Preventive intervention with infants in multi-risk-factor families. *Children Today, 10*(4), 27-31.

Nuckolls, K.B., Cassel, J., & Kaplan, B.H. (1972). Psychosocial assets, life crises and the prognosis of pregnancy. *American Journal of Epidemiology, 95*(5), 431-441.

Piaget, J., & Inhelder, B. (1969). *The psychology of the child.* New York: Basic Books.

Powell, D.R. (1980). Personal social networks as a focus for primary prevention of child mistreatment. *Infant Mental Health Journal, 1,* 232-239.

Pridham, K.F., & Hansen, M.F. (1980). An observation methodology for the study of interactive clinical problem-solving behavior in primary care settings. *Medical Care, 18*(4), 360-375.

Pridham, K.F., Hansen, M.F., Bradley, M.E., & Heighway, S.M. (1982). Issues of concern to mothers of new babies. *Journal of Family Practice, 14*(6), 1079-1085.

Pridham, K.F., Hansen, M.F., & Conrad, H.H. (1977). Anticipatory care as problem solving in family medicine and nursing. *Journal of Family Practice, 4*(6), 1077-1081.

Pridham, K.F., Hansen, M.F., & Conrad, H.H. (1978). *A paradigm of problem-solving behavior.* Unpublished paper.

Pridham, K.F., Hansen, M.F., & Conrad, H.H. (1979). Anticipatory problem solving: Models for clinical practice and research. *Sociology of Health and Illness, 1*(2), 177-194.

Pridham, K.F., Hansen, M.F., Heighway, S.M., & Bradley, M.D. (1980, October). *Anticipatory care of the problem-solving behavior of the parents of new babies.* Final report, Grant No. RO1-NU-00606, Division of Nursing, DHHS.

Robertson, W.O. (1961). An investigation of maternal concerns by mail survey. *Child Development, 32,* 423-436.

Russell, C. (1974). Transition to parenthood: Problems and gratifications. *Journal of Marriage and the Family, 36,* 294-301.

Ryan, T.A., Joiner, B.L., & Ryan, B.F. (1980). *Minitab reference manual.* University Park, PA: Pennsylvania State University.

Shavelson, R.J., & Stern, P. (1981). Research on teachers' pedagogical thoughts, judgments, decisions, and behavior. *Review of Educational Research, 51*(4), 455-498.

Shulman, L.S., & Elstein, A.S. (1975). Studies of problem solving, judgement, and decision making. In F.N. Kerlinger (Ed.), *Review of research in education* (Vol. 3). Itasca, IL: F.E. Peacock.

Sonnen, B. (1980). *Problems identified by parents who telephone an ambulatory pediatric care setting.* Unpublished master's thesis, University of Wisconsin-Madison.

Spivack, G., Platt, J.J., & Shure, M.B. (1976). *The problem-solving approach to adjustment.* San Francisco: Jossey-Bass.

Sumner, G., & Fritsch, J. (1977). Postnatal parental concerns: The first six weeks of life. *Journal of Obstetric and Gynecologic Nursing, 6*(3), 27-32.

Thomas, A., & Chess, S. (1977). *Temperament and development.* New York: Brunner/Mazel.

Tversky, A., & Kahneman, D. (1974). Judgment under uncertainty, heuristics, and biases. *Science, 195*(1), 124-131.

Tyler, N.B., & Kogan, K.L. (1977). Reduction of stress between mothers and their handicapped children. *American Journal of Occupational Therapy, 31*(3), 151-155.

Vaughn, W.T., Huntington, D.S., Samuels, T.E., Bilmes, M., & Shapiro, M.E. (1975). Family mental health maintenance: A new approach to primary prevention. *Hospital and Community Psychiatry, 26,* 503-508.

Walcer, C.S., & Slaughter, D. (1979, March). *Ego development and parenting style: A developmental framework for understanding of maternal attitudes.* Paper presented at the Biennial Meeting of the Society for Research in Child Development, San Francisco, CA.

Walker, L.O. (1976, June). *Identifying nursing needs of adoptive parents.* Final Report, Center for Health Care Research and Evaluation, The University of Texas, School of Nursing, Austin, TX.

Walker, L.O. (1982, May). *The present state of nursing research.* Paper presented at the Nursing Research Conference Honoring Mabel Wandelt, R.N., Ph.D., The University of Texas at Austin School of Nursing, Austin, TX.

Wandersman, L., Wandersman, A., & Kahn, S. (1980). Social support in the transition to parenthood. *Journal of Community Psychology, 8,* 332-342.

Wolkenheim, B.J. (1982). *A descriptive analysis of the problem-finding operations of nurses in a secondary care setting.* Unpublished master's thesis, University of Wisconsin-Madison.

Social Networks and Social Support of Primigravida Mothers and Fathers*

Linda R. Cronenwett, R.N., Ph.D.

Most researchers have examined the effects of stress and social support on pregnancy outcomes without identifying the relationship between social support and social network factors. While the type and amount of support have been shown to be related to pregnancy outcomes, the sources of that support and the influence of network structure on a person's supportive resources have not been defined. Network factors, in fact, may predict perceived support or may explain more of the variance in pregnancy outcomes than social support does alone. The objectives of this study were to describe the social networks of primigravida women and their husbands; to determine if there are any differences in social networks based on gender, education, or income; and to examine the relationships among network characteristics, demographic characteristics, and perceived availability of support from network members.

The 54 couples who composed the sample for this study were recruited through local physicians who provided the names of all clients who were primigravidas, living with the father of the child, and residing within 25 miles of Ann Arbor, Michigan. During the third trimester of pregnancy, couples were interviewed in their homes, and each parent completed a Social Network Inventory (SNI). The SNI obtained information about the size of the network, role relationships, frequency of contact, percent of uniplex relationships, and degree of overlap with spouse's social network. In addition, parents were provided with definitions of each of House's (1981) four types of social support and asked to indicate which forms of support they received from each network member.

*Preparation of this presentation was supported in part by a grant from the Division of Nursing, US DHHS, R01 NU-00856, awarded to William Wilson.

This paper was revised after the conference in response to some of the comments noted in the Critique presented by J. Fawcett.

Both individual variables (age and educational level) and network structure variables (size, percent kin, percent females, frequency, and density) were significantly associated with the amount of perceived social support. For each type of support, the independent variables associated with support were different for men and women.

SOCIAL SUPPORT

Early investigations of the relationship between health and social support focused on the interplay among specific stressors, social support, and various measures of physical and psychological well-being. By and large, access to social support was found to be associated with a variety of positive health outcomes (Cobb, 1976; Dean & Lin, 1977; Nuckolls, Cassel, & Kaplan, 1972). A thorough understanding of this phenomenon, however, was limited by the fact that researchers failed to employ a common conceptualization of social support and made few attempts to document the specific relationships from which support was assumed to be derived (Thoits, 1982). Fortunately, these shortcomings are gradually being corrected. For example, conceptualizations of social support used by many investigators are now notably similar (see Table 1). A more important advance, however, has been the application of the concepts and techniques of social network analysis to studies of social support (Barnes, 1972; Mitchell, 1969; Gottlieb, 1981; Wellman, 1981).

Researchers who have applied social network analysis to the study of social support and health outcomes have studied subjects in a variety of stressful contexts, such as adolescents who are pregnant (Barrera, 1981), recently bereaved widows (Hirsch, 1980; Walker, MacBride, & Vachon, 1977) older women returning to school (Hirsch, 1980), single parents (McLanahan, Wedemeyer, & Adelberg, 1981), new parents (Richardson & Kagan, 1979), and recently divorced women (Wilcox, 1981). On the whole, these studies indicate that network structure is associated with different levels of perceived support, depending on the specific life context and the type of support in which the person is interested. This occurs in part because social ties that are considered supportive in one context can be stressful in other situations (Wellman, 1981). Even social networks themselves may change as a result of certain life situations or transitions (Thoits, 1982). In order to understand the relationship between social network structure and perceived social support more fully, additional effort must be focused on gathering data which pertain to many different stressful like contexts.

EFFECT ON TRANSITION TO PARENTHOOD

As clinicians responsible for helping couples integrate parenthood into their lives, nurses need to understand how network structure and perceived support are related to a couple's ease and satisfaction during the period of transition to parenthood. Most researchers have examined the effects of stress and social support on pregnancy and outcomes without identifying the rela-

Table 1
Comparison of Social Support Conceptualizations

House (1981)	Barrera (1981)	Hirsch (1980)	Kahn & Antonucci (1980) Norbeck, Lindsey & Carrieri (1981)	Mitchell & Trickett (1980)	Power & Parke (in press)	Walker, MacBridge, & Vachon (1977)
Emotional	Intimate interaction	Emotional	Affect Affirmation	Emotional	Relational	Emotional
Instrumental	Material and physical assistance	Tangible assistance	Aid	Task-oriented assistance	Physical	Material aid and services
Information	Guidance	Cognitive guidance		Access to new information and social contacts	Information	Information
Appraisal	Feedback Social participation	Social reinforcement Socializing	Affirmation	Communication of expectations, evaluation, and shared world view	Ideological	Access to new social contacts

tionship between social support and social network factors. Social support has been found to have a positive direct or interactive association with both physical (Nuckolls et al., 1972; Norbeck & Tilden, 1983), and psychological (Paykel, Emms, Fletcher, & Rassaby, 1980; Carveth & Gottlieb, 1979) outcomes of pregnancy. In these studies, the type and amount of support have been demonstrated to be related to pregnancy outcomes, but the sources of that support and the influence of the structure of the social network on a person's supportive resources have not been defined. At this point, then, the relationship between social network structure and perceived support during the specific life context of becoming a parent is not clear. Network factors, in fact, may predict perceived support or explain more of the variance in pregnancy outcomes than social support does alone.

The information gained from two studies that have attempted to describe the relationships among all three types of variables has been limited by the research design and sample selections involved. Barrera (1981) studied only pregnant adolescents and collected all his data at one point during the pregnancy. Richardson and Kagan (1979), on the other hand, studied older, college educated, primiparous couples and collected data only during the time period of 3-7 months postpartum. No one has yet done a longitudinal study to determine how expectant parents' social networks and perceived social support prior to delivery relates to postpartum outcome measures. Furthermore, with the exception of Richardson and Kagan (1979) who included fathers in half of their study, the subjects in all of the studies of parents mentioned previously have been mothers. Almost no information, therefore, is available about social support, social network structure, and fathers' responses to parenthood.

The majority of psychological outcome measures in the studies cited previously were measures of general symptomatology related to affect, anxiety, somatic complaints, depression, and self-esteem. The only exceptions were found in studies by Carveth and Gottlieb (1979) and Richardson and Kagan (1979), both of which included one measure that was specifically related to parental stresses or satisfactions. While the generalized measures do provide information about a certain form of health outcome, it is not clear how these measures relate to a person's adaptation to the parental role in particular.

While literature reviews by both Cronenwett and Kunst-Wilson (1981) and Power and Parke (in press) contained hypotheses regarding relationships between type of support, sources of support, and specific outcomes, neither reviews included the influence of social network characteristics in their hypotheses. Due to the limitations of the studies by Barrera (1981) and Richardson and Kagan (1979) in which these relationships were addressed, there is little empirical basis for hypothesizing about the nature of the interrelationships among network structure, social support, and psychological outcomes of the transition to parenthood for either mothers or fathers. Research in this area of study, then, is essentially exploratory in nature, although the general hypothesis supported by the stress paradigm will be tested; i.e., that interrelationships among social network structure, perceived social support, and outcomes of pregnancy do exist.

STUDY

The purpose of this paper is to summarize the data on the relationships found between two sets of variables: social network structure and perceived social support. The data presented in this paper are derived from a larger study which was designed to examine the interrelationships among three sets of variables for couples having their first child (Cronenwett, 1983). Specifically, the objectives in this paper cover the first phase of the larger study and are to: describe the social networks of primigravida women and their husbands; determine if there are any differences in social networks based on a person's gender, educational level, or income; and examine the relationships among network characteristics, demographic characteristics, and perceived availability of support from network members.

Sample

To obtain a sample that was representative of primigravida couples living within 25 miles of Ann Arbor, Michigan, letters requesting assistance in recruiting subjects were sent to all obstetrical and family practice groups in the area. Of the 22 group practices or individual physicians contacted, representatives of 6 groups (8 physicians) agreed to participate. One physician was a university faculty member, whereas the rest were in private practice. Their clients were delivered at one of the three different hospitals that operate within the designated geographical area. From October 1981 to May 1982, these physicians provided the names of all clients who were 5 months' pregnant, having their first child, living with the father of the child, and residing within 25 miles of Ann Arbor. Clients were subsequently contacted by project investigators, first by mail, and then by telephone. In addition, since a few more subjects were required during this time period than were obtained by the above procedure and since all the couples recruited by the above method had chosen to attend childbirth classes, one Lamaze-sponsored program was used for the purpose of recruiting additional subjects.

A total of 142 referrals were received from participating physicians. Eleven couples were sent letters, but could not be reached by telephone and did not respond to the letters. Another 26 couples were ineligible for participation due to losing their baby, separation or divorce, not speaking English, plans to leave the area, living outside the designated area, or already having a child. Of the 105 eligible couples, 50 (48%) initially agreed to participate in this longitudinal study.

At the Lamaze-sponsored program where a childbirth film was being shown, the opportunity to participate in the study was offered to a group of 44 couples. After the project was described in detail, each couple was asked to indicate on a sign-up sheet whether or not they were interested in becoming subjects. Twenty-one couples were ineligible for the project because their expected dates of confinement were either too early or too late. Of the remaining 23 couples, 8 (35%) agreed to participate, bringing the total subject pool to 58 couples. Of these 58 couples, 4 couples dropped out before completing the first phase of this longitudinal project, 2 couples delivered prematurely, 1 husband took an out-of-town work assignment, and 1 couple changed their minds about participating. This left 54 couples who composed the sample for this study.

Instrument

The Social Network Inventory (SNI), the instrument used to collect data on network structure and perceived social support, was developed by the investigator. The SNI required straightforward information about members of the subject's social network: gender; age; marital status; role relationship to the subject (relative, coworker, neighbor, or any other kind of friend); whether or not the person had children and those children's ages; and the frequency of face-to-face, telephone, or letter contact the subject had at that time with each network member.

Two issues of concern in this and other studies are: how the subjects define network members, and how the researcher ascertains the types of support derived from network members. Barrera (1981) and Wilcox (1981) obtained their subjects' lists of network members by asking for the names of people to whom subjects turned for various forms of support such as to borrow money or to talk about a personal problem. In contrast, Brim (1974), Hirsch (1980), Norbeck, Lindsey, & Carrieri (1981), and Richardson and Kagan (1979) asked their subjects to list their important network members first and then asked what forms of support were received from each member. The latter approach was used in this study, with the following opening instructions to the subjects:

> In column A we would like you to list at least one and at most ten people who are important in your life right now. These people may be family members, including your spouse, or they may be neighbors, coworkers, or friends. The people you list should be those with whom you share something significant. Do not write out the whole names of these people. Instead, just enter three letters for each person--the first letter of their first name and the first two letters of the last name. For instance, if the person's name was Mary Smith, you would enter MSM. It is not necessary to enter ten names. Only list people who are truly meaningful to you. On the other hand, if you have more than ten people you would like to name, just list the ten most important ones.

No requirement was made for a certain frequency of contact with network members.

The conceptualization of social support advanced by House (1981) was adapted for use in the SNI. Rather than compiling a list of supportive behaviors which would hopefully tap a subject's access to social support, the approach used here was to present subjects with a written description of the types of support. Instrumental support was labeled material support and appraisal support was called comparison support in the SNI in an effort to increase the clarity of meaning of these terms for lay subjects. The definitions and the format used by the interviewer follow:

> Now we would like you to think about the people you have listed in terms of what kinds of support they give you. On this card, we have listed four kinds of support which I will go over with you now.
>
> A. Emotional. The person communicates love, caring, trust, or concern for you.
> B. Material. The person directly helps you, such as through gifts of money, help with house chores, help with your work, etc.
> C. Information. The person tells you things you need to know, and helps you solve your problems by sharing information or finding out things for you.
> D. Comparison. This person helps you learn about yourself just by being someone with similar experiences. He or she is like you in some important way, and you feel supported because you can share ideas and feelings with someone like yourself.
>
> Do you have any questions about what we mean by any of these kinds of support? (If not, the interviewer continues.)
>
> Now, thinking about the people you've listed, show which kind or kinds of support you get from each person by writing A, B, C, and/or D in the column.
>
> If you receive none of these forms of support from a person, enter an X in that person's space.

After completing their SNIs and returning the card with the definitions of support to the interviewer, 22 subjects were asked to write, in their own words, what they understood to be the definition of each type of support. In this check on the clarity of the definitions used, two judges rated the percentage of complete and correct answers for the definition of emotional support to be 100%, material support as 91%, informational support as 86%, and comparison support as 82%.

Perceived support for each subject was calculated by totaling the number of persons in the SNI from whom the subjects indicated they obtained each of the four types of support. The network structure variables derived from the SNI were:

1. **Size.** Total number of persons listed.
2. **Frequency.** Total number of contacts per week with network members.
3. **Percent** of the network who were relatives.
4. **Percent** of the network from whom the subject received only one form of support (uniplex relationships).
5. **Boundary density.** The degree to which the subjects' network members overlapped with the network members named by their spouse.

Procedure

An outline of the project requirements was sent to each couple with an introductory letter. If the couple indicated an interest in the project, they were visited in their home by one of two project staff members during their seventh month of pregnancy. A consent form approved by the Human Subjects Review Committee was read by each parent, and questions, if any, were answered. If the consent form was signed, demographic data were collected and a SNI was completed by each parent. The time required for the total interview was approximately 45 minutes.

Table 2
Characteristics of Primigravida Couples[a]

Characteristic	Descriptive Values			
	Men		Women	
	Mean	(SD)	Mean	(SD)
Age	28.9	(4.1)	26.9	(3.6)
Number of Years of Formal Education	16.2	(2.7)	15.4	(2.6)
Annual Family Income			Percentage	
Less than $10,000			3.7	
$10,000-$13,999			3.7	
$14,000-$17,999			11.1	
$18,000-$21,999			3.7	
$22,000-$25,999			11.1	
$26,000-$29,999			18.5	
$30,000-$33,999			13.0	
$34,000 or more			35.2	

[a]N = 54

RESULTS

Descriptions of Subjects

Table 2 contains age, educational, and economic levels for all study subjects. When both men and women were considered, the mean age was 27.9 years, with a mean educational level of 15.8 years of formal schooling. The gross income of 52% of the study families was under $30,000 a year, with the remaining 48% earning over that amount. Two subjects were black, two were oriental, and the rest were white. All couples were married.

Social Network Characteristics

The size of subjects' social networks ranged from 4 to 10, with a mean of 8.5 members. Most network members were married (mean = 73%). While an average of 64% of network members had children, only 16% had children under 5 years of age. The mean number of people from each category of role relationship was: relatives 5.5, coworkers .7, neighbors .2, and friends .2.

A mean of 50% of the network members were the same age as the subject, plus or minus 5 years; 7% were more than 5 years younger, 9% were 6-15 years older, and 34% were more than 15 years older (parent and grandparent-age relatives). Networks were composed of a mean of 55% females and 45% males. The percentage of network members who were already parents themselves and in addition, who were the same gender and same age, plus or minus 5 years as the subject, ranged from 0-67%, with a mean of 13% of network members.

Frequency of contact was determined by asking subjects to indicate the average number of times per week that they had letter, telephone, or face-to-face contact with each network member. If, on the average, they had less than once a week contact, they were instructed to put an X next to that person. Total frequency, then, was obtained by adding up the numbers in the frequency column of the SNI, including adding a value of one for every two Xs. Excluding their spouses, subjects averaged 11.8 contacts with network members per week (range 1-35).

Finally, network members listed by spouses were compared to determine the boundary density of their social networks. The percentage of network members listed by both members of a couple ranged from 0-100%, with a mean of 27%. While the same neighbors were never listed by both spouses and only one couple had a coworker of one spouse appear in the other's network, 17% of the couples listed the same friend, and 74% of the couples listed at least one common relative.

Impact of Gender, Education, and Income

Gender. While a subject's gender did influence some network characteristics, the similiarities between the networks of men and women in this study were more remarkable than the differences. Men and women did not differ significantly in the size or boundary density of their networks nor in the mean frequency of contact with network members. Their networks were made up of persons similar in age, marital status, role relationship, and percent who were parents. Husbands and wives did not differ in the frequency with which they had contact with parents versus nonparents, or married versus single persons. Finally, male and female subjects perceived similar access to social support. The number of network members from whom they received instrumental, informational, and appraisal support did not differ significantly, although women's mean sources of emotional support totaled 7.7 while men claimed only 6.4.

The differences found between male and female networks were based on the fact that there were significantly more men in men's networks and more women in women's networks (see Table 3). Sixty-four percent of the persons in women's networks are females, compared to 46% females in the men's networks. Table 4 shows the composition of men's and women's networks by gender and role relationship. Although all subjects list male and female relatives in about the same proportion, coworkers, neighbors, and friends are generally the same gender as the focal person.

In terms of frequency of contact, men had a mean of 7.3 contacts per week with men in their networks compared to women's rate of 2.9 ($t = 5.9$, df $= 106$, $p < .001$). In contrast, women saw women members of their networks a mean of 8.7 times per week, while men had contact only 4.0 times per week with women. The only other significant difference between male and female subjects was their source of emotional support. While 81% of men's emotional support came from relatives, only 71% of women's emotional support was derived from that source ($t = 2.4$, df $= 105$, $p < .05$). Women indicated that a mean of 24% of their emotional support came from friends, whereas the corresponding figure for men was only 14% ($t = 2.4$, df $= 105$, $p < .05$).

Table 3
Distribution of Men and Women in Networks by
Gender of Focal Person

Gender of Focal Person	Mean Numbers in Network	
	Men	Women[a]
Male	4.6	3.9
Female	3.0	5.4

[a] $t = 5.24$, df $= 106$, $p < .01$

Table 4
Gender and Role Relationship Composition
of Networks for Males Versus Females

Gender of Focal Person	Mean Percentages							
	Relatives		Coworkers		Neighbors		Friends	
	Male	Female	Male	Female	Male	Female	Male	Female
Male	26	39	8	2	3	0	18	4
Female	30	36	1	6	0	2	4	20

Education. The number of years of formal schooling was significantly correlated with only two of the network and support variables for women and with none of these variables for men. For women, the higher the educational level, the lower the total number of contacts per week with network members ($r = -.30$) and the lower their claimed sources of instrumental support ($r = -.34$). Educational level was not associated with the size, composition, or density of the social network, nor with access to emotional, informational, and appraisal support or the percentage of uniplex versus multiplex ties. In this sample, educational level was also not associated with the subject's age or income level, although income level and age were significantly correlated for both men and women.

Income. Income was positively correlated with age for both men ($r = .37$, $p < .01$) and women ($r = .42$, $p < .01$). No other network, social support, or demographic variables were associated with income level.

Perceived Social Support

Levels of support for each of the four categories — emotional, instrumental (material), informational, and appraisal (comparison) — were obtained by summing the number of people from whom the subject said each type of support was received. Values for these four variables were associated with one another ($r = .21$ to $.53$) (see Table 5).

The mean number of sources of each type of support per subject was: emotional 7.1, instrumental 3.3, informational 4.7, and appraisal 4.7. As mentioned previously, mean emotional support for fathers (6.4) was lower than for mothers (7.8), but means for men and women were essentially the same for instrumental, informational, and appraisal support. Table 6 shows the percent of each kind of support obtained from relatives, coworkers, neighbors, and friends. By comparing the mean percentage of each type of member in the total network to the mean percentage of support they provide, it is seen that relatives provide more than their share of emotional and instrumental

Table 5
Intercorrelations among Social Support Variables

Dependent Variables	Pearson r values (n = 107)		
	Instrumental	Informational	Appraisal
Emotional	.27**	.29**	.35**
Instrumental		.41**	.21**
Informational			.53**

**p<.01

support. For instance, even though relatives comprise only 66% of the total network, they are claimed as sources for 77% of the emotional support and 85% of the instrumental support. In the same way, coworkers give relatively higher amounts of information and appraisal support, and friends are more frequent sources of appraisal support.

Multiplex as opposed to uniplex relationships are characterized by two or more distinct exchange contents such as types of support (Barnes, 1972; Pilisuk & Froland, 1978). For the subjects in this study, the percentage of relationships where only one form of support was received (uniplex) ranged from zero to 80%, with a mean of 23%. The size and boundary density of the network and the subject's age, gender, and education were not associated with the extent to which a network was made up of uniplex relationships. The composition of the network, however, was related to the multiplexity of relationships with the existence of higher percentages of relatives in the network associated with lower percentages of uniplex relationships (r = -.23, p<.05).

Table 6
Sources of Four Types of Social Support by Role Relationship
with Network Members

Type of Support	Relatives (66)[a]	Coworkers (8)[a]	Neighbors (2)[a]	Other friends (23)[a]
Emotional	77	3	1	19
Instrumental	85	7	1	7
Informational	66	13	2	20
Appraisal	56	11	3	29

[a]Mean percent of each type of member in network.

Relationships between Network Structure and Social Support

The final question to be answered is how important are network characteristics in predicting perceived levels of support for men and women. Each potential network variable (percent kin, percent females, number of males, number of females, frequency divided into total frequency, and frequency of female and male contact, size, and boundary density) plus the individual variables (age and educational level) were first examined for the strength of their bivariate relationships with the support variables and for their intercorrelations with each other. Tables 7 and 8 contain the intercorrelations among these variables for men and women separately. Because of the high correlation between the frequency variables, they were never used simultaneously in a regression equation. Likewise, percent females was chosen over number of males or females because it represented in one variable most of the information derived from the other two. To check for problems with multicolinearity, the independent variables were regressed on each other to determine how much variance in each was explained by the rest of the independent variables. The percent of explained variance varied from 5-39%, with a mean R^2 of .24. No statistical problems, therefore, were expected in regressions using these variables.

Access to each type of social support was regressed on first the network structure variables and then on the individual and demographic variable sets. Variables with t values of less than 1.5 were removed from further regressions in order to create the most parsimonious equations for predicting perceived support. Independent variables from both sets of variables were then combined into the final equations for each type of support. Tables 9 and 10 summarize the equations that resulted.

Forty-eight percent of the variance in perceived emotional support for men was accounted for by size, percent kin, education, and age. Size explained 37% of the variance, with percent kin adding another 13%, education adding 5%, and age an additional 3%. For women, size accounted for 72% of the variance. The only other variable to remain in the equation was percent females which, surprisingly, was negatively correlated with total emotional support, adding 4% to the explained variance.

Instrumental support was not as strongly associated with network and individual variables. For men, boundary density accounted for 15% of the variance, with total frequency of interaction with network members bringing the total explained variance up to 19%. Frequency of contact with males was the factor most strongly associated with women's perceived instrumental support. In addition, education and age were both negatively correlated with instrumental support, with all three variables together accounting for 20% of the variance.

Table 7
Means, Standard Deviations, and Intercorrelations of Antepartum Variables for Mothers

Independent Variables (Mean, S.D.)	Correlations (N = 53)										
	1	2	3	4	5	6	7	8	9	10	11
1. Size (8.4, 1.7)											
2. Density (28, 23)	.15										
3. % Kin (67, 20)	-.20	.35a									
4. % Females (65, 11)	-.16	-.38a	-.20								
5. Frequency (12, 7)	.40a	.24	.05	-.18							
6. Female Frequency (8.7, 5.0)	.24	-.04	.00	.13	.84a						
7. Male Frequency (2.9, 3.4)	.40a	.40a	.11	-.47a	.75a	.33b					
8. Number Females (5.4, 1.4)	.73a	-.13	-.30b	.55a	.20	.28b	-.01				
9. Number Males (3.0, 1.2)	.59a	.37a	.07	-.88a	.35b	.02	.58a	-.12			
10. Age (27, 3.6)	-.05	-.12	-.16	.06	-.15	-.12	-.08	.02	-.09		
11. Years Education (15, 2.6)	-.14	-.10	-.16	.06	-.26	-.22	-.16	-.06	-.13	.20	
12. Emotional (7.8, 1.9)	.85a	.26	-.12	-.37a	-.39a	.15	.47a	.46a	.69a	-.02	-.10
13. Instrumental (3.0, 2.1)	.15	.17	.10	-.14	.27b	.11	.31b	.02	.20	-.29b	-.29b
14. Informational (4.5, 2.6)	.46a	.23	.14	-.13	.25	.10	.32b	.28b	.34b	-.25	-.28b
15. Appraisal (4.9, 2.1)	.44a	.11	.02	.07	.08	-.06	.15	.42a	.15	-.02	-.12

a p < .01
b p < .05

Table 8
Means, Standard Deviations, and Intercorrelations of Antepartum Variables for Fathers

Independent Variables (Mean, S.D.)	Correlations (N = 54)										
	1	2	3	4	5	6	7	8	9	10	11
1. Size (8.5, 1.7)											
2. Density (27, 21)	.08										
3. % Kin (64, 50)	.07	.31[b]									
4. % Females (46, 16)	-.01	.23	.46[a]								
5. Frequency (11, 6.2)	.16	.14	-.15	.10							
6. Female Frequency (40, 3.5)	.17	.14	.05	.38[a]	.67[a]						
7. Male Frequency (7.3, 4.2)	-.01	.06	-.24	-.22	.78[a]	.17					
8. Number Females (3.9, 1.5)	.53[a]	.20	.37[a]	.82[a]	.19	.46[a]	-.19				
9. Number Males (4.6, 1.5)	.58[a]	-.10	-.28[b]	-.79[a]	-.01	-.26	.17	-.39[a]			
10. Age (29,4)	.17	-.16	.03	.00	-.24	-.25	-.18	.07	.11		
11. Years Education (16, 2.7)	.04	-.09	-.13	-.12	.02	-.16	.08	-.10	.14	.07	
12. Emotional (6.4, 2.6)	.61[a]	.29[b]	.40[a]	.23	.10	.08	-.09	.49[a]	.20	-.07	.20
13. Instrumental (3.6, 2.3)	.14	.39[a]	.25[b]	.15	.26	.17	.13	.19	-.03	-.12	-.17
14. Informational (4.9, 2.1)	.15	.32[b]	-.03	.07	.21	.27[b]	.00	.13	.03	.12	-.17
15. Appraisal (4.6, 2.4)	.33[b]	.15	-.05	.00	.14	.19	-.06	.17	.20	.15	.20

[a] $p < .01$
[b] $p < .05$

Table 9
Variables Associated with Emotional and Instrumental Support

Type of Support	Gender	Independent Variables[a] (N = 54)	Partial r[b]	Increase in R^2	F	p
Emotional	Male	Size	.68	37		
		% Kin	.52	50		
		Education	.34	55		
		Age	-.29	58	17.2	< .01
	Female	Size	.84	72		
		% Females	-.44	76	66.6	< .01
Instrumental	Male	Density	.37	15		
		Frequency (Total)	.22	19	6.1	< .01
	Female	Frequency (Male)	.29	10		
		Education	-.23	16	4.2	< .05
		Age	-.20	20		

[a]Variables included if adding them increased R^2 by at least 3% and if t value > 1.5.
[b]r values when all variables listed are in the equation.

Table 10

Variables Associated with Informational and Appraisal Support

Type of Support	Gender	Independent Variables[a] (N = 54)	Partial r[b]	Increase in R^2	F	p
Informational						
	Male	Density	.29	10		
		Frequency (Female)	.24	15	4.6	< .05
	Female	Size	.47	21		
		Age	-.27	27	9.2	< .01
Appraisal						
	Male	Size	.33	11	6.4	< .05
	Female	Size	.44	19	12.3	< .01

[a]Variables included if adding them increased R^2 by at least 3% and if t value > 1.5.
[b]r values when all variables listed are in the equation.

Density was a significant factor for men a second time by explaining 10% of the variance in informational support. Frequency of interaction with females brought the total R^2 for men's informational support to .15. For women, informational support was best explained ($R^2 = .27$) by size and age, with age being inversely related to women's informational support.

Appraisal support for both men and women was associated only with the size of the network. Network size accounted for 11% and 19% of the variance, respectively.

In summary, the individual variables of education and age were associated with men's emotional support and women's instrumental support. Age was also associated with women's informational support. These findings support the notion that properties of the individual are related to perceived social support. Properties of the social network are also associated with perceived social support, as demonstrated by the fact that each of the network variables were a factor in at least one of the eight final equations. Because the SNI required only significant others to be named as part of the network, size was one of the variables that remained in five of the eight equations. Only instrumental support for men and women and informational support for men were not associated with the size of the network. The degree of overlap between spouse networks played a significant role for men in both instrumental and informational support. Density was never an important factor in explaining women's perceived support. The remaining network variables appeared only once among the eight equations for men and women.

SUMMARY

Kahn and Antonucci (1980) describe a person's support network in terms of three concentric circles. The smallest circle around the focal person includes people whose support is so highly valued that they remain quite stable throughout the years. Geographical proximity is not necessary to maintain these relationships. The second circle consists of family, friends, and coworkers with whom intimacy is somewhat dependent on the role relationship. The final circle of membership includes people named as supportive, but whose relationship with the focal person is definitely role-dependent, and the relationship would change dramatically if they were no longer coworkers, neighbors, etc. Members from the first circle tend to provide more than one type of support, whereas Kahn and Antonucci (1980) believe that members of the third circle are more likely to provide only one type of support.

In limiting the size of our subjects' networks to 10 and in instructing them to list only those members who were truly important to them at this time of their lives, the intention was to tap only the first two levels of network membership. Subjects indicated, however, that they received only one form of support from an average of 23% of their network members. Does this mean that these members are on the periphery of a person's network? When the SNI is completed again at 8 months' postpartum, will the network members dropped from a person's SNI be those where support ties were uniplex?

The social networks of all our subjects were dominated by kin. Whether this is an accurate picture of social networks for same age married couples before they become pregnant is not known. It is possible that by the third trimester of pregnancy, the importance of family members in one's life has been made salient by one's focus on having a child. A comparison needs to be made between our subjects' networks and the networks of a comparable sample of married couples who are not pregnant.

In a similar study, but one where network and social support data were collected when new parents were 3-5 months' postpartum, Richardson and Kagan (1979) found that friends constituted the largest percentage of social network members. They allowed their subjects to list 15 names. Their subjects were slightly older (mean age for men 33.2 years, for women 30.7 years), and most had completed a college degree. These differences in method and subject characteristics may possibly be responsible for the differences in makeup of social networks; or the differences could reflect a change in what kind of persons are most important prior to and after one has a child. Documenting the change or lack of change in our subjects' social networks may help explain these discrepancies.

The findings of this study indicate that men perceive as much access to support in their intimate social networks as women do. The consequences of receiving most of their emotional support from relatives are not clear. At 4 months' postpartum, these subjects will be asked which social ties have become more supportive to them since they became parents and which ties have been characterized by increased stress and conflict. Analyzing these data, along with the original SNI information, may indicate how social networks can predict satisfaction with the transition to parenthood.

The data reported here, unfortunately, are subject to many of the limitations of previous studies. The high refusal rate limits the generalization of the results to a larger population. In addition, when asking subjects to list the kinds of support they receive from network members, one has to acknowledge that perceptions of support may differ depending upon some unknown characteristic of the subject. For instance, even if the definition of emotional support is clear to both men and women, they may differ in their perception of what characteristics of a relationship constitute the exchange of love, caring, trust, or concern. These problems only emphasize the necessity for many studies using different samples of the same population.

This presentation contains the first description of the social networks of primigravida couples, along with descriptions and data on their access to emotional, instrumental, informational, and appraisal support. While valuable in and of itself, the data presented here also serve as base line information for a longitudinal study. When considered along with the results of similar studies, these descriptive data will hopefully lead to the development of theories that will explain the relationships among network structure, social support, and the ease of and satisfaction with becoming a parent.

CRITIQUE

Jacqueline Fawcett, R.N., Ph.D., FAAN

The following critique was prepared for the original presentation, "Social Networks and Social Support of Primigravida Mothers and Fathers," by Linda Cronenwett. Subsequent to the critique, Professor Cronenwett revised the paper, addressing several areas presented in the original critique. A comparison of the published paper and this critique will be helpful to the reader to reinforce how the concerns presented in the critique can be addressed and add substance and clarity to the presentation of research. Such efforts will strengthen nursing research and facilitate the development of nursing knowledge.

Content previously omitted and now included in Professor Cronenwett's paper is an explanation of changes in wording used to describe the four social support variables; an expanded literature review; and the intercorrelations among social support variables (Table 5) and those among network structure and demographic variables (Tables 7 and 8).

It is a distinct honor to have been invited to this conference, and especially to have been asked to comment on Linda Cronenwett's study, "Social Networks and Social Support of Primigravida Mothers and Fathers." My critique of this research is directed by guidelines derived from the criteria for innovative nursing protocols developed for the Conduct and Utilization of Research in Nursing project (Haller, Reynolds, & Horsely, 1979). The guidelines are made up of questions related to the study's scientific merit, clinical relevance, and contribution to nursing knowledge (see Table 1).

These guidelines are in keeping with the purpose of any critique — discussion of the scientific merit of the study and its implications for further study of clinical application. Moreover, use of the guidelines facilitates achievement of this conference's objective which is directed toward reaching an operating consensus of what advances are needed to bring the knowledge of social support to a level useful for professional practice.

SCIENTIFIC MERIT

Replication

Professor Cronenwett's study was designed to collect base line data describing the social networks of primigravida women and their husbands, as well

Table 1
Guidelines to Critique Nursing Research

Scientific Merit

Has the study been replicated? If so, are the findings similar in all situations?

Is the theoretical structure of the study explicit? Is it logical?

Does the research design flow from the theoretical structure? Is the design appropriate for the research question(s)? Are the research instruments valid and reliable?

Does the data analysis answer the research question(s)? Are the statistics appropriate?

Do the findings of the study confirm or refute the theoretical structure? What do the findings mean?

Clinical Relevance

Does the study focus on a significant clinical practice problem?

Do nurses have clinical control of the study variables?

Contribution to Nursing Knowledge

What overall contribution to nursing knowledge does this research make?

What further steps must be taken to develop this area of knowledge for use in nursing practice?

Note. Adapted from: 1) "Utilization of Nursing Research Findings" by J. Fawcett, *Image,* 1982, *14,* 57-59. Copyright 1982 by Sigma Theta Tau. 2) "Contemporary Nursing Research: Its Relevance for Nursing Practice" by J. Fawcett. In N.L. Chaska (Ed.), *The Nursing Profession: A Time to Speak.* Copyright 1983 by McGraw-Hill. Reprinted by permission.

as the types of social support provided by members of the networks during the seventh month of pregnancy. This investigation is not a true replication, although it apparently follows from and is an extension of the unpublished work by Richardson and Kagan (1979), who collected social network and support data from parents 3-5 months after the birth of their child.

Theoretical Structure

The study described in Professor Cronenwett's presentation augments her ongoing research program dealing with social aspects of the family experience of pregnancy (Cronenwett, 1980; Cronenwett & Kunst-Wilson, 1981; Cronenwett & Newmark, 1974; Kunst-Wilson & Cronenwett, 1981). In particular, this presentation expands her empirical work from descriptions of fathers' responses to childbirth and of outcomes of mothers' postpartum support groups, to identification of relatives, friends, and associates who provide various types of social support for both mothers and fathers.

The need for the study is obvious; no other such data exist. The theoretical structure of the study, however, is not explicit. One can speculate that there is some connection between this study and the theoretical paradigm of transition to fatherhood previously described by Cronenwett and Kunst-Wilson

(1981). The place of this presentation in the empirical testing of this paradigm needs to be identified.

Moreover, no rationale is given for the choice of study variables. What led the investigator to suspect that differences in social networks exist for individuals of different gender, educational level, and income? What led her to suspect that the network characteristics of size, frequency, and density; the percent of kin in networks; and the demographic variables of age, education, and income might be differently related to types of social support? And, what led her to suspect that these relationships might differ for men and women?

Additional theoretical questions are raised by this study, as well as by other similar investigations. What is the theoretical link between social networks and social support? Is a social network ipso facto a social support? In other words, it is redundant to include both social network and social support measures in a study?

Furthermore, what are the theoretical definitions of social networks and social support used for this study? Perusal of the literature dealing with these two concepts reveals many different definitions. One, therefore, is forced to question the connections among studies. Just how related is the related literature?

Although Professor Cronenwett has not supplied a theoretical definition of social networks, she has presented an adequate operational definition. Likewise, although the investigator has not provided a theoretical definition of social support, she has presented a clear and concise operational definition, in the form of four categories of support—emotional, material, informational, and comparison. Confusion arises, however, when the terms, "instrumental" and "appraisal" support, are introduced in the discussion of study findings. The confusion is alleviated somewhat when the definitions of "material" and "comparison" used in this study are contrasted with those of "instrumental" and "appraisal" provided by Cronenwett and Kunst-Wilson (1981). The conclusion reached by this reviewer is that the terms, "material" and "instrumental," are analogous, as are "comparison" and "appraisal."

These comments should not be construed as semantic quibbles. Consistency in terminology is an important part of research programs. This is especially so in the case of the social support literature, which is characterized by diverse definitions and attempts to reconcile the diversity. Readers should no longer be expected to shuffle various research reports to determine what definition is denoted by what term.

In summary, the articulation of a theoretical structure for this and other studies dealing with social support is needed. A strong, logically consistent rationale for the selection of correlates of social support would advance this important area of research.

Research Design

The design of this study is in keeping with its goals. The subjects were selected in accordance with study delimitations, and despite the high refusal rate, the sample size was adequate for a descriptive study. In fact, power analysis (Cohen, 1977) of the reported statistical values carried out by this reviewer revealed that power values ranged from approximately .30 to .99.

The survey instrument provided data needed to answer the research questions. Unfortunately, no validity or reliability data were provided for the investigator-constructed Social Network Inventory. Furthermore, no explanation was given for development of this new instrument, rather than use of an established tool. Professor Cronenwett's description of her instrument suggests it is similar to the Norbeck Social Support Questionnaire (Norbeck, Lindsey, & Carrieri, 1981), which has acceptable levels of validity and reliability. Why, then, was a new instrument needed?

Data Analysis

The statistical tests employed in this study are appropriate and provide answers to the research questions. Despite the adequacy of the data analysis, questions remain. What were the intercorrelations among the independent variables? More specifically, what was the correlation between education and income, two variables that usually are found to be highly related? What were the correlations among the network characteristics of size, frequency, and density? What were the correlations between each of these network characteristics and percentage of kin in the network? The answers to these questions are needed for the reader to determine if multicolinearity existed, because this situation confounds the interpretation of multiple regression equations (Kerlinger & Pedhazur, 1973, p. 396).

Furthermore, what were the correlations among the four types of social support? Were these independent of one another, or are there overlaps? These data would help to establish the empirical validity of House's (1981) theoretical notion of categories of social support, as well as the validity of Professor Cronenwett's Social Network Inventory.

Finally, what were the values of all statistical tests? A more comprehensive understanding of the magnitude of relationships would have been possible if the values for all statistical tests were given, rather than just for those values that reached statistical significance. Reporting of all obtained values is necessary for investigators to determine the overall effect of size or the combined probability level of a group of related studies (Glass, McGaw, & Smith, 1981; Pillemer & Light, 1980). These data synthesis techniques should begin to be applied to the rapidly increasing volume of studies of social support, to provide fuller understanding of this phenomenon.

Research Findings

The findings in Professor Cronenwett's presentation provide knowledge of the network characteristics and types of social support available to married couples during the seventh month of pregnancy. These findings support the existence of social networks during pregnancy. However, as Professor Cronenwett pointed out in her summary, the research instrument limited identification of network members to 10; thus, it may have precluded a comprehensive description of social support networks during the childbearing period.

Linda Cronenwett noted the limitations imposed by the sample of volunteers for the study. Another limitation was imposed by the timing of data collection. Since the study design precluded collection of data at several points during pregnancy, findings cannot be generalized to the entire period of childbearing.

CLINICAL RELEVANCE

Significance of the Problem

Professor Cronenwett's study clearly falls within the domain of nursing research by addressing one of the three major themes of nursing's metaparadigm, viz., the patterning of human behavior in interaction with the environment in normal life events and critical life situations. The larger project conducted by Professors Cronenwett and Wilson (Wilson & Cronenwett, 1981-1983), of which the present study is a part, addresses another of the themes, the process by which positive changes in health status are affected (Donaldson & Crowley, 1978; Gortner, 1980).

More specifically, findings that social support is related to health indicate that Professor Cronenwett's presentation focuses on a significant clinical problem (Cobb, 1976; House, 1981). Further, conflicting findings about the extent of crisis during the transition to parenthood (McCubbin, Joy, Cauble, Comeau, Patterson, & Needle, 1980) support the need for the present study, as well as the larger investigation.

Control of Study Variables

The frequency of contact between nurses and childbearing families in many settings, such as physicians' offices, prenatal clinics, and childbirth education classes, permits the nurse to control the variables involved in many different studies of social support. Nurse investigators do not have to rely on other health professionals to collect data or to interpret study findings in this area of research.

CONTRIBUTION TO NURSING KNOWLEDGE
Overall Contribution to Nursing Knowledge

The major contribution of Professor Cronenwett's presentation to nursing knowledge is the inclusion of both mothers and fathers in one study. Although many authors have claimed that pregnancy is a family experience, few investigators have studied the responses of both partners to the childbearing experience. Lack of empirical evidence for the involvement of both women and men in the childbearing experience makes the concept of "family-centered maternity care" no more than another appealing idea having no basis in fact. At this time of retrenchment in the economy and shortages of health professionals, such ideas, no matter how appealing, will be subject to criticism without supporting data. Thus, Professor Cronenwett's findings lend credence to the thesis that pregnancy is a family experience, and they provide a rationale for the inclusion of pregnant and postpartal women, as well as their partners and other supportive persons, in nursing care.

Further Steps

Knowledge of the nature of social networks and the types of social support available to childbearing couples is a first step toward utilization of knowledge of social support in nursing practice. The next step should be to assess the adequacy of the social network in meeting the perceived needs of the couple. Linda Cronenwett's findings provide quantitative knowledge of the network, but her data do not tell us anything about its quality or effectiveness.

We need to know the extent to which a couple's network meets their needs for social support. If couples already receive all the social support they need, there is no reason to invent a nursing intervention that would provide direct support or enhance support given by friends and relatives.

We need to know whether couples need additional support, and if so, from whom. It is necessary to learn if support given by relatives and friends is less effective, as effective, or more effective than that provided by nurses or other health professionals.

We also should determine how couples establish social support networks. Do they actively seek support when a need is perceived, or is an external catalyst required? If a catalyst is necessary, is a health professional more effective than a lay member of the community?

In addition, we need to learn if there are patterns of change in social networks and types of social support from early pregnancy to the late postpartum. Although the larger research project being conducted by Professor Cronenwett and Wilson will include data from the seventh month of pregnancy, as well as the sixth week and fourth and eighth months postpartum, knowledge of social support during the first two trimesters of pregnancy still will be needed.

It is necessary to learn if social support network characteristics and perceived needs for various types of social support change with each pregnancy. We need to know if there are differences in the composition of the social network and in perceived social support needs for pregnant, not-pregnant-now, and never-pregnant couples. We also should learn if there are relationships between social support networks and length of marriage, age at first pregnancy, and marital status.

Finally, we must determine if there are critical periods during which provision of social support is most effective. If so, when, how much, and what kind of nursing intervention is effective?

I urge Professor Cronenwett and other researchers to build a strong base of descriptive knowledge about the nature, quality, and effectiveness of couples' extant social support networks prior to testing specific nursing interventions designed to make available or augment social support. Such information would allow nurses and other researchers to make reasoned judgments regarding nursing's role in the provision of social support. The present era of cost containment mandates this knowledge. I also urge all researchers interested in social support to construct their studies on a firm theoretical foundation, so as to avoid a collection of unrelated empirical facts and to facilitate a clear understanding of this phenomenon.

DISCUSSION

N. Jackson: I think we agreed on every point in the critique except the last one concerning experimental research, and perhaps, our disagreement about the role of experimental research comes from the relative importance that each of us might place on theoretical and practical implications for research. I see an important role for experimental work even if it is premature in the practical sense, because I think there are some questions that are never going to be answered by descriptive work alone. One instance is the issue of understanding the nature of tangible aid. Is tangible aid as effective when it is given in a totally impersonal context—a check through the mail—as when it comes in a network of interpersonal communication? It seems to me that this would be an important question to answer in terms of figuring out whether tangible aid is part of the social support context, and it is a question that is relatively easy to answer in an experimental context. I think there are a lot of situations like that where it just becomes more efficient and more cost effective to disentangle some theoretical issue in an experimental context.

L. Walker: I'd like to respond to Dr. Fawcett's critique. I could see descriptive research as a first phase of intervention if the purpose of that research was to determine the critical values for normal development and function. That certainly helps to establish the priority of where resources, if they are limited, are going to go, and I think that is a very valuable utilization of descriptive or predictive research.

I also think that you are really talking about more than just a disease prevention context. If we get beyond that disease model and are really interested in enhancement and development, I don't think we may even know the parameters at which people may be able to function. It's like breaking what used to be the 4-minute mile record. If no one had kept trying, we never could have achieved it. We would have just assumed that 4 minutes was the top level of performance.

It may be that everyone could achieve a higher level of wellness or family functioning if we shifted to an enhancement model of human development. Choosing an enhancement versus prevention model depends on the value structure—the value orientation of that research. I think we may be able to raise human levels of development, but we might not be able to know what these levels might be if we don't do the intervention across all levels of functioning.

T. Antonucci: Along those lines, I am struck by the fact that we are confronted with several levels of problems. If we lived in a so called ivory tower of academia, we could design ideal studies and solve all the problems, but I think cost effectiveness is a prime criterion. When funding agencies are not giving lots of money for large studies, we have to find some short cuts, and the reason I say that is because whether or not we have data, the policy makers are going to make the decisions. I think this is particularly true in the kind of work we're talking about today. I'm a purist at heart. I like the idea of an experimental design that's perfect; you solve the problem at the first level, then you go to the second, and then maybe you explore special problems indicated by your results. That would take a long time. Meanwhile, those policy people are out there with or without the data, so I really think that it's incumbent upon us to try to be true to our design and experimental criteria. At the same time, we must try to move things along so that we can get some useful information to people who are going to be making the decisions whether or not they have the data. This is really important these days when money is such an issue and services are being cut. The only way they're going to make interventions to give money to people who want to do research is if they think it's going to save money. Policy makers are not going to approve research and programs which are costly. We must prove an intervention is cost effective, or it will simply be eliminated.

G. Anderson: Someone mentioned earlier that descriptive and experimental research are complementary. This has been my experience, and I consider the interweaving of the two to be very productive. Usually, my experiments are based on a rationale that has led me to define the intervention, and usually we have tested the hypotheses successfully. Yet, at the same time, unanticipated questions have been raised. Some of these questions cannot be tested experimentally, but require more descriptive work instead. The answers to the questions then make possible new rationales leading to new interventions. This is exciting and productive science.

T. Antonucci: I didn't mean to imply that experimental research was the best way. It's going to be useful, however. Reality kind of forces us in this direction.

 G. Anderson: I believe that we really need both kinds at different stages, depending on which questions are paramount for us at that time.

R. Lederman: I have a question concerning reliability of the measure. Dr. Cronenwett reported a number of significant correlations of a high magnitude, which to some extent attests to the reliability of the instruments being utilized, in spite of the fact that she has not conducted formal reliability studies. Another concern discussed here is the reporting of significant correlations, some of which may have been obtained due to chance. The relevant question here is whether the data are really significant and whether they significantly contribute to theory development and to new knowledge. To address this question, perhaps a more meaningful approach is to examine the pattern of relationships and whether there is a pattern of significant relationships. Do they make a contribution to theory? Is there repetitiveness in the patterns of relationships? If repeated measures are done, are they similar to earlier findings? Is there evidence of convergent and discriminant validity? In sum, is there a pattern which is repetitive and consistent and lends confidence to the interpretation of the data? This may be an additional and more meaningful way of determining whether the results are significant, or whether they are possibly due to chance. One other measure to provide confidence that some significant results are not due to chance is to compare results to other findings in the research literature; consistency with other findings then adds additional confidence concerning the results obtained.

J. Fawcett: My point in the critique was that it is important to report the values of all statistical tests, whether they are significant or not. It is also important to report the exact probability values whenever possible. These values are needed for meta-analyses of related studies. Meta-analyses are, I think, especially important in nursing, because research findings could have implications for changes in clinical practice. Thus, it is important to know the magnitude of the effect of an experimental intervention or the magnitude of the association between two variables. This is what a meta-analysis will determine for a group of related studies.

My other point has to do with multicolinearity. Dr. Cronenwett did not report the correlations among the independent variables, and so it was not possible to determine if a colinearity problem existed. When two or more independent variables are highly correlated, the interpretation of the results of the multiple regression are confounded. In the case of high correlations between two independent variables, only one of the variables should be entered into the multiple regression.

L. Cronenwett: I think you're absolutely right. I should have indicated what process I used in making sure that I did not have a statistical problem with multicolinearity, but I did not include that in this paper. With respect to education, however, I did report the variables with which it was correlated. You are correct that I did not show the correlations between education and the other network and social support variables with which it was not associated. I could have done that. The intercorrelations among the social support variables were in the .2 to .4 range. I will add them to the paper—an excellent point.

K. Barnard: What was your criteria for rejecting multicolinearity? The computer program manual for the Statistical Program for the Social Sciences (SPSS) is incorrect in the criteria because they suggest too high of a relationship as being acceptable for rejection of multicolinearity.

L. Cronenwett: The statistical consultant told me to regress each independent variable on all the other independent variables. If the amount of variance explained was not greater than 40-50% for any variable, there would be no statistical problem of multicolinearity. Based on that criterion, I did not have a problem using the social support variables in multiple regression equations.

T. Antonucci: But you didn't use the Statistical Program for the Social Sciences (SPSS), did you?

L. Cronenwett: No, we don't use the SPSS Program.

R. Lederman: We find that the thing to look for is a pattern of relationships that makes sense theoretically which can be supported by the existing literature and by other findings in your study, as well as related studies. That lends more power to the whole theory that you're considering.

L. Cronenwett: I wanted to address two other issues which Dr. Fawcett pointed out. One is that I would have used either Dr. Norbeck (1981) or Dr. Brandt's (1981) tool, but I developed my instrument in the summer of 1981. It wasn't until the fall of that year that the work was published in *Nursing Research*. In relation to the labeling of social support concepts, I did change House's labels from instrumental and appraisal to material and comparison support respectively, because I didn't think subjects would understand House's terms. I did not change the definition of the concepts, just the labels. Your point is very well taken that I should use a consistent label when I'm reporting data.

J. Fawcett: I thought that was what happened. I do not disagree with what Dr. Cronenwett did, but rather that the report did not make clear that this was done. The literature in many areas suffers from this problem; I would like to avoid the problem at the outset for the social support literature.

D. Magyary: Linda, you indicated being surprised that you had not found sex differences when examining the mean score values obtained on several support variables. Do you think that sex differences would have been evident if you had measured perceived support, especially nurturance and emotional support?

L. Cronenwett: Perhaps.

D. Magyary: I am not familiar with the research literature on social support and sex differences.

J. Norbeck: In my instrument, normative data were obtained from employed adults. I found that for every functional and structural property of the social network, the means were slightly lower for males than females, but in no case did this ever reach statistical significance.

I'd like to return to the issue in Linda Cronenwett's research that really fascinates me—the fact that she is measuring conflict free versus the conflicted support. I think that's going to provide very valuable data, and I'd like to tie-in some of the other literature that comes to mind.

Perhaps we can discuss this a little bit to gain some theoretical guidance on how you might approach those scores when you come to analyzing them. What comes to mind first of all is Elizabeth Bott's (1957) work in which she found that social networks of very high density, insular, very interconnected family relationships differed from the people who had loose connections and included more nonkin people in the network. It's a value judgment as to which is better, because when you look at Hirsch's (1980) work, then you move into the same kind of issue of high insular networks transcending the value judgment in terms of actually having less optional outcomes. Certainly, you're finding in your measure that there's a high number of kin in your network, and I would think that would be some indication to look at density, not the boundary density, but the other density measure, as well as at the proportion of kin to nonkin in the conflict free area.

S. Eyres: I was interested, too, that Professor Cronenwett's presentation is part of an experiment that's ongoing. Do you think, based upon what is included in the larger experiment, that you will be able to make some of the process links that Nancy Jackson was talking about last night—not just in terms of does the intervention make a difference, but does the intervention change something about the people, and is it related to the outcomes that give us more clues about what is support? Is that built into the work?

L. Cronenwett: The only chance we have for that is the fact that we're video-taping the groups and, to that extent, we'll have their comments. I haven't looked at more than a small percentage of the videotapes, but we're getting fathers when they are alone in their same sex groups. They have made remarks like, "I wouldn't have done certain things with the baby this week, but then if I didn't do it, I'd have come here and tell everybody else and look like a bad father." These anecdotal reports will be all we're getting, but they should give us some hints for what to test after that.

A. Spietz: As a practitioner in the field serving a population with low incomes and low education, we're grappling with how to track certain types of support that we're providing as well as our interventions.

One of the overall goals of the clinical nursing models project is to evaluate the type and amount of support available to subjects beginning during the first trimester of pregnancy and ending with the child's first year of life.

During this time we are providing a nursing protocol using many of the instruments discussed here today. We're using, for instance, Dr. Cranley's tool as a measure of maternal-fetal attachment, and Drs. Brandt and Weinert's (1981) social support measure. We have adapted Dr. Antonucci's support circle (Kahn & Antonucci, 1980) to be used with subjects. Each subject is asked to write in the names of those most and least supportive to them.

We're overwhelmed by the task of how to go about tracking this information. How are we going to show that our intervention may have changed their support network or may have influenced their outcome at the end of the first year? Some people have suggested single case analysis in order to look at the individual differences of the subjects rather than group differences. I'd like some of your ideas or insights as to how we, as nurses, overloaded with paperwork, can work this out. Does anyone have suggestions?

T. Antonucci: There are lots of levels to that question. I assume that you don't have the luxury of a control group. That's a helpful solution, but it's not always practical, especially when you're doing interventions. You think the intervention will help, but sometimes you can create, sort of artificially create, your control group through drop outs, through people who come for certain parts of the intervention, but not others, and by tracking your interventions and looking at their effects.

We did some very small pilot studies using three concentric circles with young teenage mothers. You know that they are at risk, but some were worse off than others. Some seemed really extreme because they had one person in their network—their baby. Now, you know a person like this is in trouble. You can compare that person at the beginning of your intervention and at the end and be able to note substantial improvement. Comparisons can then be made with less extreme cases. There are ways to compensate for the situation.

N. Jackson: I think another thing might help. It's ideal to plan this sort of thing I'm suggesting in advance, but sometimes one can look back and do exploratory post-hoc analyses of this sort. Think in terms of all the interventions you're doing and the information you're collecting across time as a casual chain. You start out with people who are in a certain state, and you do something that is expected to change that state. If a subgroup of people were not in the group on the day a particular intervention happened, you wouldn't expect the absent subgroup to progress to the next state. In the kinds of treatments you're administering and in the kinds of measures you're collecting, there are probably a lot of implicit sequential dependencies. If you can track how the individuals in your group are progressing along these sequences, maybe you'll be able to prove the only people who make it through to the ultimate goal of wellness, whatever that may be, are those who were doing okay every step along the way. You may be able to see where, for certain people, the chain has broken. This is the kind of thing that shows up in a lot of the more sophisticated contemporary program evaluation research, and I think it's a very helpful way of thinking.

S. Feetham: I would like to reinforce what Dr. Antonucci said. In the longitudinal study of families with children with myelodysplasia (spina bifida), we found that although the mean family discrepancy score was lower for families of infants with myelodysplasia than with families with healthy infants, the variance for the families with the child with myelodysplasia was greater (Feetham, 1980). Some families had very high discrepancy scores, indicating that what they had expected was not what they perceived they were experiencing in family functioning. On further examination, we found the families with the high discrepancy scores were also the families who were described by clinic staff as having difficulty. These observations suggest the potential clinical validity of the Family Functioning Survey (Feetham, Knecht, & Kai, 1982; Feetham & Humenick, 1982).

L. Cronenwett: Ms. Spietz, I was wondering when talking about measuring outcomes for your three separate groups, is it possible to see if one group had reduced variance? In other words, while you may not have shifted the mean outcomes for the treatment group as a whole due to your intervention, you may have reduced the number of people on the extremes, thus creating a more predictable response from your intervention and less families who did very poorly.

K. Barnard: Actually the project your're talking about is the Models of Newborn Nursing Care research.

We had three comparison groups, and we had specific hypotheses and defined standard outcome measures. The frustration is that we see individual change, but these microchanges are not always duplicated in group measurement. We've been struggling with how we can get clinical meaning out of some of the progress that does take place, because we all have a sense—even though we carefully chose the outcome measures—that some of the changes are happening on a different level.

A new study we are now doing involves a more homogeneous sample. The subjects are pregnant women with inadequate social support. Perhaps it will be possible to learn more by starting with subjects at the same end of the continuum.

S. Feetham: I wonder, though, clinically when you say they don't have any supports, isn't that self-selected by the individuals? Sometimes I think persons build their own boundaries so that they don't have supports and, therefore, are not perceived as healthy in our value system. As interventionists, I believe we must determine if a family has selected to have more closed boundaries yet is actually coping, or if it is a family with closed boundaries who is not coping. The lack of apparent support may not be a deficit to some families at some times. There are many reasons a family may be a multiproblem family. The lack of apparent social supports may or may not be a reason the family is multiproblem.

I just finished reading Jane Howard's book *Families* (1976), and she reinforces the concept of given families (families we are born into) and chosen families (persons who fulfill family roles but who do not meet the generic, legal definition of family). We are talking about measures of social support. Most closed format studies of social support differentiate between family and friends, not giving the respondent the opportunity to perceive the concept of the chosen family. For some persons, the chosen family may be more functional in meeting family roles than the related family. Persons who may not be in a position to chose family members may then isolate themselves from their given families as these families may not be helpful to them. The professional may then see this person as "isolated" when the isolation may be a protective response. Nursing research that provides for this differentiation of family may substantiate a category of relationships that supports the concept of the chosen family. This research may also delineate the chosen family as an important resource in nursing interventions.

T. Antonucci: Sometimes these families take a little while. It strikes me, if you have your classic multiproblem families, you're talking about a lifetime of really negative patterns of behavior, and you're trying to use support as intervention. Eventually they should be able to be picked up with the standard measures. This is comparable to certain health studies. Some people report that they are sick before it can be picked up with standard clinical tests. They know before the clinicians know, so maybe this is a similar case.

J. Norbeck: I think that the area of research on the networks for the chronic psychotic population is a good example here. Base line data for this group show that their networks are really almost nonexistent. There may be four people in their interconnected networks, because the network consists of their nuclear family of origin. There are examples in the literature of half-way house programs for these people (Budson & Jolley, 1978). Over time, these programs teach them the social skills and the kind of interaction exchanges that you go through to build a network—the kind of things that most people learn as children. Very concrete kinds of teaching are provided about what it means to be a friend and what ordinary interactions mean. You would have to develop much more sensitive ways of tracking whether such persons are making much progress, because at the end of a whole year they may have somebody they could rather loosely call a friend, but for the previous 20 years, they've never had anybody but a nuclear family member in their network. So that is progress. It sounds as if you're talking about that end of the continuum with the multiproblem families you described.

K. Barnard: One theory we have is that these women lack social competence. In the Infant Family Focus project, one treatment group involves training in social skills and relationship building. In another group, we're providing the information and resources pregnant women might need, but in this group, we do not emphasize the social skills. On the surface, it looks as if they haven't learned these social skills. Then you have case situations where all of a sudden one day the mother uses skills you never thought she possessed. It is almost as if with the right conditions and pressing the right button, there is a storehouse of ability available for use. We're tapping into very interesting aspects, but it's a struggle to understand the process.

I think we're all listening to this discussion about support networking, certainly with an appreciation of the importance of networking, but also with an attempt to figure out the role of the health care system. In terms of the professionals' role, as we have conceptualized it in the research we are now doing, they are to get the persons in a state which fosters their competency and in an environment that will allow them to begin to build their social network. The professionals are not the social support system, but they are the vehicle.

P. Brandt: Networking skills develop throughout one's lifetime, with the early beginning of friendship skills evolving during early childhood. When working with families who are deficient in networking skills, one can probably expect that considerable time would be needed to develop these skills so that ample demonstration, rehearsal, and feedback are provided during the learning period. At times of stress or fatigue, newly learned skills are often forgotten unless consistent support and reinforcement for actions are provided.

K. Barnard: It does create a huge problem in terms of measurement when you test them in one of those down phases versus testing them in one of their up periods. You're going to get a whole different picture, and I don't think we've even begun to be sensitive to that in terms of measurement.

S. Feetham: You said this morning, Dr. Barnard, that the perception of having been taught certain things by the nurses was higher with the intervention group. Were the visits done at the families' discretion, or were community health nurses used who tend to have a more set schedule? Are you more flexible with your families? You were referring to their receptiveness, and that might be one reason they are receptive. If your visits are done when the families want them and when they can handle them, then that would also affect the receptiveness they indicated.

A. Spietz: Following up on what Dr. Barnard indicated earlier, in addition to talking to them about subjects such as birth control, we also provide handouts on the topics that we thought were important to them as individuals. Birth control was the topic of the handouts; that probably reinforced what we were teaching, and gave them an opportunity then to use it at their own discretion when they felt they could absorb it better.

S. Feetham: A key thing that I believe I heard you say was that the intervention was directed toward the identification of things that were important to your mothers or related to them. What may be important is the context in which you presented your information versus what might happen with the community health nurse who may not have the same level of need-focused relationship with the family. Another concept refers to what you were saying, Dr. Barnard—how do you measure all of this? We have been talking about cues, receptivity, and reciprocity; and I would think these are basic elements of your model that may not be evident in other studies of nursing interventions.

G. Crawford: I'd like to ask a question about the community health nursing component of that. One published study has shown that people receiving community health nursing visits often did not know why the nurses were visiting or what kinds of things they were doing during the visit (Mayers, 1973). We have tried to remedy that situation by emphasizing the importance of setting goals, making appointments with clients, and making sure we get there when we say we will. Have these factors been built into the community health nursing component?

K. Barnard: Pretty much so. In fact, in that same 6 month questionnaire to the mother, one of the interesting findings was a nonsignificant tendency for the mothers in the public health model to indicate that the nurse had increased her own confidence.

K. Pridham: In terms of the measurement question that Dr. Barnard raised concerning the different results that are obtained when measurements are made in the client's down versus up times, I was hearing you talk about assessing problem solving capabilities in a broad sense. I wonder about the possibility of analyzing the down and up times for critical aspects. Then you could treat the major aspects as extraneous variables and block your design for analysis on them. One could examine down times to see if a specific type of problem is occurring during these times or whether the type of problems with which clients are dealing vary widely and are seemingly random. It makes sense to examine the type of problems with which a client is dealing since problem solving skill, at least for some types of problems, is reported to be specific to the problem (Newell & Simon, 1972). Another question that might be asked about the up and down times in order to assist the measurement task is— how many problems are currently ongoing?

G. Anderson: Your comments bring to mind the traditional view of development as having a period of disequilibrium preceding qualitative change. When this occurs, some acquired skills seem to become lost, at least temporarily, before the new gains are made. This principle is set forth very well by Bower (1974). He also discusses specific versus more general disequilibrium.

K. Barnard: We'll let you know when we've solved the problem.

REFERENCES

Barnes, J.A. (1972). *Social networks* (Module in Anthropology #26). Reading, MA: Addison-Wesley.

Barrera, M.J. (1981). Social support in the adjustment of pregnant adolescents: Assessment issues. In B.H. Gottlieb (Ed.), *Social networks and social support.* Beverly Hills: Sage.

Bott, E. (1957). *Families and social networks.* London: Tavistock.

Bower, P.G.R. (1974). Repetition in human development. *Merrill-Palmer Quarterly, 20,* 303-318.

Brandt, P.A., & Weinert, C. (1981). The PRQ: A social support measure. *Nursing Research, 30,* 277-280.

Brim, J.A. (1974). Social network correlates of avowed happiness. *Journal of Nervous and Mental Disease, 158,* 432-439.

Budson, R.D., & Jolley, R.E. (1978). A crucial factor in community program success: The extended psychosocial kinship system. *Schizophrenia Bulletin, 4,* 609-621.

Carveth, W.B., & Gottlieb, B.H. (1979). The measurement of social support and its relation to stress. *Canadian Journal of Behavioural Science, 11,* 179-188.

Cobb, S. (1976). Social support as a moderator of life stress. *Psychosomatic Medicine, 38,* 300-314.

Cohen, S. (1977). *Statistical power analysis for the behavioral sciences.* New York: Academic Press.

Cronenwett, L.R. (1980). Elements and outcomes of a postpartum support group program. *Research in Nursing and Health, 3,* 33-41.

Cronenwett, L.R. (1983). *Relationships among social network structure, perceived social support, and psychological outcomes of pregnancy.* Doctoral dissertation, The University of Michigan, Ann Arbor.

Cronenwett, L.R., & Kunst-Wilson, W. (1981). Stress, social support, and the transition to fatherhood. *Nursing Research, 30,* 196-201.

Cronenwett, L.R., & Newmark, L.L. (1974). Fathers' responses to childbirth. *Nursing Research, 23,* 210-217.

Dean, A., & Lin, N. (1977). The stress-buffering role of social support. *Journal of Nervous and Mental Disease, 165,* 403-417.

Donaldson, S.K., & Crowley, D.M. (1978). The discipline of nursing. *Nursing Outlook, 26,* 113-120.

Fawcett, J. (1982). Utilization of nursing research findings. *Image, 14,* 57-59.

Glass, G.V., McGaw, B., & Smith, M.L. (1981). *Meta-analysis in social research.* Beverly Hills: Sage.

Gortner, S.R. (1980). Nursing science in transition. *Nursing Research, 29,* 180-183.

Gottlieb, B.H. (1981). Social networks and social support in community mental health. In B.H. Gottlieb (Ed.), *Social networks and social support.* Beverly Hills: Sage.

Haller, K.B., Reynolds, M.A., & Horsely, J. (1979). Developing research-based innovation protocols: Process, criteria, and issues. *Research in Nursing and Health, 2,* 45-51.

Hirsch, B.J. (1980). Natural support systems and coping with major life changes. *American Journal of Community Psychology, 8,* 159-172.

House, J.S. (1981). *Work stress and social support.* Reading, MA: Addison-Wesley.

Kahn, R.L., & Antonucci, T.C. (1980). Convoys over the life course: Attachment, roles, and social support. In P.B. Baltes & O. Brim (Eds.), *Life span development and behavior* (Vol. 3). New York: Academic Press.

Kerlinger, F.N., & Pedhazur, E.J. (1973). *Multiple regression in behavioral research.* New York: Holt, Rinehart and Winston.

Kunst-Wilson, W., & Cronenwett, L. (1981). Nursing care for the emerging family: Promoting paternal behavior. *Research in Nursing and Health, 4,* 201-211.

Mayers, M. (1973). Home visit: Ritual or therapy? *Nursing Outlook, 21*(5), 328-331.

McCubbin, H.I., Joy, C.B., Cauble, A.E., Comeau, J.K., Patterson, J.M., & Needle, R.H. (1980). Family stress and coping: A decade review. *Journal of Marriage and the Family, 42,* 855-871.

McLanahan, S.S., Wedemeyer, N.V., & Adelberg, T. (1981). Network structure, social support, and psychological well-being in the single-parent family. *Journal of Marriage and the Family, 43,* 601-612.

Mitchell, J.C. (1969). The concept and use of social networks. In J.C. Mitchell (Ed.), *Social networks in urban situations.* New York: Humanities Press.

Mitchell, R.E., & Trickett, E.J. (1980). Task force report: Social networks as mediators of social support: An analysis of the effects and determinants of social networks. *Community Mental Health Journal, 16,* 27-44.

Newell, A., & Simon, H.A. (1972). *Human problem solving.* Englewood Cliffs, NJ: Prentice-Hall.

Norbeck, J.S., Lindsey, A.M., & Carrieri, V.L. (1981). The development of an instrument to measure social support. *Nursing Research, 30,* 264-269.

Norbeck, J.S., & Tilden, V.P. (1983). Life stress, social support, and emotional disequilibrium in complications of pregnancy: A prospective, multivariate study. *Journal of Health and Social Behavior, 24,* 30-46.

Nuckolls, K.B., Cassel, J., & Kaplan, B.H. (1972). Psychosocial assets, life crises, and the prognosis of pregnancy. *American Journal of Epidemiology, 95,* 431-441.

Paykel, E.S., Emms, E.M., Fletcher, J., & Rassaby, E.S. (1980). Life events and social support in puerperal depression. *British Journal of Psychiatry, 136,* 339-346.

Pilisuk, M., & Froland, C. (1978). Kinship, social networks, social support and health. *Social Science and Medicine, 12B,* 273-280.

Pillemer, D.B., & Light, R.J. (1980). Synthesizing outcomes: How to use research evidence from many studies. *Harvard Educational Review, 50,* 176-195.

Power, T.C., & Parke, R.D. (in press). Social network factors and the transition to parenthood.

Richardson, M.S., & Kagan, L. (1979, September). *Social support and the transition to parenthood.* Paper presented at the meeting of the American Psychological Association.

Thoits, P.A. (1982). Conceptual, methodological, and theoretical problems in studying social support as a buffer against life stress. *Journal of Health and Social Behavior, 23,* 145-159.

Walker, K.N., MacBride, A., & Vachon, M.L.S. (1977). Social support networks and the crisis of bereavement. *Social Science and Medicine, 11,* 35-41.

Wellman, B. (1981). Applying network analysis to the study of support. In B.H. Gottlieb (Ed.), *Social networks and social support.* Beverly Hills: Sage.

Wilcox, B.L. (1981). Social support in adjusting to marital disruption: A network analysis. In B.H. Gottlieb (Ed.), *Social networks and social support.* Beverly Hills: Sage.

Wilson, W.R., & Cronenwett, L.R. (1981-1983). *Nursing interventions to promote paternal behavior.* Grant R01 NU-00856, US DHHS, Division of Nursing.

Social Support and Negative Life Events of Mothers With Developmentally Delayed Children*

Patricia A. Brandt, R.N., Ph.D.

The purpose of this study was to obtain an understanding of social support and its relationship to negative life events experienced by mothers of developmentally delayed children.

The subjects were 91 mothers of children aged 6-months to 3-years-old with developmental disabilities. Questionnaires were completed anonymously by the respondents and returned by mail to the investigator. The measure of social support, the Personal Resource Questionnaire, provided three estimates of support: the availability of a number of resources, the satisfaction with help obtained during problem life situations, and perceived support. The Life Experience Survey provided the estimate of negative life events.

The findings of this study indicated that the mothers with a high impact of negative events over the past year felt less supported as measured by perceived support and felt less average satisfaction with the help obtained during problems. The relationship between negative life events was maintained whether negative life events were measured subjectively (impact) or objectively (number). Thus, the more struggles these mothers had, the less they felt supported.

The birth and rearing of a child with a developmental dysfunction present acute and long-term stressors for the family members. As new family members are integrated into the family, reorganization and adjustment are necessary. A handicapped child, however, demands adaptation from the family beyond what is required for a normal child. The responses by individual family members to the child's defect, the caretaking responsibilities, and the economic cost of raising

*This study was supported by a training grant, No. 3F31 NU-05106-03S1, from the Division of Nursing. This paper was written while the author was funded under a National Research Service Award Grant, No. T532 NU 07004-05, from the Division of Nursing, U.S. Public Health Service, Department of Health and Human Services.
This paper was revised after the conference in response to some of the comments noted in the critique presented by S.L. Feetham.

a handicapped child seriously test the family unit's adaptive ability. The family's adaptation to the child's handicapping condition is influenced by specific characteristics of the child, as well as by the family's social and economic resources, coping abilities, and concurrent negative life events.

The purpose of this paper is to identify the adaptive difficulties faced by parents of children with handicapping conditions and to describe the social support and negative life events of a sample of mothers with developmentally disabled children who ranged in age from 6 months to 3 years old.

ADAPTIVE DIFFICULTIES

Marital tension has been found to be higher in families of children with handicapping conditions than in families with normal children. In a study by Gath (1977), 30 families with Down syndrome infants were matched with families of normal infants by socioeconomic and family structure. Ratings of the marital relationship obtained through interviews indicated that the quality of the marriage was higher for the control group than for the parents of Down syndrome infants. Tew, Laurence, Payne, & Rawnsley (1977) reported a higher divorce rate for families 10 years after the birth of a child with spina bifida than for families of similar age (20-34 years) in communities in England and Wales. Neither study measured marital satisfaction prior to the birth of the child; thus, a selection bias may have contributed to the differences obtained in the stability of marital relationships. In a review of the effects of a handicapped child on the parents' marital relationship, Howard (1978) suggested that the level of marital harmony may be a reflection of the degree of integration achieved prior to the birth of a handicapped child. Family stresses associated with raising a handicapped child may heighten the vulnerability for marital relationship difficulties rather than cause marital instability. Parents of a handicapped child may be experiencing stressors, such as financial difficulties (McAndrew, 1976), problems with caregiving responsibilities (Beckman-Bell, 1981), or behavioral problems with the handicapped child or his/her sibling (Gath, 1974; Schroeder, Mulnick, & Schroeder, 1980). If these stresses are experienced within a limited time period, the negative consequences of stress are more likely to evolve (Holmes & Rahe, 1967). In studies of normal children, a stressful family milieu appears to negatively affect the mother's attitude toward her child (Stress and Families Project, 1980) as well as to decrease the quality of mother-infant attachment (Vaughn, Egeland, Sroufe, and Waters, 1979).

Caregiving demands have been found to be the main contributor toward the stress experienced by parents of handicapped infants (Beckman-Bell, 1981). Feeding and handling children with abnormalities of muscle tone and posture demand time and skill. Visual or learning difficulties may influence the child's ability to signal clear cues and to respond contingently to parental care. The child's medical conditions may require repeated professional health care and/or specific home treatments. If these caregiving responsibilities are coupled with a lack of financial resources, families may be limited in obtaining services that would enable them to become more competent in caregiving or to be relieved for short periods by trained babysitters. In a study by Holroyd (1974), single mothers of physically or mentally handicapped children reported more financial and caregiving time demands than married mothers.

The parent-child relationship also may be a stressful experience for the parents, as well as for the handicapped child. Interactive difficulties between parents and high-risk infants have been characterized as hyperactivity by the mother and hypoactivity and visual inattentiveness by the young infant (Field, 1980). The follow-up of these mother and infant dyads 2 years later reported that mothers who were previously hyperactive toward their infants now exhibited overprotective and controlling behavior. At 2 years of age the child's behavior reflected verbal unresponsiveness and language delay. Field (1980) indicated that parental overcompensation may have been a reaction to the infant's unresponsiveness and the mother-child noncontingent interactive style subsequently encouraged the child to be less actively involved in communication exchanges.

Studies by Greenberg (1971) and Jones (1980) corroborated findings of disruptive interactive styles between atypical infants and their mothers. Greenberg (1971) found that mothers of atypical infants had less rhythmical responses and used fewer modalities for stimulating their infants than did mothers of normal infants. Mothers of normal infants used auditory, kinesthetic, and visual modalities; whereas mothers of atypical infants primarily used the kinesthetic form of stimulation. In comparison to mothers of normal children 8-24 months of age, Jones (1980) found that mothers of Down syndrome children were more directive in their child's play, initiated more interactive events likely to be unresponded to by the child, and expected the child to have fewer communication skills. The children were matched on developmental age, sex, social class, and family position. Greater external control by mothers also was found in a study by Marshall, Hegrenes, & Goldstein (1973) that compared 2 groups of 20 mother-child pairs, one of retarded 3 to 5-year-olds and one with normal 3 to 5-year-olds. These studies suggest that the interactive styles of atypical children and their mothers are not as mutually reinforcing or as varied in the stimulative and exploratory experience which is typical of normal mother-infant dyads. Interactive styles between fathers and atypical infants have not been a focus of research.

Parental responses to the birth and rearing of a handicapped child may affect the evolving relationship with the child, as well as influence other family interactions and behaviors. The recognition of the child as handicapped is accompanied by a variety of grief responses. Depression, anxiety, guilt, anger, and/or denial of the child's defect or its severity are expressions of grief that the parent may experience at the time of diagnosis and periodically throughout the child's development. According to Olshansky (1966), parents of handicapped children experience chronic sorrow throughout their lifetime, with varying levels of acceptance. D'Arcy (1968) found that it took mothers of Down syndrome children months, and for some mothers, years to adjust to the fact that the child was not normal. Throughout the handicapped child's development and progression into adulthood, the parent is confronted with reminders of the child's limitation and differences. For some handicapping conditions, the degree of severity of the child's defect or the child's future competency is unclear, which heightens the parents' anxiety and increases a chronic mourning phase of grief. In a study of 32 families with mentally retarded children, Wikler, Wasow, & Hatfield (1981) found that the majority of families reported difficult adjustment periods during the developmental crisis points, such as the diagnosis of the disability, entry into school, puberty, and guardianship. Few parents reported an adjustment period that was restricted in length or limited to a grief phase experienced only after diagnosis. These families were not randomly selected; thus, further study is needed to document the grief phase characteristic of families with handicapped children. However, an awareness of indicants of chronic mourning and the stress involved in continual adaptation should encourage the periodic assessment of families with handicapped children and intervention relevant for the individual family.

Prolonged, regular exposure to stress reportedly creates high attentional demands upon individuals and reduces the capacity to adapt to subsequent stressors (Baum, Singer, & Baum, 1981). Studies which have compared parents of normal children with parents of handicapped children indicate that the fathers and mothers of a handicapped child have more negative feelings about themselves and less positive feelings about the child's ability or appearance than do parents of normal children (Cummings, Bayley, & Rie, 1966; Cummings, 1976; Waisbren, 1980). In addition, the siblings of developmentally disabled children have been reported to be more likely to have emotional disturbances than siblings of normal children (Howard, 1978). Parents are faced with the difficult challenge of integrating the handicapped members into their family while maintaining a growth producing milieu for each member.

In a review of research on child abuse, Frodi (1981) indicated that preterm and physically and mentally handicapped children are at risk for abuse. Frodi indicated that abuse is multiply determined by interrelating factors such as parent-child interaction styles, parental characteristics, child characteristics, and stressful environments. In addition to having interactive difficulties, the parent of an atypical child may perceive the child's cry as aversive and be unable to develop effective soothing techniques. According to Frodi (1981), the cries of atypical infants are often unpleasant and have a higher or lower pitch than cries of normal infants.

Physical characteristics of handicapped children may be quite different than expected by parents. As the child develops in interaction with the environment, the child's behaviors may present challenges that the parent is unprepared for or unable to manage. Misunderstanding of the child's cues or difficulty soothing the child may influence the evolving parent-child relationship. A study of 15 mothers regarding the early infant cues which enhance the development of attachment revealed that disturbances in one or more infant behaviors were reported by each of the mothers (Stone & Chesney, 1978). The infant behaviors studied included smiling, crying, vocalizing, eye contact, eliciting attention, response to being handled, and activity level. This study did not include a follow-up of the attachment relationship obtained between the mothers and infants later in infancy.

STRESS MEDIATORS

The adaptive difficulties associated with having a handicapped child affect families differently. If the parents decide to integrate the handicapped child into the family unit rather than institutionalize the child, previous experience with normal children may be of little assistance in parenting the handicapped child. A study of 116 parents of handicapped children indicated that previous child rearing experience and knowledge of normal children did not eliminate the child care difficulty for parents of handicapped children (McAndrew, 1976). The limitations of the child may necessitate or encourage caretaking approaches and relationships which may further increase the child's differences rather than encouraging normalcy. For those parents and families who are able to adapt and effectively integrate the handicapped child into the family system, the adaptation can be growth producing for the child and other family members (Gabel, McDowell, & Cerreto, 1983).

Why are some families more stress resistant and adaptive than others? The family's income, community response (Burr, 1973), and the severity of the child's dysfunction (Holroyd, 1974) are important factors which can interfere with or encourage adaptation. In addition, personality characteristics (Kobasa, 1979), coping strategies (Pearlin & Schooler, 1978) and social support (Turner, 1981) have been found to be major factors that differentiate the stressed who remain healthy from the stressed who suffer negative or maladaptive consequences. This research has focused upon the influence of single categories of stress mediators such as social support, personality characteristics, or coping strategies, but the combined or interactive effects of these stress mediating variables have not been studied. The emphasis of this paper is on the stress mediator--social support.

The support available from relationships with family and friends has been associated with beneficial parenting and child outcomes. Studies have linked a strong social support system with positive maternal-fetal attachment (Cranley, 1981) and secure mother-infant attachment (Crockenberg, 1981). Waisbren (1980) found that support from parents and friends was associated with more positive feelings by fathers and mothers about their developmentally disabled child. A study by Friedrich (1979) indicated that the security of the marital relationship was a significant predictor of coping behavior for mothers of handicapped children aged 2-19 years. Marital security accounted for 79% of the variance in coping behavior, and it was associated with positive coping.

The beneficial functions of social support appear to become evident especially if stressful conditions operate in the family environment. Nuckolls, Cassel, & Kaplan (1972) found that women with high psychosocial assets and high life change scores experienced one-third of the number of pregnancy complications as compared to women with low assets and high life changes. Eyres (1979) reported that mothers with high support in association with stressful environments demonstrated more positive infant feeding and teaching techniques toward their infants than mothers with low support.

Indicators of social support have varied in studies from the presence or absence of an intimate other (Brown, Bhrolchain, & Harris, 1975) to the degree a person's social needs are met through emotional comfort or exchange of services (Caplan, 1976). A multidimensional social support instrument with valid and reliable psychometric properties has not been characteristically used in studies of parental support. Furthermore, there is a paucity of empirical evidence regarding the social support of parents with developmentally handicapped children.

STUDY

In order to obtain an understanding of social support and its relationship to negative life events, the substudy reported in this presentation was conducted using data obtained from a multivariate study (Brandt, 1981) on the influence of maternal social support and negative life events on maternal discipline and maternal stimulation for children with developmental disabilities. The conceptual framework for this study was developed from an ecological approach to parenting, and it is described in the study by Brandt (1981). Since the purpose of the multivariate study by Brandt was to obtain information on the impact of support and negative life events on maternal caregiving, no data were requested from the child's father. The father's participation in future studies would provide needed clarity to issues related to environmental influences on parenting.

The following major questions were addressed in this substudy on social support and negative life events:

1. What were the patterns for choosing resources to help?
2. Was there a difference in the number of resources between groups of mothers:
   a. Younger versus older?
   b. With partners or without partners?
   c. Homemakers versus employed?
   d. Low versus high income?
   e. Low versus high education?
   f. Of children with one to two disabilities versus three to five disabilities?
   g. Of children who attend school and/or clinic for a few versus high number of hours per month?

3. Did the level of satisfaction with help differ with the type of problem situation experienced?

4. Was there a difference in perceived support between groups of mothers (same groups as identified in question 2)?

5. What resource category predicted perceived support?

6. How are the three estimates of social support related?*

7. What types of negative life events were experienced by the mothers in this study?

8. Was there a difference on negative life events between the following mothers:
    a. Younger versus older?
    b. With partners versus without partners?
    c. Homemakers versus employed?
    d. Low versus high income?
    e. Low versus high education?
    f. Of children with one to two disabilities versus three to five disabilities.

9. Was social support related to the negative life events experienced?

10. Does the relationship between perceived support and negative life events persist if relationship loss events are controlled statistically?

Subjects

The subjects in this descriptive substudy included 91 mothers of children aged 6-months to 3-years-old with developmental disabilities. Individuals were asked to volunteer if they were natural or adoptive parents, English speaking, 18 years of age or older, had completed 8 years of education, and had a child who attended a developmental school or disabilities clinic in Everett, Washington or the greater Seattle area.

The majority of the respondents were white, married, full-time homemakers, and had completed 12 years of education. The respondents' median age was 28.8 years, with a median family income range of $15,000-$20,000. The children in the study had a median of 2.4 disabilities that included large muscle, fine muscle, language, sensory, or learning problems. Fifty of the children were male and 41 female. The median age was 24 months. In 43% of the families the disabled child had no siblings.

Method

Social support and negative life events were two of the self-administered measures in a questionnaire completed anonymously by the respondents and returned by mail to the investigator. The return rate of the questionnaires was 40%. The Personal Resource Questionnaire (PRQ) by Brandt and Weinert (1981) was the measure of social support. The PRQ provided three estimates of sup-

*These estimates are the availability of a number of resources, satisfaction with help during problem situations, and perceived support.

port: the availability of a number of resources, satisfaction with help obtained during problem life situations, and perceived support. The psychometric properties of the PRQ are described in a study by Brandt and Weinert (1981) and by Dr. Weinert at this conference. The Life Experiences Survey (LES), developed by Sarason, Johnson, and Siegel (1978), is a widely used stress tool with established reliability and validity, and it provided the estimate of negative life events. The LES allows for individualized ratings of the degree of impact of an event experienced within the past 12 months and whether the event was a negative or positive experience at the time of occurrence. Undesirable events have been found to be consistently and positively related to mental health indicators, whereas positive or total events have not been consistently related to stress outcome measures (Johnson & Sarason, 1979; Zautra & Maio, 1981).

The social support variable, number of resources, was obtained by summing each resource indicated across seven problem situations: emergency, help needed for handicapped child care, interpersonal difficulty, loneliness, family concerns, upset with conditions of life, and general problems. The options available for resource selection were spouse or partner, relative, friend, neighbor, spiritual advisor, prayer, professional, agency, or books. Scores of 0-56 were possible for the variable, number of resources. A high score indicated a high number of resources available.

The support variable, satisfaction with help, was obtained for each of the problem situations experienced by the respondent. A rating scale of very satisfied (5) to very dissatisfied (1) was used to determine the satisfaction level. An average satisfaction score was also computed for use in correlation analyses since few respondents had experienced all the given problem situations. Average satisfaction was obtained by first summing the responses to the satisfaction with help items for all the problems experienced and then dividing the total satisfaction score by the number of problem situations experienced. A high score indicated high satisfaction or high average satisfaction.

The support variable, perceived support, was obtained by summing the 30-item, 7-point Likert scale that measures the five relational functions of support defined by Weiss (1974). Six items are included for each of the five relational provisions of intimacy, nurturance, social integration, self-worth, and guidance. A score of 0-210 can be obtained on perceived support, with a high score representing a perception of being highly supported. A rating of "7" indicated "strongly agree," whereas a rating of "1" indicated "strongly disagree."

A score for negative life events was obtained by summing the degree of impact (no effect to great effect) for the total negative events experienced on the LES during the past year. The events listed included such items as death of a family member or friend, loss of a job, borrowing money, and pregnancy. A high score on negative life events indicated a high impact for the total negative events experienced.

In addition to descriptive statistics, univariate and multivariate data analyses were performed; t tests (two tailed separate variance estimates), Pearson correlations (two tailed), partial correlations, and stepwise multiple regression methods were used to analyze the substudy data. Results significant at $p < .05$ were accepted.

RESULTS

Social Support: Number of Resources

The average number of resources that the respondents reported for each of the seven life situations was three. The majority of respondents selected the option, partner, as one of their resources for each life situation except interpersonal. However, partners were still chosen more frequently to help during interpersonal problems than were other resources such as relatives, friends, or professionals. Table 1 indicates the percentage of respondents who selected each resource according to the given life situation. The respondents appeared to be selective in their choice of support for a specific type of problem. For example, 63% of the respondents would count on professionals during an emergency, but only 20% would count on professionals for help with the handicapped child's care; 74% would count on friends when they were lonely, but only 35% would count on friends during interpersonal problems. Few respondents utilized books or agencies for the seven problem situations.

In order to determine if there was a difference in the number of resources among groups of mothers, t tests, two tailed separate variance estimates, were used. Data were analyzed to see if there was a difference in the number of resources among the following groups of mothers: younger versus older, with partners versus without partners, homemakers versus employed, low versus high income, low versus high education, of children with one to two disabilities versus three to five disabilities, and of children who attend school and/or clinic for few versus a high number of hours per month.

Fewer resources were available to:
a. employed mothers, $t(85) = -2.54$, $p < .05$, than to mothers whose work was homemaking.
b. mothers aged 19-28 years than to mothers aged 29-45 years of age, $t(78) = -2.37$, $p < .05$.
c. mothers who were divorced, separated, or never married than to those who lived with a partner, $t(27) = -3.12$, $p < .01$.

No significant differences were obtained on groups determined by education, income, number of child disabilities, or number of hours the child attended school or clinic.

Table 1
Resources for Life Situations

Situations	Resources								
	Partner	Child	Relative	Friend	Spiritual Advisor	Prayer	Professional	Agency	Books
Emergency	81%	4%	58%	54%	27%	43%	63%	11%	12%
Help for Handicapped Child	55	4	64	43	7	13	20	18	0
Interpersonal Problem	49	3	35	35	27	35	34	10	5
Loneliness	73	30	52	74	14	34	12	14	8
Family Problem	57	10	4	42	14	32	47	9	2
Upset With Life	66	10	40	44	23	44	30	13	11
General Problems	65	65	35	56	13	20	18	10	0

N = 91

Social Support: Satisfaction with Help

The substudy also determined if the level of satisfaction with help differed with the type of problem situation experienced. The median number of problem situations experienced by the respondents during the previous 3-4 months was 2.1; 17% of the respondents had not personally experienced any problem situations, and 7% of the respondents had experienced all 6 of the problem situations. The following information identifies the number of mothers who experienced each problem situation and the percentage of those mothers who were quite/very satisfied versus the percentage of mothers who were dissatisfied/little satisfied with the help obtained for the problem situation:

1. Thirty-two mothers reported emergencies; 75% were quite/very satisfied, and 25% were dissatisfied/little satisfied.
2. Thirty-seven mothers needed help to care for their disabled child; 70% were quite/very satisfied, and 30% were dissatisfied/little satisfied.
3. Twenty-nine mothers indicated interpersonal problems; 42% were quite/very satisfied, and 58% were dissatisfied/little satisfied.
4. Forty-eight mothers indicated they were lonely; 52% were quite/very satisfied, and 48% were dissatisfied/little satisfied.
5. Twenty-one mothers reported family problems; 62% were quite/very satisfied, and 38% were dissatisfied/little satisfied.
6. Fifty-two mothers were upset with the conditions of their lives; 42% were quite/very satisfied, and 58% were dissatisfied/little satisfied.

These results indicate that there were some mothers who experienced problems and were dissatisfied or only a little satisfied with the help obtained. In situations which appear to require informational or task help such as emergencies and child care, higher percentages of mothers were quite satisfied with the help received. However, in situations conducive to emotional or affirmational support, such as upset with life condition or interpersonal problems, the majority of mothers were either only a little satisfied or dissatisfied with the help received. In addition, 53% of the 91 mothers in the study reported being lonely and 57% reported being upset with the condition of their life during the past 4 months. In this particular sample, some degree of emotional turmoil appears to be operating in these mothers' lives. For the 69 mothers who had experienced at least one of the life situations, the average satisfaction score was 3.7. A rating of "3" indicated "a little satisfied," and a rating of "4" indicated "quite satisfied."

Social Support: Perceived Support

The average score on the measure of perceived support was 168.6, SD 23.9, with a range of 93-210. Most of the subjects in this study perceived themselves as having a moderate level of the relational provisions of support as measured by the Personal Resource Questionnaire.

Table 2
Regression Coefficients Predicting Perceived Support Level

| | | | Standard | | Simple | | | Adjusted |
Step	Predictor	B	Error B	F (df)[a]	R	R^2		R^2
1	Partner	3.97	1.24	10.32 (1, 82)*	.39	.152		.142
2	Spiritual Advisor/Prayer	1.16	.65	3.17 (1, 82)	.23	.179		.159
3	Professional/ Agency	-.68	.79	.74 (1, 82)	-.04	.188		.159
4	Books	-2.42	3.14	.59 (1, 82)	.23	.190		.152
5	Child/Relative/ Friend	.54	.73	.55 (1, 82)	.21	.196		.147

[a]F ratios for the equation after the last step.
*p < .01

Differences were apparent in perceived support among groups of mothers. Mothers with incomes of $19,999 and below perceived their support to be significantly less than mothers with incomes of $20,000 and above, $t(75) = -2.2$, $p < .05$. There were no statistically significant differences between groups for age, education, employment, marital status, number of disabilities in the child, or number of hours/month the child attended a clinic or school.

Stepwise multiple regression was used to determine what type of resource predicted the mother's perceived support. Availability of a partner was the only significant predictor of the mother's perceived support, accounting for 15% of the variance. Spiritual advisor/prayer, professional/agency, books, or child/relative/friend as predictors did not significantly increase the explained variance (see Table 2 for regression coefficients).

Relationship among the Three Estimates of Support

Using a Pearson correlation, the number of resources and perceived support were positively related, $r = .29$, $p < .01$. Mothers with a higher number of resources across life situations were more likely to feel higher levels of perceived support (see Table 3). The number of resources mothers would turn to was not significantly associated with the mothers' average satisfaction with help obtained during actual problem situations. Average satisfaction with help was positively related to the perceived support of the mother, $r = .50$, $p < .01$. If the mother felt satisfied with the help she obtained during problems actually experienced, she was more likely to feel supported. The two support variables, number of resources and perceived support, share approximately only 9% of the same information. Therefore, different dimensions of support appear to be measured by these variables, and this allows for the following different interrelationships among support variables:

1. The number of resources and perceived support are related (9% shared variance).

2. The number of resources and average satisfaction with these resources during problem situations are not related.

Table 3
Correlations among Support Variables

Variable	Number of Resources	Average Satisfaction	Perceived Support
Number of Resources	—	.16	.29*
Average Satisfaction		—	.50*
Perceived Support			—

*$p < .01$

3. The average satisfaction with resources during problem situations and perceived support are related (25% shared variance).

Negative Life Events

The concurrent life stressors experienced by the respondents during the previous 12 months were assessed by the Life Experience Survey. The scores on negative life events ranged from 0-76, with a median of 5.7, a mean of 9.3, and a SD of 11.7. During the previous 12 months negative life events were not experienced by 15.7% of the mothers in this sample.

Type of negative life events experienced by mothers. Examples of negative life events that the respondents in this sample experienced during the past year and rated as having a bad impact on their lives included partner-related problems, child-related problems, and self-related problems (see Table 4).

Difference in negative life events. There was some difference on negative life events among groups of mothers. Mothers of children with three or more disabilities obtained higher scores on negative life events, $t(51) = -2.22$, $p < .05$, than mothers of children with one or two disabilities. There were no statistically significant differences on negative life event scores between younger and older mothers, homemakers and employed women, low and high income mothers, women with partners or without partners, and low and high education mothers.

Table 4
Negative Life Events

Problems	Percentage
Partner Related Problems	
Sexual difficulties	11
Separation due to conflict	14
Major changes in arguments	13
In-law difficulties	14
Child Related Problems	
Child illness	23
Having handicapped child (write-in)	8
Little money for child care	6
Self-Related Problems	
Sleep difficulties	22
Change in closeness with others	17
Eating habit change	13
Personal illness/injury	10

Table 5
Correlations between Negative Life Events and Support Variables

	Perceived Support	Average Satisfaction	Number of Resources
Negative Life Events (qualitative score)	-.51* (91)	-.39* (69)	-.17 (88)
Number of Negative Life Events (quantitative score)	-.48* (87)	-.42* (68)	-.14 (85)

*p<.001
The number of subjects are listed in parentheses.

Social support, as measured by perceived support and average satisfaction, was significantly related to the negative life events that were experienced (see Table 5). Pearson correlations obtained between negative life events and each support variable indicate that negative events were associated with perceived support, r = -.51, p<.001, and average satisfaction, r = -.39, p<.001. Mothers with high negative event scores were more likely to feel less supported or less satisfied with help obtained. Negative life events and number of resources were not significantly related.

Evidence of the relationship between negative life events and the two support variables, perceived support and average satisfaction, was also found when the number of negative events rather than the impact of these events was used as a variable. The higher the number of negative events, the lower the perceived support or average satisfaction with help obtained (see Table 5 for correlation coefficients). Therefore, the relationship between negative life events and these support variables is maintained whether life events are measured subjectively (impact) or objectively (number).

Relationship between perceived support and negative life events when relationship loss events are controlled statistically. Since life events have the potential to influence losses or gains in supportive relationships, partial correlations between negative life events and/perceived support (r = -.45, p<.001) and negative life events and average satisfaction (r = -.27, p<.05) were obtained controlling for loss events experienced. The negative events included in the loss variable were deaths of a family member or friend, jail, change of residence, separation or divorce from a partner, loss of a job, dropping out of school, alienation from friends, and leaving home (self or children). By controlling for losses, the shared variance between negative life events and the two support variables, perceived support and average satisfaction, decreased somewhat from the shared variance obtained with no control for losses. The variance shared between negative life events and perceived support decreased from 26% (no control) to 20% (control); whereas the variance shared between negative life events and average satisfaction decreased from 15% (no control) to 7% (control). These results suggest that known losses do influence the relationship between support and life events; however, a significant inverse relationship is still maintained when controlling for relationship losses or changes.

IMPLICATIONS

Number of Resources

The respondents were selective in choosing resources for help according to the problem situation listed. Friends were more likely to be chosen for lonely situations than for interpersonal problems. One wonders if friends may offer emotional support during lonely times but may not be as likely to be perceived to offer problem solving or the informational aid necessary for interpersonal problems. The strength of a friendship may not potentiate the sharing of interpersonal problems as easily as lonely situations do. During emergencies, the respondents were more likely to elicit help from partners or professionals rather than from spiritual advisors or books. In an emergency situation, the strength of relationships is probably not as critical an influence as is the type of support available from the individual resource. In a review of research on job-related stress, Cohen (1982) reported that co-workers provided more effective support than family or friends. Different stressors may demand different coping requirements and respond better to certain types of support.

Another example of a differential selection response was shown as informal helping sources, and they were chosen by more mothers than were professional sources. Only in one problem life situation, emergency, did the majority of mothers select professionals as resources to whom they would turn. In a review of research on natural support systems, Cowen (1982) reported that informal caregivers are more likely to be sought out during interpersonal distress than are mental health professionals. Reliance on natural caregivers may be due to the cost of professional help; the belief systems of the individuals needing help; or network characteristics such as the location of the resource and the strength, symmetry, or content of the relationships. For example, is the natural caregiver emotionally committed to the individual (strength), less controlling (symmetry), and offering self-worth relational provisions (content)? If these characteristics match the individual's needs for support and are more likely to be obtained from a natural caregiver, professional help will not be sought.

Satisfaction with Help

Mothers were more likely to be satisfied with help obtained when the situation was conductive to instrumental or task support rather than emotional support. These results raise several questions:

1. Do emergency situations require different coping strategies than interpersonal problems?
2. Is informational or instrumental support easier to elicit from others?

3. Are the expectations for emotional aid different from the expectations for instrumental or informational support?

One of the major problems with supportive interactions is that the needs of the person who requires help may not be matched with the helper's response (Brickman, Rabinowitz, Karuza, Coates, Cohn, & Kidder, 1982). If a person attributes responsibility for the problem as well as the solution to the problem to oneself, the supportive interactions may differ quite markedly from interactions with a person who blames others for the problem and expects other to solve the problem. Brickman et al. (1982) noted that people who try to be supportive may apply the wrong model of helping; thus, efforts to help may be ineffective. At times when a person needs someone to listen to them using self-blame, the helper's response may be to encourage problem solving or attribution of the blame on others. However, self-blame at that time may be a positive coping strategy, because it is often an indicant of a need to control one's life.

Mothers with lower incomes had significantly lower scores on perceived support than mothers with higher incomes. These group differences demonstrate the importance of controlling for financial status in studies of social support.

Interrelationship of Support Variables

Different aspects of support appear to be measured by the three indicators: number of resources, average satisfaction, and perceived support. The number of resources was not significantly associated with the person's satisfaction with help when the activation of these resources was required. In addition, the two variables, the number of resources and perceived support, shared only 9% of the same information. These findings raise the following questions for future research:

1. Which of the social support indicators best measures the construct that potentiates a person's adjustment to stressors?

2. What network dimensions are important to measure in order to clarify the complexities of the social support construct?

3. Do certain dimensions of support predict different outcomes more effectively than other dimensions?

Wellman (1981) suggests that it is essential to study individuals' social support within the context of their network and the situations in which help is required. Relational and structural network dimensions influence the flow of support. The situation creates different needs for help and possibly different people to help. The three estimates of support used in this study only sample a few of the dimensions of a person's network. The support variable, perceived support, appears to be an indicator of the content category of the relational network dimension. The relational dimension categories of strength and symmetry were not measured. The support variable, number of resources, could be interpreted as an indicator of network size and diversity, which are structural network dimensions. Structural categories not included were personal interconnectedness and stability. The support variable, satisfaction with help, investigates the actual support experienced during a recent problem situation. Further study of the structural and relational network dimensions which affect the support obtained during specific problem situations will contribute to the knowledge needed to construct the appropriate assessment tool.

Negative Life Events and Social Support

Although the Life Experience Survey (LES) does not assess problems necessarily specific to parenting a handicapped child, the effects of commonly experienced life events are obtained. Adaptive difficulties with the parent-child relationship, caretaking, sibling behavior, or parental responses to the birth and rearing of a handicapped child are not included as items on the LES. The results of this study, however, do provide information about life events that have had a negative impact on the respondents' lives. The percentage of mothers who experienced: 1) partner-related problems ranged from 11-14%; 2) child-related problems ranged from 6-23%; and 3) personal health or psychological problems ranged from 10-22%. Life conditions were especially difficult for mothers whose children had multiple disabilities; a higher negative impact of events was experienced for these mothers in comparison to mothers whose children had one or two disabilities.

Mothers with a high impact of negative events over the past year felt less supported as measured by perceived support and felt less average satisfaction with the help obtained during problems. The relationship between negative life events and these support variables is maintained whether life events are measured subjectively (impact) or objectively (number). Thus, the more struggles the mothers had, the less they felt supported. These results raise several issues:

1. Do individuals have a greater need for support during stressful conditions than during nonstressful conditions?
2. Why is a person dissatisfied with help? Is dissatisfaction due to a high need level, a lack of social skills needed to obtain help, or inadequate financial or coping resources?
3. Does a third variable, such as mother's mental health status, influence the relationship obtained between negative life events and the two support variables, average satisfaction and perceived support?

The inverse relationship between negative life events and social support is maintained when the obvious relationship losses due to life events are statistically controlled. However, the variances shared between negative life events and perceived support decreased somewhat when controlling for relationship losses. These results indicate that clarification of the interactive effects of support on life events and life events on support will enhance our knowledge of support as operationalized in our daily lives. Thoit (1982) recommends that measures of support should be obtained before and after the occurrence of events in order to "disentangle" the interaction of support and life events. In a study of parents with developmentally handicapped children, a longitudinal study with an onset preferably during the early neonatal period would be one approach to assess the relationship between support and adaptive difficulties involved with parenting.

SUMMARY

Although the results of this substudy cannot be generalized due to such factors as the 40% questionnaire response and the absence of random selection, the information obtained consistently highlighted that the mothers in this substudy were faced with adaptive struggles. Over 50% of the mothers, for example, were upset with the conditions of their lives, and most of these were dissatisfied or only a little satisfied with the help received for this problem. Life conditions were especially challenging for mothers of children with multiple developmental delays. Any further study of social support and negative events will be facilitated by the development of a measure of stressors specific to families with handicapped children. By identifying the coping requirements of adaptive difficulties such as caregiving demands, the type of support needed at the onset and during the process of adaptation may then become more clearly understood. Since support is only one of many coping strategies, the content and source of support would be best studied in the context of other problem solving or adaptive methods and an association with parental competencies such as caregiving abilities and communication skill. An overdependence on others for support may actually induce stress by decreasing self-reliance, control, and problem solving, or it may be an indicator of the lack of individual competencies.

The selectivity in choosing resources for specific kinds of problem situations affirms the need for nursing research, which can determine what individuals and families as a unit profit from support, what type of support, and from whom. Nursing practice will also benefit from studies of effective models of social support offered by both lay and professional sources during high-risk situations.

The conceptualization and implementation of support demands continued attention. The three estimates of support utilized in this study appear to assess different dimensions of social support and yet are not comprehensively providing a total picture of support within the context of a person's network. The symmetry, strength, interconnectedness, and stability of relationships also affect the support actualized from relationships, and these aspects need to be defined in terms of the situational challenges of parenting a developmentally handicapped child.

CRITIQUE

Susan L. Feetham, Ph.D., R.N., FAAN

The following critique was prepared for Dr. Brandt's original presentation of

"Social Support and Negative Life Events of Mothers of Developmentally Delayed Children" at the conference. Subsequent to the critique, Dr. Brandt revised the paper, addressing several areas presented in the original critique. A comparison of the published paper and this critique will be helpful to the reader to reinforce how the concerns presented in the critique can be addressed and add substance and clarity to the presentation of research. Such efforts will strengthen nursing research and facilitate the development of nursing knowledge.

Content previously omitted and now included in Dr. Brandt's paper is the identification of the conceptual framework for the study; clarification of the discussion of social support; the specification of the research questions; and clearer reference to the reliability and validity of the instruments. These revisions add to the conceptual clarity of the study and show overt evidence of the scientific rigor applied in this study but not clearly described in the original paper.

INTRODUCTION

The primary task of this conference is to identify the advances needed to bring knowledge of social support to a level useful for professional practice. I found that Dr. Brandt's paper provides an important base to identify issues of social support research in relation to children with developmental disabilities and their families. Her presentation has strengths to build on for future nursing research, and it exemplifies some of the issues common to nursing research. My analysis will focus on both the conceptual and research issues identified in this study and reviewed within the context of both nursing practice and research. I will review the strengths of the study and use these to first identify conceptual issues and secondly to identify research issues. Dr. Brandt's sections, Implications and Summary, clearly show her own identification of several of the issues I will address in this review. This research makes a contribution to the knowledge of social support by linking earlier research on children with developmental disabilities and their families to the concept of social support.

STRENGTHS

The purpose of Dr. Brandt's paper was to identify adaptive difficulties faced by parents of children with handicapping conditions and to describe the social support and concurrent life events of a sample of 91 mothers with children, aged 6 months to 3 years, with developmental disabilities. The examination of the relationship of social support to stressful life events in families with handicapped children is also presented as a purpose of the study. One strength of this study was the use of previous research related to children with developmental disabilities and their families as a basis for the study. Dr. Brandt clearly reviewed the variables examined in earlier studies and directed this review toward the concept of social support. This review implied the multivariate nature of the responses of families and children with developmental disabilities. The conceptual linking of the responses of these families to the variable of social support was consistent with the methodology which tested these linkages. While the linkages were made between the social support literature and studies of children with developmental disabilities, a unifying conceptual framework was not presented.

The design also included the collection of data related to the multiple variables identified from previous studies. It was implicit that it was not possible in the design to examine all of the multiple variables identified in the review of studies. Explicit attention to the issues of multivariate design and analysis would have strengthened the paper while adding to the conceptual clarity of the multivariate nature of research on these children and their families.

Another support of the multivariate design is that although not presented in this paper, the references cited for the instruments used in this study report the multidimensional nature of the primary instrument (Brandt & Weinert, 1981). The other reports on the Personal Support Questionnaire instrument suggest Dr. Brandt's sensitivity to the multivariate nature of the study of children with developmental disabilities and their families.

Data Analysis

Another strength of Dr. Brandt's paper is that the analysis attended to the multiple concepts identified in the literature review. Although repeated univariate analysis was used, there was consistency between the review of the literature and the analysis. The analysis also reinforced the need for multivariate analysis derived from a multivariate conceptual framework, something not done in this study.

Dr. Brandt appropriately used stepwise multiple regression analysis. This analysis was used as an additional examination of factors related to single social support variables. In the regression analysis, the lack of significance of the various resources as predictors of mother's perceived support may be related to the conceptualization and method of measuring support in a fixed item format. The significance of a partner as a predictor of the mother's perceived support is consistent with the literature and practice. It also reinforces the need to possibly expand this construct of partner conceptually and methodologically to the family in future research. An increase in the variance accounted for may occur by having the respondent define partner and other personal support systems which constitute their family. While in other work Dr. Brandt clarifies family as a source of support, the construct family is not measured in this study.

The use of partial correlations to control for possible intervening variables and to identify possible relationships in such a complex issue strengthens the research and further attends to the multiple factors possibly affecting social support. Additional possible intervening variables that I have noted from my practice with families who have children with developmental disabilities which clinically affect their use of social support systems include: the family member's stage in responding to the birth of the child, their perception of the defect and its effect on their child, their perception of their previous experiences with support systems, and their family relationships. Also empirically, it is reported that previous experiences with any type of group is related to the parent's use of parent groups as a form of support (Feetham, 1976).

Another strength is that the questions for future research and the conceptual issues identified by Dr. Brandt provide important direction, and they reinforce her understanding of the issues related to this area of research. Discussion of some of these conceptual issues related to social support would have further strengthened the presentation if they had been presented prior to the methodology and results.

CONCEPTUAL ISSUES

While recognizing the strengths of Dr. Brandt's research, there are several conceptual issues for nursing practice and research derived from review of this study. These issues include the need for conceptual/theoretical frameworks consistent with and clearly deriving from nursing practice, and that these frameworks should support a multivariate research design and analysis. The nursing research using such practice based conceptual frameworks would provide a basis for programs of research; would examine process in addition to outcome; and by design would examine the interaction of the child, family, and environment. While this statement may appear to be a "chicken or egg" dilemma concerning practice based research versus research based practice, I will briefly review what I believe is the origin of much of our nursing research and what direction our research needs to take in order to be useful to practice. The basic premise for my ensuing comments is that nursing practice (clinical decisions) requires the processing of multiple factors/variables; therefore, nursing research may be more appropriately addressed through multivariate frameworks and designs (Grier, 1981). The question is--while nursing practice requires the processing of multiple variables, why is it that nursing research has adopted the research methods of other disciplines which tend to use univariate models?

One basis for the univariate model in nursing research, but particularly in examining children with developmental disabilities and their families, is the derivation of this research from the medical model (Feetham, 1980). A medical model follows the process of delineating the symptoms, diagnosis, and treatment. Etiology has been sought through the study of biology, anatomy, and physiology. As researchers in other professions began to study children with developmental disabilities and their families, they maintained the univariate (linear) approach of the medical model, but they also examined a different set of variables resulting in a univariate analysis of very complex multivariate situations. Traditionally, research on families who have children with developmental disabilities follows the univariate linear models which examine the presence of the child with a developmental disability as the independent variable and suggest the child as the causation of the dependent variables of family functioning, marital disruption, sibling problems, etc. Dr. Brandt's study suggests multivariate relationships and that the presence of the child with a developmental disability is but one variable interacting with family outcomes. Dr. Brandt's study does advance from the traditional univariate research of children with developmental disabilities by implying the multivariate nature of the study.

The result of the traditional univariate research is that pieces of the family, child, and/or the developmental disability are examined. Univariate research, including univariate analysis, does not provide the basis for examining the interactions of the multiple variables affecting children with developmental disabilities and their families. When nursing research does use a more multivariate design, as was done to a degree in this study, the analysis is often univariate, reducing the power and interpretation of the data.

Another possible reason for more univariate designs is the difficulty in achieving explicit clarity from the conceptualization of a multivariate study through the methodology, particularly through analysis. In any research, the clarity of the research variables is essential. However, the research variables, as modeled in nursing research textbooks (Polit & Hungler, 1983), as evident in nursing research reports (Denyes, in press), and as presented in this study, lack clear development of operational definitions of the research variables. Hopefully, the volumes of the new reviews of nursing research will provide some clarification of this issue (Werley & Fitzpatrick, 1983). This conference is also making a major contribution in establishing the collaborative research networks needed to advance nursing research, including the clarification of definitions of research variables such as social support.

I am not negating the state of the art in measuring nursing practice and families, but I believe nursing does have adequate knowledge and a practice base for nurse researchers to use their practice to develop multivariate conceptual frameworks with clear operational definitions for nursing research. For example, in working with children with developmental disabilities, we know clinically that it is more than the interaction of the mother and child that determines the use of support systems. Therefore, the conceptualization for research should be one that addresses the interdependence of the child, family, and environment. If the research must examine only a few of the variables perceived to affect the child and family, the rationale for selecting the limited variables can be addressed and future studies in the program of research derived from the multivariate conceptual framework can examine other pieces of the conceptual whole. As long as nursing continues to adopt the more linear research models from other disciplines when examining complex questions such as children with development disabilities and their families, the application to practice will continue to lag.

A conceptual framework that addresses the interdependence of the child, family, and environment is the human ecological framework proposed by (Bromfenbrenner 1977a; 1977b). This framework has received further interpretation and presentation as a family ecological framework by Paolucci and others (Paolucci, Hall, & Axinn, 1977; Andrews, Bubolz, & Paolucci, 1980). Eyres (Barnard & Eyres, 1977), Lancaster (1980), and Melson (1980) have provided further interpretation of this framework to nursing. The strength of the framework is that it uses an open system developmental model, addresses the environment, and is interactional. The framework also focuses on strengths and resources. While it is not possible to measure every variable which we perceive affects children and families, the family ecological framework can guide the researcher in identifying the whole, from which the researcher can then examine the variables pertinent to the study of a component of the whole. The family ecological model, I believe, is more consistent with the multivariate process used in nursing practice (Feetham & Humenick, 1982; Roberts & Feetham, 1982).

Social Support Definitions

Other conceptual research issues that will move research to practice are related to the lack of clarity in the operational definitions of the social support research. It is frequently reported that there is no consistent definition of social support networks (Norbeck, Lindsey, & Carrieri, 1981). Dr. Brandt used the number of resources as one measure of support, while perceived support was measured through the five relational functions of support defined by Weiss (1974). The physical (tangible) construct of social support was also measured in this study. Based on my clinical practice this construct is an important construct to measure in research on families who have children with developmental disabilities.

Descriptive research continues to be needed that will contribute to the clarification of the definitions of social support. Methodologies which provide for the subject defining social support versus the researcher are recommended. Dr. Brandt used a fixed format to measure resources (social support). Meister (1982) and others (Norbeck et al., 1981) have used a free choice of format. Although the free choice format has its own set of limitations, it is needed to further clarify the contextual definitions of social support. Dr. Brandt's work suggests a fixed format for examining social support has limitations in the study of families who have children with developmental disabilities.

Another issue related to social support is that there is a contextual nature to the perception of support. In other words, support which is helpful in one context may not be helpful in another. There needs to be continuing research, preferably longitudinal, that examines the patterns of use of support, using the respondent's definition (free choice format) and perception of support, and this research should use a variety of populations.

The issue of context is also related to who constitutes the samples in our research on social support. The process of using social support needs to be examined within the context of the family. When only mothers or other individual family members are used as subjects, the influence of other family members and the family as a whole in the identification and use of social support may not be examined. It has been suggested that we do not have a cadre of family research, but research on mothers' perceptions of their families (Safilios-Rothschild, 1970). Whenever possible, multiple family members should be included in our research. When this is not possible, I believe the researcher should identify why only mothers or fathers were sampled and then identify the limitations from such a sampling. Work by Meister (1982) and Norbeck et al. (1981) suggests that as researchers we should not even assume who is family, but include the subject's definition of their family, including pets if identified as part of the social support research.

Perceptions of Social Support

Another conceptual area important to social support research is the area of resources. While Dr. Brandt's instrument is a measure of personal resources, there are some considerations related to resources that may provide guidelines in future research. There are several criteria about resources identified in the family ecological framework that are applicable to social support research. Using the family ecological framework, resources must meet the following criteria to be available (Paolucci, et al., 1977). They must be:

1. perceived as available.
2. perceived as needed.
3. allocated among (family) persons.
4. transferable between individuals, family, and other groups.

These four criteria are implicit in the social support research that examines the respondents' perception of support. I believe, however, that the research would be strengthened if each of these criteria was measured overtly. Such measures would provide data on process which is fundamental to determining what social support is applicable to practice.

The four criteria related to the availability of resources are consistent with the work of Lazarus and others (Lazarus, 1974). The work of Lazarus examines the processing of data which is a conceptual base useful to further research on social support (Folkman, Schaefer, & Lazarus, 1979). This work also provides a conceptual link to the issue I have raised on nursing research which is consistent with the multivariate decision process of nursing practice. The work by Lazarus and others is also related to the concept of decision making by Fjellman (1976). Fjellman examines unnatural decisions which are a component of decisions in families of children with developmental disabilities. I believe Dr. Brandt's work, coupled with the conceptualization of resources from the family ecological framework, will provide a process for the social support research related to children with developmental disabilities and their families.

Summary Regarding Conceptual Issues

I will summarize the issues I have reviewed related to social support research; then I will briefly review components of Dr. Brandt's study which I believe exemplify the state of the art of reporting nursing research. The following conceptual and research issues have been identified as a basis to advance knowledge of social support for practice:

1. A conceptual framework such as that derived from human ecology is necessary to examine such multivariate problems.
2. Social support needs to be defined contextually by the subjects studied.
3. There needs to be more descriptive research that is processed based and preferably longitudinal.
4. The basic unit of measure of our research needs to be families.
5. The subjects need to be multiple family members. When this is not possible, the rationale and limitations of the researcher's sample selection need to be explicit.

The reality of the state of the art for multivariate research is recognized. However, nurse researchers should acknowledge the appropriateness of grounded research and define the major variables for study from their practice.

The limitations of continued adoption from other disciplines need to be recognized, and a blending of the knowledge from the disciplines is needed. It will take time for nursing to develop reliable and valid measures, but recognition of the strengths of our studies and our practice, while also overtly addressing the limitations, will advance the knowledge of social support from research to practice.

RESEARCH METHODOLOGY ISSUES

While recognizing the strengths of this research, there are some omissions that I have found not only in this paper but also in the 40 plus research papers I have reviewed elsewhere in recent months. I will review some of the more frequent omissions, because I believe attention to these conceptual and methodological concerns are necessary to advance and bring knowledge of social support and all nursing research to a level useful for professional practice.

Research Questions and Variables

The presentation of research is facilitated by an early, clear statement of the research questions. While a general statement of the purpose of the study, as done in Dr. Brandt's presentation is helpful, the statements of the research questions or hypotheses provide more clarity and direction to the reader. In addition, each presentation of the purpose and/or research questions should use the same terminology to avoid having the reader question the introduction of additional variables. For instance, in this study the terms--concurrent life events, stressful life events, and negative stressors--were all used within various statements of the purpose of the paper and/or study. When multiple terms are used, the reader is not sure if this indicates creativity or lack of conceptual clarity.

Intervening Variables

One area of omission, that if included would have contributed to the conceptual and methodological rigor, is the identification of possible intervening variables. The state of the art of research is not now, nor is it ever expected to be, refined enough to measure all possible intervening or confounding variables. Brief attention to what these variables are would add conceptual clarity. Methodological clarity would be achieved by identifying the possible intervening variables, and either explaining why they are not addressed in the design, or at least identifying that they exist but that it is not feasible to control for these variables.

In this study, recognition of possible intervening variables, such as the age range of the children with a developmental disability (6 months to 3 years), the perception of the child, and the mother's responses to a child with developmental disability would have strengthened the presentation. In addition, identifying other factors affecting the study, such as the sampling issues of using only mothers and the potential bias of a 40% return rate, would have strengthened the presentation. Every study has some limitations, whether it is inability to control for intervening variables or other factors. An overt quick acknowledgment of these limitations frees the reader to focus on the strengths of the study and teaches the novice researcher.

Instruments

Another methodological issue omitted is the evidence of the reliability and validity of the instruments. When not overtly addressed, the reader is left to ponder if the researcher is not aware of the importance of the issue, and/or if such data are not available on the instruments. While Dr. Brandt did reference the instruments, more overt attention would have been helpful. Even if instruments are used that have limited or no reported data on reliability and validity, recognition of this with a statement as to why the instruments were used reaffirms to the reader the researcher's attention to these basic methodological considerations.

Literature Reviews

An issue related to conceptual clarity can also be identified under the category of omissions. It appears that as nursing research is evolving, the reports of nursing research may be bypassed when the literature is reviewed for previous research. I encourage nurses reporting their research to make explicit their knowledge of the literature, both in nursing and other disciplines. What is required within a review of the literature is the statement that reports of related studies are not reported by nurse researchers and/or in the nursing literature. In addition, as part of the literature review, for conceptual clarity, it is helpful when the nurse researcher identifies the relevance of related research in other disciplines to nursing and particularly to the nursing research in question. I have found the relationship of other research to nursing is often so obvious to the nurse researcher that the relevance is not made explicit in the report of nursing research. In order to advance nursing knowledge, to communicate the uniqueness of nursing, and to educate nurses and professionals from other disciplines, however, these relationships should be made explicit in the conceptual development of nursing research. In this study, a few statements as to why nurses and nursing research need to examine the relationship between social support and negative life events of the mothers who have children with developmental delays would have added conceptual clarity and reinforced the relevance of the study to nursing.

SUMMARY

As indicated, the points of omission I have just reviewed are not unique to this study. The areas of omission I have cited are common conceptual and methodologic concerns in both nursing research and research from other disciplines. They may be perceived as given and, therefore, implicit, but I believe their implicitness diminishes progress in a scientific discipline. We were asked to identify what advances are needed to bring the knowledge of social support to a level useful for professional practice. I believe these basic issues are fundamental to this quest. The frequency with which I have observed these omissions suggests that they are not mundane, but perhaps contribute to the discrepancy between research and practice and the building of nursing knowledge. Consistent attention to these areas in all research presentations provides a basic rigor necessary in a developing discipline.

Dr. Brandt has addressed an important area relevant to nursing and also to children with developmental disabilities and their families. Her study provided further testing of an instrument that has been recognized for its potential in nursing research. In her own summary statement, Dr. Brandt articulately reviews issues relevant to future research in social support and children and families. By building on the earlier research of children with developmental disabilities and their families, Dr. Brandt has contributed knowledge by examining a linkage between the earlier research and the construct of social support. I believe her study provides an important base for future research.

DISCUSSION

L. Walker: In research studies where complex theoretical relationships are proposed, it is often quite helpful to self-consciously identify the theoretical network and its corresponding operational network of variables. Both Gibbs (1972) and Hinshaw (1979a, 1979b) have described methods for moving from the theoretical model underlying a research project to the vast network of variables that serve to connect the theoretical model with empirical phenomena. Graphic depictions of models across theoretical and operational levels can be very helpful in locating errors, ambiguities, and gaps in hypotheses tested and their theoretical interpretations.

J. Fawcett: One problem with a lot of our research is we assume that the person is a holistic being; yet we use mechanistic methods of investigation. This is especially so in the choice of statistics. Most, if not all statistical procedures, including multivariate techniques, are based on adding sums of squares. This reflects a mechanistic, quantitative, additive view of the person. That is, the person is treated as a sum of parts, rather than as a unified whole. We need new statistics to measure the person as a holistic being. Overton and Reese (1973) point this out in one of their papers on the mechanistic and organismic (holistic) views of the world, but they do not identify the statistics that should be used.

S. Feetham: I agree with Dr. Fawcett regarding the need for statistical procedures that can more accurately address what she calls holistic measures. A strength of Dr. Brandt's paper was that her work conceptually implies what Dr. Fawcett calls a holistic viewpoint and I have referred to as a multivariate or full theoretical model. Another strength of Dr. Brandt's paper was to suggest where to go from here. I hope my point was made clear--that I realize the complexity and formidible task ahead of us. I do think the issue of the holistic view is something that we can try to communicate through a multivariate conceptual framework (full theoretical model). As long as we use A + B conceptual models, we are implying a limited thing that I don't think we practice as nurses.

P. Brandt: The presentation today was based on a substudy of a multivariate study. The purpose of the major multivariate study was to investigate whether social support and negative life events influenced maternal discipline and environmental stimulation of the handicapped child. Analysis was performed by means of multiple regression. The research questions were formulated to study maternal parenting issues. However, in the future, it would be beneficial to address fathering, as well as family system issues. The aims of the substudy were to enhance the understanding of the interrelationship of support and negative life events and to describe the conditions experienced by mothers of handicapped children.

R. Lederman: How would you deal methodologically with the problem of administering similar instruments to both husband and wife, particularly those that measure social support or the couple's relationship? It is likely that there will be communication about how each partner responded to questions. If while the instrument is being filled out, there is an explicit request or even some implicit knowledge that the respondent is going to be asked how she replied, this is likely to confound the results. How do you deal with this issue if you want to elicit objective responses from the whole family, including children and the extended family?

J. Fawcett: One solution to the problem mentioned by Dr. Lederman is to use instruments with many items. For example, I have used a semantic differential questionnaire to measure spouses' strength of identification. The semantic differential includes 10 concepts, each of which is differentiated along a 7-point scale on 9 bipolar adjective pairs (Lazowick, 1955). The questionnaires are completed separately by each spouse. I think it is unlikely that either spouse could remember his or her responses to all the items, so I don't think that their discussion of the questionnaire would influence results.

M. Cranley: There is another way to approach that, depending on what you consider to be the unit of research. If the unit of research is the family, then what you want is the consensus view, and family researchers are using single instruments that are administered, not separately and equally, but simultaneously. We're using one of these instruments that's a life-stress measure (McCubbin, n.d.b). You administer it to both partners together, and the couple complete the list together. They agree upon things that have occurred in their life; then, they agree on the amount of stress or reorganization that these events caused. The researcher has to serve as a counselor sometimes to help them come to an agreement. We use a coping skill inventory that operates in the same way (McCubbin, n.d.a), and the couple fill it out together. The couple complete these instruments together because the philosophical belief is that the information you're interested in is the family view and the family as a research unit--not his view, her view, or the difference between their views.

K. Barnard: But then you have to ask if the agreed upon view is the family view.

M. Cranley: That's true. That's a particularly troublesome conceptual issue when the family includes older children. Should the instrument be administered to parents and children together? Do you have to get a consensus? Obviously issues of family power come into play in getting a group response, especially with children. I haven't tried to grapple with that issue yet. I'm challenged enough right now just dealing with the couple.

S. Feetham: I think the points you're making on the family instrument are very true. We found that when these instruments are distributed simultaneously, one parent completes it before the other one. There are also other dynamics.

In the last study that we did, there were multiple activities for both parents which were not done simultaneously; that worked better. There was still some comparison of time, but at least the fathers were involved in some activities while the mothers were doing the family functioning. We found that when they both completed the family functioning at the same time, it created all kinds of problems. One partner wanted to see what the other one put down. Some parents required less time than the other. I still believe that we do need to obtain family data, but I'm not sure about the state of the art in doing this. We need data from all family members, but as indicated in my critique, if we can't get the information for very practical reasons, then we must acknowledge that we know why we're not obtaining full family data and how this may affect the results.

L. Walker: I'd like to congratulate Dr. Brandt in one thing that she did methodologically which I find really interesting; that was testing multiple competing hypotheses about the impact of stressors. You stated explicitly there were competing alternate hypotheses to explain outcomes. That's rarely done. Testing competing hypotheses doesn't require a lot extra in terms of design, except thinking in advance of the alternate hypotheses and making sure the measures are there to address these hypotheses.

L. Cronenwett: I thought Dr. Brandt's finding of an inverse relationship between negative life events and perceived support was interesting. Two things occurred to me. The negative life events you illustrate were often partner-related problems. Perhaps then you were in a sense measuring the same thing. In other words, if a person's negative life events included, for instance, sexual difficulties, major changes in arguments, in-law difficulties, or a change in closeness with others, you would certainly expect to find less perceived support because it's the same thing they're reporting on the LES Scale. On the other hand, maybe people develop social support networks, and there's a certain amount of give and take that goes on that is comfortable for everybody. When one person's needs increases dramatically, however, the network can't respond. The equilibrium of the support network is disrupted, and that's why you get a perception of decreased support. That would happen to everybody, regardless of whether they were socially competent or not.

P. Brandt: The reason for analyzing the relationship between perceived support and negative life events while controlling for losses is that the person's support may be influenced by interpersonal losses experienced through events such as divorce, jail, or death. If the number of helpful persons in one's network decreases, there may subsequently be a decrease in one's level of perceived support. The findings of the study of support and negative life/events of mothers with disabled children revealed, however, that the relationship was maintained between support and negative life events when interpersonal loss events were statistically controlled.

L. Cronenwett: The other interesting thing was that only 55% of your sample could count on their partner for help with the handicapped child. I thought that was astonishing, especially when the presence of a partner has been rated as a big predictor of support.

S. Feetham: In the analysis, have you controlled for the amount of partner help and the age of the child? In the longitudinal study (Feetham, 1980), a pattern was seen in the level of the father's involvement in the care activities related to the special care of the child. The fathers were very involved in the care, but by 18 months, their involvement in normal infant care activities was less than the fathers of healthy infants.

In relating your data to these findings, I wonder if the high level of the father's involvement in special care of the child begins to diminish after 18 months, eventually leaving the mother to do this care alone. If the father's involvement does decrease, then what does that mean in relation to nursing intervention and resources to the family.

An important finding is when comparing families of healthy infants and families of infants with myelodysplasia, the parents of children with myelodysplasia (spina bifida) reported the same level of enjoyment, playing with their infants, etc., as the parents of healthy infants. I think it is important to look at these data and the strengths of families and resources because we are so often reporting the negative kinds of data. We need to emphasize these positive data, such as the pattern of high level of enjoyment and those fun kinds of things our parents were experiencing with their children.

T. Antonucci: How long is the longitudinal study?

S. Feetham: We only did it for the first 18 months.

T. Antonucci: I wondered. Perhaps the fathers who helped least early on are lost to both the family and to the study through divorce. The ones who remain would then be those most likely to help with the care of the child.

S. Feetham: I think your point is very well taken because by 12 months we were having a significant difference between the mothers' and fathers' scores on the family functioning discrepancy score (Roberts & Feetham, 1982). There were different perceptions of what is, what should be, and what was going on within the family. And those families that had the high ranges on the family discrepant scores were the ones that we identified clinically as being families with difficulties. Also, clinically we were seeing that when the child was 4-5 years of age, the mothers were overwhelmed as they realized that these children were not going to get better. My sense was that our study was beginning to pick up these responses from those very early months, and perhaps with an intervention study, we could hopefully do something with those families that were showing problems at the first year of life. As a result of the intervention, the families would now stay together, but also perhaps there are things we can do to facilitate those families working together.

D. Magyary: Dr. Brandt's results suggest that parents of handicapped children do not necessarily perceive professionals as being supportive. Very few mothers identified health professionals as members of their support system. You know, we sit around and talk about providing support in sort of an abstract way, but it would be interesting to go right in and say to parents, "Why are you not seeking out professionals?" or "Why is it that when you do, you get very little satisfaction?"

At times, developmentally delayed children are seen by an interdisciplinary health team without having one health professional responsible for coordinating their health care. This type of fragmented care may result in the family's feeling nonsupported. Often the nurse is designated as the case manager, but in some health facilities this may not occur.

K. Barnard: The professional is sometimes viewed as an obstacle that one has to cope with, not as a support.

D. Magyary: This is interesting, because supposedly we see ourselves as patient advocates, but obviously, I'm not sure they do.

S. Feetham: Our study (Feetham, et al., 1982) supports what you're saying, Dr. Barnard, because when we ask the parents "What is most helpful?" and "What is most difficult for you now?" at 3 and 6 months, they identified the professional as part of that cadre of being helpful. At 12 months, the professional, particularly the physician, emerged as least helpful. Part of that, I believe is because with children with myelodysplasia that is the time they're going into braces or parapodiums for the first time. This may be the time of orthopedic surgeries, and it is the time of the anniversary of the birth. Parents are bringing the child back into clinic and being reinforced about a lot of things that are wrong with the child, while their day-to-day life with the child is focusing on what is right with the child. Our parents identify how exhausted and devastated they are after clinic visits, and I believe part of it is that we focus on those things that are wrong. I do think that that is one reason why professionals present as not being as helpful because we are those reminders about what the parents least like to be reminded.

P. Brandt: It is critical to study the helping process and the model used by individual professionals. We also need to become enlightened about the outcomes for clients whose style of coping conflicts with the style of helping provided by the professional. Thus, the match between client coping styles and professional helping styles warrants further analysis.

S. Humenick: It seems to me that we're experiencing a lot of ambivalence about our role in the social support system. I hear periodically that we don't want to make people dependent on us; yet, if they don't see us as a support, we are not quite sure where we fit in. Dr. Feetham has used a discrepancy scale to construct what people think should be with what actually is. Has this format been used to measure the client's perception of the support of health care professionals?

S. Feetham: It was used in several formats. Originally, Porter (1962) used it in business management studies to measure self-actualization in regard to control and decision making. The Porter format was used at Wayne State University College of Nursing in relation to a nationwide family planning study. This study examined the knowledge base of health professionals in family planning. I think the format does have applicability to a variety of measures.

S. Humenick: We need to know when patients need our support and when they want our support. When do they see us as providing too much or being too forceful, and when do they see us as not there when they need us?

P. MacElveen-Hoehn: Dr. Lederman and I were talking this morning about the kind of approach to helping that we use, and we were speculating about how problem focused we are as nurses. Nurses are always going to go in there, find out what's wrong, and fix it, which is kind of a mental set that is fairly common in our profession. Part of what we do is contrary to learning theory in that whatever is going all right and smoothly in the family is rarely acknowledged by nurses. If it's okay, we don't pay any attention; we move that issue aside, and we look for the problems. People with whom we have contact rarely receive any positive feedback or reinforcement for anything that's going well as a result. In a small study I did with women who had disabilities, they talked about never getting any affirmation about any part of them that was normal, okay, or healthy, and this was a loss to them in their interactions with professionals (MacElveen-Hoehn, 1981). And when anyone said "Gee, your cervix looks healthy," they were just so excited because they heard so little of that in the system. I think the question of how we interact with people is really something that we need to look at as we investigate support. We need to know more about how to assess the kinds of nursing behaviors and interventions that are experienced as supportive by families. I think we have underestimated the influence of expressed concern, acknowledgment, and affirmation to empower and enable people.

J. Fawcett: Additionally, it seems to me that in our zeal to reduce or avoid patients' dependence on health professionals that we place too large a burden on the patient. We say, "If you need us, call us; we are here." Instead, I think we should be more accessible to our patients. For example, we tell new mothers to call us if they have any problems after they are discharged from the hospital. We do this even though we know that the first several days at home with a new baby frequently are so chaotic that the women cannot even find our phone number. I think it would be more reasonable for us to call the new mother to ask how things are going, rather than to expect her to call us.

S. Humenick: We can't expect overwhelmed depressed people to call us, because a symptom of depression often is the inability to make a phone call.

G. Anderson: I'd like to elaborate on what was said a couple of minutes ago. Throughout the conference, my thoughts have returned to Haim Ginott (1956) and his parent effectiveness therapy. Ginott offers a way of communicating which is nonjudgmental, involves the other person in the decision making process, and helps that person to cope more effectively. The person providing support avoids active coping. The process fosters mutual respect, can be amazingly energy giving, and leads to acceptance of responsibility by the person being supported. This process can be generalized, and thus is useful for teachers in interaction with their students, for one spouse in interaction with the other, and for any person wishing to be supportive. We, as a group, are able to cope very well, but Ginott's perspective may explain some of the findings reported here, i.e., that the support has not been satisfying. I wonder if there has been active coping by those providing support, and if those who needed the support might have benefited more from the kind of approach that Ginott espouses.

G. Crawford: I wanted to return to what Dr. Brandt was saying about nurses being problem-focused. There are some of us who are interested in getting away from that orientation and who prefer to use the conceptualization that Rozella Schlotfeldt (1975, 1981) developed in which the focus is on health seeking behaviors and health seeking mechanisms. Her point is that you look at what is going well for a person, and then the nurse's role is to enhance those factors. We're really neglecting positive coping factors when we limit our focus to problem solving. In Schlotfeldt's view, problems are recognized, but the nurse focuses on identifying and enhancing the assets people have to deal with those problems.

J. Norbeck: I'd like to continue that line of thought. As we talk about measuring social support, there's always the image of the researcher or the clinician examining the network list or total score and saying, "This person is surely isolated," when in fact the persons get an indication of their status from filling it out. Linda Cronenwett mentioned there was a lot of insight as people filled out the questionnaires. I've certainly had that experience when people first fill out a life stress scale, then fill out the social support scale, finally put those two things together, and think, "No wonder it seems like everything is falling apart at the edges." It seems like self-examination could also be a very good vehicle for a clinical intervention, particularly if you took a collegial approach with the patient and didn't say, "Well, everyone should have at least 12 people in their network, and of that, 40% should be friends." The collegial approach would permit patients to just talk about their stresses and supports, they would come to some conclusions, and then use these from which they would build. This approach does require nursing to change its stance in terms of the use of the information.

D. Magyary: I'd like to add some realism. Nursing care activities are directed toward promoting and maintaining a state of wellness. But often, the provision of financial reimbursement per third party payment does not occur for nursing activities related to health promotion and maintenance. Thus, within many health care facilities, the nurse is forced to use a medical model directed toward the treatment of problems in order to receive third party payment for nursing services. We, as nurses, need to educate our legislators about the need to broaden third party payment to include nursing activities to prevent illnesses as well as treat illnesses.

M. Curry: I would certainly agree that we need both second and third order change in how we define and operate our health care systems. I would also like to follow up on Dr. Norbeck's comments regarding the use of the research process as a clinical intervention. I have had a similar experience in my study of antepartum hospitalization (Curry, 1983), in which women complete both Sarason's Life Experience Survey (Sarason, et al., 1978) and the NSSQ (Norbeck, et al., 1981). Many women have commented that they found completing the questionnaires helpful, both in terms of helping to pass the time and in helping them to gain a different perspective on their situation. Further, after delivery, most sample women describe participating in the study as one of their most effective coping mechanisms. It is clear that we need to systematically document these effects and begin to describe both their positive and negative effects.

J. Fawcett: One potential problem with the measurement of social support is that many of the instruments use quantity as an important variable. What happens when an individual identifies just one person as supportive? It may be that that person provides sufficient support, so others are not needed or wanted. I think that both quantity (the number of people identified as supportive) and quality (the extent to which each person is supportive) have to be considered in the measurement of social support.

T. Antonucci: You would have done very well on perceived support, and that's what we're finding out is the most predictive measure of social support to overall well-being.

S. Humenick: This leads us back to Dr. Feetham's discrepancy scale work. If one perceives no discrepancy in what is needed and what is received, then one feels adequately supported regardless of the actual level of support.

J. Fawcett: That refers to what Dr. Brandt has said, "Support is not support unless you want or need it." When support is not wanted or needed, the people who are trying to be supportive are just bothersome.

P. Brandt: The results of a study on social support are heavily influenced by the measure of support used to obtain information. The three estimates of support used in this study provided different indications of support. Thus, one needs to carefully examine not only the psychometrics of the instruments used but whether they are quantitative, qualitative, concurrent, global, or situation specific.

REFERENCES

Andrews, M., Bubolz, M., & Paolucci, B. (1980). An ecological approach to study of the family. *Marriage and Family Review, 3,* 29-49.

Barnard, K., & Eyres, S. (1977). *Child health assessment. Part II: Results of the first twelve months of life.* Seattle, WA: University of Washington Press.

Baum, A., Singer, J., & Baum, C. (1981). Stress and the environment. *Journal of Social Issues, 37*(1), 5-35.

Beckman-Bell, P. (1981). Child-related stress in families of handicapped children. *Topics in Early Childhood Special Education, 1,* 45-53.

Brandt, P. (1981). *The relationship of the mother's negative life experiences and social support to the restrictive discipline and environmental stimulation of her developmentally disabled child.* Unpublished doctoral dissertation, University of Washington.

Brandt, P., & Weinert, C. (1981). The PRQ--A social support measure. *Nursing Research, 30,* 277-280.

Brickman, P., Rabinowitz, V., Karuza, J., Coates, D., Cohn, E., & Kidder, L. (1982). Models of helping and coping. *American Psychologists, 37*(4), 368-384.

Bronfenbrenner, U. (1977a). *The experimental ecology of human development.* Cambridge, MA: Harvard Press.

Bronfenbrenner U. (1977b). Toward an experimental ecology of human development. *American Psychologist, 32,* 513-531.

Brown, G., Bhrolchain, M.N., & Harris, T. (1975). Social class and psychiatric disturbance among women in an urban population. *Sociology, 9,* 225-254.

Burr, W.R. (1973). *Theory construction and the sociology of the family.* New York: John Wiley & Sons.

Caplan, G. (1976). The family as a support system. In G. Caplan & M. Killilea (Eds.), *Support systems and mutual help.* New York: Grune and Stratton.

Cohen, S. (1982). *Social support, stress and the buffering hypothesis: A review of naturalistic studies.* Unpublished manuscript, Department of Psychology, Carnegie-Mellon University.

Cowen, E. (1982). Help is where you find it. *American Psychologist, 37*(4), 385-395.

Cranley, M. (1981). Development of a tool for the measure of maternal attachment during pregnancy. *Nursing Research, 30,* 281-284.

Crockenberg, S. (1981). Infant irritability, mother responsiveness and social support influences on the security of infant-mother attachment. *Child Development, 52,* 857-865.

Cummings S. (1976). The impact of the child's deficiency on the father: A study of fathers of mentally retarded and chronically ill children. *American Journal of Orthopsychiatry, 46*(2), 246-255.

Cummings, S., Bayley, H., & Rie, H. (1966). Effects of the child's deficiency on the mother: A study of mothers of mentally retarded, chronically ill and neurotic children. *American Journal of Orthopsychiatry, 36*(4), 595-600.

Curry, M.A. (in progress). *The effects of long-term antepartum hospitalization on maternal behavior and the family.* Research funded by NIH Division of Nursing, # ORS1088C.

D'Arcy, E. (1968). Congential defects: Mother's reactions to first information. *British Medical Journal, 3,* 796-798.

Denyes, M.J. (in press). Critical review of nursing practice research related to school age children and adolescents. In H. Werley and J. Fitzpatrick (Eds.), *Annual review of nursing research* (Vol. 1).

Eyres, S. (1979). Instrumentation and findings: Life change. In K. Barnard & S. Eyres (Eds.), *Child health assessment. Part 2: The first year of life.* Washington, DC: U.S. Department of Health, Education, & Welfare.

Feetham, S. (1976). *Parent expectations of parent groups and of professionals--A research report.* Paper presented at the Annual Meeting of the Association Care of Children's Health, Denver, Colorado.

Feetham, S. (1980). *The relationship of family functioning to infant, parent and family environment outcomes in the first 10 months following the birth of an infant with myelodysplasia.* Unpublished doctoral dissertation, Michigan State University. (University Microfilms No. 80-20697)

Feetham, S., & Humenick, S. (1982). The Feetham family functioning survey. In S. Humenick (Ed.), *Analysis of current assessment strategies in the health care of young children and childbearing families.* New York: Appleton-Century-Crofts.

Feetham, S., Knecht, L., & Kai, S. (1982, April). *Comparison of family functioning in families of infants with myelodysplasia and families of healthy infants at 6 and 18 months.* Paper presented at the Fifth Biennial Eastern Conference on Nursing Research, Baltimore, Maryland.

Field, T.M. (1980). Interactions of high-risk infants: Quantitative and qualitative differences. In D. Sawin, R. Hawkins, L., Walker, & J. Penticuff (Eds.), *Exceptional infant: Psychosocial risks in infant-environment transactions* (Vol. 4). New York: Brunner-Mazel.

Fjellman, S.M. (1976). Natural and unnatural decision making: A critique of decision theory. *Ethos, 4*(1), 73-94.

Folkman, S., Schaefer, C., & Lazarus, R. (1979). Cognitive processes as mediators of stress and coping. In V. Hamilton & D. Warburton (Eds.), *Human stress and cognition: An information process approach.* New York: J. Wiley & Sons.

Friedrich, W. (1979). Predictors of the coping behaviors of mothers of handicapped children. *Journal of Consulting & Clinical Psychology, 47*(6), 1140-1141.

Frodi, A. (1981). Contribution of infant characteristics to child abuse. *American Journal of Mental Deficiency, 85*(4), 341-349.

Gabel, H., McDowell, J., & Cerreto, M. (1983). Family adaptation to the handicapped infant. In S. Garwood & R. Fewell (Eds.), *Educating handicapped infants: Issues in development and intervention.* Rockville, MD: Aspen Systems Corporation.

Gath, A. (1974). Sibling reactions to mental handicap: A comparison of the brothers and sisters of mongol children. *Journal of Child Psychology and Psychiatry, 15,* 187-198.

Gath, A. (1977). The impact of an abnormal child upon the parents. *British Journal of Psychiatry, 130,* 405-410.

Gibbs, J.P. (1972). *Sociological theory construction.* Hinsdale, IL: Dryden Press.

Ginott, H.G. (1956). *Between parent and child.* New York: Macmillan.

Greenberg, H. (1971). A comparison of infant-mother interactional behavior and normal infants. In J. Hellmuth (Ed.), *The exceptional infant* (Vol. 2). New York: Brunner-Mazel.

Grier, M. (1981). The need for data in making nursing decisions. In H. Werley & M. Grier (Eds.), *Nursing information systems.* New York: Springer Publishing.

Hinshaw, A.S. (1979a). Planning for logical consistency among three research structures. *Western Journal of Nursing Research, 1,* 250-253.

Hinshaw, A.S. (1979b). Theoretical substruction: An assessment process. *Western Journal of Nursing Research, 1,* 319-324.

Holmes, T.H., & Rahe, R.H. (1967). The social readjustment rating scale. *Journal of Psychomatic Research, 11,* 213-218.

Holroyd, J. (1974). The questionnaire on resources and stress: An instrument to measure family response to a handicapped family member. *Journal of Community Psychology, 2*(1), 92-94.

Howard, J. (1976). *Families.* New York: Simon & Schuster.

Howard, J. (1978). The influence of children's developmental dysfunctions on marital quality and family interaction. In R. Lerner & G. Spanier (Eds.), *Child influences on marital and family interaction: A life-span perspective.* New York: Academic Press.

Johnson, J.H., & Sarason, I.G. (1979). Moderation variables in life stress research. In I.G. Sarason, & C.D. Spielberger (Eds.), *Stress and anxiety* (Vol. 6). New York: Hemisphere Publishing.

Jones, O. (1980). Mother-child communication in very young Down's syndrome and normal children. In T. Field, C. Dabiri, N. Hallock, & H. Shuman (Eds.), *High risk infants and children: Adult and peer interactions.* New York: Academic Press.

Kobasa, S. (1979). Stressful life events, personality and health: An inquiry into hardiness. *Journal of Personality and Social Psychology, 37,* 1-11.

Lancaster, J. (1980). *Community mental health nursing: An ecological perspective.* St. Louis: C.V. Mosby.

Lazarus, R. (1974). Psychological stress and coping in adaptation and illness. *International Journal of Psychiatry in Medicine, 5,* 321-333.

Lazowick, L.M. (1955). On the nature of identification. *Journal of Abnormal and Social Psychology, 51,* 175-183.

MacElveen-Hoehn, P. (1981). *Disabled women seeking care during health and illness.* Unpublished manuscript, University of Washington.

Marshall, N., Hegrenes, J., & Goldstein, S. (1973). Verbal interactions: Mothers and their retarded children vs. mothers and their nonretarded children. *American Journal of Mental Deficiency, 77,* 415-419.

McAndrew, I. (1976). Children with a handicap and their families. *Child: Care, Health and Development, 2,* 213-237.

McCubbin, H. *Family crisis oriented personal evaluation scales (F-COPES).* St. Paul, MN: (Author) Family Stress Project, University of Minnesota, n.d. (a)

McCubbin, H. *Family inventory of life events and changes (FILE)*. St. Paul, MN: (Author) Family Stress Project, University of Minnesota, n.d. (b)

Meister, S.B. (1982). *Perceived social support sub networks and well being at life change*. Unpublished doctoral dissertation, University of Michigan.

Melson, G.F. (1980). *Family and environment: An ecosystem perspective*. Minneapolis: Burgess Publishing.

Norbeck, J.S., Lindsey, A.M., & Carrieri, V.L. (1981). The development of an instrument to measure social support. *Nursing Research, 30,* 264-269.

Nuckolls, K., Cassel, J., & Kaplan, B. (1972). Psychosocial assets, life crisis and the prognosis of pregnancy. *American Journal of Epidemiology, 95,* 431-441.

Olshansky, S. (1966). Parent responses to a mentally defective child. *Mental Retardation, 4,* 21-23.

Overton, W.F., & Reese, H.W. (1973). Models of development: Methodological implications. In J.R. Nesselroade & H.W. Reese (Eds.), *Life-span developmental psychology: Methodological issues*. New York: Academic Press.

Paolucci, B., Hall, V.A., & Axinn, N.W. (1977). *Family decision making: An ecosystem approach*. New York: John Wiley & Sons.

Pearlin, L.I., & Schooler, C. (1978). The structure of coping. *Journal of Health and Social Behavior, 19*(1), 2-21.

Polit, D.F., & Hungler, B.P. (1983). *Nursing research: Principles and methods* (2nd ed.). Philadelphia: J.B. Lippincott.

Porter, L.W. (1962). Job attitudes in management. *Journal of Applied Psychology, 46*(6), 375-385.

Roberts, C., & Feetham, S. (1982). An instrument for assessing family functioning across three areas of relationships. *Nursing Research, 31*(4), 231-235.

Safilios-Rothschild, C. (1970). The study of family power structure: A review, 1960-1969. *Journal of Marriage and the Family,* 539-552.

Sarason, I., Johnson, J., & Siegel, J. (1978). Assessing the impact of life changes: Development of the life experiences survey. *Journal of Consulting and Clinical Psychology, 46,* 932-946.

Schlotfeldt, R.M. (1975). The need for a conceptual framework. In P.J. Verhonick (Ed.), *Nursing research I*. Boston: Little, Brown.

Schlotfeldt, R.M. (1981). Nursing in the future. *Nursing Outlook,* 295-301.

Schroeder, S.R., Mulnick, J.A., & Schroeder, C.S. (1980). Management of severe behavior problems of the retarded. In N.R. Ellis (Ed.), *Handbook of mental deficiency,* (2nd ed.). Hillsdale, NJ: Erlbaum.

Stone, N., & Chesney, B. (1978). Attachment behaviors in handicapped infants. *Mental Retardation, 16,* 8-12.

Stress and Families Project. (1980). *Lives in stress: A context for depression*. Boston: Harvard School of Education.

Tew, B.J., Laurence, K.M., Payne, H., & Rawnsley, K. (1977). Marital stability following the birth of a child with spina bifida. *British Journal of Psychiatry, 131,* 79-82.

Thoit, P. (1982). Conceptual, methodological, and theoretical problems in studying social support as a buffer against life stress. *Journal of Health and Social Behavior, 23,* 145-159.

Turner, R.J. (1981). Social support as a contingency in psychological well-being. *Journal of Health and Social Behavior, 22,* 357-367.

Vaughn, B., Egeland, B., Sroufe, L., & Waters, E. (1979). Individual differences in infant-mother attachment at twelve and eighteen months: Stability and change in families under stress. *Child Development, 50,* 971-975.

Waisbren, S. (1980). Parents' reactions after the birth of a developmentally disabled child. *American Journal of Mental Deficiency, 84*(4), 345-351.

Weiss, R. (1974). The provisions of social relationships. In A. Rubin (Ed.), *Doing unto others.* New York: Prentice-Hall.

Wellman, B. (1981). Applying network analyses to the study of support. In B. Gottlieb (Ed.), *Social networks and social support.* Beverly Hills: Sage Publications.

Werley, H., & Fitzpatrick, J. (Eds.). (1983). *Annual review of nursing research* (Vol. 1). New York: Springer Publishing.

Wikler, L., Wasow, M., & Hatfield, E. (1981). Chronic sorrow revisited: Parent vs. professional depiction of the adjustment of parents of mentally retarded children. *American Journal of Orthopsychiatry, 51*(1), 63-70.

Zautra, A., & Maio, J. (1981). Life events and life quality variability. *Journal of Community Psychology, 9,* 148-152.

Social Support of Teenage Mothers*

Ramona T. Mercer, R.N., Ph.D., FAAN, Kathryn C. Hackley, M.S.N., and Alan Bostrom, Ph.D.

The purpose of this paper is to report the social support perceived as available by teenage mothers during their first year of motherhood and the correlation of perceived social support with maternal role attainment variables. Social support was one of 11 independent variables studied for their impact on the maternal role for three age groups of first-time mothers: 15-19, 20-29, and 30-42 years. Social support described was categorized into four types--informational, emotional, physical, and appraisal--and by the network size.

Sixty-six teenagers agreed to participate in the study, and they were interviewed in the hospital during early postpartum and in their homes or a setting of their choice at 1, 4, 8, and 12 months after birth. This highly mobile population was difficult to follow, and there was a subject loss over the year of 39.4% (N = 26).

During early postpartum, the only type of support to correlate with maternal attachment (one of the two maternal role attainment variables measured at that time) was informational support, and teenagers had received significantly less than older women. There were no significant correlations of any of the support variables with the teenagers' perceptions of their neonate, the second measure of maternal role attainment. Teenagers received less emotional support from mates and from parents than older women.

At 1 month postpartum, teenagers received less emotional support than older mothers, but reported more informational support. Support variables failed to correlate with maternal role attainment measures of perceptions of the neonate, ways of handling irritating child behaviors, or infants' growth and development. Physical and emotional support correlated positively with feelings of love for the infant, and informational and emotional support correlated positively with gratification in the mothering role. Physical support correlated positively with maternal competency behaviors.

*This report is from the project, "Factors Having An Impact on Maternal Role Attainment the First Year of Motherhood," supported by Maternal and Child Health (Social Security Act, Title V), Grant No. MC-R-060435-03.

Appreciation is expressed to Dr. Gilbert A. Webb, Children's Hospital, for his support in recruiting subjects and help with the project.

This paper was revised after the conference in response to some of the comments noted in the critique by Dr. Crawford.

At 4 months after birth, teenagers continued to receive less emotional support than older mothers, but there were no differences in other types of support received. Physical support correlated positively with maternal gratification in the role, infants' growth and development, and maternal competency behaviors. Other types of support and the size of the network did not correlate with any of the maternal role attainment variables.

Teenagers continued to receive less emotional support than older mothers at 8 months after birth, although there were no differences in other types of support received. The support variables failed to correlate significantly with any of the five maternal role attainment variables at this time.

At 1 year after birth, teenagers perceived more informational support than older mothers, but there were no differences in other types of support. Emotional support correlated positively with maternal competency behaviors and ways of handling irritating behaviors. Other types of support failed to correlate with the role attainment variables. There was a negative correlation between informational and emotional support, suggesting a possibility of some conflict in the support system. A greater percentage of mates were listed as supportive and fewer mothers than at earlier test periods, suggesting movement toward independence from parents.

The teenager who becomes a mother deals with several potential conflicts regarding independence because of her developmental stage. First, the infant's absolute dependency on the mother and the mother's relative need for the infant (Benedek, 1959) may cause difficulty for an immature woman who has not achieved independence from her own parents. Second, a mother's identification with her infant if it permits her to regress by repeating and satisfying her own passive, dependent, receptive needs (Benedek, 1949) may be a severe threat to one who has only recently asserted, or is in the process of asserting, independence. Third, the adolescent's need to break away or move out from the nuclear family (Gould, 1972) may be superseded by the need for physical and financial help with an infant. Single parenthood may conflict with the adolescent's developing personal value system and result in lower sense of self-worth (Josselyn, 1971).

Parenthood may facilitate areas of development for the adolescent, however. The early transition to motherhood has the potential of facilitating the young woman's achievement of a sexual identity and feminine role (LaBarre, 1968). Motherhood may lead to more mature, gratifying relationships with family members (Mercer, 1980). Support, especially from mates and mothers, has appeared to contribute to the more mature relationships.

The needed support from the mate or parents may not be available, however, as alienation from family may have contributed to the early pregnancy (Rosenstock, 1980; Welches, 1979). Additionally, it seems that a changed relationship with the mother is a prerequisite for the mother to be of support (Barglow, 1968). This presents special problems for her own mother, since the teenager's pregnancy precipitates her mother's premature movement into and acceptance of grandmotherhood (Bryan-Logan & Dancy, 1974; Poole & Hoffman, 1981; Smith, 1971).

This paper reports on the correlation of social support as perceived by teenage mothers with maternal role attainment over the first year of motherhood. Social support was one of 11 independent variables studied. The theoretical framework for the study was derived from role theory from an interactionist perspective and relevant literature (Mercer, 1981b). The methodology for the study is described elsewhere in more detail (Mercer, 1981a; Mercer, Hackley, & Bostrom, 1982).

LITERATURE REVIEW

Research to date portrays social support "as a ubiquitous yet indistinctly defined concept" (Barrera, 1981, p. 70). Many approaches have been used to study support, but there have been few replications of any measure. Nearly all the studies of social support require refinement of the social support measures. There has been little correlation observed between different types of support, indicating that the different types of support are measuring very different concepts (Barrera, 1981; Crawford, 1980; Wandersman, Wandersman, & Kahn, 1980).

An individual's social network provides sources of the social support, whatever types they may be. Abernethy (1973) found that the social network correlated positively with maternal satisfaction and a sense of competence among 41 middle and upper-class women (ages not given). Social network was measured by having the mother list her four most frequently seen friends or relatives. The mother then described the relationship between herself and each of the four members in terms of: "(1) kinship or friendship, (2) frequency of contact, (3) physical distance between their residencies, and (4) time depth of the relationship" (p. 88). Linkages among the four network members were also measured, and all of these components made up the total social network score. Women with a tight network tended to have more confidence in their competence, while those in looser networks were more frustrated by motherhood. Abernethy reasoned that the tighter network provided positive feedback from neighbors and relatives whose behaviors were similar to these women. The strongest single predictor of a woman's sense of competence was the frequency of the contact with her own mother. Since the adolescent mother most often remains with her family, the potential for her sense of competence and, thus, gratification in mothering would appear to be great. However, Barrera (1981) notes that the teenager's major source of support is also her major source of strain. Accordingly, he included conflicted network size (those support network members with whom there was interpersonal conflict) in his measure of support, i.e., the Arizona Social Support Interview Schedule (ASSIS). In Barrera's study of the relationship of social support in the adjustment of 86 pregnant adolescents, he used both the ASSIS and the Inventory of Socially Supportive Behaviors (ISSB). The ISSB was positively correlated with total symptom score and stressful life events, leading to the conclusion that the ISSB was a barometer of the amount of stress experienced by the adolescents. Hobbs (1965) also observed that for situations in which mothers (ages 16-36) had extra help, five times as many were categorized as experiencing extensive-to-severe crisis in the transition to parenthood compared to the slight-to-moderate crisis category. Distressed women in single parent families also have been found to have unusually large networks, which was interpreted as an unsuccessful attempt to establish security through seeking more network members (McLanahan, Wedemeyer, & Adelberg, 1981).

Barrera (1981) found that the size of the conflicted network was positively related with total symptoms (somatic and psychic), depression, and anxiety, but the size of the unconflicted network was negatively related to symptomatology. This led to the conclusion that the unconflicted network has a buffering effect, as opposed to the conflicted network that does not. However, the role of social support was not delineated and was deemed as dependent upon the way in which it is conceptualized and measured.

Others have stressed the importance of the support relationships as well as the amount of contact and problem-centered feedback with the support person (Cronenwett & Kunst-Wilson, 1981). Coletta and associates (1981) observed that only 6.25% of the 64 black adolescent mothers in their study reported conflict with parents as a major concern; however, 17.19% reported that it was a moderately serious concern. The major coping strategy for these young mothers was to ask for assistance, which is congruent with the notion that the size of the social network may be a barometer of the amount of stress experienced. Asking for assistance was most common when faced with task-oriented problems, but avoidance was the major strategy in coping with interpersonal problems. Adolescent females reportedly also tend to disclose negative experiences to their mothers and peers more readily than males (Burke & Weir, 1978), but it is questionable if they are able to do this if relationships are poor.

Other research noted that teenage mothers who had separated more from their family at 6 weeks were doing more infant care, were less depressed, and felt more positively about infants and their own pregnancies (Wise & Grossman, 1980). The ego strength of these teenagers, along with their infants' health status and temperament, were more closely related to their adaptation to motherhood than their relationship with others, or their feminine identification. This suggests that the developmental status of the young woman, her self-concept, and characteristics of her infant outweigh perceived relationships with others in facilitating early adaptation to motherhood.

Achievement of independence is difficult; adolescent mothers are often economically unable, as well as unprepared, to form independent relationships apart from family. Zitner and Miller (1980) found that 76% of the 185 teenage parents they studied lived with families, and over half received financial assistance from them. Zuckerman and associates (1979) observed that 95% of the 23 adolescent mothers they studied lived with extended family compared to none of the older women studied. Adolescent mothers were also more insecure in their role as mothers than older mothers. LaBarre (1972) noted that married adolescent mothers faced more problems in living situations than single mothers living with parents.

Single adolescent mothers had higher conflict scores, higher neurotic scores, and lower personal worth and personality integration scores than married adolescents in Zongker's (1980) study. In another study, teenagers 17 and younger rated themselves as average on self-esteem, but rated their mothers as more important than themselves and also were highly disapproving of their pregnancy (Held, 1981). One could question if their lower self-concept and disapproval of the pregnancy are a result of lack of support.

Conclusions cannot be drawn about the support from the spouse, however. Marital support does not provide the appropriate norms and social comparison, such as Abernethy (1973) described as contributing to a woman's competence. The first-time father is usually as uninformed as the mother. Wandersman and associates (1980) correlated group, instrumental, marital, and network support with general well-being, marital interaction, and sense of competence over the first year of parenthood. They defined group support as special parenting classes conducted over the year. Group and instrumental support failed to correlate significantly with the three measures of adjustment. Network support correlated positively with feelings of relaxation. Instrumental marital support did not correlate significantly with postpartum adjustment; however, marital cohesion (emotional support) was predictive. Support accounted for only 7% of the variance in the adjustment measures for mothers (age range not given). Grossman and associates (1980) observed that interpersonal support did not predict the quality of mothering, but added that they believed support makes a difference and both the conceptualization and measurement of interpersonal support were the cause of the lack of predictability. They found that the marital relationship was the strongest predictor of adaptation throughout pregnancy and the first year of motherhood for these mothers 21-34 years of age. Women who perceived a positive relationship in the marriage were less anxious and depressed in late pregnancy, and at 2 months and 1 year postpartum.

STUDY

Although social support has failed to predict adaptation to pregnancy and motherhood or to account for a large portion of the variance explaining it, there is consensus that social support is a multidimensional construct which is important in buffering stress and facilitating mothering. The problem appears to remain in the conceptualization and operationalization of stress.* Data reported here were collected before the more recently reported measures and the current knowledge base were available. However, the descriptions of the type of support received from others were given by the subjects as they perceived the supports. These data, grounded in subjective experiences, hopefully will contribute to the growing knowledge base about social support.

*The word "support" had been intended originally, and "stress" has been retained due to the Critique.

The questions addressed in this paper are--what social support does the teenage mother perceive available at early postpartum, and at 1, 4, 8, and 12 months after birth; and are some types of social support (network, physical, emotional, informational, or appraisal) more highly correlated with measures or maternal role attainment than others?

Method

Three groups of first-time mothers, Group 1 (15-19 years), Group 2 (20-29 years), and Group 3 (30-42 years) were studied at 5 test periods early postpartum (T1), and at 1 (T2), 4 (T3), 8 (T4), and 12 (T5) months after birth. The study was conducted from December 1979 through June 1982. The purpose was to determine the form and strength of major maternal and infant variables on maternal role attainment at each of these test periods. Maternal role attainment was defined as attachment to the infant, gratification in the role, competency in the role, the infant's growth and development, and ways irritating infant behaviors were handled. This paper focuses on the independent variable, social support, and the dependent variables for Group 1 (15-19 years) only.

Sample

The following criteria were used to select for the sample.
1. The mother was between 15-19 years of age.*
2. This was the first live-born infant.
3. The pregnancy was 37 or more weeks' gestation.
4. The infant had no diagnosed physical anomaly at birth.
5. The mother could speak and read English.
6. The mother lived within an hour drive of the university setting.

Only one person under 15 met criteria for sample selection but refused to participate. Of the 66 15-19 year olds recruited, only 2 were 15, 8 were 16, 13 were 17, 20 were 18, and 23 were 19. The refusal rate was 52.9%.

With the high refusal rate and fewer numbers of teenagers delivering, three Bay Area hospitals were utilized to recruit teenage subjects.

The ethnic background included 30.3% (N = 20) Caucasians, 40.9% (N = 27) Blacks, 9.1% (N = 6) Hispanics, 7.6% (N = 5) Filipinos, and 12.1% (N = 8) others. Almost one-third (30.8%, N = 20) had a high school diploma, 41.5% (N = 27) had some high school, and 27.7% (N = 18) had some college. Almost one-third (32.3%, N = 21) were married, 67.7% (N = 44) were single, and no information was provided on 1 subject. Eighty-five percent (N = 56) were clinic patients, and 15.2% (N = 10) had a private physician. Based on Hollingshead (1957) criteria, 35.4% (N = 23) were in the socioeconomic Class V, 40% (N = 26) were in Class IV, while 20% (N = 13) were in Class III, 1.5% (N = 1) in Class II, and 3.1% (N = 2) in Class I, and no information is available for 1 subject.

*The age of the mothers in the 3 groups was 15-42 years.

Of the 66 teenagers, 79.7% (N = 51) delivered spontaneously, while 6.3% (N = 4) were delivered by low forceps, 3.1% (N = 2) by mid forceps, 4.7% (N = 3) by vacuum extraction, and 6.3% (N = 4) had cesarean births. Forty-seven percent (N = 31) had problems during pregnancy, 43.9% (N = 29) experienced complications during labor and delivery, and 18.2% (N = 12) had postpartum complications. There were no significant differences in complications experienced by teenagers during any of these periods versus those experienced by older mothers. Older mothers had more cesarean births, however (17.5% of Group 2 and 31.1% of Group 3). There also were no differences in infant Apgar scores; however, the teenagers' infants weighed significantly less (N = 3,264.6 gm, 197.2 gm less than Group 2 infants and 195.1 gm less than Group 3 infants).

MEASURES

Social Support

Support variables were measured differently for the early postpartum and 1 month periods, but the same measures were used at 4, 8, and 12 months. At early postpartum, support received during pregnancy and anticipated support were used. At 1 month, the support a mother receives is different because she usually has more support making the transition from hospital to home, but it does not represent the amount and kind of support received after she has passed the 4-6 week postpartum period. At early postpartum, measures of social support were derived from items included in a personal and social history questionnaire completed by subjects and two items on the interview schedule (see Appendix A). At 1, 4, 8, and 12 months, both open-ended questions and questions rated on a scale of 1-5 were used to measure social support (see Appendix B). A content analysis of the open-ended questions was done by listing, "Who had been most helpful in the mothering," "In what way was this person most helpful," and "Anything else besides people that has helped you?" There were 12 randomly selected interviews at each test period. Interrater reliabilities on coding of the entire interviews were: early postpartum (T1) 86.8%, 1 month (T2) 87.4%, 4 months (T3) 88.4%, 8 months (T4) 88.4%, and 12 months (T5) 89%. The principal investigator coded all interviews after reliability was established. The types of social support described by subjects fell into the four types of supportive acts defined by House (1981):

1. Emotional support. The provision of empathy, caring, love, and trust.
2. Instrumental (physical) support. The provision of direct help via doing the individual's work, paying bills, etc.
3. Informational support. The provision of information that can be used in coping with problems.
4. Appraisal support. The provision of information for use in evaluating self.

Appraisal support was not coded separately from emotional support until 4 months (T3), 8 months (T4), and 12 months (T5).

Maternal Role Attainment

Table 1 summarizes the measures of the dependent variables reported in this paper for the five test periods. Available reliabilities are reported with the measures.

RESULTS

The Early Postpartum Period (T1)

Available support. Although less than one-third (N = 21) of the 66 teenagers were married, 40 (60.6%) stated the infant's father (FOB) would be living with them the entire month. Thirty-one (47%) listed their mother as living with them, and 20 (30.8%) noted their mother would be with them the entire month. Only 9 (13.6%) noted their fathers would be with them during the month. The first bar among the four categories in Figure 1 shows the percentage of persons identified who would be providing them with help when they went home. In response to whether they thought they would have enough help, 49 said yes, 3 said yes with others available on call, 12 didn't know, and 1 said no. More teenagers perceived having enough help than older mothers, X^2 (10) = 18.961, p < .05.

The teenagers perceived positive interpersonal relationships except with their fathers. On a scale of 1-5, with 5 being excellent, the mean for the relationship with the FOB was 4.19, 4.18 for the relationship with their mother, and 3.61 for the relationship with their father. The scale 3 reflected the response, "not sure," and this lower rating for fathers was probably due to lack of contact with them. Fifty-one (77.3%) of the teenagers stated they had more than one close friend in the area; 11 (16.7%) said they had no close friends.

Correlates with support. Spearman rho correlations were done with dichotomous or ranked data; Pearson product moment correlations were utilized with interval data. Initially, correlations were done with individual support items from the questionnaires. Only two items correlated significantly with the Neonatal Perception Inventory at early postpartum (NPI-I): how often the subject visited with neighbors, r = 0.27, p = .03; and how often subject and friends had picnics and parties together, r = 0.27, p = .03. It could be that close relationships with neighbors provided information about the newborns that led to more positive perceptions of these neonates. Not a single support item correlated significantly with the mothers' emotional responses to the question, "Tell me about your baby." Only two support items correlated significantly with responses to the same question, indicating the mother was identifying unique features of her infant (acquaintance responses)-- the presence of the mate in the labor room, r = 0.31, p = .02; and the presence of the mate in the delivery room, r = 0.26, p = .05. It is noteworthy that the quality of the relationship with the mate, mother, or father, or the presence of a person other than mate (usually the mother) in the labor or delivery room did not correlate significantly with the

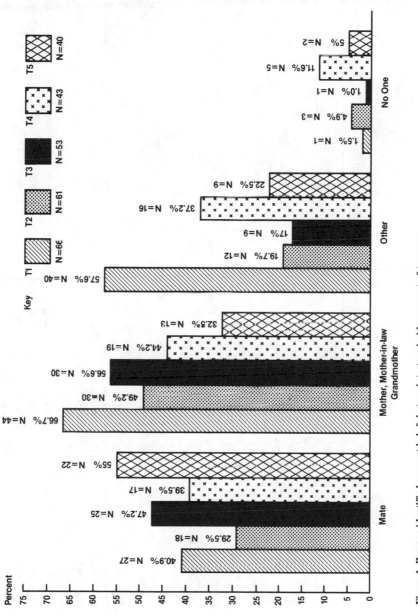

Figure 1. Persons identified as most helpful at each test period by percent of teenagers.

Table 1
Dependent Variables Reported by Test Period and Available Reliabilities

	T1	T2	T3	T4	T5
	NPI-I[a] (Early Postpartum) alpha reliability average baby, 0.63; your baby, 0.74, N=100.[b]	NPI-II[a] (1 month) Cronbach alpha reliability, average baby, 0.61; your baby, 0.65, N=279.[c]	...	...	...
	Cronbach alpha, average baby 0.56, your baby, 0.68, N=245.[c]				
	Test-retest, 0.22, N=20.[d]	Test-retest, 0.82, N=20.[d]			
Attachment Factor Emotional response	Factor Loading .687	Leifer's (1977) Feelings About Baby (LOVE). Cronbach Alpha reliability, 0.51, N=240.[c]	LOVE Cronbach alpha, 0.65, N=239.[c]	LOVE Cronbach alpha, 0.64, N=228.[c]	LOVE Cronbach alpha, N= .[c]
Refers to baby by name, he/she, it	.643	Russell's (1977) Gratification in Role (GRAT). Cronbach alpha, 0.80, N=240[c]	GRAT Cronbach alpha, 0.78, N=240[c]	GRAT Cronbach alpha, 0.78, N=231.[c]	GRAT Cronbach alpha, 0.77, N=219.[c]
Acquaintance behaviors	.649	N=240.[c]			

T1	T2	T3	T4	T5
	Blank's (1964) Maternal Behavior Scales (MABE). Interrater Spearman Brown mean, 0.73-0.92 for 13 items.[c] Cronbach alpha = 0.80, N = 275.[c]	MABE Cronbach alpha, 0.83, N = 264.[c] Interrater Spearman Brown reliability mean, 0.48-0.93 for 14 items.[c]	MABE Cronbach alpha, 0.85, N = 248.[c] Interrater Spearman Brown reliability mean, 0.55-0.92 for 14 items.[c]	MABE Cronbach alpha, 0.86, N = 240.[c] Interrater Spearman Brown reliability mean, 0.66-0.94 for 14 items.[c]
	Disbrow's (1977) Ways of Handling Irritating Child Behaviors (WHIB).		WHIB	WHIB
	Motor & Social Development (GROW)[e]	GROW	GROW	GROW

NPI = Neonatal Perception Inventory (Broussard & Hartner, 1971).
[a]Broussard & Hartner (1971).
[b]Blumberg (1980).
[c]Reliabilities as determined within the project sample.
[d]Freese & Thoman (1978).
[e]Ross Laboratories (1973).

NPI-I maternal emotional responses telling about their infant, or descriptive responses of unique characteristics (acquaintance responses).

To reduce the number of variables, principal components analyses were done to derive network, mate emotional support, parent emotional support, mate physical support, informational support factors, and a single attachment factor (ATTACH). See Table 2 for factor loadings for each of these variables.

Only one of the support factors, informational support, correlated significantly with attachment, r = 0.43, p = .02. No support factor correlated significantly with NPI-I. Groups 2 and 3 received significantly more informational support than Group 1, $F(2,273) = 17.47$, p = .0001, and significantly more support from mates, $F(2,286) = 17.56$, p = .0001. Group 2 received significantly more emotional support from parents than Group 1. Group 3 did not differ from Groups 1 and 2 in emotional support from parents.

Stepwise multiple regression analyses were done with all of the independent variables for ATTACH and NPI-I. Because of the small number of subjects with complete data (N = 28), the models must be viewed with extreme caution. No support variable entered the model to predict ATTACH. The only variable to enter the model to predict NPI-I was mate physical support, and it accounted for 8.9% of the variance.

It is of interest that Broussard's Neonatal Perception Inventory (1971) at T1 was selected as a proxy measure of attachment, and it did not correlate significantly with the attachment factor, r = 0.05 for the total sample, r = -.18 for the teenage Group 1. This supported Anderson's (1981) argument that perceiving one's infant as below average on crying, eating, spitting, sleeping, elimination, and rhythmicity does not necessarily mean that the mother is not attached. At T2 the NPI-II correlated modestly, but significantly with feelings about the baby (LOVE), r = 0.17, p = .003 for the total sample, but not with the teenage group, r = .08, p = .53.

One Month Postpartum (T2)

Available support. Fifty-four (88.5%) of the 61 teenagers remaining in the study at 1 month said they were the primary caretaker of the infant, 5 (8.2%) said their mother or another person was, and 2 (3.3%) said that the infant's care was shared 50-50 with a mate.

Half of the teenagers (N = 30) stated that their mother, grandmother, or mother-in-law had been among the persons most helpful to them in the mothering role. Almost one-third (N = 18, 29.5%), stated their mates were, 6 (9.8%) listed siblings, 5 (8.2%) listed friends, and 3 (4.9%) stated no one. As seen in Figure 1, the teenagers anticipated more help during early postpartum than was forthcoming the first month.

In response to what way these persons were most helpful, the teenagers responded, "answered questions," "showed me how to do things," "understanding," and "took care of the baby." The responses were categorized into three types of support: physical (took care of baby), emotional (understanding), and informational (showed me how to do things). Twenty-four (39.3%) of the young women described receiving emotional support, and 22 (36.1%) indicated informational support.

Forty-three (70.5%) described physical support. Five teenagers (8.5%) indicated that they had a lot more help than needed the first postpartal month, 7 (11.9%) had more than needed, 34 (57.6%) had as much as needed, 11 (18.6%) had less than needed, and 2 (3.4%) noted they had a lot less than needed.

Correlations of support variables. Three measures of social support were correlated with the dependent variables (see Tables 2 and 3).

Group 1 received significantly less emotional support than Group 2 and Group 3, $F(2,223) = 19.3$, $p = .0001$. There were no differences in network of physical support. Group 1 received significantly more informational support than Group 3, $F(2,275) = 4.23$, $p = .02$. Group 2's informational support did not differ from Group 1 or Group 3.

There were no significant correlations between NPI-II, the ways mothers handled irritating behaviors (WHIB), the infant's growth and development (GROW), and the support variables. A factor made up of motor and social development, weight gain, and length grown discriminated Group 1 and 3 infants as exceeding Group 2 infants, $F(2,241) = 4.33$, $p < .02$, Duncan's multiple range test (see Table 3 for factor loadings). Group 1 infants gained significantly more than Groups 2 and 3 infants, $F(2,264) = 5.73$, $p < .004$, Duncan's multiple range test, although there were no differences in head circumference or length grown. The greater weight gain in Group 1 may be a result of information teenage mothers received from their own mothers concerning adding cereal to the infant's bottle.

The measure of feelings about the infant (LOVE) correlated significantly with the physical support factor, $r = .44$, $p = .0005$, and the emotional support factor, $r = .26$, $p < .05$. The young woman's gratification in the mothering role correlated significantly with informational support, $r = .34$, $p < .007$, and emotional support, $r = .32$, $p = .01$. Her competency in the maternal role correlated significantly with physical support, $r = .35$, $p = .006$.

Unlike other reports in which types of support failed to correlate, emotional support correlated significantly with informational support, $r = .28$, $p < .04$, and physical support, $r = .33$, $p < .02$. Although the correlations are modest, it seems that the teenage mothers' support systems were related at 1 month. Physical support appears especially important to teenagers at 1 month. It appears that the help with the infant and household chores enables them to have more positive feelings about their infant, as well as to enhance their competency in mothering behaviors.

Table 2

Factor Loadings for Factors Utilized in Analysis at T1, Early Postpartum
Network, Mate Physical, and Informational Support and Attachment

Factor	Factor Loading	Communalities	Eigenvalue
Network Support			2.07
Number of neighbors recognized	-.345*	.119	
How often chat neighbors	-.507	.258	
Friends in area	.408	.167	
Outings with friends	-.707*	.500	
Frequency friends visit	.714	.510	
Frequency see women friends	.724	.525	
Mate Physical Support			2.62
Mate attended prenatal class	-.745*	.555	
Married to mate	.698	.487	
Mate labor room	.888	.788	
Mate delivery room	.889	.790	
Informational Support			1.45
Attend prenatal class	-.745*	.555	
Close friends here	.507	.257	
Review birth experience	.800	.634	
Attachment Factor			1.31
Emotional Response	.687	.473	
Mother Refers to baby	-.643[a]	.413	
Aquaintance behaviors	.649	.421	

MATE AND PARENT EMOTIONAL SUPPORT FACTORS

Variables	Factor Loading Factor 1 Mate Emotional Support	Eigenvalue	Factor Loading Factor 2 Parent Emotional Support	Eigenvalue	Communalities
How useful mate labor	.915	1.92	.082	1.48	.843
How useful mate delivery	.902		.053		.816
Quality relationship mate	.486		.156		.264
Quality relationship mother	−.122*		.846		.731
Quality relationship father	−.118*		.852		.740

*Scoring reversed in items.

Table 3
Factor Loadings for Factors Utilized in Analysis at T2

Factor	Factor Loading	Communalities	Eigenvalue
Physical Support Factor			
As much help as needed	.231	1.000	1.678
How much partner helps care for infant	.900	1.000	
Number who help with household	.288	1.000	
Number of things mate/ others do to help in care	.858	1.000	
Emotional Support Factor			
Number of emotional supports to manage mothering	.669	.447	1.31
Number who boost morale	.717	.515	
Number of ways persons are helpful	.588	.345	
Infant Growth Factor			
Motor development	.799	1.000	1.99
Social development	.782	1.000	
Weight gain	.653	1.000	
Length grown	.557	1.000	

The younger the teenager, the more informational support she tended to receive, $r = -.27$, $p < .04$. The more positive her self-concept, the less informational support she tended to receive, $r = -.31$, $p < .03$. The type of support received by the young woman was unrelated to whether she was married.

The sample size was too small for valid results (N = 40 with completed data), and the support variables that entered the regression models are reported as a matter of interest. No support variable entered the model to predict NPI-II. Informational support entered the model at Step 1 after the forced variables (Caucasian-non-Caucasian, educational level, and married) and contributed 17.1% of the variance in predicting gratification in the mothering role. Emotional support entered the model at Step 1 after the forced variables, and it predicted 12.3% of the variance for feelings about the infant. Physical support entered the model at Step 3, after child rearing attitudes and perception of the birth experience, to contribute 11.4% of the variance for maternal competency behaviors. Informational support entered the model at Step 2, after total positive self concept, predicting ways parents handle irritating behaviors, and it predicted 12.1% of the variance.

Four Months Postpartum (T3)

Available support. By 4 months, 13 teenagers (19.7%) had dropped out of the study, leaving a remaining total of 53 (80.3%). We were unable to contact seven of the young women; two stated they were too busy after canceling several appointments, and one stated her husband wanted her to withdraw. One young woman left her infant son with her parents, and they were unsure of her whereabouts.

All but 4 (92.5%) of the teenagers said they took care of their infants most of the time. One each listed the infant's father, her mother, and the babysitter as the major caretaker; another said she divided time 50-50 with the infant's father.

Thirty teenagers (56.6%) observed that their mothers were among those most helpful to them in the mothering role, and 25 (47.2%) mentioned their mates. The young men seemed more involved at 4 months than earlier at 1 month (see Figure 1). The others who had been most helpful at 1 month were less helpful at 4 months. Two responses included God with the list of others who helped. The most common help apart from persons was books/magazines, and only 13 mentioned these. Five teenagers listed television, and two listed classes and previous experience as most helpful.

Only 23 young women (43.4%) described receiving emotional support. Even fewer described informational support (N = 8, 15.1%), or appraisal support (N = 4, 7.6%). The majority (N = 42, 79.3%) described receiving physical support. Fewer in Group 1 received emotional support than older groups X^2 (2) = 6.45, p = .04 (43% of Group 1, 56% of Group 2, and 65% of Group 3 received emotional support). No differences in informational or appraisal support were found.

A range of 0-4 was given for the number of persons helping in day-to-day situations. This was used as indicator of the size of the support network. Seventeen (32.1%) listed one person, 13 (24.5%) mentioned 2 persons, 11 (20.8%) mentioned 3 persons, and 4 (7.5%) mentioned 4 persons. Eight (15.1%) said that no one helped in daily problems. There were no group differences in network support.

Nine persons (17%) stated they had a lot more help than needed, 9 (17%) had more than they needed, 23 (43.4%) had as much as they needed, 10 (18.9%) had less than they needed, and 2 (3.8%) noted they had a lot less help than they needed.

Correlates of support variables. Principal components analysis of potential physical support variables (as much help as needed, how much mates/others do to care for baby, physical support in the mothering role, and number of helpful persons in day-to-day situations) indicated that the number of helpful persons in day-to-day situations was a different type of support. The number of helpful persons was called network support. The factor loading of the described physical support in the maternal role was too small for inclusion with physical support variables and was not used as a measure for subsequent correlations. The factor loading of the first two variables (as much help as needed and how much mate and others do to care for baby) was equal, and since women often limit the amount of infant care the mate or others do, the "as much help as needed" scale was selected as the measure for physical support. These same measures for types of support were used for the remaining test periods.

The more that the mate or other person in the household did to take care of the infant, the more gratification the teenager derived from the mothering role, $r = .32$, $p < .02$, and the more competent her mothering behaviors tended to be, $r = .28$, $p < .05$. Physical support correlated significantly with the infant's total development score, $r = -.38$, $p = .005$ (lower score = greater support). Group 1 infants scored significantly higher on motor and social development at 4 months, $F(2,263) = 5.50$, $p < .005$, Duncan's multiple range test. There were no group differences in infant weight, length, or head circumference.

Emotional support, informational support, appraisal support, and network support did not correlate significantly with any of the dependent variables at 4 months.

Physical support correlated significantly with how much the mate or other persons did in taking care of the infant $r = -.42$, $p < .002$. There were no significant correlations between the physical, emotional, informational, and appraisal support variables at 4 months.

The number of infant illnesses correlated significantly with emotional support, $r = .41$, $p = .002$. Teenage mothers who were lower on maternal temperament adaptability tended to have a mate or other who did more in taking care of the infant, $r = -.30$, $p < .04$. Mothers with a lower intensity of response also tended to report more emotional support, $r = -.38$, $p < .007$. Caucasians tended to report more emotional support than non-Caucasians, $r = .38$, $p = .005$. At 4 months postpartum, emotional support tended to be perceived by teenagers with an ill infant who also were lower on adaptability, suggesting that the persons in their environment were sensitive to their needs. However, the more intense or forceful individual may tend to turn off emotional support.

When the stepwise multiple regression analyses were done ($N = 37$ with complete data; sample size too small for valid results), appraisal support entered the model predicting gratification in the role at Step 5 (after the forced variables, educational level, marital status, Caucasian, maternal illness, infant adaptability, maternal adaptability, and infant related stress), contributing 3.7% unique variance. The support network variable entered the model for feelings about the baby at Step 7, (after the forced variables, infant related stress, empathy, rigidity, infant stress removed, total positive self-concept, and infant adaptability), contributing 6.8% of the unique variance.

None of the support variables entered the model for maternal competency behaviors. Physical support entered the model predicting infant growth at Step 1 after the forced variables, accounting for 19.1% of the unique variance. Emotional support entered the model at Step 7, (after forced variables, physical support, infant persistence, maternal quality of mood, maternal adaptability, perception of birth experience, and maternal intensity), accounting for 3.2% of the variance for infant growth.

Eight Months Postpartum (T4)

At 8 months, 43 teenagers continued in the study. We were unable to contact 5 of the 10 lost since 4 months; mail was not forwarded and persons at phone numbers did not know where subjects were. One 19-year-old abandoned her infant with "an old lady from the carnival circus with nothing but cookies to eat," and a neighbor called the infant's grandmother who came from the eastern part of the United States and took the infant home with her. A 16-year-old was pregnant again, babysitting several infants, and "too busy to continue." One 18-year-old moved to Brazil with her infant. Two withdrew after five to seven broken appointments and many evasive tactics.

Thirty-five of the mothers (83.3%) stated they took care of the baby most of the time; 3 (7.1%) named babysitters although they were with the infant over 50% of the time, 3 (7.1%) shared care 50-50 with another person, 3 (7.1%) took care of the infant 12.5-25% of the time, and 1 (2.4%) said the grandmother took care of the infant all of the time. Fourteen (36.8%) of the young mothers were working, 7 (18.4%) were in school, 1 (2.6%) began work but quit, and 2 (5.3%) went back to school and quit because of difficulties managing babysitters and schedules.

Mothers or mother figures were most often named as one of the persons most helpful in the mothering role (N = 19, 44.2%). Mates (N = 17, 39.5%) and others (N = 16, 37.2%) were listed next most frequently.

Others included fathers, brothers, friends, and neighbors. There was movement at 4 months toward others for support and away from the teenagers' mothers somewhat. This could indicate maturation in gaining independence, or it may reflect an expanding social life, or both. An alternative explanation is that the grandmother found the increasingly active infant more of a challenge than she wished to assume responsibility for. Five young women (11.6%) did not list anyone who was helpful to them in the mothering role. The size of the network who helped in day-by-day situations was: 0 for 1 subject (2.3%), 1 for 12 subjects (27.9%), 2 for 12 subjects (27.9%), 3 for 8 subjects (18.6%), 4 for 7 subjects (16.3%), and 5 for 3 subjects (7%).

In describing helpful things, 15 (34.9%) mentioned books or magazines, 4 (9.3%) mentioned television, 2 (4.7%) mentioned religion, and 2 (4.7%) thought classes had been helpful, 1 each (2.3%) mentioned the walker, disposable diapers, the pacifier, instincts, and previous experience.

Thirteen teenagers (30.2%) said those who had helped them provided emotional support, 11 (25.6%) reported informational support, only 3 (7%) described appraisal support, and 36 (83.7%) received physical support. Group 1 (34.2%) reported significantly less emotional support at 8 months than Group 2 (46.2%) or Group 3 (60.2%), $X^2 (2) = 8.12$, p< .02, but no group differences were found for other types of support.

Three (7.1%) of the teenagers stated they had a lot more help than needed, 8 (19%) had more than needed, 22 (52.4%) as much as needed, 7 (16.7%) less than needed, and 2 (4.8%) a lot less than needed.

Correlates of support variables. At 8 months, there were no significant correlations between any of the support variables (network, physical, informational, emotional, and appraisal) and any of the dependent variables measured (GRAT, LOVE, WHIB, GROW, and MABE). In the stepwise regression models, (N = 36 with complete data sets; sample size too small for valid results) physical support entered at Step 1 after forced variables, and accounted for 26.2% of the variance in gratification in the role. None of the support variables entered the model for LOVE, WHIB, GROW, or MABE.

There were no group differences on the factor GROW, motor or social development, and growth in length and head circumference. However, there were group differences in weight gain, $F(2,223) = 5.14$, p =< .05. Group differences were not great enough for the Duncan's multiple range test to discriminate, although the weight gains were 2,128.3 gm for Group 1, 2,067 gm for Group 3, and 1,840.6 gm for Group 2.

Eight months was the only test period at which Group 1 had a significantly higher illness score than Groups 2 and 3. Group 1 had significantly less emotional support at this time, although there was no relationship between the two. The relationship between the network size and maternal illness approached significance, however, r = - .30, p = .059, N = 41. It would appear that with fewer persons available for support, the tendency for illness increased.

One Year Postpartum (T5)

Available support. Forty teenagers were interviewed at the final test period at 1 year, an attrition rate of 39.4% over the year. This contrasts strikingly with the older mothers; Group 2 had a 17.4% attrition rate and Group 3 a 2.2% rate. We were unable to contact one of the three teenagers lost since 8 months, and two refused numerous appointments before finally stating they were too busy to be interviewed or to complete forms.

Two teenagers had delivered a second child at 1 year, and one was pregnant. Another feared she was pregnant, and one had a therapeutic abortion between 8 and 12 months.

Thirty-one (77.5%) were primary caretakers for their infants, 8 (20%) were sharing caretaking 50-50, 1 (2.5%) was sharing less than 50-50, and not one teenager named another as primary caretaker. (Two 19-year-olds who had abandoned their infants over the year were lost to the study.)

The mate was the modal person named as one of the persons most helpful in the mothering role (N = 22, 55%). Thirteen (32.5%) named their mothers as most helpful, and 9 (22.5%) named another person. The percentage of teenagers finding mates most helpful to them in the mothering role increased from 40.9% at early postpartum to 55% at 1 year (see Figure 1). During this time there was a decrease in those seeing their mothers or the mother figure as most helpful, from 66.7% early postpartum to 32.5% at 1 year. The help anticipated from others (57.6%) was apparently unrealistic early postpartum when contrasted with help received for the rest of the year (19.7%, 17%, 37.2%, and 22.5%, respectively). Beginning at 8 months there seemed to be movement toward more helpful support from others, which could reflect an increased ability to elicit and receive help. Twenty-seven (67.5%) of the sample are older adolescents 18-19, 12 (30%) are middle adolescents 16-17 years old, and only one (2.5%) is an early adolescent (15 years old), and these changes toward more helpful relationships with others appear to reflect healthy maturation toward independence and the ability for intimate relationships with others.

There were 3 (7.5%) of the young women listing 4 persons in their support network, 17 (42.5%) listing 3, 9 (22.5%) listing 2, and 11 (27.5%) listing one person. Two (5.1%) rated that they had a lot more help than needed, 8 (20.5%) rated they had more help than needed, 21 (53.9%) rated they had as much help as needed, and 8 (20.5%) had less than needed. No one rated herself as having a lot less than needed. From 1 month to 1 year, those having as much help as needed and less help than was needed tended to remain constant over the year, while those rating in both extremes diminished.

Two young women (5%) of the 40 remaining clearly had social support deficits. One was a victim of mate physical abuse, and one physically abused her infant. The former's family provided support, and the latter was happy and relieved to have a social worker become involved and enlist help so that she could be a better mother.

Fifteen (37.5%) of the young mothers described receiving emotional and informational support. Only 3 (7.5%) described receiving appraisal support. Very few from the total sample, 18 (7.4%) out of 242, described appraisal support. Since the maternal role is usually internalized earlier, perhaps reassurances regarding one's performance are no longer given as much importance. The modal time listed by teenagers as really feeling like a mother and being comfortable with their decisions as a mother was 4 months (N = 8); however, 4 stated 1 year, and 2 said they were still working on it.

Twenty-eight (70%) described help with child care, and 7 (17.5%) described help with chores. Informational support was the only type in which there were differences by age group, X^2 (2) = 6.31, p = .05. More teenagers (N = 5, 39.5%) received informational support than 20-29 year olds (N = 23, 20.4%) or 30-42 year olds (N = 18, 20.9%).

At 1 year, half of the infants' fathers (N = 20) were contributing to their infant's financial support. Infants' fathers were a source of stress also, because two mothers said they were in the process of a custody battle for the child.

Correlates of social support variables. Emotional support correlated significantly with maternal competency behaviors, r = .37, p < .03, and ways irritating behaviors were handled, r = -.37, p = .02. (the higher WHIB score indicates more unfavorable way of handling behaviors). Network, physical, appraisal, and informational support failed to correlate significantly with any of the dependent variables. Emotional support correlated significantly but negatively with informational support, r = -.32, p < .05, and positively with appraisal support, r = .36, p < .03. This suggests that as emotional support increased, informational support decreased and that appraisal support and emotional support are somewhat overlapping. A significant correlation between network and physical support, r = -.34, p < .04, suggests that the larger the network the greater the physical support (a lower physical support score means greater support).

Emotional support correlated significantly with three maternal attitude factors, from Cohler's Maternal Attitude Scale (Johnson, 1976), and 42 had been included as independent variables. Emotional support was associated with the factor depicting more adaptive responses to control of the child's aggressive responses (r = -.44, p = .007); to encouragement of reciprocity with the infant factor (r = -.56, p = .0004); and to the appropriate closeness factor, i.e., not seeing the infant as a narcissistic extension of self (r = .33, p = .05). (Lower scores in control and reciprocity indicate more adaptive behaviors.) Informational support was positively associated with encouragement of reciprocity with the infant (r = .38, p = .03). The maternal attitudes, in turn, were more strongly correlated with the dependent variables. More adaptive response to control of the child's aggressive responses was correlated with the way the mother handled irritating behaviors (WHIB) at 1 year, r = .62, p = .0001. More adaptive encouragement of reciprocity was positively related to maternal behaviors (MABE), r = .46, p = .004; LOVE, r = -.32, p = .05; and WHIB, r = .49, p = .002.

There were no group differences in the infants' motor development. Group 2 infants scored significantly higher in social development than Groups 1 and 3 infants, F(2,222) = 6.20, p < .003, Duncan's multiple range test. At 1 year, although there were no significant differences in weight, Group 1 infants weighed M = 10.4 kg more; Group 2, M = 9.8 kg; Group 3, M = 9.9 kg.

SUMMARY

At least one type of social support as perceived by the teenage mothers correlated with one or more of the maternal role dependent variables at each of the test periods except at 8 months postpartum. At early postpartum, greater informational support appeared to contribute positively to attachment behaviors, as did the presence of a mate in the labor and delivery rooms. At 1 month, support variables appeared to have much influence on mothering. Emotional support seemed to foster gratification in the role, as well as positive feelings for the infant. Informational support also played a positive role in gratification. Physical support appeared important for both positive feelings about the infant and competent maternal behaviors.

While fewer types of support correlated with dependent variables at 4 months, physical support appeared important for the infant's development. The physical help a mother receives understandably provides her with free time to play with her infant and for other activities to stimulate the infant. The person providing physical help with the infant also provides additional stimulation.

The lack of correlation between support and maternal role attainment variables at 8 months is puzzling. The infants did not lag behind other infants in development and growth. The young women tended to be less reliant on support from a mother figure at this time, but the crude measures do not reflect whether this may be due to more conflictual relationships with their mothers. Since mothers/mother figures were a large source of informational support (only one named a health professional as helpful at 8 months), the weak negative correlation between informational and emotional support at 1 year supports the possibility of some conflict. The higher illness rate among the teenaged mothers at 8 months and the significantly less emotional support provided to Group 1 suggest the support teenagers received from their mothers was inadequate.

At 1 year, emotional support appeared to be more important than other types of support in maternal role attainment behaviors. The relationships between emotional support and informational support and maternal attitudes and maternal role behaviors suggest it is the interactive effect of support with other variables that may be more influential than support alone. It is critical for health professionals to encourage adolescent mothers to develop relationships that provide emotional support to sustain them over the first year of motherhood and as the infant moves to toddlerhood and becomes increasingly active.

The failure of the types of support to correlate more consistently with the dependent variables may lie in the crudeness of the measures. The data derived, however, support continued work to refine measures for the different types of support and to measure conflicts with support persons in the social network.

Appendix A

Social Support Items on Personal and Social History Questionnaire and Interview Schedule at T1.

1. **A.** Did you attend prenatal class?
____1. Yes, I went to all the classes
____2. Yes, I went to 3/4 of all the classes
____3. Yes, I went to 1/2 to 3/4 of the classes
____4. Yes, I went to less than 1/2 of the classes
____5. No, I didn't take any classes. If no is checked, go on to question 2.

   B. Who attended class with you (check one)?
____1. No one   ____4. Friend
____2. Baby's father   ____5. Other, describe
____3. My mother

2. Relationship with the baby's father (Check *all* items that apply):
____1. At the time of conception, I was living with the baby's father.
____2. Currently I am living with baby's father.
____3. I am legally married to baby's father.
____4. None of above apply.

3. In my opinion, my relationship with the baby's father is:
____1. poor   ____4. good
____2. fair   ____5. excellent
____3. not sure

4. In my opinion, my relationship with my mother is/was (if deceased):
____1. very poor   ____4. good
____2. poor   ____5. very good
____3. not sure

5. In my opinion, my relationship with my father is/was (if deceased):
____1. very poor   ____4. good
____2. poor   ____5. very good
____3. not sure

Note. Items 1-6 from *Personal Information Form* by S.B. Virden (1981). "The Effect of Information About Infant Behavior and Primiparas' Maternal Role Adequacy," unpublished doctoral dissertation, University of California, San Francisco, California, pp. 144-146. Items 7-14 were taken from "The Adaptive Potential for Pregnancy Score (TAPPS)" by K.B. Nuckolls. In K.B. Nuckolls, J. Cassel, B.H. Kaplan "Psychosocial Assets, Life Crisis, and the Prognosis of Pregnancy," *American Journal of Epidemiology,* 1972, *95,* 431-441. Copyright 1972 by the School of Hygiene and Public Health of The Johns Hopkins University, Baltimore, MD. Reprinted by permission.

6. For the next month, who will be living with you? Check *all* persons that apply, and indicate whether for whole month or only part of the month by placing another check mark in the appropriate column.

Person	Whole Month	Part of Month	Don't Know
_____ Baby's father			
_____ Friend			
_____ My mother			
_____ My father			
_____ My relatives other than father/mother, specify _____			
_____ Relatives of baby's father			
_____ Other, specify _____			

* * * * * * *

Answer next set of questions in terms of community where you are now living, like San Rafael, Oakland, etc.

7. About how many of the people who live in your neighborhood would you recognize by sight if you saw them in a large crowd?
____1. None ____3. Many of them
____2. Some of them ____4. Almost all of them

8. About how often do you chat or visit with your neighbors?
____1. Never
____2. Rarely (less than once a month)
____3. Sometimes (once a week to once a month)
____4. Often (more than once a week)

9. Do you have any friends here?
____1. Yes, one
____2. Yes, more than one
____3. No

10. Are any of these people close friends with whom you would feel comfortable discussing things like pregnancy, child rearing, etc.?
____1. No ____2. Yes

11. Do you and your friends ever have picnics or parties together?
____1. Never
____2. Rarely (less than once a month)
____3. Sometimes (once a week to once a month)
____4. Often (more than once a week)

12. How often do you as a couple have friends in your home?
____1. More than once a week ____3. Less than once a month
____2. Once a week to once a month ____4. Never

13. How often do you have women friends in your home in the daytime or evening?
____1. More than once a week ____3. Less than once a month
____2. Once a week to once a month ____4. Never

14. Is there anyone in the Bay area, other than husband or relatives, on whom you can count for help if you should need it?
____1. No
____2. Yes. If YES, how much could you count on that person?
   ____ 1. Would do everything possible
   ____ 2. Would help some
   ____ 3. Would not help much
   ____ 4. Would help very little

15. My husband (mate) was in the labor room with me.
____1. Yes ____2. No

16. My husband (mate) was in the delivery room with me.
____1. Yes ____2. No

17. Other person specify _____ in labor room.
____1. Yes ____2. No

18. Other person specify _____ in delivery room.
____1. Yes ____2. No

19. Who is going to help you when you go home?
____1. Mate only ____3. Mother-in-law
____2. Mother ____4. Other (list)

20. How do you feel about it; i.e. will you have enough help?
____1. Yes ____2. Unsure
____3. No

Appendix B

Support Items on Interview Schedule at T2, T3, T4, and T5

T2 PERIOD

1. Who takes care of the baby most of the time?
____1. Self ____5. Neighbor
____2. Mate ____6. Friend
____3. Mother ____7. Other
____4. Sister

2. Who helps you with household chores?
____1. Mate ____4. Neighbor
____2. Mother ____5. Friend
____3. Sister ____6. Other

3. Who can you rely on for help in a bind? (financial: in a spot for quick cash; emergency: baby sick)
____1. Mate ____4. Neighbor
____2. Mother ____5. Friend
____3. Sister ____6. Other

Note. Items 1, 5-9, 12-20 from *Family Assessment Interviews, Child Health Assessment Part 2: The First Year of Life,* by K.E. Barnard and S.J. Eyres. DHEW Publication No. HRA 79-25, pages 203, 207, 209-210.

4. Who bolsters your morale by letting you know they care about you, value you?
____1. Mate   ____5. Friend
____2. Mother   ____6. No one
____3. Sister   ____7. Other
____4. Neighbor

5. In thinking back over the last month, *what* or *who* has been the most helpful to you in your role of being a mother and caring for your child? (HELP: physically or emotionally).
____1. Mate   ____6. No one
____2. Mother   ____7. Other
____3. Sister   ____8. Past experiences with babies
____4. Neighbor   ____9. Baby care
____5. Friend

6. In what ways was this person or situation the most helpful?

7. Was this as much help as you needed?
____1. A lot more than I needed   ____4. Less than I needed
____2. More than I needed   ____5. A lot less than I needed
____3. As much as I needed

8. How much would you say your husband or partner does in connection with taking care of the baby?
____1. None   ____4. A good bit
____2. Very little   ____5. A great deal
____3. Moderate amount

9. Which of the following activities does your husband or partner do in connection with taking care of the baby? (Read list. May record more than one.)
____1. Changing diapers   ____4. Playing
____2. Feeding   ____5. Other (describe)
____3. Bathing   ____6. None

T3, T4, T5 PERIOD

10. Who helps you manage the day-by-day situations in mothering?
____1. Mate   ____4. Neighbor
____2. Mother   ____5. Friend
____3. Sister   ____6. Other (name relationship with subject)

11. Do you see friends often?
____1. Yes   ____2. No
How many?
When?

12. In thinking back over the past months, what, or who has been the most help to you in the role of being a mother and caring for your child?
    (HELP: Physically and/or emotionally)

13. Is there anything else besides people that helped you in your role of being a mother and caring for your child?

14. In what way was this person, or situation the most helpful?

15. Was this as much help as you needed?
____1. A lot more than I needed   ____4. Less than I needed
____2. More than I needed   ____5. A lot less than I needed
____3. As much as I needed

16. Who takes care of the baby most of the time?
____1. Mother   ____3. Other (relationship)
____2. Father

17. How much would you say your mate/mother/other does in connection with taking care of your infant? (read list)
____1. None   ____4. A good deal
____2. Very little   ____5. A great deal
____3. Moderate amount

18. Is he/she doing as much as you feel he/she should be doing? (in connection with taking care of your child)
____1. Yes (list kinds of things done)
____2. No (could you explain?)

19. Has the father of your baby worked steadily since the child was born?
____1. Yes
____2. No (could you explain?)
____3. I don't know.

20. Is he contributing to the financial support of your child?
____1. Yes
____2. No
Comments, if any.
If no, who helps with support?

CRITIQUE
Gretchen Crawford, R.N., Ph.D.

The following critique was prepared for the original presentation of "Social Support of Teenage Mothers" by Dr. Mercer. Subsequent to the critique, Dr. Mercer revised portions of the paper addressing several areas presented in the original critique. A comparison of the published paper and this critique will be helpful to reinforce how the concerns presented in the critique can be addressed and add substance and clarity to the presentation of research. Such efforts will strengthen nursing research and facilitate the development of nursing knowledge.

Dr. Mercer's investigation contributes a great deal to theory development on social support as it relates to health. The study is one of the first to examine how receipt of various types of support is related to healthful outcomes. It is also a valuable heuristic study in that directions for future research are suggested.

The purpose of the investigation was to examine the correlation of social support with maternal role attainment as perceived by teenage mothers over the first year of motherhood. The research questions were:

1. What social support does the teenage mother perceive available at early postpartum and at 1, 4, 8, and 12 months?

2. Are some types of social support more highly correlated with measures of maternal role attainment than others?

The report of the investigation stimulated some questions which form the basis for this critique. In general, these questions arose from a desire for more information about conceptualization and indicators of social support, or about decisions made during the course of the study. The critique includes comments on the scientific merit of the research questions, method, findings, and interpretation. The contribution of this study to nursing knowledge is also discussed.

SCIENTIFIC MERIT OF THE RESEARCH QUESTIONS

Three questions were addressed in order to critique the scientific merit of the research questions set forth in this report:

1. Do the research questions fill a gap in knowledge, or do they push knowledge about social support into new areas?
2. Is the theoretical structure explicit and logical?
3. Is there an explanation of where the study fits in with regard to the building and testing of theory about social support?

Two problems are identified and emphasized in the literature review. These problems are that social support is a concept that is not well defined, and that measures of social support need to be refined. In summarizing the literature review, Dr. Mercer noted, "Although social support has failed to predict adaptation to pregnancy and motherhood or to account for a large portion of the variance explaining it, there is consensus that social support is a multi-dimensional construct that is important in buffering stress and facilitating mothering." According to Dr. Mercer, "The problem appears to remain in the conceptualization and operationalization of stress."* The social support literature demonstrates that there is little agreement about the meaning of social support or how to measure it.

Certainly differences in conceptualization are readily apparent. Some define social support as positive or negative input that moves a person toward or away from goals (Caplan et al., 1976). Others recognize only positive aspects of support in their definitions of the term (Caplan, 1974; Cobb, 1976; Moss, 1973; Galloway & Dillon, 1973)). Conceptualization definitions also vary in scope. Some include only emotional support (Moss, 1973) or information (Cobb, 1976), while others mention physical or instrumental help with tasks along with information and emotional support (Dean & Lin, 1977). Probably the definition that is most broad in scope is the typology proposed by House (1981). It includes four kinds of support: instrumental help with tasks for personal care, informational support to help people cope with problems, emotional support, and appraisal support in which opinions of others are used to evaluate one's actions. House's definition has been used in this investigation to categorize kinds of support received by teenage mothers.

*The word "stress" was used in error in Dr. Mercer's presentation, and "support" had been intended.

Although we are beginning to develop valid and reliable measures, much of the early work on social support suffered from lack of such instruments. Thoits (1982) called attention to this problem. In her review of social support research, she found that some investigators used available data, such as presence or absence of a spouse, and called this social support. Others have selected indicators of social support that are not directly tied to interpersonal contacts. Examples of these indicators include lack of money or having too many responsibilities.

Dr. Mercer's investigation, however, does not seem to be an attempt to solve these conceptual or measurement problems, although these problems are recognized. Rather, the aim of the study was to add to knowledge about types of social support that are available and how these supports are related to maternal role attachment.

The theoretical framework selected for the study is described as "derived from role theory from an interactionist perspective and relevant literature." This framework seems to have been used to guide the investigator in selecting variables to measure maternal role attainment, but not for social support. It is not clear what framework was used to conceptualize and select indicators for social support at the time the investigation was planned. The types of social support selected as variables were network, physical, emotional, informational, and appraisal support. The question needs to be raised as to why "network" is considered as one type of support in the second research question. In the literature review it was noted that, "An individual's social network provides sources of the social support, whatever type it may be." Here the social network is seen as the source of support rather than as a type of support. In addition, House (1981), whose typology was used to categorize kinds of support received by subjects in this study, distinguished sources of support (those persons who are members of the social network) from types of support received. It is not clear, then, why "network" is viewed as a type of support in the research question or in the subsequent analysis. However, Dr. Mercer pointed out that data collection began in 1979 and that the investigation thus lacked the benefit of newly developed instruments and the current knowledge base concerning social support. The lack of clarity as to whether the social network is a source of or a type of social support probably reflects the lack of clarity in the knowledge about social support that existed in the late 70s when the study began.

METHOD

The method described in the report is critiqued in terms of the research design, sample, instruments, and data collection procedures.

Research Design

The design selected for this study is not discussed. It is apparent from the purpose and questions that this is a descriptive study and that a longitudinal design was used, since the investigator examined social support and maternal role attainment over the first year of motherhood.

Sample

Subjects were grouped according to age, and the group focused upon in this report consisted of 15-19 year olds. Criteria for sample selection were described, but the rationale for the criteria are not presented. Some are obvious and are related to practicality in terms of carrying out the research, e.g., the ability of subjects to speak and read English. An explanation of the setting of some of the other criteria would have been helpful. For example, why was the sample limited to first time mothers whose infants had no diagnosed physical abnormality at birth?

The sample was described in detail in terms of age distribution, ethnicity, education, marital status, type of care (clinic or private), and social class using the Hollingshead (1957) index. A high refusal rate of 52.9% was mentioned. A discussion of possible reasons for this high refusal rate would have been helpful. Although no attempt was made to generalize from this sample to the population of first time teenaged mothers since this is a convenience sample, one wonders how characteristic this sample was given the high rate of refusal. Since the age distribution within the 15-19-year-old group shows that the number of participants increased as age increased (only 2 subjects were 15 years old), was the refusal rate higher for younger women than the rate for those 18 or 19 years old, or were fewer younger teens not delivering? A comment was made that "fewer numbers of teenagers (are) delivering," but this statement does not speak to the issue of whether or not this is particularly true for younger teens.

Instruments

Several instruments were used to measure social support and maternal role attainment. In regard to social support, different instruments were used to measure support at early postpartum and 1 month; and 1 instrument was used to measure social support at 4, 8, and 12 months. Although a rationale for use of separate instruments was provided, the use of one instrument might have been more helpful in order to draw inferences about changes or stability in social support over time.

Both social support instruments included notations that several other instruments were "sources" for many of the items. Does this mean that these items were taken from the other instruments, or that the content of items in other instruments inspired the writing of items for the instruments used in this study? How were these instruments constructed? Were they pretested with teenage mothers? Were the reliability (in terms of internal consistency) and validity of the instruments determined?

Interrater reliabilities for coding of the interviews ranged from 86.8% for early postpartum to 89% for the interviews conducted at 12 months. Once reliability was determined, all the interviews were coded, and the investigator explained that types of support reported by subjects "fell into the four types" of support mentioned by House. If all of the data were coded according to that typology, it would have been helpful if an Appendix had been included showing items and responses which were viewed as indicators of each type of support. In reading the items in both social support instruments, it is sometimes not clear what type of support a question addresses. For example, one item reads, "Are any of these people close friends with whom you would feel comfortable discussing things like pregnancy, child rearing, etc.?" Is the intent here to measure an aspect of the social network, i.e., having close friends, or is the intent to identify a type of support? If it is the latter, it is not clear what that type is. The phrase, "discussing things like pregnancy, child rearing, etc." could mean any one of the four types.

Instruments used to measure the group of dependent variables, conceptualized as maternal role attainment, were noted in a table along with reliability coefficients. Samples of the instruments or descriptions of them would have been useful. Such information would have been especially helpful in understanding NPI-I and NPI-II. Unlike titles of the other instruments, these do not offer a clue as to what is being measured.*

Data Collection Procedures

Data collection procedures are not discussed in this report. Since one sampling criterion was that subjects live within an hour's drive of the university, it is assumed that interviews were conducted in subjects' homes. One wonders if there was anything about the data collection procedures that might have contributed to the high rate of refusal in this investigation. Is it possible that home visits for purposes of asking questions might have been viewed as threatening in some way?

FINDINGS

The next section of the critique addresses data analysis and findings. Data analysis procedures are described in the "Results" section of the report. To answer the first research question concerning social support available at early postpartum and at 1, 4, 8, and 12 months, frequency distributions and percentages were calculated. Findings were presented in terms of categories of persons (such as mate or mother) perceived as most helpful or available to help, whether or not enough help was anticipated or received, kinds of support received, and number of helpers. These findings adequately answer the research question. The only comment to be made here is that lack of consistency in reporting findings across the different time periods is confusing. For example, at T1 the percentages

*The full names of the instruments have been added to the presentation after the conference.

of types of persons providing help and whether or not enough help was anticipated were reported. At T2 the kind of support received was also examined. At T3 and T5 the number of helpers was also reported.

The second research question examined correlations between types of social support and measures of maternal role attainment. Principal component procedures, used to derive support and attachment factors, were described. To answer the research question, Spearman rho and Pearson product moment correlations were calculated along with building of multiple regression models to determine the proportion of variance in maternal role attainment explained by the social support factors. In reporting the multiple regression models constructed at T1 and T2, the investigator noted that the models should be viewed with caution due to the small number of subjects with complete data. Such statements did not appear in discussion of models for T3, T4, or T5, but it seems likely that the problem still existed due to the attrition of subjects at each time period. It would have been helpful to know the total number of subjects upon which these computations were based at each time period. For example, at T5, 40 teens were interviewed. Out of those 40 subjects, how many had complete sets of data?

INTERPRETATION

Interpretation of the findings were discussed in both the "Results" and "Summary" of the report.

In the "Results" section, the investigator commented that few subjects mentioned receiving appraisal support. The interpretation given for this is that subjects seemed to internalize the maternal role by about 4 months postpartum, and perhaps reassurance regarding one's performance as a mother is not very important from that time on. However, the findings about appraisal support do not seem to lend themselves to this interpretation. Appraisal support was not directly examined until 4 months (T3). At that time and at T4 and T5, appraisal support was received by only 7% of the teenage mothers. Given the statement that the maternal role was usually internalized by 4 months postpartum, it seems likely that appraisal support would have been received by a larger proportion of subjects at early postpartum (T1) and 1 month (T2). Unfortunately, these data were not available.

Two different interpretations were set forth to explain the movement away from subjects' mothers and toward use of others for support beginning at 8 months (T4). In the "Results" section of the report, it was suggested that this might indicate healthy maturation toward independence and increasing ability to establish relationships with others. In contrast, in the "Summary" of the report, the possibility of a "conflictual" relationship between subjects and their mothers was mentioned as an alternative explanation for the decrease in support received by subjects from their mothers. Evidence given for this suggestion was the weak negative correlation between informational support and emotional support at 12 months (T5).

The possibility of conflict within support relationships was described in the literature review. Size of a conflicted network was found to be positively related to number of symptoms, depression, and anxiety (Barrera, 1981). There was also some agreement that network size may be a barometer of the amount of stress experienced (Barrera, 1981; Hobbs, 1965). The data in Dr. Mercer's study provide some support for the presence of conflictual relationships as already noted, and there is also some evidence to suggest that network size may be negatively correlated with maternal role attainment. This inference is based on the following findings. The number of helpers the teenage mothers had was determined at T3 and T5, and at T3 the number of helpers ranged from 0-4 and the mode was 1, whereas at T5 the range was 1-4 and the mode was 3. Thus, the size of the network increased from T3 to T5. At the same time, the number of relationships between support factors and maternal role attainment decreased. At T3 physical, emotional, appraisal, and network support were related to the dependent variables. At T5, emotional support was related to only two measures of maternal role attainment.

These findings indicate a need for more research to examine conflict within support relationships, as was suggested in Dr. Mercer's report, and to examine the influence of network size. One early definition of social support indicated that support can be positive or negative, moving a person toward or away from goals (Caplan et al., 1976). However, most definitions have focused on positive aspects. Findings in this study suggest that it would be worthwhile to conceptualize social support as including both positive and negative components. Future investigations can determine what the negative as well as the positive components are, conditions under which positive and negative components exist, how these components influence the kinds of social support received, and how they affect outcomes such as maternal role attainment.

Another important finding that was commented upon in the "Summary" of the report was that there were few relationships between social support and maternal role attainment. This finding was consistent throughout the time periods and methods of analysis. The greatest number of relationships between social support and maternal role attainment were found at 1 month (T2). At that time, two significant correlations were found between physical support and the dependent variables, and one relationship was found for informational support. In addition, informational support entered two of the regression models, emotional support entered one, and physical support entered another.

Given the amount of social support received at each time period it is difficult to understand why the support factors were not more consistently related to maternal role attainment. The amount of support received was first examined at 1 month (T2). At each of the time periods from 1 month to 12 months, over half of the subjects received physical support, 30-40% received emotional support, 15-40% received informational support, and appraisal support was received by 7% of the teenage mothers at T3, T4, and T5.

The investigator suggested that the failure of the support variables to correlate more consistently with maternal role attainment may be due to the "crudeness of the measures." However, there are some other possibilities as well. It may be that the lack of correlation may be due to the way social support is conceptualized, or there may be problems in the way the theoretical framework was developed.

CONTRIBUTION TO NURSING KNOWLEDGE

At the end of the report the investigator stated that it is crucial for health professionals to encourage teenage mothers to develop relationships that can provide emotional support. This statement emphasizes only a part of the contribution that this study makes to the body of nursing knowledge. In examining the various types of social support that may be received, the study emphasizes the importance of knowing about different kinds of support. This knowledge should be of use to practitioners. Early knowledge about social support, by and large, was limited to knowing about social support systems or networks, so it was not uncommon for nurses to assess whether or not patients had significant others to rely on for help. The assumption seemed to be that if a support system was in place, a person was then supported. This study provides new knowledge about social support to question that assumption. The study is a beginning in knowing how different kinds of support may be related to healthful outcomes, in this instance to maternal role attainment.

More research is needed to add to and confirm knowledge about the effectiveness of different types of social support in promoting health. At the same time investigators need to develop better conceptualizations of social support and continue instrument development.

It seem likely that social support research conducted by nurses will be directed toward answering some questions of concern to nurses:

1. What types of support are needed by people who face actual or potential threats to their health?
2. What conditions affect the kinds of support people receive?
3. Does the source of support make a difference as to whether or not people perceive themselves as supported?
4. In what ways is receipt of support related to health outcomes?

Questions such as these will serve to focus research and lead to the development of a theory about social support from a nursing perspective. This knowledge base will provide a firm foundation for taking the next step--the designing and testing of nursing interventions to assist patients in obtaining the support they need.

DISCUSSION

S. Humenick: I'm not certain I remember accurately all the figures from Dr. Mercer's presentation. Wasn't the percentage of those adolescents that were clinic patients quite different as compared to the older age group?

R. Mercer: Yes, it was. In Group 1, 84.7% were clinic patients; in Group 2, 73.7% were; and in Group 3, 40.5% were (X^2 = 40.04 (2), p = .001).

S. Humenick: It would then seem that many of the comparisons made between age groups might also represent or be confounded very strongly with socioeconomic factors. For example, in surmising why younger mothers didn't have as many cesarean births, it may not be that they are healthier. Others have suggested it may be that there is no financial incentive for a cesarean in clinic patients. Still, there may be an intervention mindset in private care versus public care that influences the number of interventions.

T. Antonucci: Teenage mothers may not appear until they are in labor, whereas older mothers may be more likely to have complete prenatal care.

R. Mercer: Those are all valid interpretations, but I'd like to go to a point made in the critique. Dr. Crawford mentioned that the appraisal support findings did not lend themselves to the interpretation that few responses of appraisal support suggested that since most had internalized the maternal role at 4 months, perhaps reassurance about the role wasn't as important, because appraisal support had not been examined at early postpartum and 1 month. Appraisal support could be classified from the raw data since those responses had been included with emotional responses at 1 month, such as responses describing how persons had helped them by, "Telling me I was doing a good job," or "Telling me I was a good mother." However, it is interesting how few times that type of response was made as compared to responses such as "Clean the house," or "Help take care of the baby." I think that maybe teenagers are less articulate because of their educational level, but across the board all subjects tended not to give the appraisal kind of support answers. So I don't know whether appraisal support is related to internalizing the mothering role, or is more difficult to describe than the other areas where persons were of help.

J. Fawcett: Findings from Kishi's study of clients' recall of information provided by health care professionals are relevant to this discussion (Kishi, 1981). These findings revealed that the mothers of the children seen in the well baby clinics were never directly praised. Rather, the praise was directed at the baby; for example, "Oh, what a beautiful baby you are; look how well you are gaining weight; how bright you are; isn't that a cute smile." This suggests that when we say these things to the baby, we are indirectly telling the mother what a good job she has done. However, the mother is not getting appraisal support in any direct fashion, and so she may never report that she perceives this kind of support.

T. Antonucci: I would like to expand on that. We've observed the same thing, and now when we're teaching residents and medical students how to do a well baby exam, we tell them, "Say something about the kid, and say something good about the mother." Unless things are really bad, you should be able to find something positive to say. It makes people feel a lot better. They are then much more likely to tell you what's on their mind, and will seek information from you. When you say, "Well, is there anything you want to ask me," they will not say, "No," when they've got a long list and if they really feel comfortable. So we just tell our staff to throw in a compliment if they can find something to compliment, and if they can't, maybe there should be a referral.

L. Cronenwett: I think that if you had asked, "In what way was this person supportive of you" versus "What kind of help did you get," you would have obtained different responses. I think the word, "help," in our society triggers us to think of instrumental or tangible forms of support because that form is so rare and so valuable. Asking how a person has been supportive, on the other hand, causes subjects to think of more intrapsychic phenomena.

J. Bumbalo: I'm interested if you know anything about your subjects that were lost to the study. It's roughly a third that you didn't get to follow through the T5 period; isn't that correct?

R. Mercer: Yes, 39.4%. Those teenagers who were lost to the study did not differ by self-concept, personality integration, marital status, ethnicity, or level of education.

You made the comment about reasons for not participating in the study. I do have that compiled, and I have a full report of it elsewhere. Overall, 35.2% of those who refused gave no reason. Among the 74 teenagers choosing not to participate, 22 (29.7%) gave no reason, 12 (16.2%) said they were moving out of the state, 12 (16.2%) said they were not interested, and 9 (12.2%) were too busy. Two (2.7%) of the teenagers indicated that their parents didn't want them to participate. One (1.4%) gave as a reason that she was putting her infant in a foster home, one (1.4%) said she was involved with another nurse, and one (1.4%) said her husband did not approve. Fourteen (18.9%) agreed to be in the study during postpartum hospitalization, but when we tried to follow up after they went home, they dropped out. This really raises the question of informed consent. Perhaps they didn't feel safe refusing to participate until they were in their home setting.

T. Antonucci: Maybe they were more mobile. Maybe they were moving around.

R. Mercer: They were. Of those lost to the study, we were unable to contact 22 (84.6%) for the appointments. We'd visit them sometimes at the boyfriend's apartment and sometimes at their mothers. It was very difficult to keep in contact with them. Some interviews were even held in pizza parlors; we used any setting that we could to make the interview attractive. In contrast, the older mothers seemed to enjoy the study, and used interviews as learning opportunities. For example, in response to "What are you teaching your baby now?" many would say,

"Oh is there something I could be teaching my baby?" The next time we visited and asked the question, there would be a big long list of things they were teaching the baby. At the end of the study, we did ask the question, "Has participating in this study changed anything you've done," and there was a halo effect. Several of the mothers said it had stimulated them to think about more things that they could do for their baby as a result of participating, and several said it had helped to talk about what had concerned them. Significantly, more of the teenagers (N = 26, 65%) replied that participating in the study had had no effect on them, compared to 53 (46.5%) of Group 2 and 45 (57.1%) of Group 3.

If I were interviewing the teenagers again, I would pay them $10 an interview, because compared to the older women they were poor, and I think they really didn't see any value to the study. We would have to interview them with the stereo on. They were doing us a favor; we were imposing on their time. There were some times when the researchers would go there five times before they caught the teenager at home. We would call before we left the office and say, "We are just checking to remind you that your interview is coming up now, and I'm going to leave." When we arrived, we would be told, "Oh, she had to go to the beauty parlor, or she had to go...," or else there would be no answer when we arrived. There were a lot of evasive tactics.

We also lost some subjects who just dropped out and we couldn't follow on them. What I was naive to was the number of people who give fake addresses to the hospital. I was really not aware that when some people check into the hospital, they don't give the right address or phone number.

J. Fawcett: How old were the data collectors?

R. Mercer: The interviewers were 24-30, except for me. I didn't collect a lot of data, but I did a few of the interviews, and I was by far the oldest.

J. Fawcett: The reason I was asking about the age of the data collectors is because I think age may influence the client's reaction to the health care professional. For example, a teenager may view a nurse or physician who is older as an authority figure or a mother or father figure. In other words, this is just the person she does not want to deal with at the same time she is working out her relationships with her own parents and other authority figures. I think we have to find ways to establish effective relationships with our clients, relationships that carry over from the time they are in the hospital to when they are at home, yet still in need of health care. Furthermore, I think that some clients may want a relationship that is both professional and personal. This seemed to be the case in my longitudinal research of spouses' body image changes during and after pregnancy (Fawcett, 1978). I found that some couples would inconvenience themselves to find time for me to visit them for the data collection; others would call me, sometimes long distance, to postpone an appointment. Only once in a great while was someone not at home at the time of the appointment. I think that these reactions were influenced by the relationship I established with each couple.

I began to realize this when I found that several couples asked me to stay after the data collection for coffee or lunch or dinner. They wanted something more than just to be part of a study; I think they wanted to have a relationship with someone they could view not only as a nurse, but also as a friend.

R. Mercer: Our research assistants were served lunch or coffee quite often too by women in Groups 2 and 3 because this sort of relationship was established. The initial refusal rate regarding participation was not peculiar to age; however, the 20-year-olds had a 53.2% (N = 157) refusal rate. The highly educated 30-year-olds were in the group who had the lowest refusal rate (31.3%) and this group was easy to study longitudinally. Out of ninety 30-42 year olds, there were 88 at one year, a 2.2% attrition rate. They seemed to be more responsible and to enjoy participation more, and they shared more data. The older women were more open and told us when they thought the measures weren't valid. The teenagers answered questions with one or two words, would require probes and rephrasing of questions, whereas the older women would respond quite verbosely to an open-ended question.

S. Eyres: Getting back to social support, what can you tell us after you've done your study? You have your findings, and you've reconceptualized them. How would you go about measuring social support differently? What is your current thinking about social support?

R. Mercer: I'll be honest. I didn't have a conceptual framework about social support in 1979. I would really want to use two measures described by Barrera (1981), the Inventory of Socially Supportive Behaviors and the Arizona Social Support Interview Schedule, which measures conflict. I would want to measure conflict, because the teenager is dealing with developmental tasks and the reported antecedents to teenage pregnancy. All suggest conflict. I would want to know who were in her support system and what her relationship was with those people.

I do think that there's a big difference in emotional support, and I think some kinds of support make a difference when given earlier. I think physical support had a very critical impact during the first 4 months as far as their feelings about everything. I really feel strongly that at 8 months and 1 year emotional support probably is the most nurturing or sustaining to an individual.

In talking with the older women and looking at the total study, it seems that the nurturant relationship meant more at this time because they were feeling their nonpregnant selves again and had mastered the maternal role so to speak, so that they could manage all of the physical or instrumental kinds of things. They had found babysitters and were very competent in managing the kinds of things that they weren't able to manage the first 4 months. It would be important to look at the four different kinds of support: physical, informational, appraisal, and emotional. The fact that they would not fit into one factor and at several test periods failed to correlate with each other makes me say that they are different kinds of concepts. The size of the network was important, and I didn't mean that as a type of support, but the way it was reported here was confusing. We correlated the size of the network with dependent variables to see if we could learn something about the extent of support. I'm not sure that network size was always reported reliably. The teenager would sometimes say, "Oh my mother, my aunt, my uncle, and my grandfather" in response to, "Who has been most helpful," and you'd wonder about her sincerity in their helpfulness. On the other hand you would feel very badly when one would say, "No one." Indeed at 1 year, one teenager who had no one as a support person was abusing her child and was very happy to be referred to Children's Protective Services because the social worker could find help for her. In these cases the network size was not a barometer of the amount of stress experienced as suggested by Barrera (1981). In summary, I would take advantage of some of the new support measures, and I would definitely want to look at the types of support in any future study.

L. Cronenwett: Our refusal rate was almost identical with a different population. Similar to you, we are not having too much of a problem with attrition in the 30 + year old subjects. The four couples who did drop out of our study by choice were all lower socioeconomic group couples. The major problem is that when we conduct studies that require data collection on a number of variables, either the subjects have to read a lot, or they have to sit there and listen. If you go in and do one quick measurement on one variable, I think you could get lower socioeconomic people to participate; but that's not what we're trying to do. We're trying multivariate and longitudinal approaches, and they get tired of it. They don't want to read the same scale and fill it out repeatedly. Hooray for you and that you tried to reach this hard-to-reach group, that you tried to follow them for a year, and that you kept going back. I think that's marvelous. For all the problems you have with your data analysis, I still think it's wonderful that you tried.

R. Mercer: Did you pay your subjects?

L. Cronenwett: We paid our participants $30 for the entire study.

L. Cronenwett: On the project Dr. Antonucci and I are working on now, we're definitely going to give out $5 at each measurement point.

K. Barnard: Our drop-out rate for subjects in the Newborn Nursing Models Study was 85% at 3 months. The nursing intervention was during the first 3 months. At the 10 month follow-up we had 65% of the sample. I think if there is some payoff, service, reimbursement, etc. for the subject, it is helpful.

It is confusing to me at this time about what strategies we should use in nursing research. We talk about needing holistic, multivariant approaches. We talk about the need for a large, random sample. I think we're just kidding ourselves. There's little money to do research, and the subjects are hard to get. In some ways, we're existing in a dream world. My good colleague and friend, Mary Neal, often says that what has to happen is we have to develop research as a way of life and not just in relation to when we are funded. I know how hard Dr. Mercer and everyone else who reported today has worked in terms of doing the study, getting funded, etc.; and yet when we look at it, there's just so much more to do. I don't think we're making the best use of small samples and single case studies, however. I've recently reviewed all nursing case studies concerning children under the age of 5 for the last 5 years. There are, as near as I can calculate from the literature, 20 case studies a year published about children under 5. There is no common format; most of them relate to the medical diagnosis, and there really are no conclusions drawn in most. The best one I've ever found (and I'm partially biased because I helped her with it) is Barbara Durand's work (1975) on failure to thrive. She did an excellent study on a hospitalized child, with observation and experimentation, tied strongly to the conceptual and theoretical knowledge, which raised some additional questions. I think some things are becoming clear in the whole area of social support at this conference, but I think we're going to have to move in some different methodological directions to enhance our research.

M. Cranley: One of the things that I've been playing around with but have not fully developed is the utilization of clinicians in the collection and recording of data in a systematic fashion. If you talk with a number of clinicians, you'll find that they always ask the same kinds of questions, and they always elicit the same kind of information from every pregnant woman, for example. But if you look at the record, it's not recorded there. It seems to me that we could systematically formulate some things we want to know about patients, whether that was descriptive information or whether it was intervention kinds of things. Then we could work with clinicians not only to collect the data (which they may be doing anyway), but also to record that data in a way that's retrievable.

L. Walker: I think there are some other alternatives. One which doesn't get a lot of press is a survey. I did a one parent survey study that cost $350 (Walker, 1976). While not a landmark study, I think it came up with some important information. A second alternative has been proposed by Sieber (1973). It involves the combination of survey and case study techniques, i.e., qualitative plus quantitative. One thing he recommends is doing intensive interviews on selected survey subjects. An investigator can use case studies for debriefing what happened to survey subjects, or to pull out one or more modal subjects and then go for some intensive interviews with them to illustrate specific processes or characteristics in more depth. I think that that's another way of getting the numbers you may need for multivariate research with large numbers when you're in between grant money. Because paper/pencil surveys are subject to what people actually do, this weakness may be addressed by qualitative data gathered by interview and observation of small subsamples of survey subjects. Our current economic crunch may facilitate the development of a more economical way to handle some of those issues.

G. Anderson: Let me suggest another alternative, something I call clinical collaborative implementation research. In a sense this is my own idea, but it draws heavily on the work of Campbell and Stanley (1963), Cook and Campbell (1979), and the nonequivalent control group design that they describe. The alternative design is useful when you choose to replicate an intervention that has been documented as effective, or when you have come upon an intervention in your practice that you would like to test. In either case, the first step is to collect and systematically record base line (control group) data for a prespecified period of time. Ideally the data would be the kind we collect anyhow, or something additional that requires very little time to do. This way clinicians can be involved with virtually no increase in workload, and costs of additional personnel can be kept to a minimum. The next step is to introduce the intervention and collect the same kind of data as before, for the same time period, or until an equal number of subjects are obtained. Because the groups are nonconcurrent and nonequivalent, the design is not a perfect one, especially for a single study. However, if the same protocol is used, with the same intervention, in several settings, and if the same kind of results are obtained, these cumulative findings would be fairly convincing. In a busy clinical setting this design is more feasible than an experimental design because it is much easier to carry out. The staff doesn't have to be responsible for two groups at the same time, or worry about which patients belong in which group, or remember one procedure for one group and another for the other. Also there is no danger of cross-contamination of the intervention between groups; and if the intervention is shown to be desirable, it can be implemented simply by continuing it. The biggest disadvantage is that some pertinent factor may be different for each group, such as summer weather for the first group, and winter weather for the second. If one is aware of this problem,

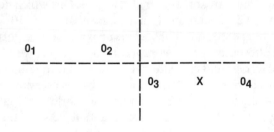

Figure 2. Change in weight

The horizontal broken line depicts that the two groups are not equivalent, and the vertical broken line depicts that the two times of data collection are not equivalent.

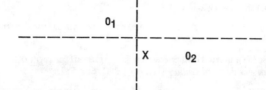

Figure 3. Total hospital costs.

The horizontal broken line depicts that the two groups are not equivalent, and the vertical broken line depicts that the two times of data collection are not equivalent.

however, much can be done to avoid, equalize, or control for such factors. The design is essentially a nonequivalent control group design, but according to Cook (personal communication, August 10, 1983), it is a special case not actually described in the book. It would be called a nonconcurrent nonequivalent control group design. Figure 2 shows the design for a dependent variable such as a change in weight. The design for a variable like total hospital costs, which can be measured only once, is illustrated in Figure 3.

Much can be said for this implementation research, especially when done at several different times, in different localities, and by different groups of investigators. Such a project will commence at the University of Florida in January 1983 by myself, Tanya Bodo, Linda Sortino, Dorothy Barrus, Myra Edens, and Ann Sipp; and we hope other investigators will want to do the same research in their own setting. We will study the effect of self-regulatory mother-newborn interaction postbirth on maternal and infant condition and behavior and maternal and nurse satisfaction.

REFERENCES

Abernethy, V.D. (1973). Social network and response to the maternal role. *International Journal of Sociology of the Family, 3,* 86-92.

Anderson, G.C. (1981). Critique (on Mercer, 1981a). In R. Lederman & B. Raff (Eds.), *Perinatal parental behavior: Nursing research and implications for newborn health.* March of Dimes *Birth Defects: Original Article Series, XVII*(6). New York: Alan R. Liss.

Barglow, P., Bornstein, M., Exum, D.B., Wright, M.K., & Visotsky, H.M. (1968). Some psychiatric aspects of illegitimate pregnancy in early adolescence. *American Journal of Orthopsychiatry, 38*(4), 672-687.

Barrera, M. (1981). Social support in the adjustment of pregnant adolescents: Assessment issues. In B.H. Gottlieb (Ed.), *Social networks and social support.* Beverly Hills: Sage Publications.

Benedek, T. (1949). The psychosomatic implications of the primary unit: Mother-child. *American Journal of Orthopsychiatry, 19,* 642-654.

Benedek, T. (1959). Parenthood as a developmental phase. *Journal of the American Psychoanalytic Association, 7,* 389-417.

Blank, M. (1964). Some maternal influences on infants' rates of sensorimotor development. *Journal of the American Academy of Child Psychiatry, 3*(4), 668-687.

Blumberg, N.L. (1980). Effects of neonatal risk, maternal attitude, and cognitive style on early postpartum adjustment. *Journal of Abnormal Psychology, 89*(2), 139-150.

Broussard, E.R., & Hartner, M.S.S. (1971). Further considerations regarding maternal perception of the first born. In J. Hellmuth (Ed.), *Exceptional infant* (Vol. 2). New York: Brunner/Mazel.

Bryan-Logan, B.N., & Dancy, B.L. (1974). Unwed pregnant adolescents. *Nursing Clinics of North America, 9*(1), 57-68.

Burke, R.J., & Weir, T. (1978). Sex differences in adolescent life stress, social support, and well-being. *Journal of Psychology, 95,* 277-288.

Campbell, D.T., & Stanley, J.C. (1963). *Experimental and quasi-experimental designs for research.* Chicago: Rand McNally.

Caplan, G. (1974). *Support systems and community mental health: Lectures on concept development.* New York: Behavioral Publications.

Caplan, R.D., Robinson, E.A.R., French, J.R.P., Caldwell, J.R., & Shinn, M. (1976). *Adhering to medical regimens: Pilot experiments and patient education and social support.* Ann Arbor: University of Michigan, Research Center for Group Dynamics, Institute for Social Research.

Cobb, S. (1976). Social support as a moderator of life stress. *Psychosomatic medicine, 38,* 300-314.

Colletta, N.D., Hadler, S., & Gregg, C.H. (1981). How adolescents cope with the problems of early motherhood. *Adolescence, 16*(63), 499-512.

Cook, T., & Campbell, D.T. (1979). *Quasi-experimentation.* Boston: Houghton Mifflin.

Crawford, G. (1980). *Teen social support patterns and the stress of pregnancy.* (Unpublished doctoral dissertation, Case Western Reserve University.) *Dissertation Abstracts International, 41,* 893B-894B. University Microfilms No. 8019335.

Cronenwett, L.R., & Kunst-Wilson, W. (1981). Stress, social support, and the transition to fatherhood. *Nursing Research, 30*(4), 196-201.

Dean, A., & Lin, N. (1977). The stress-buffering role of social support: Problems and prospects for systematic investigation. *Journal of Nervous and Mental Disease, 165,* 403-417.

Disbrow, M.A., Doerr, H.O., & Caulfield, C. (1977). *Measures to predict child abuse.* (Final Report). Seattle, WA: University of Washington.

Durand, B. (1975). A clinical nursing study: Failure to thrive in a child with Down's Syndrome. *Nursing Research, 24,* 272-286.

Fawcett, J. (1978). Body image and the pregnant couple. *MCN, The American Journal of Maternal Child Nursing, 3,* 227-233.

Freese, M.P., & Thoman, E.B. (1978). The assessment of maternal characteristics for the study of mother-infant interactions. *Infant Behavior and Development, 1,* 95-105.

Galloway, J.C., & Dillon, P.B. (1973). A comparison of family networks and friend networks in health care utilization. *Journal of Comparative Family Studies, 4,* 131-142.

Gould, R.L. (1972). The phases of adult life: A study in developmental psychology. *American Journal of Psychiatry, 129(5),* 521-531.

Grossman, F.K., Eichler, L.S., Winickoff, S.A., Anzalone, M.K., Gofseyeff, M.H., & Sargent, S.P. (1980). *Pregnancy, birth, and parenthood.* San Francisco: Jossey-Bass.

Held, L. (1981). Self-esteem and social network of the young pregnant teenager. *Adolescence, 16(64),* 905-912.

Hobbs, D.F. (1965). Parenthood as crisis: A third study. *Journal of Marriage and the Family, 27(3),* 367-372.

Hollingshead, A.B. (1957). *Four factor index of social status.* New Haven, CT: Yale University, Department of Sociology.

House, J.S. (1981). *Work stress and social support.* Reading, MA: Addison-Wesley.

Johnson, O.G. (1976). *Tests and measurements in child development: Handbook 2* (Vol. 2). San Francisco: Jossey-Bass.

Josselyn, I.M. (1971). Value problems in the treatment of adolescents. *Smith College Studies in Social Work, 42(1),* 1-14.

Kishi, K.I. (1981). *Communication patterns between health care provider and client and recall of information.* Unpublished doctoral dissertation, University of Pennsylvania, Philadelphia.

LaBarre, M. (1968). Pregnancy experiences among married adolescents. *American Journal of Orthopsychiatry, 38,* 47-55.

LaBarre, M. (1972). Emotional crises of school-age girls during pregnancy and early motherhood. *Journal of the American Academy of Child Psychiatry, 11(2),* 537-557.

Leifer, M. (1977). Psychological changes accompanying pregnancy and motherhood. *Genetic Psychology Monographs, 95,* 55-96.

McLanahan, S.S., Wedemeyer, N.V., & Adelberg, T. (1981). Network structure, social support, and psychological well-being in the single-parent family. *Journal of Marriage and the Family, 43(3),* 601-612.

Mercer, R.T. (1980). Teenage motherhood: The first year. *JOGN Nursing, 9(1),* 16-27.

Mercer, R.T. (1981a). Factors impacting on the maternal role the first year of motherhood. In R. Lederman & B. Raff (Eds.), *Perinatal parental behavior: Nursing research and implications for newborn health.* March of Dimes *Birth Defects: Original Article Series XVII(6).* New York: Alan R. Liss.

Mercer, R.T. (1981b). A theoretical framework for studying factors that impact on the maternal role. *Nursing Research, 30(2),* 73-77.

Mercer, R.T., Hackley, K.C., & Bostrom, A. (1982). *Factors having an impact on maternal role attainment the first year of motherhood.* (Final Report of Project MC-R-060435). San Francisco: University of California, Department of Family Health Care Nursing. (Available from National Technical Service, U.S. Department of Commerce, Springfield, VA 22161.)

Moss, G.E. (1973). *Illness, immunity, and social interaction: The dynamics of biosocial resonation.* New York: John Wiley & Sons.

Poole, C.J., & Hoffman, M. (1981). Mothers of adolescent mothers: How do they cope? *Pediatric Nursing, 7*(1), 28-31.

Rosenstock, H.A. (1980). Recognizing the teen-ager who needs to be pregnant: A clinical perspective. *Southern Medical Journal, 73*(2), 134-136.

Ross Laboratories. (1973). *Boys/Physical development, birth to 56 weeks. Boys/Adaptive-social development, birth to 56 weeks.* Columbus: Author.

Ross Laboratories. (1973). *Girls/Physical development, birth to 56 weeks. Girls/Adaptive-social development, birth to 56 weeks.* Columbus: Author.

Russell, C.S. (1974). Transition to parenthood: Problems and gratification. *Journal of Marriage and the Family, 36*(2), 294-301.

Sieber, S.D. (1973). The integration of fieldwork and survey methods. *American Journal of Sociology, 78,* 1335-1359.

Smith, E.W. (1971). Transition to the role of grandmother as studied with mothers of pregnant adolescents. In *ANA Clinical Sessions, 1970, Miami.* New York: Appleton-Century-Crofts.

Thoits, P.A. (1982). Conceptual, methodological, and theoretical problems in studying social support as a buffer against life stress. *Journal of Health & Social Behavior, 23,* 145-159.

Virden, S.B. (1981). *The effect of information about infant behavior and primiparas' maternal role adequacy.* Unpublished doctoral dissertation, University of California, San Francisco.

Walker, L. (1976). *Identifying nursing needs of adoptive parents.* Final Report, Center for Health Care Research and Evaluation, The University of Texas, School of Nursing, Austin.

Wandersman, L., Wandersman, A., & Kahn, S. (1980). Social support in the transition to parenthood. *Journal of Community Psychology, 8,* 332-342.

Welches, L.J. (1979). Adolescent sexuality. In R.T. Mercer (Ed.), *Perspectives on adolescent health care.* Philadelphia: J.B. Lippincott.

Wilson, W.R., & Cronenwett, L.R. (1981-1983). *Nursing intervention to promote paternal behavior.* Washington, DC: DHHS, Division of Nursing.

Wise, S., & Grossman, F.K. (1980). Adolescent mothers and their infants: Psychological factors in early attachment and interaction. *American Journal of Orthopsychiatry, 50*(3), 454-468.

Zitner, R., & Miller, S.H. (1980). *Our youngest parents.* New York: Child Welfare League of America.

Zongker, C.E. (1980). Self-concept differences between single and married school-age mothers. *Journal of Youth and Adolescence, 9*(2), 175-184.

Zuckerman, B., Winsmore, G., & Alpert, J.J. (1979). A study of attitudes and support systems of inner city adolescent mothers. *Journal of Pediatrics, 95*(1), 122-125.

Supportive Measures for High-Risk Infants and Families

Kathryn E. Barnard, R.N., Ph.D., Charlene Snyder, M.S.N., and Anita Spietz, M.S.N.

The experience of providing a 3-month nursing program of care to infants and their families with physical, health, and social-environmental risks is presented. An individualized case approach was used which first involved a nursing assessment of the family, infant, and environmental needs and then was followed by subsequent appropriate nursing intervention. Brammer's conceptual model about the helping process was used to assist the analysis of the success or failure experienced in assisting these high-risk families. The differences that emerged were in the mothers' involvement in the exploration phase which involves goal setting. Families with incomplete progression through the helping process not only participated in less mutual decision making, but they were also less open to the initial assessment phase and had higher social risk. The nurses had less total contact with the uninvolved families. A brief description of a subsequent approach to provide effective nursing to a socially high-risk group of pregnant women is given. The approach involves a more extended period of intervention and emphasizes the development of a therapeutic relationship.

This paper will describe our experience in supporting vulnerable families with one type of nursing intervention which was part of a larger research project to experimentally test three models of providing nursing services to families of newborns. The assumptions of the larger research project, "Models of Newborn Nursing Services," were that the parent-infant system is influenced by the individual characteristics of each member; and when the parent and infant are acting together in mutually dependent ways, there is optimal interaction and adaption in synchrony. We further assumed that in the development of the parent-child relationship, there is reason to believe that complex and competent functioning is extremely unlikely to occur in certain families. Some of these families include infants whose biological and physical status makes it difficult or impossible for the infants to send cues or to repond to their caregiver. Some of the families include parents who lack knowledge about infant behavior and development. Other families may not adapt because the parents' level of life stress is high, their level of support is low, and they are unable to apply the knowledge and skills they have.

We combined these assumptions into our selection criteria for the families where there were nonoptimal infant characteristics or nonoptimal parent characteristics. The nonoptimal characteristics of the infants were primarily biological factors including prematurity, low birth weight, and complications of pregnancy, labor, and delivery; while the characteristics of nonoptimal parents included those which interfere with adaptive behavior and are primarily social in nature. Although little research has been directed specifically at adaptive behavior as a function of social class or educational level, it is known that these variables are related to infant developmental test scores. Moreover, lower social class and educational level are both associated with higher levels of family disorganization.

Thus, the subjects we selected had what we termed double vulnerability; i.e., they had both biological complications during pregnancy, and they represented families with social problems. We hypothesized that if either partner in the parent-child interaction had nonoptimal characteristics, the chances for parent-child adaption, especially for synchrony, would be markedly decreased. This is most dramatically true for those families in which both the parents and the baby have nonoptimal characteristics. Several studies have shown that measures of general infant development are particularly low for children in these circumstances (McDonald, 1964; Werner, Bierman, & French, 1971; Willerman, Broman, & Fiedler, 1970).

The only empirically tested nursing approaches designed to facilitate adaptation that we are aware of have been relatively unstructured and generally supportive in nature. Most commonly, they have served as controls in research studies which tested the efficacy of other programs. Where nursing served as the control group, the children did not show any positive benefit; whereas in the experimental group which used the educational approach with the infant or parent, the infant showed cognitive gains. Before this study, no systematic study has been made of a program specifically designed to use nursing care as a facilitator of parent-child adaptation in synchrony.

In spite of the lack of research, thousands of nurses are offering care at times and in places where they might favorably influence parent-child adaptation. For example, in the newborn nursery, nurses are able to easily assess the biological characteristics of the infant which may contribute positively or negatively to adaptation in the parent-child dyad. Similarly, postpartum care nurses often have a chance to provide information to new mothers and fathers about infant care and development. The most promising service setting for the nurse to promote adaptation and synchrony, however, is in the patient's home. Whether these visits are for all new mothers or only selected ones, this entry into the home environment provides an unusually effective opportunity for promoting adaptive behaviors.

OVERVIEW

Since unstructured, general, supportive nursing programs in the home have been shown to be ineffective in producing gains in infant development, we sought to design and implement alternative nursing programs which could be used by public health nurses in home visits. We wanted to determine if nursing care programs designed to facilitate mutual adaptation between high-risk infants and their parents in the first months of life would, in fact, modify this process and improve subsequent development of the infant and the parent-child relationship. We tested three programs, all designed to be used from birth through 3 months postpartum. These programs were called the Nursing Parent and Child Environment (NPACE), Nursing Support Infant Bio-Behavioral (NSIBB), and Nursing Standard Approach to Care (NSTAC).

The NPACE, an acronym for a program conducted in the parent and child's environment, was a system for the provision of individualized nursing care to families with new babies. The NPACE program focused broadly on the whole spectrum of parent and infant needs during the first few months after birth, and it made extensive use of systematic screening and assessment.

The NSIBB, an acronym for Nursing Support of Infant Bio-Behavioral, was a program to provide more standardized nursing care to families with new babies. The NSIBB program focused specifically upon the mothers' and fathers' needs for parenting skills and their knowledge of child development, and it included explicit training for the parents in the assessment of their infant's behavior. It was based on information about the biological and behavioral course of development during the first 3 months of life and the influence that development has upon adaptive behavior on both the infant and the parent.

The NSTAC, an acronym for Nursing Standard Approach to Care, was a global designation for the general support services offered by the Seattle-King County Health Department, which are representative of many health department programs.

THE NPACE PROGRAM

The subject of the present paper is to describe more fully the process of nursing intervention with families in the NPACE program. The intent of this paper is to discuss the supportive nature of the nursing intervention in the NPACE program in relation to the characteristics of the sample population and the content of the nursing program. We will indicate the stresses these families were experiencing during the first 3 months of the postpartum period in relation to care of a newborn, the characteristics of these families, and how NPACE nurses were able to provide support to these vulnerable families during this transitional period. The NPACE program did provide support to the families.

It is important to note from the literature that support is viewed as a complex phenomenon. Cobb (1976) defines support as information leading one to believe that he is cared for, loved, esteemed, and a member of a network of mutual obligation. He further elaborates that information is a major product of support, information about self and resources. The mechanisms by which social support may negate the effects of a life stress, such as having a new baby, have not been determined. Bowlby (1977) spoke of persons being more effective when they are confident about their support system. Karen Lindner (1982) found a relationship between individuals' problem solving skills and high or low satisfaction with their support system. Individuals with low social support had a poorer quality of problem solving. She also found that when individuals with low social support were given social support during a test of their problem solving procedure, the low support individuals with supportive instructions did improve their scores on the quality of solution. The quality of solution was judged by whether the respondent had the protagonist in the story initiate action leading to the solution of the problem, or if the protagonist merely reacted to some action taken by others. A higher quality rating was given if the respondent initiated instrumental action. Therefore, there is evidence that support is potentially important in helping individuals adapt to problem situations.

METHOD

NPACE was an individualized program based upon a nurse's systematic assessment of family strengths and weaknesses. The key words are: individualized (because it was designed to meet the individual needs of family members), systematic (since it utilized a variety of assessments in a semistructured manner), and strengths (because the nurses attempted to build on the positive qualities and assets in the family rather than focusing on or working from a deficit model).

The NPACE program was designed and conducted by C. Snyder and A. Spietz, two nurses with M.S.N. degrees, for the purpose of providing services to a population of mothers and their infants who were extremely vulnerable due to biological reasons which placed them at risk during pregnancy or the intrapartum period, and because the mothers had a high school education or less. Due to lack of a sufficient number of subjects toward the end of the program, recruitment was initiated with a hospital OB clinic. Consequently, a few of those enrolled in the program achieved a higher educational level.

The program was carried out through the systematic use of approximately 15 assessment tools (see Table 1), which were developed and validated in the course of the Nursing Child Assessment Project (Barnard & Eyres, 1976) or adapted from the work of other researchers whose work was related to the early postpartum period. The assessments provided a semistructure to the NPACE approach which allowed the nurses to be flexible in meeting individual needs. The flexibility allowed the nurse to focus on either the mother, the infant, or both. The assessments used were: questionnaires that were filled out by the mothers,

Table 1
NPACE Program Assessments

Questionnaire
1. Neonatal Perception Inventory (NPI) (Broussard & Hartner, 1976)
2. Life Change Events (Holmes & Rahe, 1967)
3. Dudley-Welke Coping Scale Questionnaire (Dudley & Welke, 1977)
4. Temperament-Questionnaire (Carey, 1972)

Interviews
1. Database, mother (Seattle-King County Health Department)
2. Database, infant (Seattle-King County Health Department)
3. Developmental Expectations (NCAP) (Barnard & Eyres, 1979)
4. Psychosocial Assets (NCAP)
5. Father Involvement (NCAP)
6. Neonatal Perception Inventory (NPI)
7. Parent Mutuality Interview (NCAP)
8. Motherhood Feelings (NCAP)
9. Parent Concerns (NCAP)

Rewards
1. Nursing Child Assessment Sleep Activity Record (NCAP)

Observations
1. Nursing Child Assessment Feeding Scale (NCAFS) (Barnard, 1979)
2. Nursing Child Assessment Teaching Scale (NCATS) (Barnard, 1979)

interviews by the nurses, records that the mothers were asked to keep of their own or their infant's behavior, and observations of behavior and interactions by the nurses. Each assessment assisted in determining the physical, supportive, psychosocial, and adaptive abilities of the families.

The use of assessments in the NPACE intervention program was important for the following reasons:

1. The assessments provided a framework for:
   a. giving feedback to the family.
   b. additional assessments.
2. The assessments:
   a. were stimuli for the parents, giving them ideas for teaching and interacting with their child.
   b. provided:
      (1) a structure and organization to the visit, as well as to the time spent with the parent.
      (2) a framework for resource materials.
      (3) an environment for building rapport and trust.
   c. promoted parent participation and subsequent parent involvement.

3. Assessment results provided a:
    a. framework to determine family strengths and weaknesses.
    b. guide for mutual goal setting with the parents.

NPACE was broadly focused on the many family needs that may emerge during the period following birth. More specifically, it was based on the philosophy that parenthood is a transitional period and that parents, especially those at risk, have special needs for support, validation, new information, and direction. The nurse was used to provide support, not only through frequent contact, but also by recognizing that parents have the need to talk about feelings and concerns. By assuming the role of an active listener, the nurse could help nurture the parents' growth and strengths. It was recognized that parents have the need to know that what they are doing is right, and validation aids them in becoming more confident about their own skills and successes. New parents generally are also eager to learn all they can about their newborn and, therefore, benefit from the new information a nurse is able to provide. During this time, parents often express a feeling of confusion and can benefit from any direction or organization the nurse can supply. Nursing support ranges from asking parents to keep a 7-day sleep-awake activity record of their infant to merely reminding mothers to drink 7-8 glasses of fluid daily to maintain lactation.

The NPACE program content is best described in reference to the Nursing Child Assessment Interactional Model (Barnard, 1979, p. 19), and the components are illustrated in Figure 1. The largest circle represents the environment of the child and parent(s). The smallest circle depicts the child and the child's unique physical and behavioral characteristics. The remaining circle represents the characteristics of the mother or primary caregiver. The overlapping areas of the circle in this model represent the interactions that occur between the infant, mother, and environment.

Sample

Marital status. Most of the mothers were married or living with a partner (62% at the time of delivery). The remainder of the mothers were living alone or had a partner who was emotionally unsupportive for a satisfactory relationship.

Parity. This was the first baby for 33 (55%). The remainder of the mothers (N = 27, 45%) had 2-5 children.

Age. The age distribution for the NPACE mothers at the time of delivery ranged from 17-35 years. There were 13 (22%) adolescents. The majority of the mothers (N = 43, 71%) were 20-29 years, and only 4 mothers (7%) were over 30 years.

Race. The majority of mothers (N = 46, 77%) were Caucasian. Sixteen percent (N = 10) of the mothers were black, and the remainder of the mothers (N = 4, 7%) were Asian, Hispanic, and American Indian.

Educational level. Most of the mothers (N = 49, 82%) had 12 years or less of education. The range of educational level was 9-17 years.

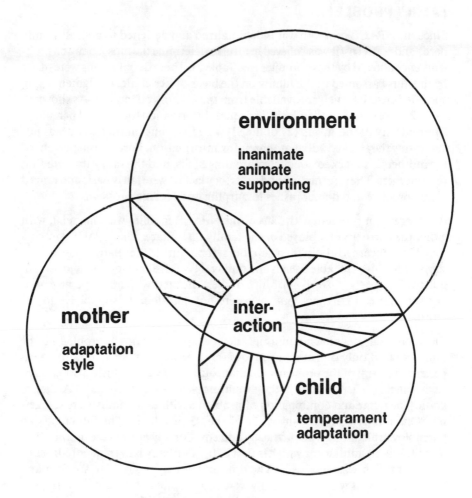

Figure 1. The child health assessment interaction model.
Note. From *Nursing Child Assessment Satellite Teaching Manual* by K.E. Barnard. Copyright 1979 by K.E. Barnard. Reprinted by permission.

FAMILY PROBLEMS

Since the NPACE program was individualized and designed to address family needs and concerns, it was believed helpful to determine the most common problems encountered by these families (see Table 2). These designations were made by the nurse assigned to the family on the basis of her clinical judgment using specified criteria which are available from the authors on request. As shown in Table 2, 52% of the mothers lacked adequate information for optimal parenting. The majority of this group (27 of the 31) were first time mothers, so it was not surprising they lacked adequate parenting information. Forty-seven percent of the mothers also lacked adequate parenting skills, and the majority were first time mothers. The information and skills they lacked were fairly basic and ranged from cord care and diaper rashes to burping and feeding problems.

Another major problem with 52% of the NPACE families was financial, with either the partner unemployed or the family on welfare. The NPACE mothers were also concerned about their support system. Either they had an inadequate support system of reliable friends and family (N = 23, 38%), or they had no supportive partner (N = 28, 47%). Many of these mothers with no supportive partner actually had partners, but they were not emotionally supportive to the mother.

These problem areas are not unusual and perhaps would not be problems if the families faced only one at a time. However, many of the NPACE families experienced several of the problems simultaneously and were living in disorganized environments. There were 16 of these multiproblem* families in the NPACE program. The range and combination of problems with each family were staggering. One family had as many as 12 of the 23 problems. The father was an unemployed alcoholic who physically and emotionally abused the mother. The mother was an adolescent with her first baby. The baby had frequent illnesses, and the mother was depressed. The time and energy required to sort out and determine a focus with such a family were considerable. In the face of this family's crisis and disorganization, the NPACE program with its systematic assessment and individualized approach was extremely valuable in providing a framework for focus and organization.

THE SUPPORTIVE PROCESS

Since we found parent participation and cooperation critical in developing and carrying out a program of care and services to these families, much time and effort were expended in building relationships. In reviewing the cases, differences were found in the amount of progress made in establishing the relationships and the degree of satisfaction gained in working with the families. NPACE nurses found that an important aspect of their program was the establishment of a car-

* Families living in disorganized environments, who were always in a crisis state and/or experiencing a lot of life change.

Table 2
Most Common Problems as Identified by NPACE Nurse[a]

Problem Areas	Number	Percent
Mother Lacked Information	31	52
Financial or Unemployment	31	52
Mother Lacked Skill	28	47
No Supportive Partner	28	47
Baby's Physical Health	26	43
Inadequate Support for Mother	23	38
Depressed or Emotionally Upset Mother	17	28
Child Rearing (child abuse, neglect)	17	28
Mother's Physical Health	17	28
Multiproblems	16	27
Adolescent Mother	14	23
Mother-Infant Interaction	14	23
Mobility	13	22
Cesarean Births	11	18
Cultural Differences	10	17
Abused Mothers	9	15
Death or Grief	7	12
Alcohol or Drug Abuse	7	12
Mother without Transportation	7	12
Intellectually Slow Mothers	4	1
Premature	4	1
Other Problems with Partner, Other Children, Relatives, Housing	21	35

[a]Problem definitions can be obtained from the authors.
N = 60 families.

ing, trusting relationship with the parents. The nurses defined it as a caring relationship, because according to Mitchell and Loustau (1981), they assisted parents to grow toward whatever aspect of healthy functioning they could attain relative to their current state. The nurses did not attempt to change or cure the parents; rather they attempted through caring to maximize the parenting potential at the parents' current level of functioning.

Framework

For the purpose of describing the NPACE program, the nurses utilized Brammer's (1973) helping relationship sequence since it incorporated many models, such as problem solving, skill development, life planning, and awareness, which have been found to be beneficial to parents during this transitional period. The goal of the helping relationship was to assist the parents to work toward independence and ultimately assume responsibility for their decisions.

The eight stages in Brammer's helping process include entry, clarification, structure, relationship, exploration, consolidation, planning, and termination. Two important points to remember about the helping relationship is: l) the process may not progress sequentially, and differing amounts of time may be given to different stages; and 2) one's ease with terminating the relationship and/or the degree of satisfaction with the relationship are often directly related to a progression through all the stages, even if this is out of sequence. A definition of each stage of the helping process and how the NPACE nurses utilized the content are presented in Table 3.

Establishment

Relationship building differed for many of the families. The nurses identified three basic relationship progressions: ideal, difficult, and incomplete (see Figures 2, 3, and 4).

The first relationship illustrated in Figure 2 depicts the "normal" or "ideal" progression through the NPACE program. The norm was generally six to seven home visits. By the end of the first visit, the nurses had a firm commitment from the mother to participate in the program, with the relationship generally well established. There was little need to focus long on the mother or her needs since she was generally confident and competent as a mother and a person. By the fourth to fifth visit, she became actively involved in making decisions and setting goals regarding types of services she desired for follow up.

In contrast, mothers in the second type of relationship illustrated in Figure 3 experienced difficult progression through the stages of the helping relationship. These mothers seemed to require much more time with the nurse, and they had a great need to talk about themselves, their problems, and possible plans for the future. They were not ready to take action, however, or to set concrete goals and follow through. Most of the time with these families was spent in the stages of relationship building and exploration in order to develop trust, explore their problems, and deal with the many crises that characterized their lifestyle (see Figure 3). These mothers characteristically withdrew, broke appointments, or became physically or emotionally ill. Termination was often problematic. Although the termination date was planned in advance, i.e., 3 months, many mothers were not at the point of terminating since it took as long to establish trust. It was frustrating for them as well as for the nurses to end the contact.

The third type of relationship, illustrated in Figure 4, depicted incomplete progression. This relationship was characterized by a fewer number of visits (two to five) and an unwillingness on the part of the mother to become involved in the program offerings. The commitment to participate in NPACE on the first home visit was rarely made. It was very difficult to see these mothers a second or third time. There was a great deal of resistance. A relationship was not established per se, although all the mothers agreed to remain in the study and

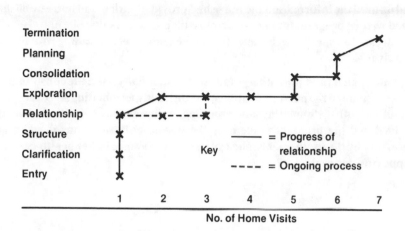

Figure 2. Ideal progression through the stages of the helping relationship.

Case example. Mrs. L is a 28-year-old, married woman with 4 children (three girls, 7, 4, and 3 years of age and a week-old son). On the first encounter Mrs. L was a very warm, outgoing, positive, and very enthusiastic about the program and how she would best be able to benefit from her involvement. Even on the first home visit, she was eager to learn and experience all she could about her newborn son. Her initial reaction to the nurse's demonstration of her infant's capabilities, such as his ability to see, hear, habituate, console, etc., was, "I never knew babies could do so much! This is exciting. What more can you tell me?" Rapport was readily established, and she openly shared information about herself and her supports, i.e., her husband, family, and religion, which were all strengths to her during this time. She exuded confidence and competence in her social and mothering abilities. By the end of the first visit, the nurse had a commitment from the mother to both the program and the relationship.

The second, third, and fourth visits were used for exploration and were focused on the mother and her needs. Her concerns during this 3-week period centered on her husband's unemployment, her problems with overeating, the 7-year-old's bed wetting, and the sibling rivalry between the 3 and 4-year- old. During this time she found the infant to be a real delight and easy to care for. He was quite predictable in his schedule, alert, and very responsive to all the family members. Despite her need to focus on her concerns, she remained eager to learn all she could about him, his capabilities, and what she could do to enhance his development and their interaction. She was cooperative, confident, and actively sought help and advice from the nurse in areas about which she knew little.

By the end of the fifth visit, Mrs. L had set specific goals for herself regarding weight loss and positive ways of coping with the unemployment situation. She had utilized the information the nurse had provided earlier and had established a bed wetting program for her 7-year-old with positive results. She had also read and decided on specific techniques that made sense to her in dealing with the sibling rivalry.

Planning and termination phases followed sequentially from the consolidation phase. Although the nurse and mother had difficulty terminating since they both found each other stimulating and rewarding, both were pleased with the benefits derived and the progress made over the weeks. Follow-up was deemed unnecessary by the mother since she expressed confidence in her health care and supportive network.

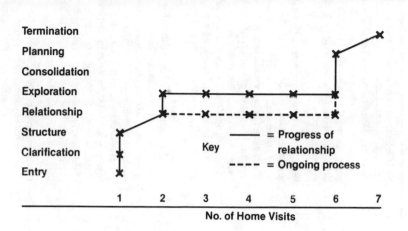

Figure 3. Difficult progression through the stages of the helping relationship.

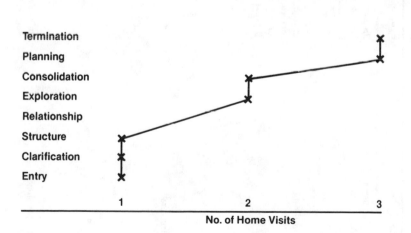

Figure 4. Incomplete progression through the stages of helping relationship.

Table 3

NPACE Adaptation of Helping Process with Supportive Nursing Measures

Stage[a]	Definition	NPACE Supportive Nursing Measures
1. Preparation and Entry	Prepare the parent, open the relationship, set the stage	Program explained to parent, i.e., what we had to offer and what benefits they could expect. Since parents were asked to select site for first visit and this was generally in the home, they were in control.
2. Clarification[b]	State problem, concern, and reasons for seeking help or giving services	We clarified why we were there and what their consent entailed. Discussed: 1) how visits would proceed, i.e., use of assessment, observation, flexibility in our approach, and length and frequency of visits; 2) role of the nurse, i.e., listening, observing, note taking, and providing feedback; and 3) our expectations of parent, i.e., sharing her observations, record keeping, goal setting, etc.
3. Structure[b]	Formulate the contract and structure	In verbal contract parent agreed to active participation by: 1) keeping scheduled appointments; 2) notifying if appointment needed to be rescheduled; 3) keeping records of infant's behavior, sleep, feeding; 4) reading suggested materials as interest and abilities allowed; 5) sharing observations about baby; and 6) engaging in play and interacting with her child in mutually agreed upon activities, i.e., teaching.
4. Relationship[c]	Build the helping relationship	Goal is to increase depth of relationship and intensity of parent's commitment. Termination is a possibility. Relationship usually established by end of Stage 4; i.e.,

trust and openness are increased, and parent is committed and ready to work toward goals of program (stage where relationship deepens and trust is established).

Stage		Description
5. Exploration	Explore problems, formulate goals, plan strategies, express feelings, learn skills	This working stage of the relationship involves assessment, intervention, data gathering, information exchange, joint problem solving, and mutual goal setting. Parent often has need to talk about self, problems, and possible plans, but is not ready to take next step, i.e., consolidation.
6. Consolidation	Explore alternatives, work through feelings, practice new skills	Decisions by parent to decide or act. Goals of this stage are to clarify feelings and pin down actions to take and new skills to practice. Flows from exploratory stage, blends into planning stage.
7. Planning	Develop plan of action, consolidate and generate new skills, behaviors, to continue self-directed activity	Time to evaluate progress, give feedback, encourage setting of new goals. Long-term goals established.
8. Termination	Evaluate outcomes and terminate relationship	This stage planned in advance and discussed several visits prior to last. Prepare for follow-up if needed and enlist mother's involvement in future needs, also anticipatory guidance for growth and development. Time for summary of progress and feedback to mother.

[a]From Brammer (1973).

[b]The first three stages take place on first visit so the mother knows what to expect and what is expected of her if the relationship is to continue.

[c]This stage may occur as early as the first visit, or it may never develop.

were seen at 3 months by the evaluation team. Their reasons for not participating ranged from being disinterested, to not having the time, or simply not fully understanding what they had signed up for in the hospital. Figure 4 illustrates the abruptness or incompleteness of this type of helping relationship.

Achievement Factors

It was more difficult in some instances and in few cases impossible to provide support to the mothers. We had additional information about these families which we analyzed and reviewed to better understand this dilemma. By doing case reviews of the families, some further characteristics of the mothers were identified. In order to accomplish this case review, we chose the process of initially reviewing all cases the nurses felt they were successful with and subsequently those cases that were deemed failures.

The differences that emerged with these families had to do with the mothers' goal setting and decision making styles. There were three categories of mothers identified: involved, less involved, and uninvolved. The involved, interested mothers (N = 27) who entered into a mutual goal setting dialogue with the NPACE nurses had goals of their own, asked questions, and readily accepted the nurses' feedback and suggestions. Most of these mothers had a mature approach to problem solving and decision making; i.e., they sought solutions to their problems and were more independent in their actions. These mothers exhibited what some authors have called an internal locus of control; they were responsible for their own actions. The nurses were able to move through the stages of the helping relationship without difficulty, and these mothers exemplified the ideal progression model of the helping relationship.

The second category, mothers who were less involved (N = 27), were not as eager or enthusiastic as the involved mothers. They merely tolerated the program and became only partially involved in setting goals for themselves. Fifteen of the 27 in this category were members of multiproblem families and demonstrated few skills in problem solving and decision making. They often let things happen and were caught up in the decisions of others. They exhibited an external locus of control. These mothers took little or no responsibility for their own actions. Nurses found it difficult to make progress in moving through the helping relationship with these mothers, and the difficult progression model exemplifies these interactions.

The third category, uninvolved mothers (N = 6), consisted of those mothers who stayed in the program but were not interested in getting involved or participating. These mothers did not set goals, and their decision making was diffused, i.e., scattered with no direction, or nonexistent. Their problem solving abilities were either finalized, inflexible, or undetermined. These mothers exemplified the incomplete progression model of the helping relationship.

Table 4 lists the three categories of mother (involved, less involved, uninvolved) and the problems they most commonly encountered. The involved mothers had fewer problem areas to contend with; thus, they had more energy to become involved in the NPACE program. They had few financial problems; therefore, they did not have to expend energy worrying about adequate food, heat, or housing. They could use their energy to seek out answers to their concerns and could become more involved in setting mutual goals with the program nurse. There was a high percentage of these mothers who lacked information (66%), and this was because they asked for information more often.

Most of the multiproblem mothers were categorized as less involved (see Table 4). These less involved mothers typically had many financial problems, no sup-

Table 4
NPACE Most Common Problems by Category of Mother

Problem Areas	Involved N = 27	Less Involved N = 27	Uninvolved[a] N = 6
Mother Lacked Information	66%	59%	33%
Financial or Unemployed	33	70	50
Mother Lacked Skill	52	59	17
No Supportive Partner	33	59	50
Baby's Physical Health	33	49	67
Inadequate Support	33	52	33
Depression or Emotional Upset	29	48	33
Child Rearing Problems	30	30	17
Mother's Physical Health	22	37	33
Multiproblems	7	48	17
Adolescents	15	26	33
Mother-Infant Interaction	4	44	17
Mobility	11	48	17
Cesarean Births	15	26	33
Cultural Differences	19	19	0
Abused Mothers	7	26	0
Death or Grief	15	15	0
Alcohol or Drug Use	7	26	17
Lack of Mobility	7	33	17
Intellectually Slow Mother	7	4	17
Premature Infant	0	11	17
Other Problems with Partner, Other Children, Relatives, Housing	26	37	33

[a]The uninvolved mothers reported less problems, but these results are believed to have been influenced by the difficulty assessing these mothers, rather than less problems.

portive partner, inadequate support systems, and were often depressed. The mothers and infants had more physical health problems, there were more interaction problems with the infant, and they were more mobile.

The lack of involvement by these multiproblem families was understandable. Since multiproblem mothers were so overwhelmed with all their problems, they had little energy to become involved with or show interest in outside sources, especially if they were depressed or had a physical health problem.

In the third category of mother, uninvolved, the nurses identified fewer problems, except for the baby's physical health, cesarean birth, intellectually slow mother, and premature birth (see Table 4). These mothers were characterized as not going beyond the third stage of the helping process (structure); therefore, the information exchange that would have allowed the nurses to identify additional problems was often missing. These mothers were not thoroughly assessed.

SUPPORTIVE MEASURES

To gain a greater understanding of the NPACE process and program, it was helpful to look at the goals of the mothers and the decision/making categories (involved, less involved, uninvolved) in relation to the nurses' supportive acts (see Table 5). Figure 5 shows each of the mothers' goals and the nurses' supportive acts as identified in a post hoc analysis by each of the NPACE nurses. There were some commonalities across all the mothers' goals; i.e., the nurses tended to devote the same amount of time to active listening, information exchange, validation, and information giving. This was to be expected since these acts were the major thrust of the NPACE program.

Since the analysis of supportive acts was done on the basis of chart review and recall by each nurse for her own case at the termination of the program, the percentage of occurrence can only be regarded as a selective perception of the aspects of support. With that as a limitation, it was interesting to see some difference between the categories of mothers. The nurses did more social sharing, self-disclosure, and mutual sharing with the involved mothers than with the other mothers. This fits expectations since these mothers were more involved and interested in the program.

A look at the less involved mothers revealed that the nurses served more as sounding boards (see Figure 5). Since a majority of these mothers were from the multiproblem families, it was not surprising that they had a lot to "sound off" about to the nurses.

The mothers who were uninvolved, although few in number (N = 6), required a different set of supportive acts from the nurses (see Figure 5). With these mothers, the nurses touched the baby more and performed more actions such as errands or giving physical help. Their babies were more often sick, which required physical touch for examination and physical assessment. Additional ef-

Table 5
NPACE Nursing Support

Nursing Support to Meet Mothers Goals	Nurses' Acts
1. Self-Disclosure	Provide input regarding personal experiences. Use of self as therapeutic entity.
2. Mutual Sharing	Easy give and take, generally on feeling level. Dialogue. Focus more on client.
3. Social Sharing	Interaction that emphasizes other family members, pets, sports/activities outside context of program goals: i.e., offering tea, coffee; showing house; conversing with grandmother; etc.
4. Active Listening	Responding to emotional message, reflection, clarification, restatement of ideas, etc.
5. Information Exchange	Back and forth exchange of information regarding infant, mother, family, or problems (problem solving). Nurse or client initiation, with client an active participant.
6. Sounding Board	Being there, taking in, listening, but not necessarily responding.
7. Validation	Praise, encouragement, positive reinforcement, feedback, or discouragement that supports current activities (common words = admired, reassured, etc.)
8. Information Giving	Program content, pamphlets, resources, anticipatory guidance, teaching, suggestions, advice, discussion, instructions, demonstration of Brazelton behaviors. Client is a passive receiver of information.
9. Actions	Demonstration of infant care skills, bringing or arranging resources (calling agencies), grocery shopping, watching sibs, running errands with mother, bringing reading materials, cutting nails, etc.
10. Baby or Mother Touch	Any nonverbal gesture that results in contact between nurse and person or infant.

fort was also required on the part of the nurses to get the mother more involved with her infant.

One additional analysis was completed from the nurses' home visit recordings. The home visit recordings were analyzed by independently trained coders. The coders were graduate students in nursing, and the code had designations for the type, area, focus, basis, and topic of the nursing measure. There were 5 types of measures, 6 areas, 3 foci, and over 68 topics. Reliability for every tenth record was done; all were above 95% interrater agreement. Table 6 describes the types, areas, and basis, since these are the only categories concerned within this paper.

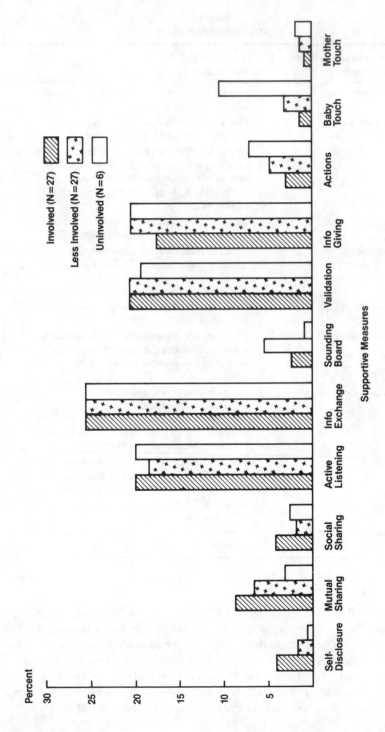

Figure 5. Nurses' supportive acts by mother category.

Table 6
Nursing Activities Log Coding Guide

Each nurse's recording of the visit in the Visit Log is analyzed with respect to her stated activities. A nursing measure is defined as a recorded activity which pertains to a discrete type, area, basis, and topic. The definitions for each category follow.

TYPE

Monitoring is:
- collecting information
- keeping track of events
- making a diagnosis
- formulating problems
- identifying concerns
- subsumed in information, support, therapy, and planning

Information is:
- providing verbal, written, or behavioral guidance to a client
- role modeling, demonstration, discussion, showing
- mass media (pamphlets, books)

Support is:
- validating behaviors, reinforcing, praising, encouraging ongoing behavior
- listening
- giving resources, supplies, (diapers, etc.)

Therapy is:
- providing methods for an identified problem, i.e., information, discussion, problem solving, prescription of medication or physical treatment regime

Planning is:
- a program action to achieve goal
- nurse gives information to client to plan so the client is the planner

BASIS
No specific assessment used

Specific assessment identified

AREA

Physical refers to body structure or physiological function due to physical growth.

Nutrition is foodstuff or nutrient intake: type, amount, frequency, method, and pattern. Does not include interaction.

Parenting is any act of taking care of a child, e.g., interacting, mediating, stimulating, caretaking, or the process of parenting or caretaking. Includes the development of role of parent.

Developmental pertains to integration of biopsychosocial systems to level of behavior.

Resources/Environment are finances, housing, material resources.

Psychosocial (Intrapersonal) includes neighbors, friends.

Table 7
Nurses' Contact with NPACE Families (Minutes)

Category of Mothers	Mean	SD
Involved	664.48	250.08
Less Involved	682.00	342.41
Uninvolved	335.66	115.19

The analysis of the nurses' recordings revealed they spent significantly more time with the involved mothers in supporting their parenting and providing information on nutrition (see Table 7). The recordings also revealed that the nurses did significantly more specific assessments with these families. Because of the support and fewer problems, these mothers were available to complete the sequence of planned assessments. Consequently, the nurses utilized more assessments.

For less involved families, the nurses spent significantly more time with these mothers than with the uninvolved mothers, and more time was spent on the telephone with the mothers about work, school, support systems, and self-esteem (see Table 7). This was not surprising since the nurses felt the need to monitor these families more closely. As was seen in Table 4, these mothers lacked basic child care information and frequently they were without partners or supportive others. In addition, they and their babies had more physical health problems, the mothers were depressed more often, and they had more alcohol or drug problems.

The time spent with the uninvolved mothers was in actual monitoring of their physical problems and assisting them with resources. These mothers were from families least available to the nurses, so when the nurses did get into the homes, they used the physical parameters of assessment which seemed more acceptable to the families and were more comfortable for the nurses to use.

Another significant difference was the total time spent with the three categories of mothers (see Table 7). Based on a Kruskal-Wallis l-way ANOVA, significantly less time was spent with the uninvolved mothers. It was interesting and enlightening that an equal amount of time was spent with the involved and the less involved mothers. It was expected that more time would have been spent with the less involved because of the many problems encountered with these families.

Variables

In attempting to further understand the factors contributing to these differences, an examination of the demographic characteristics yielded useful information. The two variables which showed significant differences among the groups were social status and social risk. Social risk included the presence of the following factors: husband/partner absent; maternal age less than 18; and mothers had no financially supportive person, no emotional help, no person to share concerns, negative feelings at birth, no phone, no contact person, and heavy use of alcohol during pregnancy. Kruskal-Wallis 1-way ANOVA showed the involved mothers had a significantly lower social risk score than the less involved mothers, who, in turn, had a significantly lower score than the uninvolved mothers.

The social status score (Hollingshead, 1975) was statistically significant in the direction expected. More of the involved mothers had the highest social status score, while mothers who were classified as uninvolved scored the lowest among the three categories.

RESULTS AND IMPLICATIONS

The purpose of this paper was to define our experience in supporting vulnerable families. Although all the families in the NPACE program were high risk, some benefited from the NPACE approach more than others. Ideally, the NPACE's individualized approach would be desirable for all high-risk families; but due to the time required and the usual public health nurse caseload, it would be highly impractical. While client outcomes are not the focus of this paper, the parent-infant outcome data suggest that the NPACE approach has the most positive influence on multiproblem families compared to the Nursing Support Infant Bio-Behavioral (NSIBB) and Nursing Standard Approach to Care (NSTAC) programs.

These multiproblem families were appropriate for the NPACE program for two reasons. First, since they were living in disorganized environments with daily crises, they required a lot of time and energy from the nurses attempting to reach them. The NPACE program design was not limited to a specific amount of time that could be spent with each family. Secondly, the families represented those most in need of services; i.e., these families were among the hardest to reach and the most difficult to provide with services. In reviewing the nurses' supportive acts, however, we found that the mothers from multiproblem families were more similar to the mothers categorized as involved than with the mothers in the less involved category who did not have multiple problems. The nurses' supportive measures for multiproblem families with the less involved mothers were similar to measures provided for involved mothers with fewer serious problems in relation to mutual sharing, active listening, information exchange, validation, and information giving. The involved mothers seemed to know they had problems, and they sought some help. To cite a cliche--support is only support when it's needed and sought.

We believe we could be more effective using the NPACE approach with high-risk families if contact would begin in early pregnancy. The first 3 months of life is a time of crisis and disorganization; therefore, the postpartum period is not the ideal time to begin nursing intervention. First of all, an effective working relationship requires the establishment of a trusting relationship. The timing to initiate such a relationship is critical to its success, and the point at which a mother is developing a relationship with her new infant is not the appropriate time to initiate a relationship with a nurse. This period is often referred to as a closed period for forming new relationships outside the family unit, and this concept led us directly to our current research in which we are studying relationship building during early pregnancy (Barnard, 1981-1987). Although we are still in the early stages, we have discovered pregnancy is an ideal time to begin intervention with multiproblem families. The pregnant women are interested and more psychologically available for a working relationship during this period.

Since our results show differences in the number of assessments accomplished with the three categories of mothers (involved, less involved, and uninvolved), we believe that a more structured approach over a longer time would prove more effective with the uninvolved families. One of the overall strategies of the current project is to continue our systematic approach and be more persistent, focused, and structured with the less involved mothers. Having a longer period of time to work with these mothers should enhance the development of the helping relationship. These changes may prove to be less threatening for those mothers who tend to become withdrawn or apathetic when faced with the task of forming a new relationship. We also will incorporate more information about infants' behavior and developmental changes during the first 3 months after birth in order to be sensitive to mothers' needs. Since a working relationship has already been established in the prenatal period with the mothers in our current project, more time can be spent on focused activities. During this time of crises and family reorganization, therefore, the family will not only have a relationship with a professional who can listen to their concerns, but they will also have someone to provide needed information and guidance in creating a more optimal environment for the newborn. Therefore, the current project with its initiation during the prenatal period, the additional time spent maintaining a relationship with the nurses, and its structured focus hopefully will allow these women to maintain a satisfactory relationship with the nurses. This experience should enable them to become more independent, confident, and competent in their parenting and social abilities.

SUMMARY

We have shared a review of the process of helping vulnerable families within the framework of testing a specific model of nursing intervention. The nursing care was offered during a transitional period for families, i.e., immediately following the birth of their infants.

The intent of the nursing care was to be supportive of the family, particularly of the mother. We found some families were difficult to support; these tended to be families who by our definitions of problems had more reasons why they could benefit from help. We also found that mothers who did not have clear goals or the ability to make decisions easily were difficult to involve as mutual participants in the helping process. These mothers came from families that tended to have higher social risk, lower social status, and less evidence of a supportive network. We have concluded that the critical elements to consider in supporting these families are when contact is established and the length of time supportive nursing measures are provided. We speculate it would be more productive to be involved with high social risk families who have low support in early pregnancy and continue the support until they begin to use a network of family, friends, and other professionals in a supportive, helping relationship. To obtain support requires individuals who actively seek the information and support they need to optimize their parenting role.

CRITIQUE
Sharron S. Humenick, R.N., Ph.D.

Kathryn Barnard, Charlene Snyder, and Anita Spietz have presented a partial report from a larger study of nursing interaction with high-risk families of newborns. They have documented what many nurses may have previously surmised; i.e., those families which appear to need the most help may be the hardest to serve.

NURSING SUPPORT

Another documented finding is that characteristics of the mother, such as her eagerness to engage in problem solving, are related to the nature of support given by the nurse. Involved mothers evoked from the nurse an increased amount of mutual sharing, active listening, information exchange, validation, and information giving. The other group who evoked these same increased nursing responses were the less involved mothers from multiproblem families (as opposed to less involved mothers from families with fewer problems).

A comparison of three nursing approaches—NPACE, NSIBB, and NSTAC—was not the major thrust of the current paper under review. However, it is encouraging to note that NPACE, a supportive approach based on systematic assessment, was described as producing the most positive outcome with high-risk families. This individualized approach, based on reinforcing strengths, is a positive approach as compared to a problem oriented deficit model.

The problems under study in this research project are most relevant. For years public health nurses have made home visits to families of newborn infants, especially to those with physical and social high-risk factors. There has been very little research available to guide the content, approach, or timing of such visits. Over the years little has been done to document the value or cost effectiveness of such nursing services. As a result, in many health departments newborn family home visiting is not the well-funded service it once was. In some areas of the country, public health nurses have even asked nursing educators why newborn home visiting is still taught to student nurses. It is clearly time to evaluate the methodology and document the value of nurses making home visits to families of newborns. Although the road to definitive answers is long, it is gratifying to note the inroads made through the present study.

Perhaps one of the most important questions raised by the reported findings is — How does a nurse provide support for hard-to-serve, high-risk parents? The report indicates that these mothers were of a lower social status and demonstrated less evidence of a supportive network in addition to being high risk. Clearly this study provides a picture of mothers needing more support than they are receiving, but not responding, or perhaps being unable to respond, well to nursing support offered.

The additional research which was described as in progress and based upon the investigation of establishing a trusting relationship with a nurse during pregnancy appears promising. This approach allows a longer time for relationship building and has several other potential advantages as well.

ADDITIONAL BENEFITS

It has been asserted that women move faster and further in a therapeutic relationship while pregnant. Thus, pregnancy may prove to be one of the most effective times for a nurse to establish a working relationship with young women who are characterized by a lack of support systems. If researchers should find that nurse-client relationships formed in pregnancy are especially productive, the common practice of casually reassigning a new nurse when the client relocates in a neighboring nursing district would be called into question. Continuity of care might receive more emphasis in planning nursing care.

Nuckolls and associates (1972) reported that in the presence of stress, pregnant women with a large amount of support were associated with a one-third decrease in the incidence of complications. Brown and Harris (1978) found in a study of 485 women that under conditions of high stress, women with support had a 25% less incidence of depression.

Thus, in providing supportive nursing acts for high-risk pregnant mothers, there is a potential to accomplish far more than establishing a relationship which will be useful in the postnatal period. If a combination of support and individualized education were to be offered at prenatal visits, there is a potential to decrease infant complications and/or depression in the mother. Either outcome might affect the number of subjects who eventually become doubly vulnerable, as were some of the subjects in the study at hand.

Furthermore, researchers have provided evidence that active participation in childbirth is associated with an increase in internal locus of control (Felton & Segelman, 1978) and instrumental personality attributes among women (Humenick & Bugen, 1981). If the prenatal nursing contacts include intervention which results in a more active, satisfying birth experience for the mothers, it is possible that prenatal nursing visits would influence mothers towards exhibiting attributes of internal control in the postnatal period. These mothers,

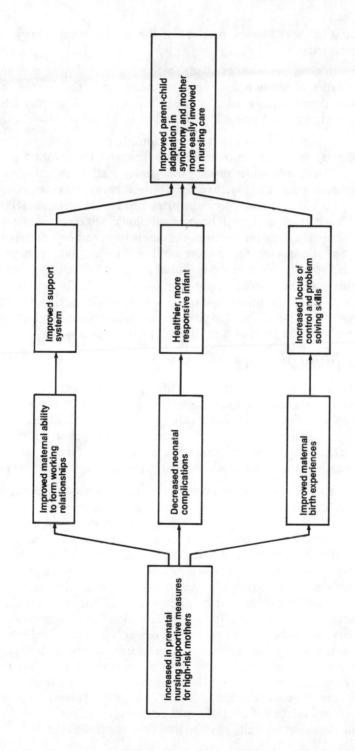

Figure 1. Hypothetical benefits of supportive nursing measures with high-risk prenatal women.

therefore, would be more like the mothers of the current study who were classified as involved.

The hypothetical, potential benefits of supportive prenatal nursing acts are described in Figure 1. In addition to the need for research to further test the implied hypotheses, there is also a need to evaluate the content, timing, approach, and cost effectiveness of such prenatal visits.

Of interest in the current study is the use of relationship progression and case reviews to differentiate mothers into categories of involved, less involved, and uninvolved. In systems theory terminology, engaging a client in active collaborative interactions is termed systems entry. The fact that systems entry is not always readily negotiated has been previously described in the literature (Hall & Weaver, 1977). Although any type of health professional is likely to find variation in ease of obtaining client involvement, the problem appears especially pertinent in relation to home visits for newborns. When the client initiates health care services, she typically comes believing she has a situation which can benefit from interaction with the health care provider. In home visits for newborns, however, the service is often initiated by the nurse or a referring agency. It is no surprise, therefore, that it is difficult to involve some mothers, especially those with an apparent external locus of control and a poor support system.

MATERNAL INVOLVEMENT

In this study, the authors found a difference in the type of nursing activity based on the level of involvement of the mother. Since we have come to accept that the infant, in part, shapes the behavior of the caregiver, it is not difficult to accept that clients, in part, shape the behavior of the nurse. The surprise in this study was the finding that less involved mothers from multiproblem families evoked similar responses from the nurses as were evoked by the more involved mothers.

In explaining this finding, the authors suggest that being faced with multiple problems led the less involved mothers to know they needed help. While this explanation is possible, rival hypotheses also exist. Perhaps it was nursing factors which led the nurses to respond differently. For example, in multiproblem situations, it is probably exceedingly clear to the nurses why they need to be there. Thus, they may be motivated to exert extra effort even when clients lack motivation to become involved. It also might be worthwhile to hypothesize that most home visiting nurses have a tendency to be internal locus of control personality types. Perhaps nurses with an internal locus of control relate better to clients with an internal locus of control such as the involved mothers were surmised to be. Although the less involved mothers appeared to be external locus of control personality types, perhaps a certain percentage were internal locus of control types whose typical responses were masked by depression resulting from the multiple problems they faced. It would be conceivable that if a number of the less involved were basically internal locus of control types, some aspect of their behavior evoked nursing responses typically given to internally controlled clients.

Whatever the actual reason for different types of nursing responses to different types of clients, this finding provides very fertile ground for future research. For example, one might ask if the differences in nursing measures were actually appropriate given the client characteristics. The answer to such a question might help to formulate guidelines for influencing nurses to respond in appropriate ways, given certain types of clients. Measures such as locus of control on both mothers and nurses might be useful.

RESEARCH IMPLICATIONS

The description of levels of mother involvement during nursing home visits brings up yet another question--What are the cost/benefit ratios for visiting each type of mother? Maternal-child nurses, on the whole, do not like to put dollar values on services they see as benefiting humanity. It may be our lack of documentation of cost/benefits, however, that has led to a general decrease in the funding of this type of service. Such a question is, therefore, an important one to research.

The family that is hard to serve may show little short-term benefit, even with extensive nursing visits. The families described in this study were doubly vulnerable through high maternal risk, high infant risk, and additionally they had poor support systems and lack of involvement with the visiting nurse. They could be hypothesized as headed for further problems which will be exceedingly expensive to society in the long run. If they can eventually become involved in nursing care, there is the possibility of cost effectiveness even though the cost of the initial service is high. First of all, nursing researchers need to document whether or not nursing support has the potential to make a significant difference with such families; then, it would be possible to determine if philosophically, preventive supportive care should be offered. Likewise, it would be useful to obtain documentation of cost/benefit ratios for intervention with high-risk involved clients, as well as low-risk families. The ground work provided by this study would be very useful as the basis for some long-term cost/benefit studies.

The remaining aspect of this study upon which I wish to comment is the positive, supportive approach used with clients. When nurses are taught problem solving skills, problem oriented charting, and problem oriented nursing diagnoses, there is the potential to become problem oriented and to lose sight of maintaining a supportive balance. In addition to solving problems, nurses can and do support client strengths, assist clients to build stronger support systems, and in general help clients become adept at self-care. Several nursing research studies have documented the benefit of supporting clients' strengths in families with newborns (Barnard & Neal, 1977; Anderson, 1980; Poley, 1979). Yet, it is not atypical for some nurses to feel that they have no role in situations where they are not given a problem to solve. Studies such as the presentation are important to continue to build a strong theoretical basis for nursing services which provide a balance between a positive approach to support and a problem solving approach.

DISCUSSION

J. Bumbalo: I was struck by the fact that the process in this study started with these families with a systematic assessment, and I would put forth the proposition that it really did not just use an assessment but a very sophisticated level of nursing process all the way through. I would ask us to look at the fact that there is an interplay between the interpersonal process, the therapeutic process, and nursing process; they do indeed interact with each other and facilitate one to the other. I think where nurse researchers run into difficulty is they don't look at the interface between what they are asking in relation to the nursing process and what they are asking in relation to interpersonal factors. For example, at the point of assessment we want the most information; and we know from an interpersonal point of view that when we're in the orientation phase in the interpersonal relationship, we're going to have people least willing to share information. At the other end of the continuum — termination of the relationship and evaluation — nursing process fits in very nicely. Using good nursing process helps with both aspects of the relationship. What I've tried to look at with a lot of graduate students relative to their clinical practice is what's the interface between nursing process and interpersonal factors, and when do you back off from your nursing process to build on your interpersonal process to allow you to go back to your nursing process. I think the study that was just described to us is a superb example of this type of interface.

A. Spietz: I think that was our monumental task, and I think we've grappled with this for a long time in trying to separate the two processes and yet maintain the integrity that is there between them. That's enlightening for us too, but I think the difficulty is in trying to teach it.

J. Bumbalo: I have a comment that relates to trying to teach it. We teach students some things about how to apply the nursing process, but I wonder if we do not avoid teaching them how to use the interpersonal process ("Interpersonal Relationships," 1966). I've found one model that is especially helpful. McGrath's (1963) group in Utah talked about three parameters that influence relationships: attraction, influence, and attitudes. They built a model that says that you very specifically try to manipulate those things that you're trying to influence; for example, show the person what common bases you have. And that would be how you would work on attitudes. Some of the attraction factors are not known, but I think that is what Dr. Humenick was alluding to when she said that maybe the attraction is that the nurses and the less involved mothers were both examples of external locus of control type personalities and they were better able to build a relationship. I think, however, that we should do a more analytical analysis of why a particular nurse is able to work very well with a certain type of patient. Maybe we don't need to change nurses; maybe we do need to be very systematic about finding the basis to interact with a certain family.

J. Fawcett: I have two comments. First, some of this discussion refers to what sociologists call interpersonal attraction. This is a very difficult area to investigate, perhaps even more difficult than social support, due to many theoretical and empirical problems. Like other behavioral research, studies of interpersonal attraction do not yield definitive and concise explanations for the reasons why people are attracted to certain people, but not others. Second, I am concerned about the apparent separation of the nursing process and the interpersonal process in some of our discussion. I think that Carper's notion of types of knowledge needed for nursing practice combines the two processes in a meaningful way. She maintains that nursing practice "...depends on scientific knowledge of human behavior in health and illness, the esthetic perception of significant human experiences, a personal understanding of the unique individuality of the self and the capacity to make choices within concrete situations involving particular more judgments" (1978, p. 22). Nursing practice, then, is a combination of science, art, the therapeutic use of self, and ethics. The nursing process is a systematic manner of applying this knowledge. The interpersonal process is what transpires between client and nurse as the nursing process is applied.

J. Bumbalo: In my previous comments, I was obviously using the term nursing process to refer to the methodology of the practice of nursing, i.e., a problem solving approach involving assessment, intervention, and evaluation. I was referring to interpersonal process as a separate phenomenon. However, let me attempt to clarify my position. In the sense that nursing process forms the basis for one's contract with the patient or client and is the basis for nurse-patient interaction, it is definitely interpersonal and therapeutic in nature. Whether or not it is possible or appropriate to empirically differentiate between nursing process and interpersonal process is debatable; however, I have found it a valuable teaching strategy to have students analyze them theoretically as separate but concurrent processes.

D. Magyary: I notice that the study indicated more adolescents in the less involved group, and I thought of Dr. Mercer's comment about how hard it is to get them to participate in a study. Did you notice the nursing process taking on a different orientation when dealing with adolescents versus middle-aged women?

C. Snyder: I would say yes. Adolescents were much more difficult. As you can see, they did fill up that group. Often times, the teenagers were living with their mother or living in disorganized environments with or without boyfriends. The increased numbers of people, as well as the disorganization, made it difficult to focus.

D. Magyary: Did you find anything that linked them with the nursing process?

C. Snyder: I think it was just a sensitivity to where they were in their developmental process more than anything else.

P. Brandt: Perhaps we need to study a variety of treatment approaches to determine what enables adolescents to adapt to parenting. For example, the helping process may be more therapeutic with adolescents if peers are utilized rather than or in addition to professionals. Group sessions versus individual sessions could also be examined in relation to selected desired child or parenting outcomes.

K. Barnard: I'd like to speak toward alternative approaches. Our approach did not work with these less involved clients. I would like to indicate that possibly one approach to working with people who find it difficult to become involved in a relationship is a type of structuring which the NSIBB program did provide, in which it was not necessary for the mother or the nurse to get as involved in a therapeutic relationship. There were certain activities that the nurse provided for the mother and the rest of the family, both in terms of talking about and leaving little pamphlets about infant crying, keeping a sleep activity record, and so forth. The nurses who were involved in this program were absolutely frustrated because they had to keep this agenda and they felt that it was not meeting the needs of the families, etc. We also almost had a major office rift because we discourage people from talking to one another during the project since we're working on opposite teams and fear contamination. This rule had a sizable effect on office morale. We did carry out the project, but the nurses were constantly coming to me and sayings "We've just got to do something different. We can't carry out this program. They have so many needs." I talked to them, but unless it was a case of murder, child abuse, or something like that, I tried to encourage them to maintain the program.

When we looked at the 3-month data, particularly for the multiproblem families, the infants in the multiproblem family group in the NSIBB program had the highest mental development. One of the things this suggests to me is that if you continue structuring for very disorganized, multiproblem families, the constant structuring and focusing allowed them to focus on the needs of those infants, maybe in a better way than all the therapeutic relationship building in the other program. However, when you looked at the 10-month outcomes, what was apparent in these multiproblem families was that the NSIBB kids had plummeted on the Bailey measurements while the NPACE infants had taken an upward shift. It was as if by focusing on the mothers, which was a predominant activity in the NPACE program, you energized them and they finally began to focus on the infants; whereas the mothers in the NSIBB were not energized, and when they lost the structure and focusing, their focus on the infant decreased.

I think there are alternatives, and it's very clear to me that the NSIBB program, although carried out with master level prepared nurses, could be modified and carried out by less trained individuals, e.g., neighborhood aides, etc. I think that we have to quickly move to begin to reconceptualize how we work with some of these multiproblem families, and I think a simpler model with less individualization might be the model to use.

B. Bishop: I wondered if you were able to look at the hard-to-reach teenagers. In my experience it is really tough to reach these teenagers. When you look at their histories, very often those youngsters, particularly if they were living in the home with their mothers, had been set up to have the baby. The baby was not their baby; it was for their mothers who could no longer have a baby. They could not take care of their baby as a mother because they were a vehicle for their mothers and their job was done. They have incubated a baby so that their mothers have a baby, and they're ready to return to school, etc.

Also, I have some reflections in relation to Dr. Barnard's comments about alternative approaches. I was a school nurse for pregnant teenagers, and maybe one of the approaches we need to look at much more is the school nurse in the high school. It's a beautiful way to monitor teenagers. They don't have to come see you; you're there, and they're there. You can keep track of them, and you can get reinforcement from the group. Other teenagers can recommend you if you work well with them, and after a while, more teenagers will come to see for themselves what the nurse is doing and the help she can offer to them. The most successful program that I know of as far as adolescents is the one in St. Paul where they put the maternal-infant care program right into the high school and the nurse was there all the time. What they found first is that the fertility rate went down for the entire population in that school since family planning was available. Second, for those teens that became mothers, they had no cases of abuse or neglect a year after the child was born and also teen mothers' fertility rate went down. In a school situation, one can cover a large population without one to one because of the grapevine and the results of teens interacting with each other to spread information. And it can affect everyone, not just the pregnant adolescents.

P. Brandt: By providing opportunities for peers to teach or support each other in parenting, we actually encourage the natural process of helping that occurs between adolescents on other topics. Peer teaching has been found to be important for the development of communication in young handicapped children and for facilitation of social competence in juvenile delinquents. There appears to be potential importance for adolescent parents also. For example, the adolescent mother I am presently seeing in the clinic demonstrates skills in contingently relating to her infant, and she is enthusiastic about sharing these skills with other teen mothers. She would be an excellent resource for a peer teaching program.

A. Spietz: That is one of the techniques we use when we distribute some of the books we want them to read. We ask them to review this particular book and let us know how it would work for them so that we could use it for other mothers in the program. They just love that because it is an esteem building type of exercise.

P. Brandt: I recently talked to a researcher in Ohio who had nurses train neighborhood/community people to develop skills in relationship building and infant care. The community people subsequently worked with new parents to develop parents' skills in infant care.

S. Humenick: There is a term that I really like which Hall and Weaver (1977) attribute to Smoyak. It is "professional hanging around," a tactic used when systems entry is not readily negotiated with the client system. Sometimes we need to give ourselves permission not to do anything that looks therapeutic, but rather just hang around in an effort to become part of the environment. Eventually, we may be seen as more acceptable and we may then be better able to negotiate a therapeutic relationship.

M. Curry: It seems that we need to put some of these approaches into operation with families whose infants fail to thrive, and perhaps use lay or community workers to do the relationship building. This approach may be much more cost effective than using nurses, and it may accomplish the same outcome. I would certainly agree that we need both second and third order change in how we define and operate our health care systems. I would also like to follow up on·Dr. Norbeck's comments regarding the use of the research process as a clinical intervention. I have had a similar experience in my study of antepartum hospitalization (Curry, 1983), in which women completed both Sarason's Life Experience Survey (Sarason, 1978) and the NSSQ (Norbeck, Lindsay, & Carrieri, 1981). Many women have commented that they found completing the questionnaires helpful, both in terms of helping to pass the time and in helping them to gain a different perspective on their situation. Further, after delivery, most sample women described participating in the study as one of their most effective coping mechanisms. It is clear that we need to systematically document these effects and begin to describe both their positive and negative effects.

K. Pridham: I think this a very rich study in many ways. One way is in the language which this study develops to describe nursing and nursing actions. I wonder if you are developing a language with which to characterize the family strengths that you have identified. It seems to me that one of the things which has been lacking in the currently available nursing diagnosis classification system is a means of identifying strengths or competencies that one wants to enhance or support.

A. Spietz: I think we are. We have developed profiles for each family whereby we will divide up each assessment tool that we do use and cite the strengths that we find from that assessment. For example, having realistic developmental expectations for her infant at birth is a strength, i.e., knowing a newborn can see, hear, and is aware of surroundings, etc. A weakness, on the other hand, might be if she perceives that talking to the baby isn't important until 12 months of age. Our assessments can lead to identifying the strengths, as well as the weaknesses. I think that the problem many nurses have is in translating and intervening from the actual assessment. We find it very easy because it is a skill we have developed in doing the research during the past 10 years. For example, if you find a mother who scores low on sensitivity to cues, we interpret it immediately and give some kind of positive feedback. We initially started collecting data, then we began to slowly intervene and collect small bits of information, and now we're intervening totally.

C. Snyder: In addition, we share the assessments freely with the mothers. We do an assessment, tell them their strengths, and show them the areas they can work on if they are interested. It seems to build their self-esteem to focus on their strengths.

In this new project (Infant-Family Focus), one major focus has been to try to help them improve their social skills and help them survive in the community so to speak. We assess their social skills at the beginning, and then reassess them to look for any improvement. They also need community skills. Many of these mothers don't even know where the nearest bus stop is; and they don't know how to use the yellow pages, the telephone book, or the library. We get some dialogue going on this skill; and some will try to develop the skills, while others won't. We also try to get them involved in building their skills, not just around the pregnancy, but as a woman. We try to build self-esteem and nurture these mothers so that they, in turn, can nurture their baby. It's very exciting.

One of the tools that we use in the new project is Dr. Cranley's Fetal Attachment Scale (1981). We've started using the scale during the latter weeks of pregnancy; and at the same time, we've also incorporated some of Jessup's work of getting the mother to focus on her unborn baby (Carter-Jessup, 1981). We ask her to talk to her fetus and try to interact by massaging or rubbing her belly. She then keeps track of these activities, as well as the fetal movements, on an Nursing Child Assessment Sleep/Activity (NCASA) record. This simple record keeping has been very helpful in promoting and enhancing the acquaintance process.

B. Bishop: One of the things that is not included very much in the nursing literature is documenting how to identify and use strengths to build nursing plans. Most of the available information is too vague. We all know how to assess weaknesses better than strengths. I think that this kind of information is available in this study, and it is time to share some of this information with colleagues.

S. Feetham: You have indicated that nurses do not know how to use the instruments for obtaining a systematic assessment as reported in your research. It would be helpful to practitioners and nurse researchers for you to publish what you have gained in your intervention research through the use of systematic assessment.

K. Barnard: I'd like to go back to something Sharron Humenick mentioned, which I call the collapse of the public health nursing services in communities. These services are disappearing. We need to find ways to support their continuance, but there is a problem proving their effectiveness and also a significant burn out problem in public health nurses. They encounter on a daily basis really hard families to work with; the way they cope is not to contact these families, or to stop visiting after one or two visits. One of the things we've been thinking about is to provide a structure for the nurse to survive in these situations. For instance, we had the nurses complete a 9 point scale after each visit to determine their satisfaction with their performance on that contact. Our data suggested that public health nurses are very dissatisfied with what they can accomplish, but the use of the assessment does increase their satisfaction. The nurses in our study on Newborn Nursing Models that were the most satisfied with their performance were the nurses that were using the NSIBB program. The NSIBB was the most structured model where the nurses had definite objectives and specific interventions for each home visit. I think that out on the battlefield, it may be necessary to have some structuring and some guidelines. I'd like to encourage those of you who are involved to begin to turn some of your energies toward developing protocols that can be used in the field by nurses who really are dealing with some monumental societal problems in the families we serve. In many respects, these nurses are holding communities together.

G. Anderson: There seems to be a common problem being reported by almost everyone here these 2 days, and I have a suggestion that may help to build both the mothers' self-esteem and the nurses' satisfaction. The common problem is the crying of an unsootheable infant. There are ways to help some of these infants, and these measures could be very easily instituted. If these infants become more sootheable, I believe many other problems will take care of themselves. Social support will still be needed, but it will have a much better chance of being more effective. One approach is based on research by Jakobsson and Lindberg (1978, 1983) in Sweden. In a double blind crossover study, these investigators found that when mothers stopped ingesting cow's milk, cow's milk products such as cheese, and products containing cow's milk, colic disappeared in 35 of 66 breast-fed infants and reappeared on at least 2 challenges (cow's milk to mother's) in 23 of these 35 infants (Jakobsson & Lindberg, 1983). A second approach is something that I learned from Jack Paradise who told me that otitis media in young infants is very difficult to diagnose because both otitis media and crying cause a very red tympanic membrane.* Because infants are likely to cry during an ear examination, otitis media can be missed, and it can become a chronic problem and the cause of much crying in some infants. The third approach is that very simple chiropractic techniques may be needed, each for different problems that may have occurred during birth, e.g., as a result of forceps deliveries or with pressure that is sometimes placed on the neck in order to deliver the infant's shoulders. At present, the best reference on this material is by Frymann (1966). The techniques she described have been modified and extended by chiropractors, but they have not been described by them in the literature as yet, in part because the techniques are so easily taught and so effective that it did not seem necessary at first (M.D. Chance, personal communication, September 1982). However, background material is available now (Walther, 1981, 1983), three more volumes are planned, and the fifth one will specifically address the pathology of colic as viewed by chiropractors and the recommended procedures for treatment. Chiropractic treatment is not symptom-oriented, the processes and rationales make sense, the results are convincing, and this alternative seems worthy of our consideration.

---

*Jack Paradise is a pediatrician in the Ambulatory Care Center, Children's Hospital of Pittsburgh. He has studied colic (1965) and has written a very fine review of otitis media (1980).

S. Feetham: I think also the work Dr. Barnard is doing on infant massage identified some areas for soothing infants. Have you used that in teaching the parents?

K. Barnard: We did teach infant massage, and we found a variable response. Some mothers cannot use infant massage well, and it sends them and their baby into hysteria. It would be very interesting to follow those mother-infant pairs later. Other mothers find it a very useful technique, and among the mothers we originally taught during the first 3 postpartal weeks, about 75% of them were still doing it at 8 months.

Our infant massage program included some techniques from the literature which use face, arm, hand, body, and foot massage in a sequence for approximately 8 minutes that we taught mothers to do (Booth, Johnson-Crowley, & Barnard, 1983).

C. Snyder: I have had experience using these techniques, although I wasn't involved in Dr. Barnard's research on infant massage. The success of the technique really depends on the mother's personality. A very nervous, uptight mother simply cannot massage, and I also think you have to teach mothers some relaxation techniques. Instruct them to relax and tune into the baby. Then guide her; otherwise, these mothers overexcite the babies. You really have to be sentitive to the mother's personality. It's just like therapeutic touch. You really have to be sensitive to those energy fields.

K. Barnard: We teach mothers little games and exercises to play with their infants. I would say that the majority of them handle the games and exercises better than they do massage.

S. Feetham: One thing I've always been so impressed with is the strong clinical base in Dr. Barnard's work. Many nurse researchers come from a strong clinical base; yet we do not often acknowledge the strength of that base and overtly identify to others that this is the source of our research. When we use instruments from other disciplines and we feel uncomfortable about what is measured, it may be because the instruments are not consistent with our practice. We, as nurse researchers, need to recognize that there may be other ways to test the questions derived from our practice. A strength of so much of what has been presented and discussed during this conference is movement towards the recognition and development of research from the strengths of nursing practice.

REFERENCES

Anderson, C.J. (1980). Informing mothers about the behavioral characteristics of their infants: The effects on mother-infant interaction. Unpublished doctoral dissertation, The University of Texas, 1979. *Dissertation Abstracts International, 40,* 1119-B. (University Microfilms No. 79-200076)

Barnard, K.E. (1979). *Nursing child assessment satellite teaching manual.* Seattle: University of Washington.

Barnard, K.E. (1981-1987). *Clinical nursing models proposal.* (Grant No. MH36894). National Institute of Mental Health.

Barnard, K.E., & Eyres, S.J. (1977). *Results of the first twelve months of life.* Final report to the Division of Nursing, Bureau of Health Resources and Development, U.S. Public Health Service, Health Resources Administration, Department of Health, Education and Welfare on the Nursing Child Assessment Project. (No. 01700200142-9). Washington, DC: Government Printing Office.

Barnard, K.E., & Eyres, S. (Eds.). (1979, June). *Child health assessment, Part 2: The first year of life.* (DHEW Publication No. HRA 79-25). Hyattsville, MD: Division of Nursing.

Barnard, K.E., & Neal, M.V. (1977). Maternal-child nursing research: Review of past strategies for the future. *Nursing Research, 26,* 193-197.

Bowlby, J. (1977). The making and breaking of affectional bonds. *The British Journal of Psychiatry, 130,* 201-210.

Booth, C., Johnson-Crowley, N., & Barnard, K.E. (1983). *A program of massage and exercise for newborns: Description of program and results.* Unpublished manuscript, University of Washington, Seattle.

Brammer, L.M. (1973). *The helping relationship process and skills.* Englewood Cliffs, NJ: Prentice-Hall.

Broussard, E.R., & Hartner, M.S.S. (1976). Neonatal prediction of outcome at 10/11 years. *Child Psychiatry and Human Development, 7,* 85-93.

Brown, G.W., & Harris, T. (1978). *Social origins of depression.* London: Travestack.

Carey, W.B. (1972). Clinical applications of infant temperament measurement. *Journal of Pediatrics, 81*(4), 823-828.

Carper, B.A. (1978). Fundamental patterns of knowing in nursing. *Advances in Nursing Science, 1*(1), 13-23.

Carter-Jessup, L. (1981). Promoting maternal attachment through prenatal intervention. *MCN The American Journal of Maternal Child Nursing, 6,* 107-112.

Chance, M.D. (1982, September). Personal communication.

Cobb, S. (1976). Social support as a moderator of life stress. *Psychosomatic Medicine, 38,* 300-314.

Cranley, M.S. (1981). Development of a tool to measure maternal-fetal attachment. *Nursing Research, 30,* 281-284.

Curry, M.A. (in progress). *The effects of long-term antepartum hospitalization on maternal behavior and the family.* Funded by NIH Division of Nursing, No. ORS 1088C.

Dudley, D.L., & Welke, E. (1977). *How to survive being alive.* New York: Doubleday & Co.

Felton, G.S., & Segelman, F.B. (1978). Lamaze childbirth training and changes in belief about personal control. *Birth and Family Journal, 5,* 141-150.

Frymann, V. (1966). Relation of disturbances of the craniosacral mechanisms to symptomatology of the newborn: Study of 1250 infants. *Journal of the American Osteopathic Association, 65,* 1059-1075.

Hall, J.E., & Weaver, B.R. (1977). *Distributive nursing practice: A systems approach to community nursing.* New York: Lippincott.

Hollingshead, A.B. (1975). *Four factor index of social status.* New Haven, CT: Author.

Holmes, T.H., & Rahe, R.H. (1967). The social readjustment rating scale. *Journal of Psychosomatic Research, 11,* 213-218.

Humenick, S.S., & Bugen, L.A. (1981). Mastery: The key to birth satisfaction: A study. *Birth and Family Journal, 8,* 84-90.

Interpersonal Relationships: A review. (1966). *Regional Rehabilitation Research Institute Bulletin, 1.* Salt Lake City, University of Utah.

Jakobsson, I., & Lindberg, T. (1978). Cow's milk as a cause of infantile colic in breast-fed infants. *Lancet, 2,* 437.

Jakobsson, I., & Lindberg, T. (1983). Cow's milk proteins cause infantile colic in breast-fed infants: A double-blind crossover study. *Pediatrics, 71*(2), 268.

Lindner, K. (1982). *Life change, social support and cognitive problem-solving skills.* Unpublished doctoral dissertation, University of Washington.

McDonald, A.D. (1964). Intelligence in children of very low birth weight. *British Journal of Preventive and Social Medicine, 18,* 59-74.

McGrath, J.E. (1963). A descriptive model for the study of interpersonal relations in small groups. *Psychological Studies, 27,* 10-17.

Mitchell, P.H., & Loustau, A. (1981). *Concepts basic to nursing.* New York: McGraw-Hill.

Norbeck, J., Lindsay, A., & Carrieri, V. (1981). The development of an instrument to measure social support. *Nursing Research, 30,* 264-269.

Nuckolls, K.B., Cassel, J., & Kaplan, B.H. (1972). Psychosocial assets, life crisis, and the prognosis of pregnancy. *American Journal of Epidemiology, 95,* 431-441.

Paradise, J.L. (1966). Maternal and other factors in the etiology of infantile colic: Report of a prospective study of 146 infants. *Journal of the American Medical Association, 12*(1), 7.

Paradise, J.L. (1980). Otitis media in infants and children. *Pediatrics, 65,* 917.

Poley, B.A. (1979). Altering dyadic synchony, maternal self-confidence, and maternal perception of the infant through a teaching-modeling intervention with primiparous mothers. Unpublished doctoral dissertation, The University of Texas, 1979. *Dissertation Abstracts International, 39,* 5313. (University Microfilms No. 79-11012)

Sarason, I., Johnson, J., & Siegel, J. (1978). Assessing the impact of life changes. Development of the life experiences survey. *Journal of Consulting and Clinical Psychology, 46,* 932-946.

Walther, D.S. (1981). *Applied kinesiology, Vol. l: Basic procedures and muscle testing.* Pueblo, CO: Systems DC. (275 W. Abriendo Ave., Pueblo, CO 81004).

Walther, D.S. (1983). *Applied kinesiology, Vol. 2: Head, neck, and jaw pain and dysfunction - the stomatognathic system.* Pueblo, CO: Systems DC.

Werner, E.E., Bierman, J.M., & French, F.E. (1971). *The children of Kauai. A longitudinal study from the prenatal period to age ten.* Honolulu: University of Hawaii Press.

Willerman, L., Broman, S.H., & Fiedler, M. (1970). Infant development, preschool IQ, and social class. *Child Development, 41,* 69-77.

SUMMARY

Sandra J. Eyres, Ph.D.

I will begin this Summary by recalling the goals of this nursing roundtable conference, i.e., to provide a forum for presenting conceptual and empirical knowledge about social support and vulnerable individuals, and to reach an operating consensus of what advances are needed to bring knowledge of social support to a level useful for professional practice.

My task is to provide an overall conclusion of the presented empirical and conceptual information and the implications for practice and future research. I will also take the liberty of reporting some personal observations that came from knowing I had the responsibility to summarize this conference. I believe I speak for all in saying this has been a very constructive roundtable conference and that we are grateful to the March of Dimes Birth Defects Foundation who funded it and to those whose hard work and vision made it possible.

CONCLUSIONS

A number of conclusions can be reached by examining the empirical and conceptual information presented during this conference. In the reviews of the research on social support, there is clearly enough evidence to show its relationship to various indicators of health, well-being, and behavior; and this finding warrants our continued attention. Throughout the conference in the papers, critiques, and discussions, we also have touched on the themes--What is social support, and how does it work? Since we are motivated by health care perspectives, we have also considered if social support is something health professionals give.

The data tell us that social support is provided by health professionals, but only for selected circumstances such as emergencies, help with pregnancy, or illness. The consensus at this meeting seemed to indicate that health professionals do not belong in personal networks except briefly and in crises and that facilitating the building of personal networks is the more appropriate role of health professionals. This finding has major implications for our future work. Implicit in this position is promoting autonomy and development instead of 'doing for' a client. If we believe this is a valid principle, it needs to be clearly stated and become part of our theoretical underpinnings.

Those who reported data on social support were quite consistent in using categories based on someone's earlier classifications of the phenomenon (e.g. House, Weiss, Kahn, and Antonucci) and on the traditional social network variables. In general, however, while there were some relationships between components, the size of the correlations does not give confidence as to their distinctness. Factor analysis has also not provided clear direction for empirical definitions of social support. There is consensus, however, that there are some usable tools to measure social support, and they have grown out of the cooperation and collaboration that arose among nurse researchers with common interests.

It is appropriate to consider these papers as reflective of the first generation of tool development to measure social support. We all agree, however, that we need to expand our understanding of social support. The complexities of social support as a concept or construct have been mentioned often, both directly or indirectly. Within the same sample, different aspects of social support seem important at different points in time. Different subsets look to different sources for various types of social support. Different samples show different levels of social support and different sources of social support. At this point in time, social support data are somewhat precariously based on how responses are elicited. For example, network size may depend on the number of people respondents are allowed to list, or on whether the word "help" versus "support" is used in the instructions to the respondent.

Responses are further complicated by the varying ability of different people to report on esoteric concepts like "appraisal," as well as by the challenge of trying to measure social support or its effects on those in greatest need of environmental support because of overwhelming problems. The question has been asked at the conference, and I believe we need to attend to it--does social support have both general and situation specific aspects? The answer may rest, at least in part, on the notion that an historical/longitudinal picture of an individual's support is critical; i.e., earlier type or ongoing support build personal competence, and additional or new social support may be needed in specific situations.

The complexity of social support is compounded by the conviction that it is, by definition, a perceived quantity. With this as part of our theoretical framework about social support, whether covert or overt, we are committed to finding out about it as it is processed through a person's thoughts, feelings, beliefs, values, and expressive capacities and in all their possible combinations. This stance leads us to questions such as, "Are different aspects of social support perceived as more supportive?"

Another complexity which has been mentioned repeatedly is the need to consider both the positive and negative components of social support. My premonition is that considering both positive and negative components could have serious implications for explicit theoretical frameworks and the resulting definitions of social support.

One of the most pervasive problems in interpreting the findings shared at this conference is figuring out which is the horse and which the cart, or whether there is something else that was not measured that is pulling both of them. For example, consider the following questions — does lack of social support cause depression, do depressed people turn off their potential sources of social support, or is there something else about people that makes them happy and well supported?

Tied to this dilemma is the fact that, in general, our attempts to relate social support to dependent variables have explained only a small amount of variance. There is consensus that we are omitting something. Actually, that is not too surprising since the focus has generally been on social support and perhaps a measure of life change, and no attempt has been made to include all possible explanatory variables.

IMPLICATIONS FOR PRACTICE AND FUTURE RESEARCH

In order to discuss the implications for practice and future research, I would like to share with you a favorite quote from one of our faculty, — "Adam looked and found things and he named them. Modern man names things and then looks to find them." I am now going to ask you to step back and look with me at where we are. In trying to understand and test our understanding, a variety of approaches are legitimate and useful.

To date, we have favored the modern man approach to deal with social support. We have taken the categories and classifications, the names others have assigned, and we are looking for something to fit them empirically. We have set social support up as a thing apart, an entity in isolation from other bodies of knowledge. Our strongest consensus is that this is a dead end street if pursued at the expense of other approaches; i.e., social support is threadbare theoretically and lacks a guiding rationale.

It occurs to me that we need to broaden our perspective of where we are headed. We must consider what we are trying to achieve. As fascinating as social support is, I think we would agree that for our discipline it would become boring as an end in itself. Our goals are to help people achieve and maintain health, including optimal development, uncomplicated pregnancies, psychological comfort, positive child rearing styles, physical health, etc. The big question for nurses, therefore, is — what factors in the social environment promote those outcomes? This is a different question than asking what is social support.

I think we have been leaving out the logical link between the social environment and health (in its broadest definition). We have not attended to the question — what facilitates, enables, or empowers individuals to work toward positive health? After all, it's the people we want to help who actually do the developing, carry the pregnancy, do the child rearing, carry out behaviors that promote health, etc. We certainly do not have to start from the beginning to answer this question. As Dr. Antonucci pointed out, there are relevant bodies of literature on such things as reciprocity, contingent behavior, and other concepts which link theoretically with control, self-esteem, and mastery. There are also other bodies of literature which link these outcomes with health.

We also must remember that health and well-being are dependent on biophysical factors. If we are to take these factors into account, we must, of necessity, include in our theoretical underpinnings the links between what are perceived as resources and threats and the potential physiological consequences. Therefore, further research would be channeled to determine which factors promote accurate appraisal of resources and threats and how to increase predictability, promote a sense of mastery or self-esteem, and so forth.

In essence, future research would determine which factors promote coping and adaptation. Both the major construct, health, and the supportive processes from the social environment need to be examined. I believe that we have a big gap in the middle of this conceptualization. In that gap are those effects which individuals experience, as well as the evidence of how they view themselves in relation to the world, i.e., whether it is a threatening, incomprehensible place, or whether there are adequate resources in the self or from others which promote a view of safety and manageability. I believe we need to examine the literature and the individuals' environments and establish supportive services to enable them to meet their life demands.

If such a course were taken, it could open new vistas for pursuing our understanding empirically. The experiments which have been encouraged at this meeting could be done using concepts such as mastery, self-esteem, etc., as the mediating process variables. We would experience a great liberation from the shackles of "perceived support." We could quit wondering why social support works because we would have some potential avenues to test.

We have a good example of what I mean in a quote from the paper by K. Barnard, C. Snyder, and A. Spietz, "The nurses did not attempt to change, heal, or cure the parents; rather they attempted through caring to maximize their parenting potential at the parents' current level of functioning . . . The goal of the helping relationship was to assist the parents to work toward independence and ultimately assume responsibility for their decisions." In Dr. Humenick's Critique of this paper, she suggested as an indicator of progress the initiation of questions by the mother. Information seeking or appraisal is part of constructive coping, and this is an example of the research focus I am proposing.

We need to approach the subject of social support from some other directions to get out of what Dr. Jackson called, "being stuck at initial conceptualizations."

Another equally important approach which has surfaced during this conference is the value of the experience and use of observations based on direct contact with patients. Recall the discussion of hesitating to rush in with reality to a pregnant woman who was denying her marital problems as a way of coping. You were expressing recognition of what was required for her to manage and complete the task of delivery. Also recall the comment that children sometimes need to be left alone without interference to carry out coping behavior. These are examples of support from the environment in the framework I am suggesting, but they would not be reflected as perceived support. Often what others do to promote our development and independence is not directly experienced as comfortable.

It would be exciting if researchers could collaborate on some efforts so as to make progress more quickly. This collaboration could include some cumulative case studies and perhaps some programmed research. I also wonder if there is some way the researchers at this conference could continue as a group to design some of the research and practice plans.

We have a wonderful opportunity to make a significant contribution in the area of social support for multiproblem families as researchers and humanitarians. My hope is that we will capitalize on it.

Index

Adolescents (*see* Social support: adolescence, and teenage mothers)
mothers, 246, 247, 248, 321, 323
Appraisal, 14
Arizona Social Support Interview Schedule, 247, 283
Attachment (*see* Bonding, Parents' attachment, and Maternal-infant attachment)

Beck Depression Inventory, 77
Bonding, 14
anxiety, 14
conflicts with the woman's mother, 115-116
depression, 14
doula support, 112
interaction with infants, 119
loss, 14
nursing care, 112
prenatal procedures, 112
social ecology, 15
somatization, 14
supportive relationships, 14
toddlers, 14
unresolved grief, 14
Brief Symptom Inventory, 56

Child abuse, 15, 101, 208, 265, 284, 323
Child development, 15-16
Clients' recall of information, 280
Cohen's CHISEL-2, 82
Cohler's Maternal Attitude Scale, 266
Colic, 326
Conduct and Utilization of Research in Nursing, 186
Conflict between the woman and mother, 120
Coping problems, 24-25
Coping process, 26-27, 324,333
avoidance, 248
confusion, 32
contingency, 38
control, 32-33
hope, 38-39
learned helplessness, 32
precoping behaviors, 38
predictability, 31-32
understanding, 32-33

Denial, 119-120
Disequilibrium, 202

Emotional concerns, 13-14
Eysenck Personality Inventory, 77

Family, 233-234, 236
Family, chosen and given, 199
Family ecological framework, 228-230
Family Functioning Survey, 198
Fetal Attachment Scale, 101, 112,325
subscales, 101, 112
Flander's Interaction Analysis System, 159
Fundamental Interpersonal Relations Orientation, 51

Infant family focus project, 200,325
Infants (*see* Supportive measures for high-risk infants)
crying, 326
massage, 327
premature, 36
preterm, 90
Information, 14, 159
Information needs and problem solving behavior of parents, study of, 125-165
adaptation, 126
conceptual considerations, 151
implications for practice, 153-154
intervention programs, 155-156
methodological and findings, considerations of, 151-153
nursing intervention, 154-155
parents' problems, 126
patient education, 159-160
problems, study of
naturally recognized by parents, 128-133, 149, 159-161
results, 130-133, 146-149, 152
simulated problem solving, 133-149, 158
results, 139-149, 152-153
problem solving, 126-128, 133-137, 149-150
social support, 153-154

Instrumental aid, 14
Interpersonal process, 320-321
Interpersonal transactions, 13-14
Inventory of Socially Supportive
  Behaviors, 247, 283

Lazarus model, 21, 26, 229
  cognitive appraisal, 21
  emotion, 21
  self-regulation, 21
Learned helplessness, 22-23
  attribution theory, 23
Life events questionnaire, 52
Life Experiences Survey, 212-213, 222,
  235, 239, 324

March of Dimes, 88, 330
Marital adjustment, 107
Marital relationships, 120-122
Marital Adjustment Scale, 63
Marlowe-Crowne Test of Social
  Desirability, 51, 70, 77
Maternal-infant attachment, 256
Maternal-fetal attachment, 325
Maternal-Fetal Attachment Scale, 107
Maternal-newborn interaction, 295
Models of newborn care research, 198,
  291
Myelodysplasia, 198, 236

Neonatal Perception Inventory, 252, 256
Networking skills, 200
Newborn Nursing Models Study, 284
Norbeck Social Support Questionnaire,
  45-57, 73, 189, 239, 324
  battered women, 56
  convoy, 46-47
  deaf, 55
  elderly, 55
  evaluation, 79-82
  findings, 56-57
  functional properties, 47
  issues concerning scores, 53-54
  measures of support, 55-56
  number in network, 54
  and the Personal Resource Question-
    naire, 78-82
  questions, 47-48
  reliability and validity, 48-53, 56, 189
  sex differences, 52-53

subjects, demographic characteristics
  of, 49
subscale versus component variable
  scores, 53-54
support network, 52
testing, 46-53
total functional support score, 53-54
total loss score, 53-54
total network properties score, 53-54
Nursing intervention, 154-155, 158

Otitis media, 326

Parent-child adaptation (see Supportive
  measures for high-risk infants and
  families)
Parent effectiveness therapy, 238
Parents' attachment to their unborn,
  99-122
  child abuse, 101
  fetal attachment and couples' dyadic
    relationship study, 106-108
    marital roles, 118
    men, 106, 107, 113, 118
    methodological concerns, 113
    results, 107-109, 113-114
    sexual relationships, 107
    stage of pregnancy, 108
    women, 106, 107, 113-114
    work, 119
  maternal-fetal attachment, 99
  maternal-fetal attachment and social
    support study, 101-106, 110-112
    fetal attachment, 104, 112
    health care support, 104, 105,
      110-112
    pregnancy advice, 105
    results, 103-106, 109, 113
    social support score, 103-104
    support from family and friends,
      103, 105-106, 110, 112
  and pregnancy, 109
  research considerations, 113-116,
    118-122
  social support,
    assumptions, 102
    components, 102
    dyadic relationship, 106
    nature of, 102
    network, 101
    nurturance, 104-105, 111

Parents' problem solving behavior (*see* Information needs)
Paternal-Fetal Attachment Scale, 107
Peer teaching, 323-324
Personal Resource Questionnaire, 51
  correlation matrix for subscales, depression, 66
  details, 62
  dyadic consensus, 76
  education, 71
  elderly, 66
  evaluation, a social support measure, 59-78, 79-83
  illness, 66
  income, 71
  internal consistency, 65
  life situations, 89
  and the Norbeck Social Support Questionnaire, 78-82
  prenatal couples, 66
  psychometric evaluation, 75-76
  psychometric testing, 76-77
  research goals, 77
  results, 66-76
    part 1, 66-69
    part 2, 68-75
  validity and reliability, 63-65, 70-77
Pregnancy complications, 100
Problem solving, 126-128, 133-134, 149, 201, 285, 319
Profile of Mood States, 52, 73
Psychosocial assets, 100
Psychotic individuals, 199

Research considerations, 155, 230-240, 291-294

Self-Help Ideology Scale, 62, 65
Social ecology, 15
Social Network Inventory, 172-174
Social networks and social support of primigravida mothers and fathers study, 167-203
  data analysis, 189
  clinical considerations, 190
  concepts, 168, 184
  instrument, 172-174, 184, 189, 195
  replication, 186-187
  research design, 189
  research implications, 191-202
  results, 175-184, 190

  education, 177
  gender, 175-176, 184, 185, 191, 195-196
  income, 177
  perceived social support, 177-178
  relationships between network structure and social support, 179-186
  sample, 171
  theoretical structure, 187-188
  transition to parenthood, 168-171, 185
Social support,
  adolescence, 17-18, 248
  affect, 46, 51-52, 61
  affection, 51
  affirmation, 46, 51, 61
  aid, 46, 51-52, 61, 92
  appraisal, 14
  assistance, 60, 64, 248
  assumptions, 102
  bonding, 14, 99
  child rearing, 16
  class differences, 116-117
  components, 102, 331
  contact, 92
  contact with woman's mother family, 247-249
  control, 31-32, 36, 51
  coping, 61, 100
  crisis, 34
  definition, 13-14, 26, 35-36, 37, 46-47, 60-62, 79, 101, 109, 168, 228-230, 240, 247, 249, 273-274, 278-279, 280, 313-314, 330, 331-333
  demanding conditions, 14
  depression, 92
  duration of relationships, 52
  effective intervention, 57
  emotional concerns, 14
  emotional support, 51, 283
  environment, 28
  as a factor in parents' attachment to unborn, 99-122
  father, 16
  fun, 14
  and function as a buffer, 84
  groups, 20, 61
  health, 60, 61, 332
  immediate family, 16
  inclusion, 51
  infant death, 55-56
  information, 14, 60

instrumental aid, 14
interpersonal transactions, 13-14
intervention programs, 155-158,
    200-201, 291-329
intimacy, 64
life-span issue, 13
looking-glass self, 13
love, 26
low income, 18
mental health, 13, 72, 73
model, 20, 90
    Lazarus model, 21
mother, 16, 19
mothering, 249
mutual obligation, 26
natural helping networks, 16, 101
and negative life events of mothers
    with developmentally delayed
    children, study of, 205-243
    adaptation, 206, 209
    adaptive difficulties, 206-209, 223
    child abuse, 208
    father, 235-236
    friends, 220
    grief, 207-208
    health professionals, 236-239
    instruments, 211-212, 231, 239-240
    marital relationship, 206, 209, 249
    method, 211-212
    natural caregiver, 220
    negative life events, 218-220, 222
    parent-child relationship, 207,
        208-209
    parenting, 210
    questions, 210-211
    research considerations, 221, 222,
        223-240
    results, 213-223
    siblings, 208
    stress, 205-207, 208, 220, 223,
        293, 316
    stress mediators, 209-210
    subjects, 211
negative support, 93
nonsupport, 61, 92
nurturing, 14
nurturance, 64, 74-75, 104-105, 111
origin, 113
physical health, 13
physical support, 283
postpartum adjustment, 249
practical applications, 33-34

predictability, 31-32, 36, 38
pregnancy outcome, 109-110, 117
psychosocial assets, 100
reciprocity, 34-35
relationships, 35, 248
relaxation, 14, 249
research considerations, 27-28, 30-33,
    61-62, 84-88, 90-94, 109, 113-114,
    186, 191-193, 195, 230-233, 234-240,
    279-287, 315-327, 330-334
resources, 19-20, 66-67, 100, 229
roles, 56
single parents, 18
social competence, 37
social ecology, 13
social integration, 14, 64
social network, 17, 37, 92-93, 167-202,
    247-248, 278, 283-284
social participation, 14
social self, 13
sociometric analysis, 13
stress, 13, 19, 26, 52, 60, 61, 92, 160,
    153-154, 168, 248, 278
    study of and persistent problems,
    82-84
suicide, 13
tangible support, 51
and teenage mothers, study of,
    245-287
    instruments (see measures)
    maternal role attainment, 250, 252,
        267, 278-279
    measures, 251-252, 262, 268-270
        267, 275-276
    method, 250, 274
    questions, 250, 251, 272-274
    reliability and validity, 252, 276
    research considerations, 274-287
    results, 252-267
        early postpartum, 252-256
        one month postpartum, 254-255,
            253, 256-260, 267
        four months postpartum, 254-
            255, 261-263
        eight months postpartum, 254-
            255, 253, 263-264, 267
        one year, 254-255, 253, 264-267
    sample, 250, 274-275
    test periods, 250
    types of supportive acts, 251-252,
        275-276

theory, 29
transitions of life, 56
understandability, 31-33, 36
usc, 13
valued, 26
and vulnerability, state of the art in
   relation to children and families,
   overview of, 11-43
worth, 64
Social Support Questionnaire, 51
Spanier Dyadic Adjustment Scale,
   72, 107, 117-118
Spanier's Marital Adjustment Scale, 72
State and Trait Anxiety Scale, 73, 77
Statistical Program for the Social
   Sciences, 195
Supportive measures for high-risk infants and families, study of, 291-329
   assumptions, 291-294, 296
   categories of mothers, 306-308
   family problems, 298-299, 307, 314-
      315, 325-326
   language, 324
   measures, 308
   method, 294-296

nursing activities, 309-312, 315-318,
   322
Nursing Parent and Child Environment (NPACE), 293-327
Nursing Standard Approach to Care
   (NSTAC), 293, 313, 315
Nursing Support Infant Bio-
   Behavioral (NSIBB), 293, 313, 315,
   322, 326
research considerations, 315-320
results, 309, 312-315
sample, 291-292, 296
supportive process, 298-308, 320-321

Testing, 88-89

Vulnerable infants, 12
Vulnerable families, 291-329
Vulnerability, 12-13

White's classification of coping
   behavior, 22

Zung's Self-Rating Depression Scale, 72

*   *   *   *   *

Special thanks to Isa Roque, without her dedication, ability, and perseverance, this volume could not have materialized.

Beverly Raff
Editor